THE SILVER EMPIRE

THE SILVER EMPIRE

HOW GERMANY CREATED ITS FIRST COMMON CURRENCY

OLIVER VOLCKART

OXFORD
UNIVERSITY PRESS

OXFORD
UNIVERSITY PRESS

Great Clarendon Street, Oxford, OX2 6DP,
United Kingdom

Oxford University Press is a department of the University of Oxford.
It furthers the University's objective of excellence in research, scholarship,
and education by publishing worldwide. Oxford is a registered trade mark of
Oxford University Press in the UK and in certain other countries

Published in the United States of America by Oxford University Press
198 Madison Avenue, New York, NY 10016, United States of America

British Library Cataloguing in Publication Data
Data available

Library of Congress Control Number: 2023945220

ISBN 978–0–19–889448–3

DOI: 10.1093/oso/9780198894483.001.0001

Printed and bound in the UK by
Clays Ltd, Elcograf S.p.A.

Preface

Some economic historians are inspired by debates among their colleagues, others by methodological innovations or current events. For me, it is most of all reading primary sources. In 2015, I discovered a document preserved in the Bavarian State Archive in Würzburg—a document of more than 200 cleanly handwritten pages that contained the minutes of a conference held in the city of Speyer in late summer and autumn 1549. At that conference, the members of the Holy Roman Empire discussed the creation of a common, Empire-wide currency. The minutes are highly detailed; in many places, they have the ring of direct speech. They offer unique insights into which monetary policy aims the members of the Empire pursued, what arguments they used to persuade their partners and opponents, and who eventually prevailed in the negotiations. One of the things that struck me was how effectively the talks were conducted. Most of the time, the participants seemed well-prepared, the chair made sure that they spoke to the point, and the results were carefully noted. The next source I found was the concluding document—the recess or, in German, *Abschied*—of a preceding meeting held a few months before the conference of the autumn 1549. Here was evidence of an entirely different atmosphere characterized not only by discord, but by what appeared as intransigence. Evidently, the style and effectiveness of monetary policy negotiations could change radically within a very brief space of time. What was going on? I knew now I had to find out more about the Empire's monetary policies, so I kept searching. Other archives soon yielded additional sources: letters, memorials, discussion papers, and so on; there was much more than I had ever dreamt of. At that point, I decided that I wanted to turn this material into a book.

The book is now finished. In it, I use the primary sources that I found not only to analyse the creation of Germany's first common currency in far more detail than was possible before, but also to reassess several hypotheses earlier research has advanced. For example, the purpose the common currency was intended to serve now appears in an entirely new light, as does the importance of the uneven availability of precious metals. Other issues have never been seen in the context of the Empire's monetary policies: princely debts, the trans-Saharan caravan trade, and the Rhine tolls, to mention only three of these. Not least, I found that in contrast to what historians—including myself—used to believe, the Empire's currency functioned not much worse than others of the time. In fact, it shared many of their characteristics, offering similar advantages and suffering from similar problems.

Writing the book would have been impossible without the support of others. The research environment of the Economic History Department of the London School of Economics and Political Science must be mentioned first. There is no larger permanent group of economic historians in Europe and probably in the world; the synergies this offers are unsurpassed. The staff of the LSE Library took pains to supply me with an endless stream of interlibrary loans; they did so extremely effectively and quickly, and I would like to use this opportunity to thank them for their support. Thanks are also due to the staff of the archives where I found the evidence on which this book is based: not only in Würzburg, but also in Munich, Berlin, Vienna, Dresden, Lübeck, Ludwigsburg, Karlsruhe, Wolfenbüttel, and Augsburg. I would also like to thank my colleagues Alex (Spike) Gibbs, Jason Lennard, and Jordan Claridge, who read the draft, commented on it, gave me advice on the use of statistical methods, and polished my English. However, greatest thanks are due to my wife Jie, who helped with the archival work, critically discussed the chapters of the book with me, and endured my obsession with sixteenth-century monetary policies with more than merely good grace. Without her support, I could not have written this book.

OLIVER VOLCKART

London
March 2023

Contents

List of Tables

List of Abbreviations

Ag.	Silver
AHL	Archiv der Hansestadt Lübeck
alb.	White *Pfennig* (*Albus*)
Au.	Gold
d.	*Pfennig*
dc.	*Ducat*
fl.	*Gulden, Florin*
GLA	Generallandesarchiv Karlsruhe
GStAPK	Geheimes Staatsarchiv Preußischer Kulturbesitz Berlin
gr.	*Groschen*
h.	*Heller* = ½ *Pfennig*
HHStA	Haus-, Hof- und Staatsarchiv Vienna
kr.	*Kreuzer*
m.	*Mark*
NLA	Niedersächsisches Landesarchiv
ÖNB	Österreichische Nationalbibliothek
ÖStA	Österreichisches Staatsarchiv
s.	*Schilling*
s.l.	*sine loco*
st.	*Stuiver*
StAA	Stadtarchiv Augsburg
StAWü	Staatsarchiv Würzburg

List of Figures

List of Maps

List of Plates

Introduction

In the first half of the sixteenth century, Augsburg was one of the cultural and economic powerhouses of Europe.[1] It was among the most populous cities of Germany, its commercial ties reached to India and America, and the splendour of its churches and palaces rivalled that of Florence a few hundred miles beyond the Alps to the south. As a centre of the northern renaissance, Augsburg was a place where even humble flysheets, which the common folk bought for a few *Pfennige* on market day, were illustrated by first-rate artists (we will get to know an example at the beginning of Chapter 2). Augsburg's merchants were princes—in some cases literally so—and its contribution to the revenues of the Holy Roman Empire exceeded that of wealthy rulers such as the dukes of Bavaria or Württemberg.[2] It was in this city, in October 1543, that a scandal broke. The affair left Augsburg's high society shaken; chronicles would keep referring to it for centuries.[3]

By mid-September, rumours had begun to circulate—rumours which Augsburg's government took seriously enough to act. We learn of this from the minutes of a meeting of the council of the city, which note that, 'as Hans Appenfelder, mint master of Kaufbeuren, is being accused by many of illegally breaking coins,★[4] the honourable magistrate has ordered to look out for him, and if he is apprehended, to imprison him in the city jail'.[5] The term 'breaking coins' referred to a widely spread practice. An eighteenth-century minting and monetary policy handbook explained that it meant not, 'in the literal sense, to break apart a coin, but rather to place one or more types of coin in a crucible, melt them and process the metal illegally and with the aim of making a profit'.[6] Appenfelder was the head of the mint of the town of Kaufbeuren, about 40 miles southwest of Augsburg. During the interrogation that followed his arrest, he quickly implicated Augsburg's own mint master Balthasar Hundertpfund, who was also duly arrested. The council minutes noted that Hundertpfund had 'for years acted against the common law, the Holy Empire's ordinances and statutes and the public proclamations of the honourable magistrate . . . thus causing notable damage to the common weal and the German nation'.[7] If this was more than hyperbole, the urban government must have feared that Appenfelder and Hundertpfund's activities would have repercussions far beyond Augsburg's city walls. In any case, Hundertpfund's interrogation triggered an avalanche of more prosecutions. By the end of November, Hans Gauger, Bartholomäus Schreiber, Lukas Müller, Hieronymus and Alexander Kraffter, Barbara Pech, Christoph Menhart, Hans Eigenmann, Sebastian Meuting, Ambrosius Stapf, Christoph Kress and his unnamed brother, Ambrosius Main, Hans Mauermüller, and Willibald Mader had been arrested and tried.[8] Seven of these people were members of Augsburg's leading merchant guilds; eight paid more than 10 *Guldens*[*] property tax, and three between 50 and 150 *Guldens*. Two—the brothers Alexander and Hieronymus Kraffter—were particularly well-connected members of the economic and social elite of the city (they would be ennobled by the emperor a few years later), and one—Christoph Kress—was a former magistrate.[9] All of the Augsburgers were convicted of supplying Appenfelder and Hundertpfund with coin—in part apparently domestic, in part minted elsewhere—that was to be broken, and all of them were fined, most heavily Hundertpfund, who had to pay 1,200 *Guldens*. The only accused whom the magistrate let off was Hans Appenfelder, and this only after a legal expert opinion they had requested pointed out that he had to be tried in his hometown of Kaufbeuren.[10]

What was all this about? How and why did Appenfelder and Hundertpfund make a profit from purchasing and melting money? Why was this something that 'many' found so disturbing that the rumours they spread reached Augsburg's magistrate? And why did the magistrate become so worried about these activities? Full answers to these questions must wait until Chapter 1. Suffice to say, for the moment, that the scandal of 1543 sheds light on a central topic of this book: on the monetary situation prevalent in Germany in the first half of the sixteenth century. Appenfelder and Hundertpfund's coin breaking operation was by no means unusual. On the contrary, what they did was done all across the country. It is one of the core hypotheses of this book that it was problems caused by this kind of 'trade in coinage'[11] which convinced the members of the Holy Roman Empire of the need to replace the many currencies circulating between the North Sea and the Alps and between Lorraine and Pomerania with one common system—a system that would make it unattractive to purchase and melt down coins in the way the two mint masters did. In this, the members of the Empire were to a considerable extent successful. Early talks in the 1520s were followed by negotiations that intensified in particular in the 1540s and that eventually, in 1559, led to agreement on a common currency.

The story allows for some more insights. The currency union agreed by the members of the Holy Roman Empire was designed to prevent practices like those the magistrate of Augsburg uncovered in 1543, rather than to support trade or economic integration. In this, it differed fundamentally from its present-day counterparts. The idea we sometimes encounter in both popular and academic writing that premodern long-distance merchants were suffering from the diversity of currencies and that monetary unions were formed to help them, simply does not stand up to the historical evidence.[12] Not only were the problems, which sixteenth-century actors faced, fundamentally different from those of the present, but the solutions they found resembled modern measures only superficially. More than that: the very parameters shaping premodern monetary policies differed radically from those to which we are used today. There were, for example, no central banks, and setting interest rates was no monetary policy instrument (which does not mean that policymakers did not worry about such rates). When this book discusses monetary policies, what is meant is primarily policies that concerned coinage: The ratio between a coin's pure precious metal content and its nominal value, the costs required to produce it, and the relative value of gold and silver were uppermost in the minds of the people planning the Empire's common currency.

Still, despite these differences, there are important parallels to present conditions. Like today, participants in sixteenth-century currency unions exchanged a certain degree of political autonomy for the advantages of membership. The contrast between the electorate of Saxony and the Low Countries shows this. During the first half of the sixteenth century, the Saxon electors successfully used monetary policies to support the external trade of their territory. After they joined the imperial monetary union, this was no longer possible. However, Saxony now benefited from the common currency that was valid all over the Empire, radically simplified monetary conditions, and reduced the costs involved in concluding contracts. By contrast, the densely urbanized Low Countries depended on food imports from further east. As these imports would have been far more difficult to finance if they had joined the common currency, it is no wonder they remained aloof.

Another similarity concerns the rules needed to stabilize a monetary union. Like in modern currency unions—think of the Eurozone—every member of the union in the late sixteenth-century Empire had the chance to make decisions that were bound to undermine the common currency. Today, the fiscal policies pursued by the members of the union pose the greatest danger. In the sixteenth century—with a monetary system based on precious metal—the problem was that each member faced incentives to increase its revenues by reducing the gold or silver content of the common money it issued. We will see that this was likely to trigger a chain reaction, and ultimately the breakdown of the currency union. We will also see that the members of the union agreed on rules designed to prevent such an event—rules which like their counterparts in the Eurozone were not enforced perfectly, but stringently enough to hold the union together.

There are political parallels, too, especially between the context of the creation of the common currency of 1559 and that of the Euro. In both cases, the monetary union did *not* join polities that had until then been completely independent of each other (for example, in the way the Latin Monetary Union of 1865 joined France, Belgium, Italy, and Switzerland).[13] Rather, the principalities and free cities that adopted the common currency of 1559 were already members of a larger political system. This system—the Holy Roman Empire—is today regularly compared to the European Union (EU), of which the Eurozone is a part. More than that: it is often held up as a model of how Europe could or should develop in future.[14] The common denominator underlying many such statements is the view that the Empire, much like the EU today, was a multilateral system explicitly based on the idea which underlies all multilateral political structures: the idea that solving important problems—whether preserving peace or providing monetary stability—works best if polities cooperate within a framework of clearly defined rules and shared values.[15] In the chapters below, we will encounter these rules (they structured, for example, processes of political decision-making) and values (such as the emphasis placed on 'order'), and we will see how they affected the creation of the common currency of 1559.

In this book, I tell the story of how the members of the Holy Roman Empire agreed on this currency and made it a success. I am a historian; my task is to understand the past and help others understand it. My conviction is that we cannot do this without focusing on what was left to us by the people whose actions shaped the past: the primary sources, which I let speak for themselves wherever possible. We have letters, edicts, minutes of discussions, position papers, memorials, memoirs, and merchant accounts. There is a mountain of material, much of it untapped. Sixteenth-century Germans were compulsive record keepers; hence many of the decisions, actions, events, and developments described and analysed here are well documented. That is relative, of course. Compared with the flood of information we have from the more recent past, the surviving material is patchy. Moreover, even if a bundle of sources seems complete, they rarely give direct answers to the questions we are asking. After all, their sixteenth-century authors had their own concerns and interests that influenced what they wrote. Knowing these concerns and interests helps in reading between the lines and in teasing out information at which the authors often only hint.

Since 2015, I have discovered many archival sources that concern the Empire's monetary policies in the sixteenth century—sources at most of which no historian had ever looked before. In 2017, I edited a selection of this material in a volume that appeared in a series published by the Historical Commission of the Bavarian Academy of Sciences,[16] the organization that also publishes the acts of the imperial diets. That monumental project started in the late nineteenth century and continued in fits and starts during most of the twentieth century. Since the 1990s, the work has gathered pace, and in the last two decades many volumes covering the diets during the reigns of Emperors Charles V, Ferdinand I, and Maximilian II have appeared. This has boosted research into the history of the Holy Roman Empire to an extent that is hard to overstate. Admittedly, most of the sources reflect politics: negotiations, dealings, treaties, agreements, and so forth, including those that concern monetary policies. Information on how people on the ground were handling money in the sixteenth century is much harder to come by.[17] That is no wonder in a largely illiterate society, where most people not only never wrote a sentence of their own, but also never figured in what was written by the few who were literate.

I have written this book based on primary sources, but that is not to say that I did not benefit immensely from the work of earlier historians and present colleagues. Scholars such as Friedrich Wilhelm von Schrötter at the beginning of the twentieth century and Fritz Blaich in the 1970s did pioneering work, exploiting the sources known to them in the full.[18] More recently, Petr Vorel used the coins, which were circulating in the sixteenth century, themselves as evidence. He added important aspects to our knowledge of the past.[19] Other authors are focusing on how early modern people used money—Philipp R. Rössner has produced a detailed volume that addresses this issue[20]—or on specific aspects of sixteenth-century monetary politics. Thus, in the 1990s Hans-Jürgen Gerhard examined the role of the ten imperial circles (the administrative subdivisions of the Holy Roman Empire)—work that Michael North is extending and deepening today.[21] Economists, too, have made crucial contributions, without which we would be unable to understand core aspects of early modern monetary politics. For example, in 1900 Gustav Schmoller examined the emergence of a (by nineteenth-century standards) modern token coinage; more recently, Thomas Sargent and François Velde have formalized and expanded his analysis.[22] For the present book, few studies proved more stimulating than Angela Redish's magisterial analysis of bimetallic* currencies.[23]

In Chapters 1 to 3 I consider the economic and political background to the creation of the common currency. We start by looking at the problems that gave rise to the desire to have such a currency (Chapter 1). In Chapter 2, we examine what people whom sixteenth-century policymakers called the 'common man' had to say about the state of the Empire's monetary economy, and the extent to which politics took public opinion into account. Chapter 3 discusses where and how politics were made in the Empire. It focuses on how it was possible to agree on decisions that could actually be implemented, on the factors that complicated political processes (especially poor communications), and on how discussions at imperial assemblies were structured to the advantage of certain participants.

Chapters 4 to 6 trace the course of the talks that eventually resulted in the creation of the common currency. The focus is first on the topic that dominated negotiations until the late 1540s (Chapter 4): the supply of silver. We examine the silver rush that gripped parts of the Empire, especially the Tyrol and Saxony, in the second half of the fifteenth century and the consequences the uneven availability of this metal had for the monetary policy-outlook of the princes and free cities of the Empire. We also analyse how and why these concerns gave way to others, notably to the problems introducing a bimetallic common currency (one where both silver and gold were used) could cause. Chapter 5 examines the supply of gold, looking at the trans-Saharan gold trade and at why some members of the Empire had better access to this metal than others. Again, the question is how and why this affected their stance in the talks about a common currency. The final Chapter 6 discusses two attempts to implement such a currency: one that failed in the early 1550s and another one that succeeded at the end of the decade, after some crucial compromises had been agreed upon. We also look at what the members of the Empire did to make their common currency a success.

This book concerns a topic, a period, and a region that many will find unfamiliar and that I want to make as accessible as possible. To do so, I avoid much of the technical jargon of monetary history. Moreover, I focus on actual people rather than on abstract concepts. After all, whatever happened in monetary history (whether prices rose, a new monetary unit became popular, or two rulers issued a common currency) was the outcome of decisions individuals made and actions they chose. Sometimes the result was what they had intended; more often it was the unplanned and unforeseen consequence of what they and many thousands of others did.

The names of persons and places are another issue. While many people who figure in this book were multilingual and styled their names differently depending on where they were—when in Spain, Charles V became Carlos I, for example, whereas he was known as Karl V in Germany—most carried German names. If they were rulers and if their name has a well-known English equivalent, that is what I use. Thus, Moritz of Saxony becomes Maurice of Saxony, his cousin Johann Friedrich, John Frederick, and so on. In the case of private persons, I decided to retain the original form. It would sound strange to talk of John rather than Hans Appenfelder, for example.

In the case of place names, I use modern English equivalents where they are well known. Köln is Cologne and Wien is Vienna, but Mainz stays Mainz because Mayence has become uncommon. If a place lies outside Germany, Austria, or Switzerland and is today known by a non-German name (or form of its name), I give this in brackets next to the German one: Straßburg (Strasbourg), Joachimstal (Jáchymov), and so on.

In terms of countries, there are some tricky cases. When I refer to the region today belonging to Belgium, the Netherlands, and Luxemburg (Luxembourg), I prefer the term 'Low Countries' for the period until the abdication of Charles V in 1555/56. From the accession of Philip II, they become 'the Spanish Netherlands'. I occasionally also use the name 'Burgundy', which is how the complex of territories the dukes of Burgundy established in that region in the late fourteenth and fifteenth century was known. This is imprecise because the Jura was part of Burgundy, too (not to mention the actual French duchy of Burgundy around Dijon), but it matches everyday sixteenth-century usage: Often, when people talked of Burgundy, what they meant were the Low Countries.

'Germany' is particularly difficult.[24] There is a whole controversy about what we should call the country in the early modern period. I steer clear of that debate. The post-Napoleonic Austrian chancellor Metternich said of Germany that the name was no more than a geographical expression,[25] and that is how I use it. In many places, 'the German lands'—a term that became popular from the mid-fourteenth century onwards—fits better, not least because it suggests the diversity of the country. The sixteenth-century style was of course 'the Holy Roman Empire', sometimes with the rider 'of the German nation'. When talking about constitutional issues or political processes, I use that term, generally in its abbreviated form as 'Empire'.

Sums of money that I mention would be meaningless if the readers were unable to relate them to modern values. Rather than giving equivalents in today's Pound Sterling—which would be hazardous given the uneven rise of prices since the sixteenth century—I put them in relation to the incomes of skilled labourers, allowing readers to draw their own conclusions. As for distances, a sixteenth-century English traveller had this to say:

> The common Germain mile, being for the most part in plaines, makes more then three English, or five Italian miles; but in some places the solitude of Woods, and the ascent of Mountaines, make the miles of Germany seeme much longer, and Suevia extraordinarily hath long miles, though it be a plaine Countrey.[26]

Having read this, I decided to opt for a unit of measurement on whose length people can at least agree: the modern international mile of 1,760 yards. The Appendix, finally, contains some technical information for readers who want to learn more about the nitty-gritty background of the story the book tells. But first let us return to Augsburg, where the story began. It continues about six years after the magistrate had so effectively dealt with the Appenfelder–Hundertpfund affair.

I

Diversity becomes a problem

Trade in coinage

Augsburg's currency under pressure

In the late summer of 1549, Silvester Raid was in deep trouble. On 18 June, his wife Anna—who lived with Raid in sleepy Donauwörth on the Danube where her husband was town clerk—had received a summons for him from the magistrate of Augsburg, Raid's original hometown. When the letter arrived, he was travelling; as Anna hurried to let Augsburg's government know, he would be back in about a fortnight.[1] On his return, Raid appeared before the magistrate of his old home. The counsellors confronted him with the claim that he had circulated strange *Kreuzer*-coins to the value of several hundred *Guldens*; they demanded to know where he had got the money. His attempts to explain himself did not convince. Some years later, he described what happened next:

> They sent me out of the room, considered a short while and then ordered a council servant to take my sword from my side and me, despite my pleas and like a common criminal, to the city's dungeons, where I was left in an underground vault chained to the stocks. And although I sent from the gaol to Leonhard Christoph Rehlinger, at that time governing mayor, humbly asking him to let my friends know that that I was imprisoned solely because of the *Kreuzers*, lest my dear housewife and friends take fright and worry, said Rehlinger answered that next morning I would learn well enough why I had been arrested, which gave me (as you can imagine) little comfort.
>
> In the morning two council servants took me like a common criminal to the torture chamber, where two magistrates, namely Master Christoph Baumgärtner and Master Dominic Honold, sat next to a chancellery clerk, with the executioner waiting outside. They started talking to me, saying that personally

> they heartily rued my imprisonment, but the honourable magistrate had given them articles in writing which they wanted to read to me and to which I should truthfully answer, or else face the torture.[2]

We have no reason to doubt Raid's account. He gave it in a letter to the magistrate of Augsburg, whose members presumably had access to evidence that allowed checking its accuracy. Moreover, their harsh and humiliating way of dealing with the suspect was dictated by imperial law. No one was allowed to be sentenced without having admitted their guilt; suspects therefore had to be given the chance to confess. If they did not take that chance they had to be prompted, if necessary, by force. Moreover, both counterfeiting and circulating counterfeit money were crimes threatened with capital punishment, specifically with burning at the stake.[3] Raid now stood accused—or so he understood the charge—of having 'deliberately minted and spent counterfeit money'.[4] He was facing first the torturer's iron, and then fire.

The question is, what exactly had he done, and was he a counterfeiter? The answer is by no means straightforward, and not only because part of the records of his trial have been lost.[5] There is more to the case, and its intricacies illuminate both the state of Germany's monetary economy and that of the country's wider political constitution in the first half of the sixteenth century. So, what had happened, as far as it is possible to reconstruct?

Raid was born soon after 1500 to a well-established family in Augsburg. Having become a notary, he gained the trust of Anton Fugger, head of Europe's most powerful trading, mining, and banking firm, who sent him on several missions to Denmark and Norway to deal with King Christian III. Raid also regularly corresponded with Duke Albert of Prussia, whom he supplied with sheet music written by his artistic Augsburg friends and with political news he gleaned as an employee of Fugger. This may be why he left—or had to leave—the firm in late 1541. Having failed to become the city of Augsburg's chief legal adviser, he practised as a lawyer, though he also put his knowledge of mining acquired as Fugger's agent to good use. He seems to have managed a mine in the Harz mountains in North Germany and acted as the agent of other large trading firms from Augsburg when they dealt with smelting businesses in Saxony.[6] In 1548, he moved to Donauwörth to take up his new appointment there.[7] His rolling days were over, or so it seemed until Anna received the summons from Augsburg's magistrate.

Now, in the dungeon of Augsburg in July 1549, Raid faced a serious predicament, and anyone in his situation had to be a courageous and resourceful character to survive. Raid was a passionate, short-tempered man, possibly with a violent streak. When he worked as a lawyer, he had been censured by the magistrate for using strong language in court; now he declared that if anyone had accused him of forgery outside the gaol, he would have answered the charge with his fist.[8] Still, courage and resourcefulness were traits he certainly possessed. His line of defence was that he had been on the point of travelling to Saxony when he was approached by Franz März, a citizen of Augsburg, who suggested a business deal. A relative of März, Hans Schaller, owned about 500 *Guldens* worth of *Kreuzers*—smallish silver coins—which he said were from Hildesheim, a place almost 300 miles away in North Germany. Five hundred *Guldens* was a hefty sum. In the mid-1530s in Augsburg, a master bricklayer earned about 8 *Kreuzers* a day; so one *Gulden* (equal to 60 *Kreuzers*) represented more than a week of skilled labour.[9] In 1541, Raid had purchased his house in Augsburg—a prestigious property he bought from the widow of the commander of the city's militia—for 600 *Guldens*.[10] Schaller's problem was that the type of his *Kreuzers* was unfamiliar in and around Augsburg, making it impossible to spend large sums easily, though he claimed that he had paid up to 50 *Guldens* in small tranches to peasants 'and other such folk'. The main thing was: the *Kreuzers* were good and genuine. Would not Raid take them back to North Germany? Schaller was prepared to let him make a good profit.[11]

At this point, Raid should have become suspicious. *Kreuzers* were current not only in Augsburg but in all Upper Germany, in fact, anywhere from Alsace to Austria—a region where in the mid-1530s many lords and cities (including Augsburg) had agreed on a common currency.[12] In North Germany, however, no one used *Kreuzers*. This is something of which Raid must have been aware; after all, he was familiar with the lands near Hildesheim, through which he would have passed when travelling to Denmark. Also, the Harz mountains, where his mine lay, are close by. So why were there *Kreuzers* from Hildesheim? Still, Schaller's money certainly looked fine. As a contemporary chronicle has it, 'on the one side it looked exactly like *Kreuzers*, with the cross on it, and the size was right; on the other side it carried a coat of arms which some said was the bishop of Hildesheim's'.[13]

Raid seems to have seen no harm in taking Schaller's money back to where it belonged. However, it soon became clear to him that he had taken on more than he had bargained for. The sum he accepted was 472

Guldens, with 6 *Kreuzers* per *Gulden* being his commission. Transporting so much cash—more than 31,000 coins with a total weight of almost forty kilograms—over miles of bad and often robber-infested roads was no mean feat. Raid soon had enough, especially as an alternative presented itself. He learnt of Cardinal Otto von Waldburg, the bishop of Augsburg, being hard-pressed by his creditors and urgently needing cash. Raid offered the *Kreuzers*; an agent of Waldburg's creditors came to collect them, tried to exchange them for golden ducats (which were much easier to transport), and became suspicious.[14] During this period, commercial centres such as Augsburg employed assayers*—officials tasked with checking the precious metal content of coins members of the public presented to them. Raid claimed later that Schaller had taken his *Kreuzers* to Augsburg's assayer and that Schaller, therefore, knew they contained nowhere near as much silver as Upper German *Kreuzers* when he gave them to Raid.[15] It is equally possible that it was the cardinal's creditors who had the money tested. Whatever the truth, when Augsburg's magistrates questioned Raid in July 1549, they presented him with the fact that the coins had been struck to a standard that at most matched that of 2½ *Pfennigs* (the official value of *Kreuzers* was 3½ *Pfennigs*). In other words, they contained almost 30 per cent less silver than they should have done.[16]

The magistrates of Augsburg considered these coins to be counterfeit money, and in fact there was little else they could do if they did not want to expose the markets in their city and its environs to serious dangers. If allowed to circulate, they ran the risk that whoever had minted the Kreuzers would regard this as an invitation to produce more of them and use them to flood Augsburg and its neighbourhood. This was entirely possible. Some people did not trust the design of the coins, but as Schaller had said, peasants 'and other such folk' were willing to accept them. After all, there were many variants of genuine *Kreuzers* that carried a cross on one side and, on the other, the coat of arms of the authority that had issued them. Encountering pieces with an unfamiliar coat of arms was probably not all that unusual. Peasants and others accepted the strange *Kreuzers* in return for their products, and apparently on the same terms on which they took genuine pieces. People such as Schaller could then sell what they had bought in exchange for Augsburg's good money. Such transactions would allow them to make a profit in terms of silver—a profit which Augsburg's city fathers understandably regarded as illicit.

However, the issue had further ramifications. Somewhere there was a mint producing money which looked very much like the genuine *Kreuzers* issued by the members of the currency union linking the lands between Austria and Alsace. How did this mint acquire the silver it needed to produce its coins? Simple: from merchants. And where—and importantly, in what form—did these merchants acquire the metal? Again, the answer is simple: This would consist either of raw silver bought at a smelting works or of Upper Germany's fine *Kreuzers* that were taken to the foreign mint, broken, mixed with a certain quantity of base metal like copper and reissued as coins that looked very much like the originals. In return for the bullion with which the merchants supplied the strange mint, they would therefore receive money that in total contained less silver. However, this mint would be able to offer them a nominal price higher than the one in Augsburg could. That was because piece for piece, the imitation *Kreuzers* contained about 30 per cent less pure silver than the originals. For the merchants involved in this practice, this still made sense if they could count on finding poorly informed consumers willing to accept the fake coins on a par with genuine ones.[17] For Augsburg, the danger was that if the magistrate allowed this to go on, the silver supply to its mint would dry up. Bullion merchants would rather turn to the foreign mint where they were being better paid, which meant that Augsburg would be unable to maintain its currency.[18]

Alternatively, whoever circulated the lightweight *Kreuzers* in Augsburg could directly exchange them for genuine ones. He could then sell these to the foreign mint, which would melt them, add copper to the alloy and reissue them as copies of the originals. In either case, Augsburg would find it impossible to maintain the output of its good coins and the bad money would begin to dominate the market. Worst of all, eventually even the common folk would notice what was going on. This could directly cause trouble: Peasants tended to react sensitively when they felt they were being systematically deceived by being offered bad money. Their complaints about 'evil' coin almost regularly played a part in the rebellions that shook large parts of Germany in the first quarter of the sixteenth century.[19] At the very least, they would ask higher prices for the products they sold in Augsburg—and that was likely to cause unrest and possibly even rioting among the many poor that crowded the city's streets and lanes. Augsburg's magistrate had every cause for alarm.

Today, the phenomenon they feared is known as Gresham's Law*. In its simplest and most widely quoted form the law says that 'bad money drives out good', and in this case, it was the bad *Kreuzer*-copies that were expected to drive out the good Upper German originals. The law got its name because a nineteenth-century economist, Henry Dunning McLeod, credited Thomas Gresham, banker and financial adviser of Queen Elizabeth I, with its discovery. In fact, by Gresham's time, people had been familiar with the phenomenon for ages.[20] By the sixteenth century, the law was widely known and many authorities responsible for making monetary policy decisions were aware of it. No wonder the magistrate of Augsburg was afraid of its consequences.

However, the city fathers did not have to deal with an ordinary case of forgery. No criminal had misused the bishop of Hildesheim's coat of arms. In fact, the arms were not those of the bishop at all; they were those of the city of Hildesheim, which seems to have enjoyed the right to issue its own coins since at least the thirteenth century. Only a few years earlier Hildesheim had concluded a contract with a new mint master that specified the range of coins he was to produce—among them a piece called 'small *Schilling*', which the master designed to look like a *Kreuzer* (Plate 1.1). Sixteenth-century authorities often left their mint officials a free hand where questions of design were concerned, but in this case, the master may have acted on the magistrate's orders. This is suggested by the fact that, in what looks like a concerted policy, the neighbouring towns of Goslar and Hameln, duke Eric of Braunschweig-Calenberg, and several other lords of that region issued similar *Kreuzer*-imitations.[21] All these authorities held the undisputed right to mint, which included, equally undisputed, the right to choose the bullion content and design of their coinage. There can be little doubt that they deliberately produced money that looked like *Kreuzers* but contained less pure silver, intending to benefit from the sale of their coins in places where genuine *Kreuzers* were current.

Hildesheim alone issued at least 1¼ million such *Kreuzer*-copies.[22] We do not know how many of them were brought to Upper Germany. Likewise, we do not know how large the share of Upper-German consumers was who rejected this money or who were suspicious enough to accept it only at a discount. It is possible that Augsburg with its public assayer and large, commercially astute population was less suited than most places for attempting to circulate underweight coins. Let us, therefore, leave Raid and his trial for a moment and consider what was going on elsewhere.

Plate 1.1. Genuine *Kreuzer* of the imperial city of Kempten in Upper Germany (left) versus imitation *Kreuzer* ('Small *Schilling*') from Hildesheim (right), *c.*1535–50
Source: © Auktionen Münzhandlung Sonntag (with kind permission); © WAG Online (with kind permission).

Mecklenburg exploits its neighbour

Take, for example, the Baltic duchies of Pomerania and Mecklenburg. We learn about them from Bartholomäus Sastrow, who is arguably one of the best-known non-princely characters of sixteenth-century Germany: A 'skilful, cunning, hot-headed, and probably often hard and partial man', as the nineteenth-century writer Gustav Freytag characterized him,[23] we are so well acquainted with Sastrow because he left an autobiography written during the last years of his life. The book is remarkable not only because there are not many memoirs from sixteenth-century Germany, but even more because of Sastrow's colourful and apparently accurate description of everyday life. A little younger than Raid, Sastrow spent some time studying the law at Rostock University. He left without a degree but still managed to become a notary at the imperial chamber court, and later a counsellor of the duke of Pomerania and burgomaster of the Pomeranian port of Stralsund.[24] His older brother Johannes was a master at Wittenberg university. Sastrow describes how in 1542 Johannes journeyed to Lübeck and Rostock to take care of some publications.

> When he travelled home from Rostock Master Heinrich Sonnenberg and a woman were his companions on the cart, and next to the cart rode Hans Lagebusch and a young, genteel fellow called Hermann Lepper, who had taken several hundred *Guldens* worth of Duke Bogislaw's *Schillings* and other coin to the mint at Gadebusch and now took home newly minted money from there; this lay on the cart. Some footpads, as such villains are called, got wind of this and went the same way, being minded to capture some good loot.

Sastrow went on to describe how

> when the cart was passing the village of Willershagen, which is under Rostock's authority and close to Rostock heath, those on the cart got off, taking their arms with them, and the two riders, who in that unsafe place should have stayed close by, went some way ahead where the footpads joined them. One, especially, rode next to Lagebusch, talking to him companionably, and when he was riding so close to him that he could reach Lagebusch's handgun (back then it was not yet the fashion to carry two guns in your saddlebags) he suddenly grabbed the weapon, which was loaded and cocked.[25]

There followed a violent scuffle, every shot, thrust, and stroke of which old Bartholomäus described with relish, and which left Johannes severely wounded.

Here we see Gresham's Law in full force. In Pomerania, Hermann Lepper was evidently in the same business as Hans Schaller in Augsburg a few years later—though Lepper seems to have been more deeply involved. We cannot be sure that Schaller deliberately deceived Raid, whereas Lepper certainly knew what he was doing. He purchased *Schillings* struck under the authority of Duke Bogislaw X of Pomerania, with which he supplied the duke of Mecklenburg's mint at Gadebusch. Once the mint had broken the money, mixed the alloy with base metal, and struck new coins, he took these back to Pomerania. The 'trade in coinage' between the two duchies was brisk, with contemporaries seeing Pomerania as its neighbour's victim. The Stralsund-born chronicler Thomas Kantzow, for example, remarked that Duke Bogislaw's *Schillings* were so good that merchants from Rostock in Mecklenburg were willing to pay a premium to get hold of them—only to take them to their hometown's mint, where they were melted and used as raw material for the town's comparatively shoddy coinage.[26]

Pomerania's coat of arms was the griffin, which also happened to be the device of Rostock. Still, with a bit of goodwill, the town would have been able to design its *Schillings* in a way that made the difference between them and their Pomeranian counterparts obvious. The lettering on the coins was not the same, but this did not help if one was as illiterate as most of the population. Rostock's de facto imitations, therefore, found a ready market in Pomerania. Kantzow, who felt strongly about the welfare of his home country, wistfully remembered the times a hundred years earlier when counterfeiters had not merely been burnt at the stake but fried in hot oil. 'If this punishment was applied in our times', he remarked sourly, 'there would be many princes and lords, yeah, even magistrates, who would have to be fried'.[27] He misunderstood the situation. Like the city of Hildesheim, the dukes of Mecklenburg and the town of Rostock did not commit a crime; they were merely exploiting their well-established and age-old rights and privileges. Counterfeiting was not the issue. It is telling, however, that educated people at the receiving end of such policies—Kantzow, but also Raid who knowingly or not got involved in spreading underweight coins—used that term to describe what was going on. From their perspective, there was little to choose between common counterfeiters and princes who behaved like the dukes of Mecklenburg.

Money traders and their profits

Other observers focused less on the authorities that produced underweight imitations of foreign money than on people like Lepper who engaged in the trade in coinage. The artful merchant who sought out the 'better' coins to sell them to a mint that restruck them as base imitations was a stock figure of late fifteenth- and early sixteenth-century literature. His practices show up in Sebastian Brant's 'ship of Fools', one of the most popular moralizing poetic works of the late Middle Ages.[28] They also occur in a rhymed booklet by Kunz Haß, a member of the guild of master singers of Nuremberg: 'Good coin is lost, with the silver standard being low in one place and high in another... Whoever understands these things strives to obtain silver by culling the heavier coins, thereby winning an ounce in the pound.'[29] Most importantly, the trade figures in many complaints raised by authorities that suffered its effects. For example, in 1539, the magistrate of the city of Hamburg declared that

> several burghers and inhabitants of this city bring whole sacks and barrels of lightweight 3- and 6-*Pfennig* pieces from elsewhere into the city to exchange them for the city's *Schillings*, *Talers**, *Marks**, and other good coin, which they export, thereby seeking their self-interest and acting against the common weal, with the result that all good coin is being driven out.[30]

At roughly the same time Lübeck complained about the same practice.[31] Some years later, the governor of the duchy of Carinthia raised the issue of foreign coins with Archduke Ferdinand of Austria, who was also king of Bohemia and Hungary, king of the Romans (and as such the designated successor of his older brother Emperor Charles V), and ruler of the Habsburg territories that form modern Austria, including Carinthia. In this case, it was small change from the county of Henneberg (more than 400 miles away across the Alps in Central Germany) that according to the governor flooded Carinthia to an extent 'that the common man cannot obtain any other money whatsoever'.[32] People were using the coins as ½-*Kreuzer* pieces; when Ferdinand's mint master in Vienna tested them, their intrinsic value turned out to be closer to that of a ¼-*Kreuzer*.[33] In Bohemia, Ferdinand faced similar problems. There, his counsellors complained that 'everyone knew his royal Majesty's silver-rich coin . . . had not benefited his Majesty's land and people, but that the money had all been exported like a commercial good, melted elsewhere and reminted into poorer coins which, together with other light coins, had then been reimported into the country and become common'.[34] Again, Gresham's Law in action.

There is a simple reason why the law played such a key role in early sixteenth-century Germany. With few exceptions (at which we will look in Chapter 5), rulers had very limited options when they wanted to supply their mints with precious metals. Some were lucky enough to control their own gold or silver mines (as Ferdinand did in Bohemia, Hungary, and the Tyrol), which solved the problem—but they were a small minority. Others depended on their territory producing goods for export, whose total value was larger than that of the goods it imported, or on providing services—for example, in the transit trade—for which the subjects of other authorities were willing to pay.[35] In short, they needed a balance of payments surplus that would result in an inflow of precious metal which could be channelled to the mint. A third option was ordering the mint to change the prices it offered for gold and silver depending on which metal it was to attract. If the ruler planned to issue more gold, the mint would offer the equivalent of more silver (in coin) for gold bullion than did the market or foreign mints, and vice versa. The downside was this meant attracting one precious metal at the expense of the other.[36] If none of this worked, the only alternative was breaking and reminting one's neighbours' money. No wonder, therefore, that historians have estimated that in parts of Germany at least half the metal used by the mints consisted of coins that people like Lepper had collected elsewhere and delivered to have them melted and restruck as underweight imitations.[37] We could consider further examples, but the gist of the argument is clear: In the first half of the sixteenth century the trade in coinage was rife. It was so rife that Germans found it convenient to have a specific term for legal but poor copies of better coins. Such pieces were called

Beischläge, a word that lacks an English counterpart. Side-strikes*, referring to the striking of coins in the mint, comes close.[38]

In the last decade, David Chilosi and I have examined the currency trade in fourteenth- to sixteenth-century Germany in depth. We started out from the idea that differences between local exchange rates of coins from throughout Germany allowed merchants to turn a profit: A merchant would purchase coins where they were cheap not only because of their low content of pure silver or gold, but also because on that market the supply of this type of coins happened to be large or demand weak. Then he would transport the money to where it was more expensive and sell it there. The more merchants engaged in this kind of trade, the more did exchange rates go up where they had initially been low and fall where they had been high. In this way differences between local exchange rates were increasingly eroded, indicating that contacts between markets became closer. What we found was that by the first half of the sixteenth century, differences between local rates in Germany had shrunk further than ever before.[39] Evidently, money was traded across the country at unprecedented and increasing rates.

While we are better informed about the trade in coinage than even a few years ago, it is worth stressing what we do not know. In line with the growth of the trade, complaints about it seem to have become more common, especially from the 1530s onwards. Most direct evidence we have is from the 1540s and 1550s. However, this evidence is not dense or systematic enough to allow us to estimate the quantity or total value of the coins traded between markets. Similarly, we are normally lacking information on the size of the output of mints that produced underweight imitations of better coins. Neither do we know how large the share of such side-strikes was in the quantity of money circulating in individual markets. Likely enough, the claim of the Carinthian governor, that 'the common man' (a term about which we will hear more below) could not get hold of any other money, was hyperbole. Michael von Kuenburg, the archbishop of Salzburg, argued some years later that 'at present the gold and silver which I am having struck and which should be in common use in my archbishopric . . . is all being exported and used for far less than one-twentieth of all payments made in my archbishopric'.[40] Again, this cannot be more than a rhetorical flourish. How would Kuenburg know that coins *not* minted in Salzburg were used in more than 95 per cent of all transactions? He had no statistical office: people engaged in collecting and processing information about what was going on in the markets of his territory. Neither did he have the resources to pay for this kind of bureaucratic apparatus, nor would he have been able to find experts to staff it. Historians talk of weak 'state capacity' in early modern Europe.[41] This captures the main point, though using the term 'state' for something as feeble and disorganized as the German principalities of the early sixteenth century smacks of a similar kind of hyperbole as that used by the governor of Carinthia and the archbishop of Salzburg in the 1550s.

How large were the profits merchants could make in the trade in coinage? There was always at least one political authority that their business harmed; hence, while common, it was certainly something one kept out of the limelight. Evidence for profits is therefore hard to find, especially as some of the persons involved managed very effectively to cover their tracks. This is true for Hans Appenfelder and Balthasar Hundertpfund's money-breaking operation that came to light in Augsburg in 1543 and that we have got to know at the beginning of this book. All we have of the case are some entries in the minutes of the city council meetings and the summary in the city's 'book of penalties'.[42] The extensive paperwork, including the minutes of interrogations, that must have existed and much of which has survived, for example, from Silvester Raid's trial, has disappeared. Still, the 'book of penalties' contains important information. It shows not only how large the sums of 'good' money were that Appenfelder and Hundertpfund's partners supplied to the two mint masters, but also how high the profits were that they claimed to have made (and on whose size that of their fine was based).[43] The sums varied widely from 70 to 3,600 *Guldens*, but the profits were tiny: between ¾ and 5 per cent, on average about 2 per cent.[44] This seems implausible given that earlier in the century big merchant firms in Augsburg and other Upper German cities typically made net profits of between 7 and 10 per cent.[45] If this was possible, why would anyone invest money for a much lower return in a shady business that could get them into deep water if their involvement became public? Overall, we can surmise that profits in the trade in coinage were at least equal to, if not higher than those in legal, everyday transactions. Kunz Haß, the Nuremberg poet's, idea was that you could win an ounce per pound in terms of pure silver; given that there were sixteen ounces to the pound this would amount to 6¼ per cent. This may be a bit low but is certainly in the right order of magnitude.

Compared to Balthasar Hundertpfund, who was fined 1,200 *Guldens*, Silvester Raid a few years later got off lightly. He escaped the torture but had to pay a fine of 120 *Guldens* and was released only once he had made and signed a formal oath not to revenge himself on the city of Augsburg and its officials. Still, the trial became a turning point in his life. Raid was extremely conscious of its effects on his reputation. He, whom everybody 'had always regarded as a man worthy of all grace and honour', had been humiliated: The magistrate had had him disarmed and chained up in gaol. Even worse, he felt he had been 'defamed and slandered' as a common counterfeiter. To crown it all, the written oath he had to sign as a condition of his release contained an admission of guilt. Raid feared Augsburg would use this against him and tried vainly a few years later to persuade the magistrate to hand the paper over to him.[46] By then, he had already lost his position as town clerk of Donauwörth. In 1552, when several Protestant princes rebelled against the emperor, he saw his chance and became a retainer of one of them: Margrave Albert Alcibiades of Brandenburg-Kulmbach, a reckless opportunist and one of the big troublemakers of sixteenth-century Germany. Raid acted as Alcibiades' 'pillage master', being responsible for determining and collecting the sums towns and villages had to pay in order not to be burnt down by the margrave's troops. It was he who negotiated the contract that allowed his master to smoothly change sides and join the emperor.[47] Later, Raid travelled several times to the court of King Henry II of France where the margrave sought further employment. If he had hoped to gain any wealth in Alcibiades' service, he was mistaken, though. All he did was make the acquaintance of various dubious characters, some of whom—members of Franconia's nobility, no less—persuaded him in 1557 to take part in an assault on a messenger who carried cash from Augsburg to Venice. This got about. An imperial commissioner arrested Raid in May 1558 and took him to Vienna where this time his interrogation did involve torture. The trial ended in his conviction, and in November of that year, he lost his head on the block.[48] Thus ended Silvester Raid, merchant, lawyer, diplomat, and highwayman: one of the most colourful characters of a century rich in colourful people.

The Empire in theory and practice

'Roman' and 'Holy'

What kind of country was this, where a successful citizen of one of its great commercial centres could join up with a group of cash-strapped noblemen to engage in highway robbery? Where assaults on travellers were so common that people went about armed with swords and handguns? Where carrying weapons was regarded as a sign of status, so that being forcibly disarmed violated one's dignity and honour? Where people found it sensible to journey large distances, only to deliver hard money to foundries that melted it and turned it into what were, to all effects, forgeries? And where, finally, princes and magistrates engaged in activities that their helpless victims thought no better than counterfeiting?

Looked at from a modern perspective, early sixteenth-century Germany barely resembles what we would call a state. It had no capital where the central government had its seat; in fact, it did not have a central government worthy of that name in the first place. It did not even have any clearly defined borders. Whether you looked east or west, in most places people found it hard to tell where the country ended and where its neighbours began.[49] What Germany had were pretentions. Take the official title of the head of the country in the years 1519 to 1556:

> Charles V, by the grace of God elected Roman emperor, at all times augmentor of the Empire, king in Germany, Castile, Aragon, Leon, of both Sicilies, Jerusalem, Hungary, Dalmatia, Croatia, Navarra, Granada, Toledo, Valencia, Galicia, Mallorca, Sevilla, Sardinia, Córdoba, Corsica, Murcia, Jaén, Algarve, Algeciras, Gibraltar, of the Canary and Indian Islands as well as of the *terrae firmae* [mainland] in the Oceanic Sea, archduke of Austria, duke of Burgundy, Lorraine, Brabant, Styria, Carinthia, Carniola, Limburg, Luxembourg, Guelders, Calabria, Athens, Patras, and Württemberg, count of Habsburg, Flanders, the Tyrol, Görtz, Barcelona, Artois, palatine of Burgundy, Hainaut, Holland, Sealand, Pfirt, Kyburg, Namur, Roussillon, Cerdagne, and Zutphen, landgrave in Alsace, margrave of Burgau, prince of Swabia, Catalonia, Asturia etc., lord of Frisia and of the Windish March, of Pordenone, Biscay, Monia, and Salinas, of Tripoli and of Malines.[50]

This was a peculiar mix of reality and spin. In some of the countries listed, Charles ruled in fact—for example, in Spain and 'both' Sicilies, which meant the island of Sicily and the Neapolitan mainland—whereas in others he had nothing to say whatsoever—for instance in Jerusalem, that is, in the old Crusader kingdom of that name that had fallen to the Muslims in the thirteenth century. In almost all places where he did rule, he did not do so in person but, more or less efficiently, through others. For much of the time this applied to Germany too, that is, to the country of which he was not only the king but to which his title of 'elected Roman emperor' was bound.

Again, this was the result of an instance of political spin, which in Charles V's times already lay some centuries in the past. The ancient Roman Empire had fallen apart in the fifth century, and it was only about 350 years later that a Western European ruler—the Frankish king Charles—was crowned emperor again. Charlemagne, as he became known, did indeed rule a substantial part of the territory of the old Roman Empire in the west, as well as large parts of Central Europe. However, his creation broke apart within a couple of generations after his death. It took about a century before a ruler of one of the splinter-territories that emerged from the wreckage felt strong enough to effectively claim the title 'emperor' again. As this splinter happened to consist of lands most of which would in later ages be collectively called Germany, that country came to be linked with the idea of the Roman Empire—a link that churchmen in the rulers' service spun as *translatio imperii*, that is, as the legitimate transfer of imperial rule from the Romans via Charlemagne's Franks to the Germans.[51]

In the twelfth and thirteenth centuries, the emperors engaged in a lengthy and at times violent dispute with the papacy about who took precedence. To stress their equal standing and their role as advocates (guardians) of the Church, they began calling their domains 'Holy' Roman Empire—another instance of political spin that would work for centuries. From now on both political theorists and the authors of popular chronicles presented the Empire as the earthly reflection of the rule of Christ; the emperors themselves appeared as essential counterparts of the popes. It was only in the fifteenth century, when their influence south of the Alps had waned, that the rider 'of the German nation' was added to the name of the country.[52]

Large parts of Western Europe faced chaotic conditions in the fifteenth century: France because the Hundred Years War with England was fought on its soil, England because it became mired in the Wars of the Roses after its defeat in France. The Empire was no different. In the 1430s, it was shaken by a religiously inspired rebellion that spread from Bohemia to devastate much of the east and centre of the country; a little later the de facto autonomous ruler of a large part of its western border regions waged a war against the equally autonomous Swiss that was no less destructive. Internecine violence among the Empire's elites was rife. Both France and, a little later, England overcame such conditions from the 1450s onwards. So did the Empire. However, whereas in Western Europe the process of consolidation led to the reconstruction of fairly centralized monarchies, in the Empire the outcome was different. There, a precarious balance between the emperor on the one side, and the princes of important territories and several autonomous cities on the other emerged. How and why did this happen?

Land-based politics and decentralization

Much ink has been spilt on this question, but we are still a long way away from consensus. This chapter cannot provide a definite answer either. It can merely survey the ideas suggested so far and point to some factors research has not yet systematically considered. One hypothesis that goes back to the first half of the nineteenth century is that the dispute with the papacy weakened the emperors' position and allowed the increase in power of the subordinate rulers of the territories that made up the Empire, that is, of the imperial princes. Another, more recent explanation points to the population growth of the eleventh to fourteenth centuries. At that time, woods were cleared throughout the country and villages, towns and lordships were founded. The argument is that this development strengthened the princes and allowed them to elude imperial control.[53] The jury is still out on whether and to what extent these views are valid. It is obvious, though, that the emperors were not the only rulers caught in a troubled relationship with the popes. The kings of France, for example, had their own disputes with the Roman pontiffs. The result was not that their position was weakened, but that they compelled the pope to settle in Avignon where they had him under close control for much of the fourteenth century. Similarly, land was cleared, and villages and towns were founded across Europe in the period up to the fourteenth century. Again, in France and England, the outcome was not a weakening of royal power. In Germany, some other factor, or a set of other factors, must therefore have been at work.

To discover these factors, we need to take a step back. When the part of the world that later was to form the core of the Holy Roman Empire first acquired something like political unity in the tenth century, neither economic nor political relations depended on money to any considerable extent. Being wealthy at that time meant being able to successfully claim land (and the labour of the peasants who worked on it). Under such conditions, anyone who tried to gain a position of political dominance needed one thing above anything else: land with which to reward supporters. This is what the tenth-century emperors had—mostly because at that time, the Empire still bordered countries further east that were productive enough to be attractive to conquer and distribute, but politically still too disorganized to offer effective resistance.[54] Once Poland had emerged as a comparatively powerful kingdom in the eleventh century, this avenue of generating loyalty was closed off. The immediate effect was that any German ruler who had followers to reward—or to attract in the first place if he was new to his office—had to fall back on his own land. Each generational change from one ruler to the next thus diminished his capacity to generate loyalty. For example, shortly after having been declared German king in 1212, Frederick II had to grant the king of Bohemia, which had been brought into the orbit of the Empire some generations earlier, parts of the emperor's lands to gain his support. Then 150 years later, Charles IV had to weigh the relative advantage of exploiting his remaining estates in Franconia himself, or of granting them to the burgraves of Nuremberg. He found himself compelled to opt for the latter course. By the fifteenth century, the resources left to the emperors were inadequate to maintain even the semblance of central governance.[55] Importantly, relations between them and the imperial princes were replicated by those between the princes and their own vassals whom they granted fiefs,[56] and again by those between the vassals of princes and the followers whose loyalty they had to purchase by offering them fiefs—and so on, down to landlords whose standing depended on how much land they could grant to peasants. In sum, this kind of land-based politics was one fundamental factor that contributed to the decentralized nature of politics in the Empire.

Since the tenth century, emperors tried to counter the danger posed by princes who demanded more and more resources in return for their support by leaning on churchmen: bishops, archbishops, and the abbots (and some abbesses) of important monasteries.[57] Unlike laypeople, churchmen would not be able to turn fiefs into inheritable rights, so at their death, their land would fall back to the emperor. The 'system' never appears to have been used as purposefully as nineteenth-century historians imagined, but whatever its original value, the emperors' protracted disputes with the popes in the eleventh and twelfth centuries put paid to it. One of the features of the settlement that was finally reached was that the emperor should no longer appoint bishops and archbishops; rather, they should be elected by their cathedral chapters and confirmed by the pope. The emperor was then obliged to invest them with their temporal rights, that is, grant them the land that their predecessors had held, which they would rule in the same way as temporal princes.[58] When, in the sixteenth century, many bishops and archbishops were key members of the emperors' clientele,[59] this was mainly because, being unable to marry and thereby add more land to their principalities, they had become weaker over time than many temporal princes. They needed the emperor's support just as much as he needed theirs.

Fifteenth- and sixteenth-century French kings managed to reverse similar centrifugal tendencies present in France by establishing an *entente cordiale* with their towns. They offered services in return for resources—law enforcement in return for taxes, to be precise—that they then used to sedate their unruly nobility.[60] Their eastern counterparts had no such chance. France benefited from the surviving remnants of the Roman road network that allowed news to travel quickly: 'Ease of communication', remarked the great French historian Fernand Braudel, 'is one of the first conditions of effective government'.[61] It allowed the kings of France to credibly offer their towns assistance wherever they learnt that this was needed. By contrast, most of Germany—roughly the area east of the Rhine and north of the Danube—had never been part of the ancient Roman Empire. There, roads were primitive in the extreme, and over the Middle Ages, improvements were few and far between.[62] How this affected the speed of travelling and transmitting news in Germany will be examined in more detail in Chapter 3. What is important here is that down to the end of the Middle Ages, and to a much larger extent than the kings of Western European countries, the emperors had to be on the move to make their presence felt.[63] In all, it seems highly probable that the poor quality of German infrastructure was a serious impediment to effective rule. Being unlikely to learn of trouble soon enough to be on the spot in time, the emperors were never able credibly to offer services such as those provided by the kings of France. Law enforcement was instead provided by the towns themselves, either individually or jointly with their neighbours.[64]

Unlike their French counterparts, German towns had (at least initially) little to offer in return for the rulers' support. Most had been founded only from the eleventh century onwards, with urbanization beginning more than a millennium later than in the regions further west and south that had been part of the ancient Roman Empire. Compared to French towns, most German ones were latecomers: small, far apart, and little developed.[65] Once they had grown and become wealthy in the later Middle Ages, it was too late for the emperors to take advantage of the change. Their position vis-à-vis the princes had already changed from effective overlord to a status more closely resembling a *primus inter pares*. Thus, poor infrastructure and late urbanization—both results of the failure of ancient Rome to integrate Europe north of the Danube and east of the Rhine—were further factors that made it hard to establish an effective central government in the German lands.

A final factor was geography. Unlike England, and to a lesser extent France, the Empire—especially its German-speaking region—was a largely landlocked country. This mattered because, other things being equal, the power of a central authority depends to a considerable extent on how difficult it is for its subjects to evade governmental control by leaving the country.[66] That is all the more the case because crossing a border is not the only thing necessary for someone trying to thwart their government. It is also necessary to have a place to go to that is more attractive than where one comes from. All this is relevant because far into the Middle Ages, the emperors' subjects enjoyed better opportunities than their French and English counterparts to escape their rulers. Britain is of course an island, which was hard to leave, while France has long coastlines and is elsewhere bordered by mountain chains, on the other side of which lay highly developed and, by medieval standards, densely populated lands. Germany, by contrast, was in the east bordered by countries that were thinly populated. With few exceptions, outright conquest was impossible after the eleventh or twelfth century, but settlers were welcome: merchants and craftsmen from the Rhineland or Westphalia who founded new towns—often with the approval and support of local rulers—and overburdened peasants who had the chance to find lords happy to grant them land and a measure of protection for a fraction of the rents they had to pay in Flanders or Swabia.[67] That the emperors found it difficult to exert control if it was so relatively easy to evade their rule seems highly plausible. The rule of the princes, who faced the same problems, was not much stronger, though due to their smaller size principalities tended to be better organized.

Talks, negotiations, and consensus building

There it is: a country where political decision-making was extremely decentralized, where authorities were generally so weak that it was hard to implement any decision that was made, where law enforcement was patchy and where in consequence life was nasty, brutish, and while not necessarily solitary, often short.[68] Still, all was not bleak. In fact, in the fourteenth and fifteenth centuries, the germs of a political culture developed that allowed the German lands to eventually emerge from the relative chaos of the late

Middle Ages. This culture was not based on violence (though violence continued to play a part in political life far into the sixteenth century); rather, its forward-looking component was a direct result of the large number of actors able to contribute to shaping politics. It was the importance placed on talks, negotiations, and consensus building.

Such talks took place at various levels and in widely differing circumstances. Princes convened their supporters—the historical term was 'estates'—to whom they had granted fiefs to ask them for political advice and increasingly money (which made it sound a good idea to invite representatives of their towns, too). In the first half of the sixteenth century, such regional diets or *Tage*, to use the German term, met in most larger territories of the Empire. The emperors did the same at least as far as their vassals north of the Alps were concerned, whom they could summon easily and who gathered at their court. Here, a group of seven particularly powerful spiritual and temporal princes—the same who monopolized the right to choose the emperor and who are therefore called electors—played a core role.[69] Over the fifteenth century, their assemblies became more regular, with rules and conventions being established that determined who else should be invited: next to the electors other important princes and the delegates of towns that were either located on what used to be the emperors' land or that had established their de facto autonomy from the lords of the surrounding territories. The more common the use of written documents became and the more often emperors listened to the advice of university-trained legal experts, the more detailed became the norms governing such assemblies and the discussions held there.[70] From the end of the fifteenth century onward, the meetings of electors, other princes, and towns organized in this way were regularly called imperial diets, and the authorities who had the right to attend imperial estates.

Altogether, there were more than 360 imperial estates: seven electors, about 280 princes of all descriptions—both spiritual and temporal, from archbishops down to the abbots and abbesses of imperial abbeys, and from dukes down to counts and barons—and *c.*80 free imperial cities of different size—from Cologne and Nuremberg, the largest with 45- and 37,000 inhabitants, respectively, in about 1500 down to Weil der Stadt and Isny in Swabia, which were among the smallest with probably fewer than 1,500 inhabitants each.[71] We should be careful, though, in assuming that conditions were in any way clear-cut. Even in 1521, when one of the oldest comprehensive registers of the imperial estates was compiled, there was much uncertainty about who should be included. This was one reason why the boundaries of the Empire were so poorly defined and blurred. Danzig (Gdańsk) and Elbing (Elbląg), for example, would have been surprised to learn that they were considered free imperial cities—they held they were autonomous under Polish overlordship. And where the lands of the mysterious 'duke of the Mase' listed in 1521 could be found was a question no one knew to answer.[72] Others were identifiable but of doubtful allegiance. In the case of the duchy of Lorraine, this was formalized in 1542–3 with a treaty that granted it far-reaching autonomy.[73] Likewise, the Low Countries had for centuries led their own economic and political life without their official membership in the Empire having much effect.[74] In 1548, Charles V negotiated a treaty that kept them within the polity but formally exempted them from the imperial diet's legislation.[75] Bohemia was another special case. Its king was one of the seven electors, but except for helping to choose the emperors his contribution to the Empire's politics was minimal. He never sat in council with the other electors at imperial diets, and in the sixteenth century, his kingdom and its fiefs in Moravia, Silesia, and Upper and Lower Lusatia were considered exempt from the diet's legislation, too.[76] If all these exceptions are taken into account, what remains is an 'inner' Empire composed of imperial estates that were entitled to take part in imperial diets and expected to contribute to defence and law enforcement.[77] This is the country with which the present book is primarily concerned (Map 1.1).

It has long been recognized that *Tage* were by no means restricted to meetings of princes with their territorial estates and formal imperial diets. At the level of the Empire, there were more assemblies, which were typically called by the imperial diet to discuss or decide specific issues. Adjusting the dues, which the imperial estates paid for military purposes or the maintenance of the imperial chamber court, required negotiations, and so did monetary policies that were the object of specific currency conferences—*Münztage,* in German. Currency conferences play an important part in this book, as do several imperial diets. However, before turning to them, it is necessary to systematically explore monetary conditions in the early years of the sixteenth century—those conditions that provide the backdrop to the activities of people like Hermann Lepper in Mecklenburg and Pomerania and Hans Schaller in Upper Germany, but that were far more important than that: Without them, Lepper's and Schaller's practices would not have been possible at all.

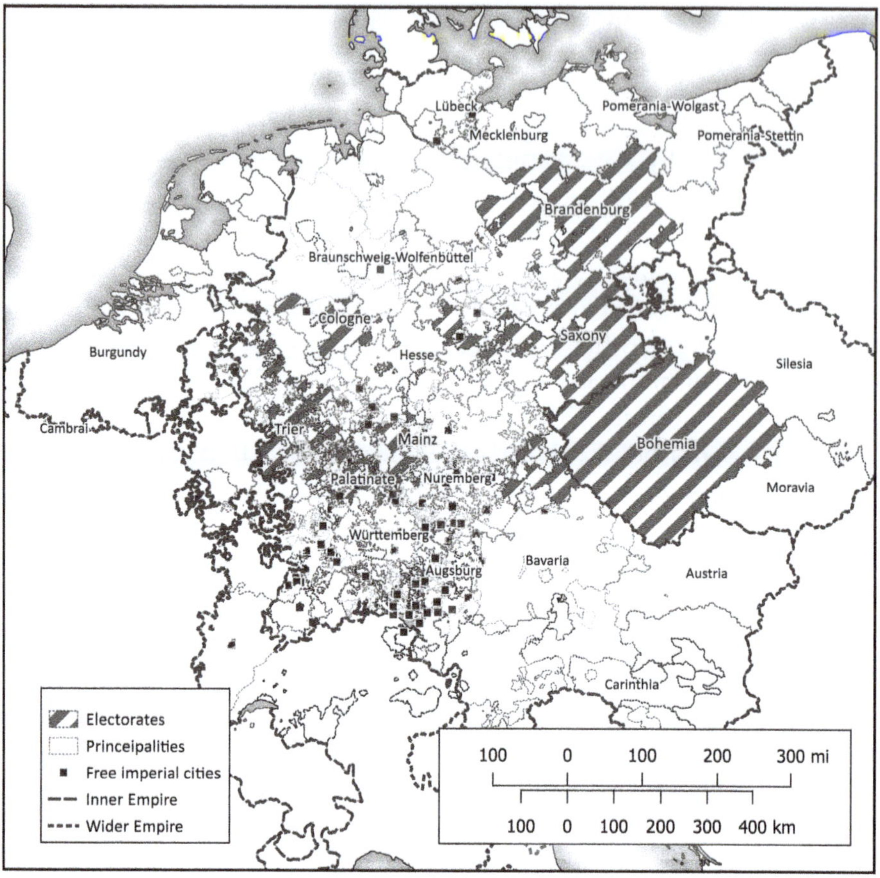

Map 1.1. The Holy Roman Empire *c.*1550

Confusion and disorder

Money without borders

If Germany was decentralized and diverse, it had money to match. To be sure, the emperors had originally regarded coinage as their exclusive prerogative. However, there had always been some rulers who did not share this view and minted their own money without imperial consent. Moreover, in areas that they controlled more closely the emperors began using the right to issue coins to reward supporters. From the eleventh century onwards, maintaining monetary uniformity proved impossible.[78]

Diversity was even larger than this would lead one to expect. As the trade in coinage considered above shows, the German lands did not consist of neatly defined currency regions separated by clear and well-monitored borders. Some estates did occasionally attempt to ban at least certain types of coins issued elsewhere, but normally it was up to the consumers to decide whether and on what terms they were prepared to accept the money they were offered. Moreover, what applied within the Empire applied to its external borders, too: They were not only poorly defined; they were wide open. People, goods, and coin crossed them without being hindered, registered, or taxed. Germany's monetary diversity was therefore not only the result of decentralization, but also of the import of money from abroad. Finally, none of the princes or towns minting in the Empire had a bureaucracy sophisticated enough to withdraw old coins from circulation when they issued new ones of a different standard. Old and new coins would then circulate side by side, and as authorities were too weak to enforce their circulation at specific values, they would normally do so at varying rates that consumers negotiated in the same way in which they reached agreements about the acceptance of foreign or unfamiliar coins.[79]

In the first half of the sixteenth century, the word that seems to have come most often to the minds of contemporaries discussing monetary conditions in the Empire was 'disorder', sometimes coupled with 'confusion'.[80] However, no one was able to tell how disorderly the coinage of the Empire actually was. No prince, whether spiritual or temporal, no magistrate, no merchant, and least of all common folk had access to information that would have allowed them to form a comprehensive idea of the multitude of types of coins of all denominations that were used across the wide geographical space the Empire covered. Charles V and the imperial diet at least tried to find out. In late winter 1551, they decided to adapt an institution created at the beginning of the century to this purpose. At that time, the Empire had been divided into ten so-called circles whose primary purpose was facilitating the enforcement of internal peace and law (for the circles see Maps 6.1 and 6.2).[81] Now, each circle was to send experts in minting and metallurgy—counsellors experienced in monetary policies and assayers such as those maintained by commercial centres like Augsburg—to a *Tag* in Nuremberg. The assayers were to analyse specimens of all coins current at that time, gold as well as silver and those minted in Germany as well as those from abroad. They and the other counsellors met in early April that year and submitted their report—70 neatly handwritten pages—at the end of May.[82]

This report is by no means comprehensive. It leaves out many aspects of the monetary conditions we would like to know, either because collecting the information did not fall under the remit of the assayers and counsellors or because they decided for one reason or another to ignore certain things. Still, imperfect as it is, it is the best guide to the money of the Empire we have, not least because it shows us what contemporaries who were considered experts in this field thought important.

The task Charles V set the assayers was determining the content of pure gold and silver in the coinage circulating in the Empire. They therefore had to collect data that were easy to obtain by weighing and testing coins. The best way to do this—the one that yielded the most accurate results—required melting the pieces. The assayers would then add lead to the alloy, which amalgamated with the base metals the coins contained and was absorbed by the porous earthenware of the crucible. The pure gold or silver remained at the bottom of the pot, with the metal's high surface tension forming it into small beads that one could weigh and compare to the original weight of the alloy.[83] Further monetary data—for example, on how many coins of which type had been issued at what time, how many were still in use, and how many were side-strikes of better originals—were left out of account, or rather, the possibility of comprehensively collecting this kind of information does not seem to have occurred to anybody. This was no doubt a realistic approach. In the fifteenth century, about five hundred mints supplied Germany with money;[84] in the first half of the sixteenth century, the number cannot have been much smaller. Attempting to obtain unbroken records of the output of all mints over a period of decades—back to when they had issued the oldest coins still in circulation in 1551—would have been futile, more so as record keeping appears to have been poorly developed at many of these mints.[85]

Even leaving aside information such as on the quantities of diverse types of coins, the participants in the Nuremberg meeting faced a formidable task which they tried to accomplish as systematically as possible. Examining every single coin-type current somewhere in the Empire was out of the question. A modern catalogue, surely incomplete, lists about 4,500 such types minted between *c.*1480 and 1550—far more than the nineteen persons who attended the *Tag*, only seven of whom were assayers, were able to analyse if they did not want to spend months on the task.[86] The panel, therefore, decided to exclude all coins below the value of roughly one *Kreuzer*, and all of which they claimed they had 'received consistent reports' that their quality was unimpeachable: silver issued by the South German authorities between Austria and the Upper Rhine who had agreed on a common currency in the mid-1530s, coins minted by the four electors in the Rhineland, that is, the archbishops of Mainz, Trier, and Cologne and the count Palatine, and those of groups of estates in Swabia, Franconia, and Saxony. Older silver coins—it was not specified how much older—from Pomerania, Lübeck, and Holstein were also assumed to be so good that testing them was not necessary.[87]

Having cut down their task to a manageable size, the assayers set about testing the gold and silver content of almost 340 different types of coins current in the Empire: *c.*190 golden ones, about 100 of which had been minted in the German lands, the rest in silver, again with *c.*100 German types. Thus, roughly 50 per cent of the gold and 30 per cent of the silver units analysed were from abroad—evidence of the fact that high-purchasing-power gold coins played a larger role in long-distance trade than silver, which tended to be more often used in local and regional exchange (for reasons discussed below this began to change in the first half of the sixteenth century).[88] All in all, 84 of the 123 imperial estates that had issued money at some point between 1500 and 1550 had at least some of their coin types tested (Figure 1.1). There were also authorities of lower status, though: mostly towns such as Hildesheim that had received minting rights not from the emperor but from the imperial estate under whose rule

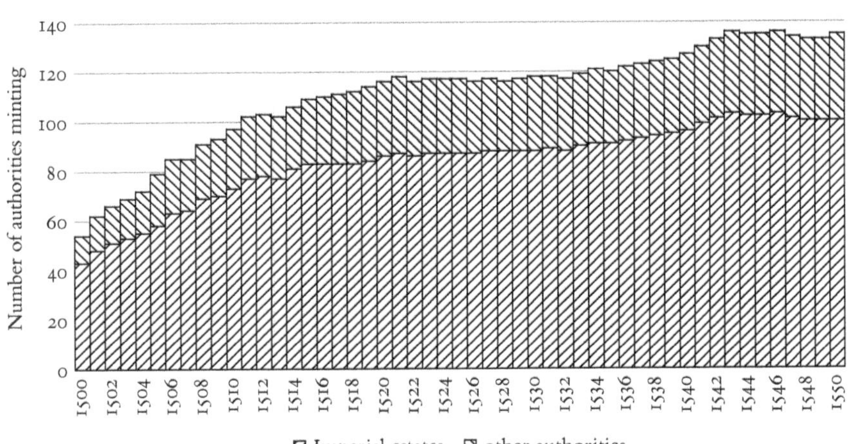

Figure 1.1. Number of authorities minting coins within the Holy Roman Empire, 1500–50

Source: Prokisch, *Grunddaten*, pp. 1–244.

they formally fell, and that were autonomous at least regarding monetary policies. We know of forty-four such authorities that struck coins in the first half of the sixteenth century; in 1551 in Nuremberg, coins of eighteen of them were analysed.[89]

From a modern perspective, one may be tempted to ask how the number of coin types issued by diverse authorities relates to the number of currencies used in the Empire. However, premodern conditions were such that answering this question is anything but straightforward. Take Württemberg, for example. In the late fourteenth and fifteenth centuries the local counts issued coins that fit into a variant of the traditional duodecimal system used elsewhere, too. In Württemberg 12 *Hellers* (the smallest coin) made up a *Schilling* and 20 *Schillings* a *Pfund*. The larger units were not minted; they were so-called 'moneys of account', that is, terms used when dealing with sums of smaller coins to simplify, for example, bookkeeping. Württemberg itself did not even issue its own *Schilling*-coins; instead, people used Prague *Groschens,* minted in Bohemia since the early fourteenth century, as 12-*Hellers*-pieces.[90] This does not imply that Bohemia and Württemberg had the same currency. The counts in Stuttgart made monetary policy decisions without coordinating them with the kings in Prague. Still, there was a degree of spontaneous harmonization. Likely the government of Bohemia was not even aware of this, and that of Württemberg possibly did not notice either. Occasionally, though, the use of 'foreign' coins was formally acknowledged. Then the pieces had to be brought to the local mint or to a goldsmith whom the magistrates had authorized, where they were counter-marked with a special sign. In the first half of the fifteenth century, there were at least 88 places in Germany, mainly in Westphalia, Swabia, and Franconia, where Prague *Groschens* were in this way integrated into the local currency.[91]

Early currency unions

Occasionally, authorities went further. In keeping with the political culture of the Empire, which as we have seen stressed talks and consensus building, some struck agreements that harmonized their coinage. Hamburg and Lübeck, both important centres of North European commerce, had concluded such an agreement already in the thirteenth century and had since then repeatedly renewed their so-called Wendish Union (the towns were called Wendish because they were located in or near areas of originally Slavic or, in German, *Wendisch* settlement close to the coast of the Baltic).[92] At the end of the fifteenth century, the largest coin they minted was the double *Schilling*, a 24-*Pfennig* piece, and there was a range of common smaller denominations, too. However, while Hamburg (like Württemberg) used the *Pfund* of 20 *Schillings* as its top unit of account, Lübeck used the *Mark*, whose value was 16 *Schillings*. Now, was this one currency or two? It turns out that under the conditions prevailing in the fifteenth and early sixteenth-century Holy Roman Empire the assumption that there is a clear distinction between currencies is anachronistic—which is why the coinage experts at the meeting in Nuremberg in 1551 did not try to make this distinction either.[93]

All this was confusing enough, but on balance, it is likely that currency unions or alignments such as those between Hamburg and Lübeck simplified the monetary economy of the German lands. There were several such unions (Map 1.2). The Upper German one that linked the imperial estates between Alsace and Austria since 1535 has already been mentioned. Another confederacy existed in Franconia. It had flourished in the fifteenth century but had come under increasing pressure from about 1500 at the latest. The growth in inter-regional trade and the increasing traffic between markets, which affected Swabia, Mecklenburg, Pomerania, Carinthia, and many other parts of the Empire, allowed the mass import of money issued by neighbouring rulers into Franconia. This made it hard for the members of the confederacy to maintain their own coinage. In 1536, they concluded their last treaty.[94]

There were some more unions, notably one in Swabia that joined Baden and Württemberg,[95] but only two that influenced the monetary economy of the Empire on a wider scale: one in the Rhineland and the other in Saxony. The union in the Rhineland was formed in the late fourteenth century by the four electors whose territories straddled the Rhine (the archbishops of Mainz, Trier, and Cologne, and the counts Palatine). It issued a gold coin, the so-called Rhenish florin, often simply called *Gulden* (German for gold coin), which began in the 1380s as a close imitation of the golden Florentine florin.[96] The Rhenish florin was debased* several times in the fifteenth century—that is, its content of pure gold was reduced—but stabilized from then on. As both coin finds and written evidence indicate, it quickly developed into the most widely used gold coin in Central and Northern Europe.[97] From the beginning of the sixteenth century, the electors on the Rhine harmonized the silver coins they issued, too. At about the same time,

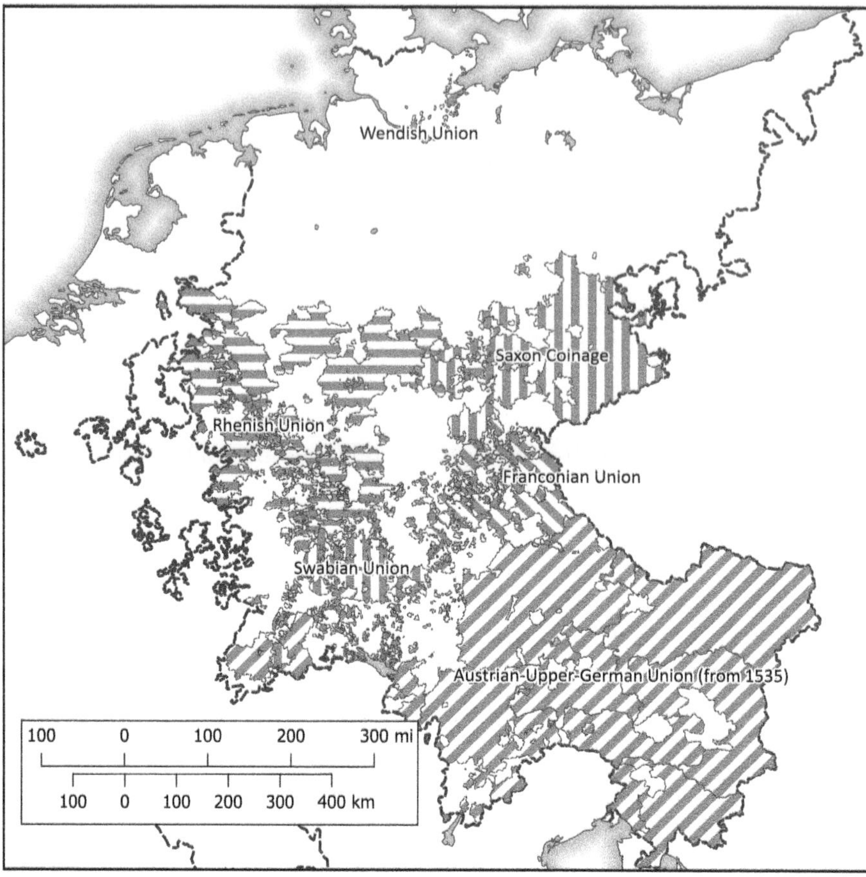

Map 1.2. Major currency unions in the Empire, *c.*1550

Note: The map shows the territories of those imperial estates that had joined a union, rather than the areas where their respective currencies were used.

neighbouring imperial estates such as the city of Cologne, the landgrave of Hesse, the duke of Jülich, Cleves, and Berg, and the bishop of Speyer formally joined their confederacy.[98] Informally, what was still its main unit—the Rhenish florin—was imitated in many other places throughout the Empire—usually with a different design and often with a reduced content of gold (Map 1.3). The assayers in Nuremberg singled out one particularly offensive piece: a coin minted by Count Oswald II of Bergh in the Low Countries that did not only contain 25 per cent less gold than it should have done, but of which they noted that it 'looked almost exactly like the Brandenburg gold *Guldens*' issued by Elector Joachim II

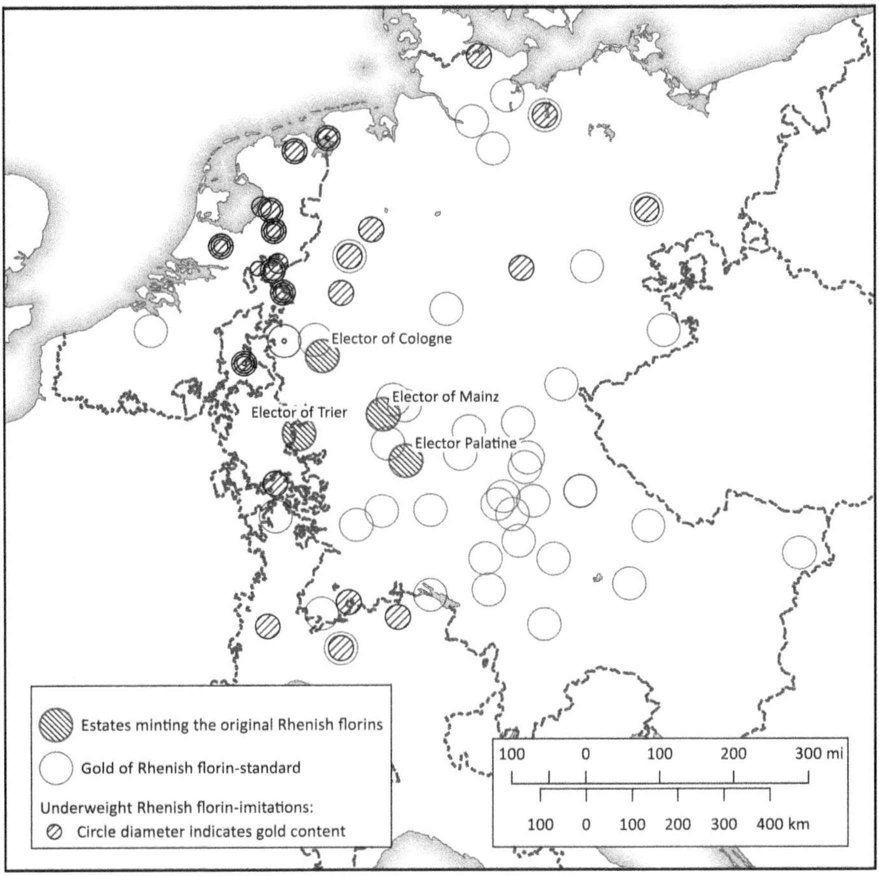

Map 1.3. The Rhenish florin and its imitations: Evidence from the assayers' report, 1551

Note: Volckart, *Währung*, no. 88, pp. 319–26. The map shows the location of the principal residences of the estates minting Rhenish florins and their imitations, rather than that of the actual mints.

(which themselves were slightly underweight copies of the Rhenish florin).[99] All in all, two-thirds of the 118 types of Rhenish florin-imitations tested by the assayers proved to be defective, many of these—for reasons we will explore in the next chapter—from the Low Countries.[100] Shortly before the assayers' meeting in Nuremberg in 1551, the electors on the Rhine explained their monetary policies to the emperor, claiming that 'the uncertain standard of the silver coinage and the import of foreign debased gold and silver money... in exchange for which good Rhenish florins are being exported, broken and melted, has not allowed us to mint considerable numbers of our gold *Guldens*'.[101] We have no reason to doubt this. There is good evidence for a steep drop in the output of the electors' gold in the first half of the sixteenth century,[102] and given the masses of in part underweight imitations that over time had entered circulation, the reason they gave was convincing enough. In short, by the mid-sixteenth century, the Rhenish union faced the same problem as the one in Franconia. Both were in imminent danger of being brought down by the trade in coinage and by the breaking and reminting of their money.

The second widely influential coinage confederacy was formed a century after the Rhenish Union as the result of the division of the territories of the elector of Saxony among his sons. The eldest son took over the electorship, while his younger brother received the rank of a duke. Both kept many parts of administration in common and issued a joint coinage. This gained prominence from the beginning of the sixteenth century onwards when Saxony adopted a monetary innovation made in the Tyrol in the mid-1480s. There, the mint at Hall near Innsbruck—located next to one of the largest silver mines of Europe—had for the first time issued a silver coin so large that its value matched that of the golden Rhenish florin.[103] In 1500, the electors and dukes of Saxony, who themselves controlled rich silver mines in the mountains between their lands and the kingdom of Bohemia, created a similar piece. The explicit purpose was offering a reliable alternative to the Rhenish florin whose underweight imitations had 'flooded' the country, as a common regional *Tag* held by the electorate and the duchy of Saxony complained in 1498.[104]

The value of the Saxon so-called *Guldengroschen** was intended to match that of genuine, correctly minted Rhenish florins. At first sight, one might therefore think that the Saxon rulers set up a situation like the one that existed when Hans Schaller tried to circulate *Kreuzer*-imitations from Hildesheim near Augsburg some decades later. Schaller claimed he had found peasants and others willing to accept the underweight money, and Augsburg's magistrate had rightly feared that such activities would undermine their currency. Why then were the Saxon *Guldengroschens* not undermined in the same way by the underweight Rhenish florin-imitations? They should have been hoarded or ended in the melting pots of the mints of neighbouring rulers; in circulation, they should have stood no chance. Yet they did. In fact, they were a resounding success.

There are two reasons why this was the case, both of which allow important insights into how money was used and are therefore worth spending some time on. First, small coins such as *Kreuzers* were always more prone to being debased than high-purchasing power pieces such as Rhenish florins and *Guldengroschens*. Historians argue that both types of coins, while interchangeable, were used for different purposes and by different groups of people.[105] Thus, small coins served day-to-day small-scale exchanges where most consumers were in no position to learn about the bullion content of the money they handled. As the representatives of the silver-producing estates at an imperial diet in 1545 put it:

> The common man, above all the peasant, uses everyday coins such as *Batzens* [4-*Kreuzer*-pieces] *Groschens*, silver *Pfennigs*, *Kreuzers* and the like in their customary values and hardly notices if the silver content of the said pieces has been reduced or increased, as long as he can spend them for as much as what he accepted them for.[106]

Guldengroschens, by contrast, were no 'everyday coins', and neither were golden Rhenish florins. They were not used in everyday small-scale transactions but primarily in the wholesale, long-distance and luxuries trade—trade that lay in the hands of professional, normally well-informed merchants.

The distinction between these two groups of consumers is important because detecting counterfeits or side-strikes required skill even if one did not aspire to a truly precise analysis such as the one conducted by the assayers in Nuremberg in 1551. One did not only need knowledge but also at least three instruments: a touchstone, a set of touch needles, and precision scales. The scales served to check the weight of the coin. The touchstone was a dark, smooth stone like basalt. If one wanted to test the quality of a coin one scraped its edge along the stone. This left a streak, whose colour one compared to that of the streaks left by the touch needles made of gold and silver of varying and known degrees of fineness. With a bit of practice, one could in this way determine the pure silver or gold content of a coin with an accuracy of up to 2 or 3 per cent.[107] Merchants active in the wholesale, long-distance, and luxuries trade were probably familiar with the touchstone and needles, and if they were not, they had the chance to turn to a public assayer like the one employed by the magistrate of Augsburg. By contrast, 'the common man, above all the peasant' who used 'everyday coins' lacked both the necessary instruments and the knowledge and experience to use them. Also, he had to think twice about spending money on the services of an assayer. He was therefore far more easily fooled by debased small change than a merchant dealing with high-purchasing power coins would have been.

Distinguishing between these two types of consumers and spheres of monetary circulation simplifies things to some extent. The reality was more complex.[108] Information about debased coins would eventually trickle down from merchants and metal experts to the 'common man', which is probably why in, for example, Nuremberg underweight small change appeared particularly often in the collection boxes of churches.[109] Moreover, peasants did not exclusively use 'everyday coins'. At least some of them handled high-purchasing power money, too. The cattle breeders on the North Sea coast did so, and elsewhere others were sufficiently wealthy to have to pay taxes on cash assets that they probably held in large coins.[110] But the fact remains that peasants were the social group in early sixteenth-century society least qualified to discover whether their money contained as much gold or silver as it legally should, and that merchants and others who handled high-purchasing power coins were normally in a much better position when it came to detecting underweight money. No wonder, therefore, that it took a long time—that is, since the inception of the Rhenish florin in the late fourteenth century—for base imitations of this coin to spread so far that they forced the Rhenish electors to largely abandon minting the originals and caused concern elsewhere. Hence the complaints voiced in 1498 at the regional Saxon diet, and the demand for a new and immediately recognizable coin of similar purchasing power as the Rhenish florin. The *Guldengroschen* satisfied this demand.

If this had been all, *Guldengroschens* would probably have been traded at or at best a little above parity with correctly minted Rhenish florins. However, there was a second factor that contributed to their success. Elector Frederick 'the Wise' of Saxony, who took the initiative on this, outsourced minting *Guldengroschens* to Nuremberg where first-rate artisans and the foremost renaissance artists active anywhere outside Italy were available. Lucas Cranach himself provided the designs for the new coin.[111] The result was superb: a piece whose artistic quality far surpassed that of the often-shoddy products of the mints of other authorities (Plate 1.2). When turning to Nuremberg, the elector was not primarily interested in supplying money that satisfied the demand voiced by the Saxon diet in 1498; in fact, he does not seem to have thought much of monetary circulation at all. What he cared about was above all 'beauty and honour', as one of his correspondents put it.[112] *Guldengroschens* were to increase his fame and reputation, and to reach this aim he was even willing to incur financial losses when issuing the new coins. As it turned out he did not have to, or at least not for long.

Plate 1.2. Saxon *Guldengroschen* minted in Nuremberg 1513
Source: © Fritz Rudolf Künker GmbH & Co. KG, Osnabrück (with kind permission).

His *Guldengroschens* proved so popular that people quickly began paying a premium to get hold of them. Their official value was 21 Saxon *Groschens*, and their content of pure silver matched that of the sum of 21 *Groschens*. However, markets not just in Saxony but throughout North Germany and Bohemia soon traded them at 24 and occasionally 25 Saxon *Groschens* or the local *Groschen*-equivalents—and those values were cost-covering.[113] That is not to say that consumers considered *Guldengroschens* solely as works of art and treated them as such. Rather, we are encountering the common phenomenon that the design of a coin has a strong influence on whether and at what conditions markets accept it.[114] In the case of the *Guldengroschen*, this worked to Saxony's advantage.

Like Rhenish florins, Saxon *Guldengroschens* were copied in many places across the Empire. Most importantly, the counts of Schlick in Northern Bohemia, who controlled a large silver mine near Joachimstal (Jáchymov) and were strongly interested in cashing in on the Saxon success, began to issue imitations in 1520.[115] They did so in such numbers that soon even the Saxon original began to be called *Joachimstaler* or simply *Taler*. North Germany seems to have taken up these coins particularly quickly. In the South, in Swabia, Bavaria, and Franconia, this seems to have taken longer. It was only from the mid-1530s that many South-German mints started to issue their own *Talers* (Map 1.4).[116]

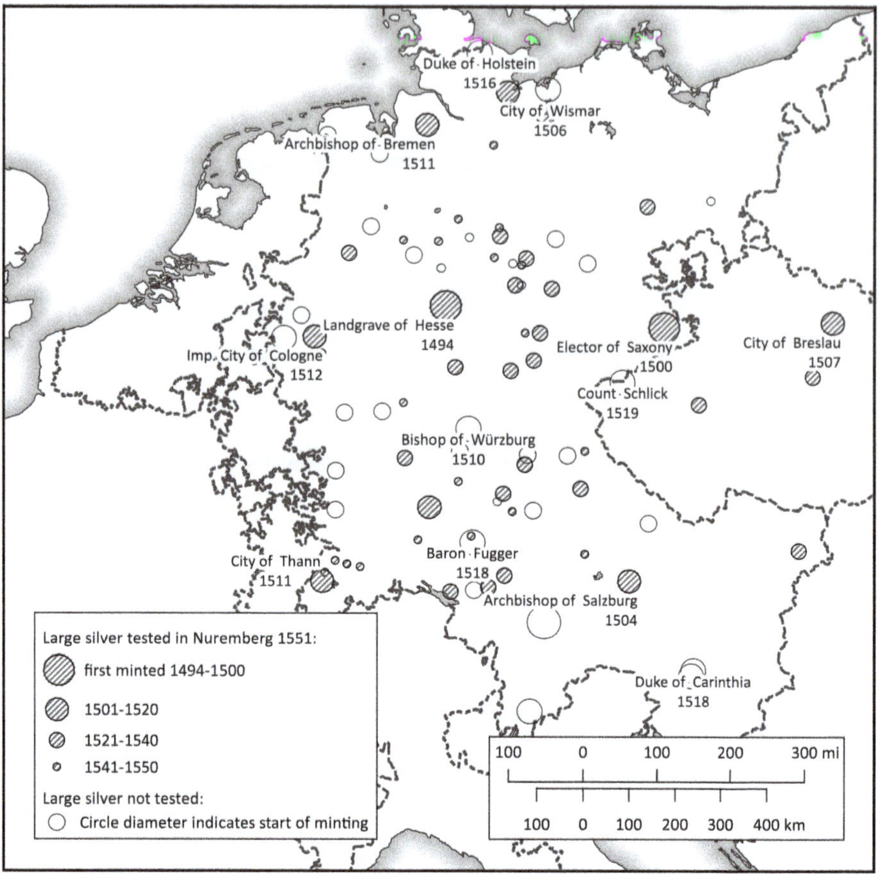

Map 1.4 The spread of silver *Guldens* and *Talers*, 1484–1550
Note: Volckart, *Währung*, no. 88, pp. 332–4; Schulten, *Deutsche Münzen*, pp. 13–472.

At the Nuremberg *Tag* in spring 1551, where the money current in the Empire was tested, the assayers analysed *Talers* minted by 77 authorities, including the kings of Denmark, Sweden, and Poland. The assayers found eight variants from within the Empire that contained less silver than the Saxon original—remarkably few considering that two-thirds of the Rhenish florin-like gold coins they tested were underweight.[117] The difference shows the extent to which monetary policies were driven by the desire to make a profit. This so-called seignorage* resulted from the gap between the production costs of a coin and the value at which the mint could 'sell' it to consumers. *Talers*, which consumers accepted as 25- rather than 21-*Groschens*-pieces, were overvalued* by 19 per cent; producing them was profitable under almost any circumstances. Rhenish florins were widely used but met with increasing suspicion. They were certainly not nearly as overvalued as *Talers*. Authorities wanting to increase the seignorage from minting them, therefore, had no alternative to cutting production costs, and the easiest way to do that was by reducing the coins' content of pure gold.

A new way of counting money

So far, we have encountered two factors which tended to make it easier for at least some consumers to cope with the monetary diversity of the German lands: currency unions and widely accepted gold and silver coins of high purchasing power. These were factors the coinage experts meeting in Nuremberg in 1551 took—at least implicitly—into account. On the one hand, they paid much attention to the Rhenish florin and its imitations as well as to *Talers*, and on the other, most of the money they excluded from their analysis because they took its good quality for granted had been issued by the currency unions in Upper Germany, Franconia, Swabia, the Rhineland, Saxony, and near the coast of the Baltic—suggesting that imperial estates could improve their monetary-policy reputation by joining up with others and agreeing on a common coinage. In the early sixteenth century, there was a third mechanism that the assayers in Nuremberg did not consider: the use of a common unit of account across much of the Empire.

Traditionally, most coins issued between the Alps and the coasts of the North Sea and the Baltic fit into variants of the common duodecimal *Pfennig–Schilling–Pfund*-system used in England (penny–shilling–pound), France (*denier–sous–livre*), and many other countries. Exceptions were some places in North Germany (e.g., Lübeck and Cologne) that preferred the *Mark* to the *Pfund*, and Bohemia and Saxony, where *Groschens* were usually summed up to units of five dozen called *Schocks*. By the fifteenth century, using common units of account did not help interregional trade. *Pfund*, *Mark*, and *Schock* were simply sums of locally produced silver coins whose bullion content varied widely; hence Baden and Württemberg's *Pfund*, for example, differed as radically from the *Pfund* used in Hamburg as the Hamburg-*Pfund* differed from the Pound Sterling. However, in the years around 1500, these traditional systems started to fall out of use in the Empire. They were at first supplemented and then replaced by new money of account that varied less and helped trade more.

The change went back to policies many authorities within the Empire pursued in the fifteenth century to overcome monetary disorder. It was widely felt that part of this disorder was caused by unstable exchange rates between gold and silver coins, and that it could be mitigated by setting fixed rates. Individual estates did so without the policy being in any way coordinated. Thus, the imperial city of Lübeck, far to the North on the coast of the Baltic, fixed the value of the Rhenish florin at 20 *Schillings* in 1433. Three years later Constance, 450 miles to the south on the border of the Swiss Confederacy, set a rate of 14 *Schillings* per Rhenish florin. Saxony determined a rate of 20 *Groschens* in 1444, and Württemberg one of 28 *Schillings* in 1472. In Vienna, from 1469 onward the Rhenish florin was the equivalent of one *Pfund* or 60 *Kreuzers*.[118] As always and everywhere in late medieval Europe, such politically fixed rates proved impossible to enforce even in the medium, let alone in the long term. In Saxony, for example, the Rhenish florin was traded at 21 rather than 20 *Groschens* by 1490.[119] However, for reasons that are not yet entirely clear but that must be related to the supply and demand of gold and silver, respectively, market exchange rates stabilized for about a generation or two over the decades around 1500. In Austria, the Rhenish florin was consistently used as the equivalent of 60 *Kreuzers* between the late 1460s and the early 1520s. It was only after 1522 that its rate started to increase to 64 *Kreuzers*. By the mid-1530s, it had reached 70 and in the early 1550s 73 *Kreuzers*. We observe a similar rise in Hamburg, Cologne, Nuremberg, and Augsburg (Table 5.1).[120]

The effect of the decades of stability around 1500 was that consumers got used to the Rhenish florin being the equivalent of a fixed number of their local silver coins. In a development that has parallels elsewhere in late medieval Europe,[121] they began using the term *Gulden* as a unit of account instead of the older *Pfund* or *Mark*. To distinguish it from the golden Rhenish florin, it was normally called '*Gulden* in coin', occasionally by people who valued precision 'Rhenish florin in coin' and by others inclined to pretentiousness in semi-Latin '*Usualgulden*'. In each case, the term indicated no gold *Gulden* but a fixed sum of locally used silver coins. As the *Gulden* in coin was everywhere based on the golden Rhenish florin, many parts of the Empire did have a common unit of account of broadly similar value in the decades either side of 1500. Not entirely so, of course, as bullion markets were not perfectly integrated: Local values of gold and silver differed to some extent. However, at the beginning of the sixteenth century they differed far less than even a few decades earlier, with divergences having been eroded by the currency trade between markets.[122] Comparing prices stated in silver in different markets of the Empire, therefore, became much easier when the values were high enough to be quoted in *Guldens* of account.

Over time—in fact, over quite a short time—the system ran into trouble. Imperial estates who held the right to mint never refrained from debasing their silver coinages if they believed this might benefit them, and these changes were rarely coordinated with those made by other estates. Local consumers kept using their (by now) customary *Gulden* in coin—only that their *Gulden* now no longer contained even broadly the same quantity of pure silver as the *Guldens* of account used elsewhere. By the middle of the sixteenth century, large gaps had begun to open between the silver equivalents of the regional *Guldens* of the Empire (Table 1.1[123]).

The problem was that this offered people like Lepper in Pomerania or Schaller in Augsburg additional opportunities to make a profit from the trade in coinage. Once again, the basis was the unequal information and bargaining power of different groups of consumers. As shown above, Hildesheim had to design its small *Schillings* as Upper German *Kreuzers* to pass them off as genuine *Kreuzers*. Rostock pursued a similar strategy when it minted coins that were outwardly practically indistinguishable from better Pomeranian pieces. However, using the *Gulden* in coin as a common unit of

Table 1.1. *Guldens* of account, *c.*1550

Region	**Coin equivalent of the regional *Gulden* of account**		**Gram silver per *Gulden* of account**
Franconia	21	*Zwölfers*	25.40
Saxony	21	Saxon *Groschens*	25.37
Upper Germany/Austria	60	*Kreuzers*	25.04
North and middle Rhineland, Hesse	24	white *Pfennigs*	24.78
Swabia	15	*Batzens*	23.86
Low Countries	40	*Grotes*	21.31
Brandenburg	32	Markish *Groschens*	21.11
Pomerania	48	*Schillings*	19.79
Southern Lower Saxony	20	*Maria Groschens*	16.49

account could make it unnecessary to imitate another estate's money, thus exposing oneself to being accused if not of forgery, then of producing side-strikes. All one needed to do was find consumers gullible enough to believe that a certain number of the coins one offered them made up a *Gulden* of account and that this *Gulden* was as good as the one they expected to be paid with. In 1545, the coinage committee of the imperial diet noted that 'in return for his bitter, hard work the poor common man receives a bad, base *Gulden* or silver coin for a *Usualgulden*, believing that one piece is as good as the other and that he has got the *Gulden*, *Batzen*, white *Pfennig*, *Kreuzer* etc. he is owed'.[124] If, for example, a Saxon peasant could be persuaded or pressured to part with a *Gulden's* worth of his grain in return for 32 Markish rather than 21 Saxon *Groschens*, he was cheated out of almost 17 per cent of the pure silver he would otherwise have received. As the silver-producing estates had pointed out at the same diet, this did not matter if he could spend the coins for as much as what he accepted them for. However, if his money were rejected by someone who recognized its poor quality, he would be in trouble. When the coinage committee of 1545 claimed that the 'fictitious *Usualgulden* that has gained so much ground next to the good, Rhenish *Gulden*' had caused 'great disorder, uncertainty and complications',[125] it was undoubtedly correct.

By the middle of the sixteenth century, people were thus juggling three different types of *Guldens*. The first was the golden Rhenish florin that came in different variants, many of which contained less gold than they should have done, the second was the *Guldengroschen* that was increasingly called *Taler* and widely imitated, too, though underweight copies were yet relatively rare. Finally, there were the *Usualguldens* or *Guldens* of account. A *Usualgulden* was a fixed sum of locally or regionally used silver coins whose value had everywhere been close to that of a correctly minted Rhenish florin at around the beginning of the century. However, by about 1550 the uncoordinated debasement of individual types of silver had caused the values of the different *Guldens* of account to become increasingly unequal. In December 1549, the counsellors of the electors on the Rhine summarized their view of the problems from which the money used in the Empire suffered:

> That the German nation has been led into notable harm with regard to the coinage, their gracious lords, the electors . . . ascribe to many estates having reduced the bullion content of their coins, having minted base money and

> having bought up good old coins, which they partly have broken and restruck more basely and partly have exported together with gold *Guldens* to foreign countries, and in exchange have imported foreign gold and silver coins that they spent at higher values than their content of bullion justifies.[126]

Altogether, the assessment seems accurate enough. The question was, what could be done about it?

2
People and politics

The common man

Ideas, rumours, public opinion

In about 1530 the Augsburg type-cutter Wolfgang Rösch published a new piece in the long series of flysheets that had become available to readers in Germany over the preceding decades.[1] These prints typically covered no more than a page; they were quick and cheap to produce, found a ready market and therefore formed the basis of the economic success of many printing workshops.[2] In particular since the beginning of the Reformation, they had developed into an important medium that helped shape the views people held on a variety of issues, most often religion.[3] Rösch's flysheet had a religious theme, too, but its starting point and presentation were unusual. The title was 'A question to a moneyer: Where has all the money gone that is minted every day?' Below this, a handsome woodcut—the work of the local artist Jörg Breu the Elder—filled the upper half of the print and suggested part of the answer (Plate 2.1). In the centre it showed the moneyer, busily minting coins and apparently answering the question posed by the flysheet, which an individual in scholarly garb is asking him. On his left sits an indulgence trader, and to the right there is a prelate of the Roman Church on mule-back with an attendant and, just visible behind him, a jester with his hand raised in the gesture that averted the evil eye. Various townspeople move about in the background.

The author of the text on the lower half of the sheet is unknown. However, he was talented enough to put it in verse, which helped contemporaries memorize it if it was read to them and thus facilitated spreading its content by word of mouth. In a largely illiterate society this

Plate 2.1. 'A question to a Moneyer', Flysheet, Augsburg *c.*1530

Source: *Ein Frag an eynen Müntzer/ wahin doch souil Geltz/ kumme das man alltag müntzet* (Augsburg: Wolfgang Rösch, *c.*1530). Online at https://ghdi.ghi-dc.org/sub_image.cfm?image_id=3300&startrow=1&language=english (accessed 13/03/2023).

was particularly important.[4] In the text, the moneyer, who is evidently considered an expert in anything related to the monetary aspects of the economy, identifies three enemies of Germany's coinage: the Pope, new fashions, and imported luxury goods. The flysheet clearly invites its readers (and listeners) to identify with him and to distance themselves from the powers that duped the 'German fools', as the text puts it (in German, 'fool' and 'jester' are the same word), out of their money: the greedy papacy and equally greedy merchants who pandered to new fashions by importing useless luxury goods.[5] None of this was particularly original; in fact, a few years earlier Martin Luther had published very similar views.[6] What was original was the short doggerel that introduced the moneyer's longer answer:

If the faith we hold was true,
God and the common weal we knew,
Had good measurements and weights,
Fair peace, justice, and common rights,
Common coins, no counterfeits,
The world would be a better place.

A common coinage untainted by side-strikes and other de facto forgeries appears as one of the essential institutions without which realizing the common weal—a concept we will encounter again—would not be possible. No doubt the author of the pamphlet expected the audience to immediately agree with the ideas his short verse expressed. Its purpose was making them receptive to the moneyer's more elaborate arguments in the rest of the text. Does this mean that there was something like a public opinion concerning monetary politics in the early sixteenth-century Empire? The fact that another version of the flysheet about the moneyer has been preserved—with the same doggerel but a different woodcut—suggests that the issue was popular.[7] This supports the hypothesis that a public opinion concerning monetary policies existed. However, most historians have looked for evidence for a public opinion in the seventeenth and eighteenth centuries, when its emergence was helped by the rise of new media like newspapers and the influence of the Enlightenment. Those who study the sixteenth century have focused on how people learnt about and helped to spread the ideas of religious reformers like Luther and Zwingli and, to a lesser extent, the way print media reflected peasant rebellions.[8] Ideas concerning monetary policies, and the possible influence of the wider population on political decision-making, have never been considered from this perspective.

One thing is obvious, however. Monetary policies were not purely imposed from above by rulers, with politics shaping the way people interacted on markets.[9] On the contrary: we have encountered several instances where monetary policies were literally made from below. The imperial estates insisted again and again that 'the value of coins should not be set high or low according to how subjects and private persons estimate them, but according to what the high and lawful authorities determine and order'.[10] However, they still had to accept that the Saxon *Guldengroschen* had 'set itself' at 24 *Groschens*, rather than maintaining its official value of 21 *Groschens*.[11] Similarly, the emergence of the *Guldens* of account was a spontaneous process. While they were ultimately based on gold–silver exchange rates that diverse authorities had determined at some point in the past, the fact that *Usualguldens* had first supplemented and then replaced the traditional units of account was the unplanned and unforeseen result of decisions made by thousands of consumers over a period of decades. Such developments did not only set part of the parameters of monetary politics; decision-makers also often perceived them as problems that required political solutions.[12]

People who changed the numerical ratios between the coins of their domestic currency or created new units of account were not the only ones who influenced politics without taking part in official decision-making. There was a complex relationship between ideology, the self-perception of the emperor and estates, and their receptiveness to views held by others—a relationship that at least in part informed their policies. Theologians and political thinkers encouraged them to see themselves as Christian authorities to whom God had entrusted the protection of the true Christian faith, the enforcement of law, and the promotion of the common weal. Their decisions were supposed not to be arbitrary, but to conform to religious and ethical norms.[13] Among these, focusing on the needs of the 'common man' took precedence. According to an anonymous author advising Charles V's counsellors on monetary policy in 1549, it was the common man who

> pleads and begs that his imperial Majesty . . . uses his imperial office to most graciously ease the heavy burden caused by the bad conditions that have arisen, and to implement a good, Christian, and useful policy, giving more consideration to the large common crowd than to the small number of self-interested people.[14]

Historians such as Stefan Brakensiek have pointed out that many rulers tried to fulfil at least some of these ethical requirements.[15] Aside from ideology and the urging by their advisers and others, there were sound practical reasons for doing so. We have seen that in the late Middle Ages, rulers were struggling to find the resources needed to enforce their decisions, and this had not changed in the first half of the sixteenth century. While some imperial estates were better off than others—for example because they had access to precious metal ore—most were still expected to live off the income of their demesnes. Elector Joachim II of Brandenburg, who from a fiscal perspective appeared as no more than the largest *Junker* of his land, is a good example.[16] Under such conditions, politics would work the better, the more willing a ruler's subjects were to accept them, or conversely, the more the emperor and estates practiced what Brakensiek calls an 'acceptance-oriented' style of rule.[17] This required rulers to communicate with their subjects, which could not be a one-sided process: Knowing how to listen was the essential complement of issuing commands. If the authorities did listen, there was a chance that their subjects would find their laws and measures reasonable or at least not unduly harsh. This would cut the costs involved in executing decisions, and that is why public opinion mattered.[18]

For the historian, discovering what both the 'large common crowd' and 'self-interested people'—in short: the public—thought about monetary policies is particularly challenging. Sixteenth-century public opinion was a complex phenomenon. In a very abstract way, we can follow Robert Scribner in defining it as 'the frame of mind of those people who constitute a "public", essentially all those concerned with an event or situation and likely to become involved with its consequences'.[19] Scribner's definition captures an essential reality, but we should not expect to find a single public with a homogeneous opinion. After all, while there were few people who never handled any money and did not experience the consequences of monetary policy decisions, different groups in society were affected in different ways. Moreover, sixteenth-century public opinion depended to a large degree on rumours that spread more easily within than between these groups.[20] Scribner has shown how this worked with religious ideas. People talked about religion in informal discussion circles, at dinner (sometimes with travellers whom they invited), during spinning bees, and above all with acquaintances and strangers they met over a beer or wine in inns. They would read pamphlets, broadsheets, and books to each other and especially to those who could not read themselves, so that the effect of the printed word reached far beyond the relatively small circle of the literate and semi-literate.[21] Likely they talked about broadsheets such as the one published by Rösch in Augsburg—and about matters of coinage in general—on such occasions, too. Scandals triggered discussions,[22] and as the money-breaking operation of Hundertpfund, Appenfelder, and their associates from Augsburg's high society kept being reported in local chronicles far into the eighteenth century, this was certainly an event that set tongues wagging in the early 1540s. Thus, the spoken word was an essential complement of printing, and reconstructing something that was essentially oral from written evidence is obviously difficult.

In recapturing popular monetary ideas, the primary sources are, as ever, our best guide. This is because they help to structure the historical material according to criteria which both those who made monetary policy decisions and those affected by them found important. These criteria are supplied by the distinction between the 'common crowd' or 'common man' on the one hand, and merchants on the other. It is these two groups who kept appearing in monetary policy discussions during the first half of the sixteenth century and to whom the political discourse attributed homogeneous political views and interests concerning the Empire's monetary economy. However, before exploring whether, or how far, political decision-makers took these views into account, it is necessary to consider who belonged to these groups and in what regard they were held.

The common man and what he thought about money

While the emperor and the estates regularly referred to the common man in their deliberations, they never defined whom they meant when they were using the term. To uncover this, we must therefore turn to other sources. A good starting point is Martin Luther, who followed a centuries-old tradition when he distinguished the Pope and the clergy, whose task was praying, the emperor and the princes, who were charged with providing protection, and the rest of the population, who had to work and whom he called the 'common man'.[23]

Historians tend to follow Luther.[24] For them, the concept refers to anyone who was not a member of the spiritual or temporal nobility. A few qualifications are necessary, though. First, as the term common man suggests, women were excluded from this group (by 'common woman', sixteenth-century hearers would have understood a prostitute). The social and economic options of women as well as their political voice were severely circumscribed in the German lands. Regional variants of 'gender guardianship', the rules of craft and merchant guilds, and the powers of local communities limited their status as legal adults. While women were therefore subject to greater constraints and had fewer possibilities than men, it would be surprising if they had not taken part in discussions of the Empire's monetary economy or monetary politics. After all, in early modern Europe women were often associated with gossip and rumour.[25] However, so far not even indirect evidence for their involvement has come to light. Tellingly, when popular pamphlets presented dialogues about economic issues in a fictionalized form, the participants were always male.[26] A second qualification concerns the politically dominant urban elites, the patricians, who partly overlapped with the commercial upper classes and whom no one considers to be in the category of the common man. And finally, servants, vagrants, and mercenaries, whom people thought dishonourable, were not in this category either.[27] They were not even implicitly considered when monetary politics were discussed.

This leaves us with the male heads of urban and rural households who depended on their own, mostly manual, labour for their livelihood and who enjoyed the honour—that is, the respect accorded to them not just by their equals, but also by the members of other social groups—specific to their station in life: essentially peasants and master craftsmen. Numerically peasants dominated, but townspeople played an important role, being more often literate and having a better chance to voice their views—with the result that we can, on occasion, glimpse what they thought about the Empire's monetary economy.

Historians have detected a fundamental change in the way the higher orders perceived the common man, especially the peasant, during the first half of the sixteenth century. Probably in consequence of Luther's teachings on the priesthood of all believers and his idea that physical labour was sanctified, the traditional negative attitude gave way to the image of the 'evangelical peasant'.[28] The change is reflected by the way the emperor, the estates, and their counsellors and advisers who discussed monetary policies perceived the common man. For example, a memorial drafted by a currency committee at the imperial diet of Worms in 1545 talked of the 'common crowd, the largest part of humanity, that is, the common man who must carry the cross'.[29] There were both Protestants and Catholics among the committee members,[30] which makes the way they placed the common man next to Christ all the more remarkable. His physical labour did indeed appear sanctified, and it conferred a dignity on him he had not had before the Reformation. Talking of 'the poor common man who must nourish all through his bitter toil and whom God the almighty no doubt has at heart' makes this even more obvious.[31] Other examples pair the common man with the 'whole German nation' in a way that suggests he was seen as representative of the population as a whole.[32] When the 'common man and weal' are mentioned in one breath, the implications are similar.[33] The conclusion is that in the eyes of the authorities involved in shaping the Empire's monetary economy, the common weal was what they believed would benefit the common man.

If we consider monetary-policy discussions at imperial assemblies between 1544 and 1559 and cases where the expression 'common man' was paired with an adjective, 'poor' unsurprisingly takes first place, while 'ignorant' and 'simple' come as distant second and third.[34] Taken together with the evidence quoted above, this suggest that the common man was seen as a person deserving of attention and of the care for the common weal. This was primarily because of his inherent dignity coupled with the helplessness that his poverty and ignorance implied—though just occasionally, we glimpse a different perspective. The instructions the delegates of the elector of Saxony received for monetary-policy talks with the other estates in early 1549 mentioned the need to mint a sufficient quantity of small change because if this was neglected, 'it would be burdensome for the common man and might easily cause an uprising in the Empire'.[35]

The Saxon counsellors who drafted these instructions were probably thinking of the series of regional rebellions that had culminated a quarter of a century before in what is traditionally known as the 'Peasants' War'. The revolt—disconnected, but all in all the largest popular uprising in Europe before the French Revolution—affected much of Southwestern and Central Germany and was put down with great brutality and bloodshed. The analysis of the written complaints the peasants submitted has shown that serfdom and its implications—such as restrictions on marriage—were the most important trigger of the revolt. The rents peasants paid to their landlords came second, and the consequences of state formation—for example increasing demands for taxes—third.[36] In addition to this, one political factor is evident. Authorities at all levels had not behaved in the way they were urged to behave in the decades after the end of the conflict: Acceptance-oriented rule had not been the hallmark of their style. In short, they had failed to listen.

The term 'Peasants' War' is today widely considered a misnomer. The urban common man was in many places involved in the uprising; elsewhere, for example in the Tyrol, miners played an important role. Moreover, the insurgents developed ideas to achieve a fundamental social and political transformation of the Empire. Their aims were as disparate as their rebellion was regionalized, but there are a number of recurring themes—the political autonomy of villages and towns, the restriction of arbitrary government—and a common underlying ideal: a social and legal system headed by the emperor, with autonomous communes as fundamental building blocks and brotherly love and the common weal as guiding principles.[37] While the peasants themselves were calling their uprising 'a Peasants' War', their far-reaching aims make it appear as a revolution, and as townspeople were involved too, following Peter Blickle in calling it a 'revolution of the common man' seems appropriate.[38] Interestingly, alongside abolishing large merchant firms which were accused of profiteering and creating monopolies, transforming the monetary economy of the Empire took centre stage among the economic policy-aims of the revolutionaries, at least as far as they were expressed in the programmatic writings of some of their leaders.[39]

One of these leaders was Friedrich Weigandt, a minor official of the elector of Mainz in the town of Miltenberg in modern Bavaria.[40] While the question of how influential he was is one of the many disputed aspects of the Peasants' War,[41] the fact remains that he envisaged a fundamental constitutional reform of the Empire. In May 1525, he argued that many authorities 'have established new coinage rights, so that the good old coinage has disappeared and poorer coins have appeared in great numbers'—exactly what Gresham's Law states. 'It would be good', Weigandt further argued, 'to investigate the origins of these privileges, and where no ancient authorization can be found, they should be abolished and the old coinage rights restored as may be required'.[42]

In so far as Weigandt started out from the idea that new rights, laws, and privileges were illegitimate and that returning to old customs meant re-establishing a just state of affairs, his demands fit the pattern of the arguments late medieval peasants used to vindicate their grievances.[43] However, he went further. He did not merely envisage a return to an imagined past but took up new ideas. 'So that the common man will not be deceived by the coinage', Weigandt demanded that all existing gold and silver money should be broken and replaced by new coins struck according to a common, Empire-wide standard. The new money was to be produced by at most 20 or 21 mints, whose regional distribution he determined as well.[44]

Weigandt had copied his ideas point-for-point from an anonymous pamphlet that had appeared in Zwickau in Saxony some years before. 'The Needs of the German Nation', ostensibly authored decades earlier by Emperor Frederick III, presented a comprehensive reform plan for the spiritual and temporal powers of the Empire.[45] Among other things, it addressed the introduction of a clear and unambiguous hierarchy of diverse authorities, the harmonization of weights and measures and, as paragraph nine out of twelve, the creation of a common currency.[46] The way Weigandt adopted these ideas shows the impact cheaply printed pamphlets could have, especially if readers then broadcast a pamphlet's ideas orally, thus multiplying its audience. Weigandt himself was no peasant; he had worked in the elector of Mainz's local tax office in Miltenberg,[47] where he must have encountered many different types of coins. However, he was writing for peasants and evidently expected his ideas to resonate with his audience. Most villages would have contained at least one or two persons able to read—perhaps the village priest or village officials—who could relay his ideas to non-readers. We also have evidence showing that peasants bought copies of other programmatic writings of the leaders of the revolt.[48] It is therefore likely that large numbers learnt of Weigandt's ideas. It is also likely that they approved of them. Think, for example, of the Saxon currency ordinance of 1511: The bill listed 37 different types of coins below the size of a *Groschen*, only four of which were domestic, and expected consumers not only to be able to correctly identify non-Saxon pieces, but also to learn their official values in Saxon money and to remember them.[49] To people treated to this kind of government directives—of which they probably learnt when their village priest read them out after the Sunday sermon—any measure intended to reduce monetary diversity must have seemed attractive.

There are other tantalizing hints that suggest the desire to overcome such diversity was widespread. Some years before the Peasants' War, the Swabian folk preacher and former monk turned Lutheran theologian Johann Eberlin von Günzburg published a collection of fifteen of his treatises. In one of these texts, he developed ideas for a set of social, economic, and constitutional reforms that were to turn the Empire into a kind of utopia he called 'Welfaria'—the 'land where all are prosperous'.[50] He advocated shutting down all merchant firms with more than three partners (which he, like Luther, suspected of profiteering) and demanded that 'in the whole Empire, there shall be a uniform coinage, that is, one standard and a common value'.[51] Eberlin called his collection of essays 'The fifteen Allies' because he expected it to provide arguments other reformist preachers could use. If they took up his monetary-policy idea in their own sermons, they are likely to have acted as 'multipliers' in the same way Weigandt did.

Do these sources illustrate that public opinion, as held by the common man, was concerned about the Empire's monetary economy? Here, we are least likely to encounter any direct written evidence, given that rumours played a core role in the formation of the views held by peasants and townspeople who were not members of the elites.[52] However, indirect evidence—references to rumours about monetary policies—is plentiful. For example, at the imperial diet of 1545 the delegates of the cities asked the representatives of the silver-producing estates to keep in mind 'what clamour and indignation' their decisions 'would cause among the common man, who has heard so many complaints, and is complaining himself, about the coinage having become so poor and bad within living memory, yeah, even within twenty years'.[53] On another occasion, the counsellors of the elector of Mainz argued that their master had pursued cooperative monetary policies because of 'the clamour that he should not hinder the common weal'.[54] Similarly, the envoys of the princes were anxious about their decisions 'gaining and having a poor repute with everyone', and the counsellors of the emperor worried about the 'malicious gossip, scandal and scorn' to which their monetary policies might expose them.[55] In 1556, the Austrian government intervened against the barons of Frohberg in Alsace (Montjoie-le-Château), arguing that because the barons had issued counterfeit coins, they had to 'be punished in a way that sets an example for others, and so that the common man may not say that one punishes the commoners and poor people only, but spares those of high standing'. The Frohbergs were fined 4,000 *Guldens*,[56] a large sum considering the 1,200 *Guldens* Balthasar Hundertpfund, the mint master of Augsburg, had to pay in 1543 for what amounted to a similar crime. In short, authorities in the Empire were evidently taking for granted that their monetary policies were the object of rumours among the wider population. While we can tell neither how political information reached the common man, nor how accurate it was or what peasants and craftsmen made of it, it is likely that when Weigandt and Eberlin von Günzburg drafted their reforms, they were taking up and further developing ideas widespread among their audience, that is, the urban and rural insurgents of 1525–6.

As always, it is worth stressing the limits of our knowledge. We do not know, for example, how strongly the common man favoured a common currency. Neither is it possible to tell whether or how peasant-public-opinion differed from that of townspeople, or to identify regional variants, though given the diversity of Germany it is likely that they existed. After all, while there were regions where peasants used large coins and owned relatively large sums of money—the North Sea coast, the bishopric of Straßburg (Strasbourg) and Thuringia are mentioned in this context—evidence from elsewhere—Mecklenburg and parts of Upper Swabia—suggests that others handled money very irregularly: maybe only a few times a year, for example after they had sold their harvest.[57] Moreover, even within the same village, peasants' wealth was unevenly distributed, with relatively well-to-do members of the village elites at one end of the social spectrum and cottagers and smallholders at the other.[58] It would be surprising if people involved in the monetary economy to such different extents had held the same views.

Still, the discussion above has yielded two findings of which we can be certain. First, a public opinion concerning the Empire's monetary economy did develop. Given the hierarchic and segmented character of German society, it was a public opinion that was specific to the common man's social stratum; possibly it was also gender-specific. And second, we know that the idea of creating a common currency was voiced often enough among the public to leave clear traces in our sources. The question now is, how relevant was this public opinion for decision-making at the level of the Empire? We have seen that the political elites held generally positive views of the common man. We have also seen that the delegates at imperial diets and other assemblies took for granted that he would learn and talk about their decisions. But did they learn what the common man was thinking? If so, how? And did they take this into account when making decisions about monetary politics?

Public opinion and monetary policies

A formal way of collecting information about the political preferences of the common man did not exist. However, there were about eighty imperial cities that were directly represented at the imperial diet, and in the first half of the sixteenth century many of them had governments dominated or strongly influenced by their respective local craft guilds.[59] Fully participating in urban government was probably difficult for master craftsmen who rarely had the necessary wealth and free time. Still, in these towns, families represented in government tended, for example, to intermarry with artisan families.[60] This must have eased the flow of information from the common man to the urban authorities. We can therefore assume that many of the delegates, whom towns sent to the imperial diets and other imperial assemblies, knew at least in outline how local craftsmen and other townspeople thought about monetary issues. Furthermore, most principalities of the Empire had their regional diets, and in some of these, notably those located in the core of the region affected by the Peasants' War of 1524–6, delegates of rural communes were present. In Tyrol and Vorarlberg, in the Austrian territories in Swabia, in Württemberg and in Baden, and in spiritual principalities such as the bishoprics of Chur and Basel and the archbishoprics of Mainz and Salzburg, the common man was directly represented in regional politics. The settlements that ended the uprising determined that he should also be admitted to the regional assemblies of territories ruled by large imperial abbeys such as Kempten (Map 2.1).[61] As in the case of imperial cities dominated by craft guilds, the envoys such principalities sent to at the imperial diets would have known how the common man felt about the monetary economy of the Empire.

Certainly, in most regional diets peasants were not represented. However, they had the chance—and used it like members of all other social groups from the very poor to the powerful—to make themselves heard by submitting petitions.[62] Also, the more important territorial towns were normally represented at regional diets, where their delegates could bring up monetary

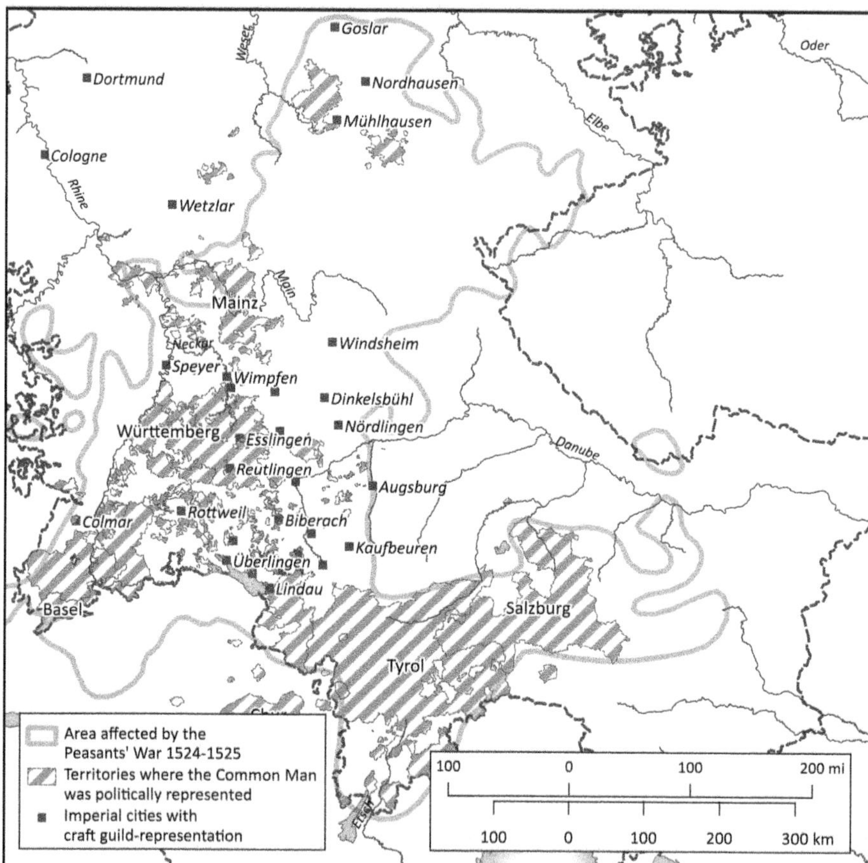

Map 2.1. The common man in politics, 1524 to late 1540s

conditions.[63] In the Bavarian diet, for example, complaints about the inflow of 'foreign' coins were voiced in 1517.[64] Electoral Saxon delegates at imperial assemblies took the views expressed at their home diet into account when discussing monetary policy issues at the level of the Empire—if only because this offered a perfect excuse for rejecting ideas they themselves did not favour. On occasion, others used the same tactic, as we will see in Chapter 5.[65]

Channels allowing information to flow from the common man to the Empire's political elites did exist. When monetary policy discussions mentioned the 'complaints of the common man', the 'great grievances of the poor man' or his 'daily crying, wailing and begging',[66] such references were more than mere rhetorical flourishes used to strengthen the elites' arguments. It is likely that they reflected views held by large parts of the population. Given the need to pursue an acceptance-oriented style of rule, taking these views into account when designing monetary policies made sense: It helped decisions gain legitimacy and reduced the costs of implementing them.

In conclusion, the evidence suggests that the interplay between a wider public whose members voiced complaints and criticism and the legitimacy of rule is something that did not develop only in the late seventeenth or eighteenth century.[67] Rather, early sixteenth-century rulers were ideologically expected to take the wishes of the common man into account. For organizational reasons they faced incentives to do so; and given the composition of regional and imperial diets they were at least to some extent able to see what the common man actually wanted.[68] Still, we have seen that the group called 'common man' did not make up more than one segment of the population. What about the rest?

Politics and trade

Hostility to trade

Typically, sixteenth-century sources juxtaposed the common man with princes, the nobility, or political authorities in general.[69] Contrasting him with any other social group was rare—but not in our context. Where monetary policies are concerned, authorities involved in making decisions at the level of the Empire set him against the merchant. We have seen that they faced incentives to take the wishes of the common man into account at least as far as they learnt of them. How about merchants, then? How did authorities see them, and did they consider the needs of trade?

The sources make it abundantly clear that the way the Empire's political elite pictured a society composed of the common man on the one hand and merchants on the other lacked any nuance. Not only did they ignore all other social groups, but this was also an aspect of their worldview where the contrast of black and white was particularly stark. In monetary policy-talks, this was expressed in no uncertain terms. Criticizing a suggested measure by rhetorically asking 'whom is this supposed to benefit except the merchants, but not the common man?' was normally expected to be sufficient to close the matter.[70]

In this, the imperial estates were at one with the common man himself and therefore able to tap into a rich vein of popular hostility to trade that had deep historical and religious roots. In the late Middle Ages merchants were increasingly suspected of giving in to the deadly sins of pride, avarice, and envy, and negative depictions such as in the broadsheet of Wolfgang Rösch discussed above were typical.[71] Eberlin von Günzburg also followed Luther in denouncing what he saw as profiteering. In 1524, Eberlin published a pamphlet with the rather elaborate title, 'I wonder why there is no money left in the land: An angry yet harmless discussion among three travellers about said title. Read this little book and you will be astonished that there is a single *Pfennig* left in this country.'[72] Eberlin did not hesitate to compare the economic consequences of trade to the devastation caused by war. The argument expanded the one presented in Rösch's broadsheet: The German lands were so rich in resources that they were in principle self-sufficient. However, devious merchants stimulated the demand for foreign luxury goods, which caused not only an outflow of money but also moral degeneracy.[73]

A group of mint masters and other experts in coinage who drafted a monetary policy-memorial for the Rhenish electors in 1529 gave the argument a further twist. Rather than merely condemning foreign cloth and spices, they demanded a ban on their import. Such goods did

> not only harm their electoral graces' lands, but the whole German nation. Their import increases the price of gold and silver. It makes other nations strong and powerful, so that they can make war upon the Germans, whereas it makes the Germans too feeble to resist, proud, rebellious, and divided.[74]

Since the late fourteenth century, bullionism—the idea that a country needed a positive balance of payments to accumulate bullion, on whose quantity its power and prosperity depended—had gained traction in Western Europe.[75] It is the doctrine the coinage experts expressed. Still, while their worries about the consequences of the outflow of bullion were coloured by ideology, there can be little doubt that there was a basis in fact. A treatise on monetary policy the electors on the Rhine sent to Charles V went to the heart of the matter. The electors claimed it was 'common knowledge that more goods are brought from neighbouring kingdoms and lands into the Empire of the German nation than from here into other countries, so that the inhabitants of this nation give more money away than they receive from abroad'.[76] We know neither whether this was really common knowledge—and if so, on what evidence it was based—nor how large the trade deficit was and how it evolved over time. However, in essence the Rhenish electors must have been right. This is demonstrated by the fact that, unlike the Empire, most European countries did not have their own deposits of precious metals. Still, France and England, among others, were able to maintain their own currencies. How would they have been able to import the bullion needed for that purpose, if not by exporting more goods to the German lands than they imported from there?[77] The Empire's trade deficit existed, and as long as it did, there was no alternative to exporting precious metals.[78]

In sum, merchants were generally suspected of draining the Empire of its bullion reserves and trading coins that were then broken and reminted in base form. Both suspicions amalgamated into a set of deep-seated anti-commercial sentiments, which regularly came to the fore when merchants were mentioned in monetary policy negotiations. Scanning the documents that reflect these discussions shows that the adjectives that went together with 'merchant' were 'clever', 'unseemly', and above all 'self-interested'—self-interested was the term authorities used for all activities that they thought might harm the common weal. Unsurprisingly, our sources mention merchants next to usurers, operators of illegal mints, and such shady characters as foreigners. Fraud and illicit profit were also concepts brought up in the immediate context of trade.[79] Very occasionally, we encounter dissenting voices. An anonymous monetary policy-report that pays particular attention to conditions in and around the imperial city of Frankfurt (and that may come from Frankfurt itself) argued that if the Empire had to export silver, it was better to export it in the form of coins. Minted silver 'passes through many thousands of hands and transactions and brings other goods of all kinds from everywhere into the Empire, and from this an untold number of people profit, whereas if silver is sold in raw form it benefits fewer than a hundred people'.[80] Between the lines, the author conceded that trade was useful. However, he stopped short of presenting merchants in a positive light, let alone in one as positive as that in which the common man was regularly shown.

Merchants and monetary diversity

That the imperial estates were so unanimous in condemning merchants may come as a surprise. One might expect that people involved in trade, especially in inter-regional trade, would suffer most from the state of the monetary economy of the Empire, and that their complaints would reach the imperial diet where they would leave at least some traces in the discussions. However, at diets the delegates of commercially important imperial cities complained about all sorts of things—the state of the roads, the security of transport, and so on[81]—but apparently not about monetary diversity. Merchants did not even do so when offering monetary policy-advice. For example, when Jacob Fugger, the uncle of Anton Fugger who took over the firm in 1525 and for whom Silvester Raid worked for a time, drafted a monetary policy-memorial for Ferdinand of Austria in 1523, he paid much attention to the costs of bullion and of minting in general. What he did not even mention were any potential benefits—commercial or otherwise—of reducing the diversity of the coinage of the Empire.[82] At around the same time Christoph Furer, one of the most important metal merchants of Nuremberg, submitted another monetary policy-report where he did recommend reducing monetary diversity. However, he did not do so to help trade. Rather, his aim was devising a way for the profits made from minting to be channelled from those imperial estates that controlled their own silver mines to the permanently underfunded Empire, which would then use them to uphold peace and law.[83] Textbooks teaching merchants about commercial practices treated monetary diversity in a perfectly matter-of-fact way—just as they treated the different weights and measures used across the markets of Europe. This applies, for example, to Lorenz Meder's 'Book of Commerce', first published in Nuremberg in 1558, but the notes merchants compiled for their own record-keeping purposes are no different.[84]

There are several reasons why we should not overstate the effect of monetary diversity on inter-regional trade in the Empire (or beyond). There is evidence for markets that preferred the same types of coins being more closely linked than others: Differences between the local prices of precious metals tended to be smaller than elsewhere, which suggests that trade between these places was more intensive.[85] But more broadly, no matter their provenance, coins could at least in principle be used anywhere, with the consumers deciding whether and on what terms to accept them. We have seen that when commercial connections became closer during the fifteenth and early sixteenth century, even small change began travelling large distances. This applied even more to high-value coins such as the Rhenish florin, on which merchants engaged in the wholesale and luxuries trade had been relying for over a century because it was known and readily accepted everywhere at least until the flood of underweight imitations started to undermine its reputation. This loss of reputation was one of the causes of the success of the *Talers* that occupied the same monetary niche: they, too, were accepted in high-volume transactions regardless of who had issued them.

In addition to this, cashless means of payment became increasingly common and versatile in the first half of the sixteenth century. Invented in twelfth-century Italy, the bill of exchange was by the fourteenth century well known in the large trading towns of the Low Countries and spread from there to other commercial centres along the coast of the Baltic and in inner Germany.[86] Bills were essentially IOUs that required repayment in a different place and different currency. At a time when the Church was still a political power and banning usury, they allowed taking out loans at interest without this becoming obvious: The interest rate was concealed in the exchange rate. Moreover, using bills gave merchants access to cash in all major markets without having to risk transporting hard money.

Until the fifteenth century, one could use each bill only once. It had to be presented to the person named on it, usually a business associate of the borrower, who would then repay the loan. There are early instances from the 1430s onward when lenders sold bills they held to someone else, but the breakthrough was a series of laws passed in the Low Countries in the late 1530s and early 1540s: Bills became fully negotiable commercial papers that could be freely traded on whatever terms the parties involved agreed, without the original borrowers having to give their consent or even to know how the bill was being used.[87] In effect, from now on they were a form of international paper money backed by hard money reserves, which the business associates of the borrowers who issued the bills had to make available on request. East of the Rhine bills spread slowly, and as late as in the mid-nineteenth century coins made up more than 80 per cent of the total quantity of money in Germany.[88] Likely, the total value of bills in circulation in the first half of the sixteenth century was tiny compared to that of hard money. However, Meder's 'Book of Commerce' shows the extent to which large merchants relied on bills.[89] They certainly played a role in reducing the uncertainty and costs resulting from monetary diversity. The upshot of all this is that our sources do not contain any evidence that allows discerning something like a public opinion concerning the Empire's coinage among the country's commercially most active social group. Merchants appear to have taken the monetary diversity of the German lands in their stride.

As most members of the Empire's political elites suspected merchants of not just coping with the currency situation in the German lands, but of benefiting from it, they tended to side line the views of the envoys of the imperial cities at assemblies with the other estates. In fact, we will see that their counsellors and delegates treated the urban emissaries in a curious way: They managed to combine the scrupulous observance of the customary rules that governed the discussions with an attitude that clearly went beyond condescension and approached contempt.[90] Much of their disdain was due to the idea that whoever represented a commercial centre must have been to some degree mixed up with trade. Regardless of whether urban delegates had any commercial interests, they were suspect by association—suspect of being governed by self-interest, of neglecting the common weal, and of pursuing policies to match. Hence, they were rarely asked for their views on monetary issues, and if they offered advice it was normally dismissed out of hand. In the sixteenth century, the Empire's monetary policies were in no way designed to help trade.

Experimenting with solutions

Taking control of one's borders

Merchants, the common man, and the members of the political elite may have disagreed on how troublesome or harmful monetary diversity was, but there was one thing on which all agreed: 'Order' was desirable; it was, according to historians, the one ideal that linked all groups in society.[91]

The mere fact that contemporaries perceived the monetary economy of the Empire as disorderly thus implies that they saw a need for action. However, there were more specific reasons and motives. Rulers whose coins served as raw material for the mints of their neighbours suffered a series of highly unpleasant consequences. After some time, the underweight money became dominant on the markets of their territory (a consequence of Gresham's Law), which meant that it tended to turn up in their revenues. In 1521, the Saxon mint master Andreas Funcke put this bluntly when he explained what consequences an inflow of small change from electoral Brandenburg would have for his princely employer:

> If this unworthy coin is being accepted in your princely grace's lands, your people will suffer palpable harm, and things will become as bad as they were when Brandenburg *Groschens* and other poor coins were circulating... Also, the *Gulden* is again gone up, and this unworthy coin will drive it up further to 21 *Groschens*. If that comes to pass, the good coins will all be exported, and these bad ones alone will stay in the land. Already now all purses are full of bad *Pfennigs*, as your princely grace will discover in your revenues from convoy services, taxes, and rents.[92]

Pomerania, whose money the neighbouring duchy of Mecklenburg and the town of Rostock reminted into their own coins, was in a similar position. For the Pomeranian dukes this was a problem not least because the Empire made significant progress in the protection of internal peace and law in the first half of the sixteenth century. This came at a price: A supreme court—the imperial chamber court—was set up in 1495, and after 1507 the estates paid a regular tax to the Empire to maintain its judges and assessors.[93] By the 1550s, the Pomeranian dukes complained about the fact that they received their revenues in bad money while the imperial officials who collected the dues needed to maintain the chamber court—the 'imperial *Pfennig*-masters'—expected to be paid in full-bodied coin.[94]

There were further consequences. Augsburg's magistrate had reason to worry that the competition of the mint which produced underweight *Kreuzer*-imitations would cause its silver supply to dry up. Similarly, with Rostock and Mecklenburg being able to offer a higher nominal price for the bullion they purchased, suppling the Pomeranian mints would become impossible.[95] No silver supply meant no minting, and no minting meant no revenues from the seignorage. The trade in coinage therefore had unambiguously negative revenue effects which were particularly painful in an age of growing governmental and courtly expenses. Being unable to issue coins with their symbols of authority moreover robbed the dukes of the chance to shape their public image—something their neighbours in Mecklenburg had successfully done since the mid-fourteenth century.[96] Finally, there was one factor to which the Saxon delegates at the imperial diet of 1555 pointed when they argued that it 'was true that every prince's rule is judged according to three things, namely the upkeep of the roads, their writs and seals, and their coinage'.[97] Not being able to exercise ones right to mint was reputationally damaging.

Solutions were widely and intensively debated among the imperial estates. One option was border controls—a topic Christoph Furer addressed in the treatise he submitted to the imperial diet in 1523. Furer argued that effective border checks were not practicable unless a 'country was closely confined by mountains and waters, so that it is impossible to evade the inspections'.[98] This was no doubt a necessary condition: After all, England had succeeded in imposing strict controls on the export of coin at the end of the thirteenth century—a success based on the fact that almost all its external trade passed through a small number of easily monitored ports.[99] However, while necessary, experience showed that Furer's condition was not sufficient. In 1559, the archbishop of Salzburg—the same who claimed that foreign money was used for 95 per cent of all transactions in his territory—stressed that his coinage was being exported because he was unable to control cross-border traffic: 'The world is wide, the people are many, the mountains high, and it will never be possible to plug every single hole.'[100] If this applied to a principality such as Salzburg, where most traffic used mountain passes that were easy to guard, it applied even more to territories that did not only lack the necessary organizational 'state' capacity, as the archbishopric clearly did, but also natural borders. Stricter controls were not even considered by relatively well-organized authorities. Think of the magistrate of Hamburg that also complained about the export of its own coin and the import of underweight foreign money—and this despite the city gates being quasi-natural points where traffic could at least in principle be monitored at low costs. As we have seen, Hamburg restricted itself to appealing to its citizens' community spirit.

From defensive to competitive debasements

If closer controls were impracticable, what other options were there? One could adapt the standard of one's coinage to that of the underweight foreign money that had come to dominate one's markets. In other words, one could implement a defensive debasement to protect one's money from being exported, broken, and reminted as base copies. In fourteenth- to early sixteenth-century Italy and Germany, urban governments in particular took this measure.[101] We can observe its effects by looking at how the Upper-German *Batzen*-coins developed. *Batzens* had first been minted by the Swiss town of Bern in 1492, with their official value being four Austrian *Kreuzers*. The fact that four *Kreuzers* contained altogether about 20 per cent more pure silver than one *Batzen* indicates clearly enough what Bern's government hoped to achieve.[102] As Bern's mint could offer a higher price for the raw material it bought than its rivals,[103] its new coin quickly spread over the Swiss Confederacy, Austria, Swabia, Bavaria, Franconia, the Alsace, the Palatinate, and to a lesser degree Northern Italy. In about 1510, there were 14 authorities that minted their own *Batzen*-variants, in 1520, 25 authorities, and in 1535 more than 40 authorities. The area where *Batzens* were used was even larger: It reached to the duchy of Prussia on the coast of the Baltic.[104] The coins were issued in large numbers. Bern alone struck more than 850,000 in 1500, the imperial city of Isny almost 700,000 in 1527 to 1531, and the imperial city of Constance almost 2.4 million between 1528 and 1533; all in all, many millions must have been minted.[105] Putting this in relation to the size of these towns—Bern and Isny had about 3,000 inhabitants each in 1500 while Constance, with a population of *c.*6,000, was the regional metropolis[106]—suggests that the *Batzens* were never intended for domestic use only. They were to flow off to neighbouring towns whose own money they were to replace. That this would happen was likely enough: After all, while each authority used a slightly different design, all *Batzens* had roughly the same size and weight and circulated interchangeably as 4-*Kreuzers* pieces, regardless of their intrinsic value. Their mere presence was an invitation to engage in the trade in coinage.

Table 2.1[107] summarizes the results of three metallurgical tests performed in 1527, 1533, and 1539. The data allow us to see both the consequences of the trade in, and breaking and reminting of, *Batzens*, and the futility of attempts to get rid of underweight variants with the help of defensive debasements.

While the early decades when the number of authorities issuing *Batzens* was still small saw relative stability, the assays of 1533 and 1539 give evidence of a rapid decline. At the same time, the coins became less uniform, as the deviations from their mean pure silver content show. Neither finding is a

Table 2.1. Three early sixteenth-century *Batzen*-assays

Place, year of the assay	Number of variants tested	Mean pure silver content (grams)	Average deviation from mean pure silver content (per cent)	Mean debasement since 1492 (per cent)
Regensburg, 1527	12	1.670	1.65	−0.01
Augsburg, 1533	20	1.601	1.60	−4.15
Munich, 1539	8	1.591	1.90	−4.71

surprise. Most *Batzens* were issued by authorities that did not control their own silver mines.[108] How were their mints supposed to acquire the large quantities of silver they needed, if not in the form of coins issued by their neighbours? To do this, they had to strike *Batzens* that looked broadly similar but contained a little less bullion. Once these began to dominate, the neighbours, who so far had minted higher-quality *Batzens*, faced strong incentives to follow suit, in other words, to implement 'defensive' debasements, hoping that this would prevent their money from being used as raw material in other mints.[109] However, any such debasement would trigger countermeasures by neighbours still interested in acquiring bullion for their mints—and these measures necessarily took the form of debasements themselves. In this way, rounds of competitive debasements followed each other, and the result was the general decline in the *Batzen*-standard that the assayers detected.

Upper Germany was not the only region suffering from competitive debasements (Map 2.2). In Lower Saxony, *Maria Groschens*—so called because their design showed the Virgin Mary—occupied the same monetary niche as *Batzens* did further south. They had been first introduced in 1505 in the imperial city of Goslar just north of the Harz mountains and were quickly and widely imitated. They, too, were issued in huge numbers: Goslar minted almost 3 million of them between 1544 and 1547, Braunschweig more than 7 million between 1543 and 1554, and Hanover 3.5 to 4 million between 1535 and 1544. Göttingen issued more than 5 million between 1545 and 1555, and Hildesheim about 3.5 million between 1542 and 1551.[110] In 1551, the assayers in Nuremberg tested ten variants; Table 2.2[111] shows the extent to which they had been debased since Goslar's original had appeared early in the century.

Maria Groschens were even more irregular than *Batzens*: In 1539, the pure silver content of individual *Batzen*-variants deviated from the mean by on

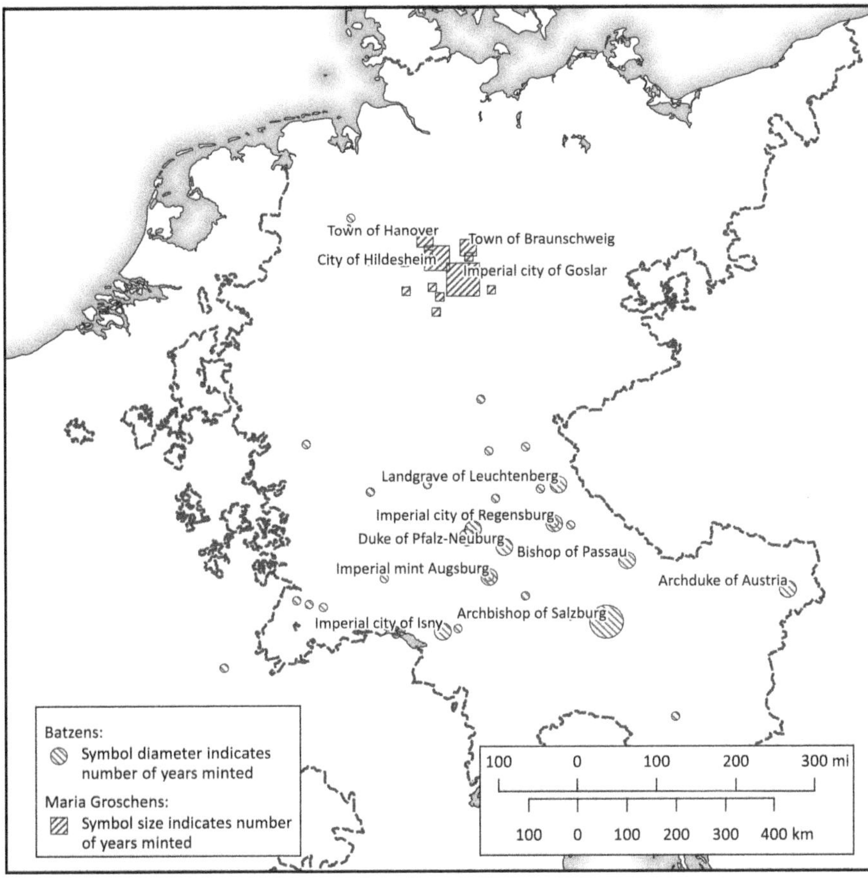

Map 2.2. Principal authorities minting *Batzens* and *Maria Groschens*, 1492–1550
Note: Schulten, *Deutsche Münzen*, pp. 17–449.

average 1.9 per cent, whereas the average deviation of *Maria Groschens* was closer to 5.7 per cent. The only authority listed in the table that controlled its own silver ore deposits was the city of Goslar, whose mines in the Rammelsberg in the Harz mountains yielded rich returns especially in the first quarter of the sixteenth century.[112] All others had to purchase the raw material for their mints in one way or the other—that is, either as raw silver or in the form of their neighbours' coins. The degree to which the *Maria Groschens* were debased suggests that the latter option played an important role and that what the assayers found in 1551 was the outcome of rounds of competitive debasements far worse than those from which the South German *Batzens* suffered. This was probably because *Batzens* spread in an

Table 2.2. *Maria Groschens* tested in Nuremberg 1551

Minting authority	Pure silver content per piece (grams)	Pure silver content deviation from mean (per cent)	Debasement since 1505 (per cent)
Imperial city of Goslar	0.913	9.7	−37.4
City of Hildesheim	0.899	8.1	−38.4
Town of Braunschweig	0.866	4.8	−40.8
Imperial abbey of Corvey and town of Höxter	0.849	2.7	−41.8
Town of Hanover	0.834	1.1	−42.8
Town of Göttingen	0.827	0.3	−43.3
Imperial abbey and town of Herford	0.776	6.2	−46.8
Town of Hameln	0.776	6.2	−46.9
Duke of Braunschweig-Calenberg-Göttingen	0.765	7.7	−47.7
Town of Northeim	0.744	10.9	−49.1
Mean:	0.825	5.7	−43.6

environment increasingly dominated by regional currency unions such as the one Ferdinand of Austria negotiated in 1535. These unions either directly prohibited minting them, outlawed the breaking and reminting of coins in general, or at least tried to ban the circulation of *Batzens.*[113] Any member of a union that violated such a rule would have had to justify its actions in front of the others, which involved at least some short-term embarrassment and a longer lasting loss of reputation. Obviously, few were willing to pay this price. By contrast, in the region where *Maria Groschens* spread, currency unions did not exist. There, it was literally every man for himself, which explains why the 'defensive' debasements here very quickly turned into rounds of competitive debasements.

A solution that worked—and why some rejected it

As we have seen, the Rhenish electors declined to further debase their gold florin. Confronted with masses of underweight imitations, minted by authorities able to offer higher nominal prices for gold than they themselves, they had given up issuing the originals. The dukes of Pomerania were in a similar position. With the mints of Rostock and Mecklenburg offering higher nominal silver prices, the supply of precious metal in Pomerania dried up. The dukes reacted by making a virtue of necessity. Thomas Kantzow, the Stralsund-born chronicler who was generally well-informed about monetary policies, tells how they 'put down the hammer'—as closing a mint was called—'trusting that one day his imperial Majesty would mandate a common coinage for all German lands'.[114] With this the Pomeranian dukes hit upon the only solution that addressed the root of the problem. What is more, it is likely that they helped trigger a chain reaction. The more estates decided to cease issuing money, the more difficult it would become for authorities that minted imitations to obtain the raw materials they needed to keep their mints in business. There can be little doubt that this contributed to the wide acceptance of the idea that creating an Empire-wide currency was the only way to eliminate the disorder that characterized Germany's monetary economy.

Some historians speculate that the common currency was a project driven by Charles V and his brother Ferdinand, and that the aim was political integration: They hoped to achieve a closer unity of the imperial estates to help increase the emperor's power.[115] Evidence, whether documentary or otherwise, that supports this idea does not seem to exist. Most scholars have located the project in the context of policies designed to foster trade.[116] In fact, this seemed the obvious thing to do. It is the angle taken by economists, none of whom doubt that monetary harmonization reduces the costs of negotiating commercial agreements between regions that used to have different currencies. Currency unions thus help interregional trade. What is disputed is whether their creation is a purely political act, or whether they can be introduced only where markets already are fairly closely connected.[117] The latter seems to be more likely, as evidence from the early twentieth century suggests.[118]

For reasons that so far have not been examined, late medieval currency unions, too, tended to form where markets were already relatively closely linked. What is evident is that once they had been established, they promoted a further growth in trade.[119] Because of this, and because medieval authorities did occasionally pursue policies designed to help commerce, it appeared obvious to historians (including me) to see the currency unions created in the Empire since the late fourteenth century in this light, too.[120] However, the evidence that has come to light in recent years leaves no doubt that whatever the imperial estates did in the sixteenth century in order to promote commerce, currency unions did not serve this purpose. They were designed not to help but to hinder trade, or at least one type of trade: that in coinage. A report submitted by Ferdinand of Austria's counsellors in 1543 stressed that a 'common, orderly and stable' currency was needed to 'prevent and supress the evil, deceitful, and self-interested business' that the diversity of coins allowed.[121] Two years later, the currency committee convened at the imperial diet argued that a 'good, honourable, upright, and silver-rich coinage' would serve to prevent 'self-interested people, who seek their own advantage and have sought and made their own unjust profit, from doing business with the irregular and uneven coins'.[122] Or as the delegates of the elector Palatine put it on another occasion: 'One thing is certain: When all estates mint according to the same standard that they faithfully observe, the breaking of coins is impossible because it can no longer be done without incurring a loss.'[123] In particular, a common currency would prevent 'abusing other minting authorities' seals, coats of arms and coinage designs'—issuing side-strikes would no longer be possible.[124] In sum: 'A uniform, good, even and stable coinage' had to be created, 'so that debasements and also the great damage, harm and deception done in the trade in coinage were averted and in future prevented, and the common weal thereby greatly advanced'.[125]

Regional currency unions that had formed since the late fourteenth century had pursued the same aims. Take, for example, the coinage confederacy that was created in the upper Rhine region at the beginning of the fifteenth century and eventually merged with Ferdinand of Austria's Upper German union of 1535.[126] The introduction to the treaty that constituted the union stated explicitly why the Austrian bailiff of Alsace, the city of Basel, and the towns of Freiburg, Colmar, and Breisach had decided to cooperate. It was 'in order to prevent and avert the large and notable ills from which gold and silver coins previously minted suffer, which are now being broken and have become poor; also because of the intruding foreign coins that have harmed this land and people and continue to do so'.[127] The treaty that renewed the union in 1498 stated that 'after many diets held in previous years because of the intrusion of coins that foreign and domestic persons have brought in and imported, which has caused noticeable harm and damage to these lands and to the common man', a debasement had finally become unavoidable.[128] Evidently this was a widespread problem and, if debasement was not a long-term solution, then it was at least an entirely typical reaction.

It is likely that by the 1540s, most imperial estates had concluded that regional unions were insufficient to prevent the trade in coinage. As we have seen, in this they knew themselves to be at one with the common man—no less so, in fact, than when it came to criticizing the self-interest that came to the fore in the activities of merchants, whether they were involved in the trade in coinage or not. Does this mean that commercial points of view were entirely neglected? There is some evidence that commerce was considered once negotiations about the Empire's common currency began. Thus, the counsellors of the elector of Brandenburg argued that without monetary unification 'little of the large damage suffered by merchants and all who trade, travel, and journey from one country to another . . . will be removed or healed'.[129] However, both the place where this remark was made and its context are revealing. The place was a draft version of the written instructions the elector's delegates received for monetary policy-negotiations with the other imperial estates in 1549. The final version of the instructions dropped the sentence. The context was a discussion about the need to include parts of the wider Empire, most importantly the Low Countries, in the common currency. This was indeed a crucial point for which commercial considerations were central. It was also a point that was reiterated again and again at imperial diets.

When the elector of Saxony drafted a memorial for the diet held in the city of Speyer in 1544, he pointed out that 'as the house of Burgundy is an immediate possession of the Empire and much poor coin is minted in its lands from good money, matters have to be turned thus that these same lands are included in the imperial currency ordinance', which was being planned.[130] However, it was the Rhenish electors who insisted most strongly on the integration of the Low Countries. At the imperial diet of Augsburg in 1547 to 1548, they brought up the topic no fewer than six times.[131] In the end, electors, other princes, and towns passed a common declaration where they 'most subserviently asked his imperial Majesty to include the Low Countries' in the common currency.[132]

Why was this so important? The Low Countries were the most urbanized part of Northern Europe, with between 19 and 20 per cent of the population living in towns of more than 10,000 inhabitants and almost 30 per cent in towns larger than 5,000 inhabitants in about the middle of the sixteenth century. By contrast, in Germany just over 8 per cent lived in towns with more than 5,000 and less than 4 per cent in towns with more than 10,000 inhabitants.[133] Urbanization is a good indicator of prosperity. This is because per person, the demand for food is relatively stable (at least, it cannot grow beyond a certain amount), so when incomes grow, people may buy a bit more or better food but will spend most of the additional money on services and manufactured products. These are typically produced in towns. The consequence is a rise in employment in urban manufacturing and in services, and this causes an increase in urbanization.[134] Fernand Braudel aptly called the Low Countries 'a second Italy, highly urbanized, "industrialized"' and therefore 'dependent upon the outside world'.[135] This was the flipside of urban prosperity. Burgundy developed a growing demand for imported food, much of which came from further east. Merchants from Antwerp and Amsterdam bought increasing quantities of grain in the countries along the south coast of the Baltic, that is, in Mecklenburg, Pomerania, Poland, and Prussia.[136] The cattle trade was also important, especially as the wealth of the Low Countries translated into a high purchasing power and a large demand for meat. Cattle was reared in relatively lightly populated regions in Northern and Eastern Europe: Denmark, Holstein, Mecklenburg, Pomerania, and North-Eastern Poland as well as Moldavia, Wallachia, Hungary, and parts of Austria and the Alpine countries. Much of it was driven west and north towards the Low Countries.[137] In 1549, the counsellors of the elector of Saxony noted in the written instructions for the Saxon representatives at a diet convened to discuss monetary policies that 'at this time, the largest and most considerable trade and business in the Holy Empire takes place in the Low Countries'.[138] There can be no doubt that they were right. When the participants in monetary policy-talks among the imperial estates a few decades later concluded that Burgundy 'can less well spare the Empire's goods than the Empire can do without those of Burgundy', they were likewise correct.[139]

We are relatively well-informed about the trade of the Low Countries because in 1567, Lodovico Guicciardini, an Italian resident of Antwerp, published a '*Descrittione di tutti i Paesi Bassi*' ('*Description of the whole Low Countries*') where he discussed the issue in detail.[140] The Belgian historian Wilfrid Brulez has analysed the text and used it to tentatively reconstruct the Dutch balance of trade in the mid-sixteenth century. It appears that yearly exports amounted to a value of about 16 million *Guldens*, whereas imports totalled at between 20 and 22 million *Guldens*.[141] How did the Low Countries cover the difference? The only way to do so was by paying cash, and this is what happened: By the end of the sixteenth century, the Dutch province of Holland alone sent at least 2 million *rijksdaalders* (or *c.*50 tons of pure silver) per year to the Baltic.[142] Where did the merchants of the Low Countries find that money? We will see in Chapter 4 that the Habsburgs had access to large amounts of silver ore not only in the Tyrol and Bohemia, but also in Upper Hungary and increasingly in the New World, so money they transferred to Brussels or Antwerp for political reasons may have helped.[143] Also, the Low Countries generated income by offering services to the subjects of other rulers, especially in the transit trade. However, where Germany and the lands along the south coast of the Baltic are concerned, our evidence points to one important factor historians have so far overlooked: the systematic production of gold coins that were essentially underweight imitations of Rhenish florins. Therefore, it is unsurprising that already in about 1500 some of the basest of these imitations—those minted by bishop John von Horn of Liège, which contained roughly half as much gold as genuine pieces—turned up as far east as Königsberg (Kaliningrad) in Prussia, where people accepted them at a value far higher than their content of gold justified.[144] All in all, there can be no doubt that it was the need to make up for their trade balance deficit which provided incentives for the minting authorities of the Low Countries to produce the many poor imitations of the Rhenish florin that the assayers in Nuremberg found in 1551.

One group of estates were in a position like Burgundy, though for different reasons: the electorate and duchy of Saxony. Both controlled some of the most important silver mines anywhere in the German lands, or for that matter in Europe. While export and import data are lacking, it is likely that the balance of trade of both principalities was in deficit. Again, monetary policies helped compensate for this. Elector Frederick 'the Wise' had rarely made a wiser economic decision than when he decided to invest heavily in the promotion of the *Guldengroschen* that soon everyone would call *Taler*. People were so keen on getting hold of *Talers* that they circulated at a premium—a fact of which the electoral counsellors were acutely aware. One of the most prominent of them was Abraham von Einsiedel, a member an influential Saxon family, early convert to the Reformation (he had heard Luther speak at the diet of Worms in 1521) and experienced politician, who regularly represented the Saxon princes at imperial assemblies.[145] We will encounter him on several occasions. In 1549 he argued that

> if in Joachimstal and further south in Bohemia the value of the *Guldengroschen* . . . is 1¼ *Guldens*, this benefits our most gracious lord's subjects, who import wine, malt, grain, wheat etc. from there, more than it harms

> them, as they may sell each *Guldengroschen* for 2 *Groschens* 3 *Pfennigs* dearer than is customary in our lands. This also encourages the Bohemians themselves to export their goods, as they receive *Guldengroschens* for 24 *Groschens*, whose value in Bohemia is 1 *Gulden* 5 *Groschen* 3 *Pfennigs*, and thus our gracious lord's subjects may obtain goods exported from there all the cheaper.[146]

Einsiedel was juggling with monetary units in a way that may baffle modern readers, but in principle his argument was simple enough. The upshot was that while in Saxony the *Guldengroschen* (or *Taler*) was overvalued at 24 *Groschens*, in Bohemia it was overvalued even more: It circulated at 1¼ *Gulden*—1 *Gulden* 5 *Groschens* 3 *Pfennigs*—or, in other words, at 26¼ *Groschens*: 25 per cent more than its pure silver content (which matched that of the sum of 21 *Groschens*) justified. With such a coin, Saxons found it easy to purchase Bohemian goods to take home. At the same time Bohemian merchants doing business in Weimar, Leipzig, or Dresden were happy to accept *Talers* for 24 *Groschens*; after all, at home they could pass them on for the equivalent of 26¼ *Groschens*. Like in the Low Countries, in Saxony up to one-third of the population was urban—mining played an important role—so that importing the 'wine, malt, grain, wheat, etc.' that Einsiedel listed was crucial.[147] The difference was that the Low Countries financed their balance of trade deficit by producing base imitations of Rhenish florins that many accepted, if not at a par with the originals, then at values higher than their content of gold justified, whereas Saxony achieved the same result by issuing *Talers* that were so popular that markets overvalued them.

The emperor and most imperial estates—or the advisers and delegates they sent to the *Tage* where monetary policies were being discussed—were aware of some of the commercial implications of what they did. However, they based their decisions on circumstances and pursued aims which differed fundamentally from those uppermost in the minds of modern politicians who consider the formation of currency unions. Trade was not what they tried to foster. Rather, they were interested in solving the problems trade had caused in an environment shaped by the lack of currency borders and increasing commercial integration. Specifically, the damage that the trade in coinage, the breaking of coins, and the minting of base imitations—in short, the effects of Gresham's Law—did to their revenues and reputation was so severe that after considering other solutions and experimenting with at least one of them—implementing defensive debasements—they realized that only a common, Empire-wide currency would address the root of the problem. In this, political decision-makers knew they would fulfil widely held wishes of the common man. Monetary diversity caused a degree of uncertainty that clearly caused resentment; measures to reduce it would be welcome. Merchants, by contrast, appeared indifferent. There is no evidence for them favouring a common currency; on the contrary: those among them who were not actively exploiting monetary diversity to make a profit from currency arbitrage seem to have been able to cope well enough with the many different types of coins in circulation.

By the 1540s, the common currency had become an ideal and an aspiration for most imperial estates. Only three remained aloof: Habsburg Burgundy and the electorate and duchy of Saxony—all three of them because they valued the chance to shape their territories' commerce with the help of autonomous monetary policies more than the chance to put an end to the trade in coinage, the breaking of coins, and the production of base side-strikes. While the ideal of monetary unification became so dominant that even the Low Countries and Saxony found it advisable to pay lip service to it (in 1549 the counsellors of the Saxon elector declared it was 'necessary and good . . . that a common, good and honourable coinage is agreed and created in the holy Empire of the German nation', and Burgundy sent delegates to monetary-policy talks),[148] integrating these dissenters would be one of the great challenges that the Empire's monetary politics faced.

3
Making politics in the Empire

Procedures and ceremonies

Rules mattered

On Friday 22 May 1551, Abraham von Einsiedel, the counsellor of Elector Maurice of Saxony whom we have encountered in the previous chapter, met Count Reinhard von Solms in Nuremberg. Solms was one of the principal monetary policy-advisers of the emperor, and as we will meet him on several later occasions, it is a good idea to become better acquainted with him at this point. He was the ruler of the small county of Solms-Lich south of the town of Gießen in modern Hesse. Lich was the capital—if that is not too grand a name for the small town where the count resided when at home—and the name was used to distinguish his lands from the splinters of territory managed by other branches of the Solms family. Count Reinhard was a military theoretician and author, an engineer, the architect of several modern fortresses, and, not least, keenly interested in monetary policies: He was the inventor of one of the first minting machines that was to reduce the labour costs involved in the production of coins.[1] Charles V had got to know him very well during a brief, sharp, and victorious war he waged in 1546 and 1547 against a league of Protestant estates that had been formed around Hesse and electoral Saxony at the beginning of the 1530s. During this 'Schmalkaldic War' (Schmalkalden was the Hessian town were the 'Schmalkaldic' league had been constituted) Solms had been field-marshal—a title that in the sixteenth century was used for the officer responsible for keeping order in the camp of the army, organizing the supply and receiving the homage of conquered places in lieu of the commander.[2] He had served the emperor in other capacities, too, representing him at two important monetary policy-conferences in 1549. Now, in 1551, Charles V had reappointed him as his representative at the general assay that had begun in Nuremberg in April.[3]

Einsiedel came on behalf of his master Maurice of Saxony, whose correspondents in Nuremberg had repeatedly reminded him of the meeting of the assayers and coinage experts; they had warned him that the absence of a Saxon representative might harm him.[4] Maurice had eventually sent Einsiedel who, having handed over his accreditation to Solms, asked submissively that he and the metal expert he had brought with him might be admitted to the assay.

Solms flatly refused. It was probably his secretary who made a note of the episode, describing how Charles V's commissioner argued that 'because the assay was almost finished and Einsiedel had not been sent by the imperial circle'—the administrative divisions of the Empire mentioned above—'as the decision of the imperial diet demanded, but only by his most gracious lord the elector, it was not meet to admit him and his assayer to this transaction'.[5] Solms' arguments were undeniably correct. The document that summarized the decisions of the imperial diet held in Augsburg between late July 1550 and mid-February 1551 determined that the directors of each circle should immediately call circle-level diets, each of which was to appoint a common assayer.[6] It was these assayers who were to convene in Nuremberg. The schedule was tight, but that the Upper Saxon circle, of which Electoral Saxony was a part, had neglected to send a representative was neither here nor there. Admitting an assayer of an individual estate, such as the one Einsiedel brought with him, was still inappropriate. Maurice's envoy was left standing and allowed to contemplate what to report back to Dresden.

At first sight this looks like a pointless issue of protocol, a pettifogging insistence on the observance of an obscure directive that lacked all factual importance. However, such a conclusion would be mistaken. The incident gives us a perfect insight into how the Empire worked, and it is to this topic that we now need to turn. This is because before examining the Empire's monetary policies, we need to know how decision-making was organized and how effective it was. The issue is particularly important because it takes us into the middle of a fundamental disagreement between historians, who have put forward conflicting interpretations of the character of the early modern Empire. Some, among them most prominently Georg Schmidt and Joachim Whaley, argue that it was a state essentially no different from its western neighbours. What was peculiar about it was merely that it operated at several levels: The imperial, circle- and estate-levels played complementary roles.[7] Other historians—for example Heinz Schilling—reject this interpretation, stressing the Empire's dysfunctional features and the at best partial success of attempts to modernize it in the first half of the sixteenth century.[8]

The debate has shaped much of the research on early modern German history over the last decades, but its intricacies need not concern us here. One thing is obvious, though, especially when we remember the sociologist Max Weber's classic definition of a state as a community that successfully claims a monopoly of force:[9] For the Empire to be such a state, the interplay between its levels of power had to function reasonably smoothly. There clearly were instances when this was the case. Take the so-called '*Policey*'-legislation—a term that has no modern equivalent, covering the regulation of markets, welfare, morals and, in part, even crime. The *Policey*-ordinances that the imperial diet passed in 1530, 1548, and 1577 were never intended to be exclusively valid. Rather, the estates were expected to 'incorporate, diminish or moderate' the institutions the Empire had set, but 'not at all to intensify or increase' them.[10] The result was that at the level of the estates, a wealth of *Policey*-legislation appeared for which imperial law provided the framework, but which was adapted to regional circumstances and left much room for the kind of idiosyncrasies with which the German lands abounded. Evidently it was possible for things to work. That the enforcement of the legislation on the ground stayed patchy is a different matter, but in this, the Empire resembled other early modern countries. In Louis XIV's France, for example, similar laws were not enforced any more strictly,[11] and if anyone knew what a state was, Louis did.

However, even during periods when the Empire functioned comparatively well, harmony was by no means universal, with the various levels of authority sometimes being at loggerheads or ignoring each other. Monetary policies give a mixed impression. We encounter instances when the imperial diet passed directives that were widely ignored or at best partially observed by the very estates that had agreed them shortly before. That the Upper Saxon circle of the Empire neglected to send a delegation to the general assay in Nuremberg in spring 1551 is just one example. On other occasions, however, the estates carefully implemented imperial legislation that pursued very similar aims—more than that, they designed and put into practice effective mechanisms to make sure no one violated the laws. Why the difference? How can we explain that sometimes, imperial law was widely respected whereas at other times it was ignored? And is it possible to discover regional patterns, that is, parts of the Empire where its writ ran strongly and others where it rarely appeared at all?

Procedures and rituals

To answer these questions, let us first return to Abraham von Einsiedel, vainly attempting to be admitted to the assayers' meeting in Nuremberg in May 1551. Why was meticulously observing rules and directives such as the one decided by the diet a few months before so important? We have seen that the emperor and the imperial estates were well advised to listen and react to complaints and desires voiced by their subjects. An 'acceptance-oriented' style of rule reduced the need to spend scarce resources on rule enforcement; in other words, it helped to cut enforcement costs that otherwise would have proved prohibitive. When the estates themselves were expected to observe decisions or pursue policies agreed at the imperial diet, allowing all present to have their say was important for the same reason.[12] It was rarely sufficient, though: After all, there were few policies that did not go against the interests of some of the estates concerned, and neither the emperor nor the diet as a collective entity had much clout to compel unwilling members of the Empire to comply with decisions they disliked.[13] Hence, if policies were to be pursued in an effective way, even those estates who felt their interests insufficiently respected had to be willing to invest time and material and personal resources in implementing what the diet had agreed. How could this be achieved?

Sociologists and historians have focused on two mechanisms that may help to solve such a problem: procedural rules and political rituals. The hypothesis that procedures are particularly important draws on the idea of the sociologist Niklas Luhmann that the mere fact that there is a framework of rules which structure the way decisions are made may lend them legitimacy.[14] This is the case if the actors, who are expected to observe and implement the decisions, take part in the decision-making procedures. By becoming 'enmeshed' in the procedures—to use Michael Sikora's term—they implicitly acknowledge not only the legitimacy of the procedures themselves but also of their results.[15] The procedures, in turn, are perceived as legitimate because they were agreed in advance, when none of those involved in making decisions knew which position they would take in the discussions. They therefore offer everyone a sufficiently large chance to realize their own interests. Such a process does not result in a consensus.[16] Rather, the result is that the actors involved in making the decisions regard even those that go against their interests as legitimate; they are therefore assumed to be more willing than otherwise to spend resources on implementing what has been decided.

Historians who refer to this kind of social theory stress three fundamental weaknesses of the procedures structuring decision-making at the level of the Empire. First, their power to bind the participants was weak because there were almost always some imperial estates that had not agreed to them from the outset, especially when they expected that the decisions which were to be made would harm their interests. As attendance at imperial assemblies was voluntary, one strategy of such estates was to simply stay away.[17] This allowed them to avoid becoming 'enmeshed', so that they could later argue that any decision made by the assembly lacked legitimacy.

Second, the Empire's procedures were poor at generating legitimacy because they lacked what sociologists call 'autonomy'. Autonomous procedures are characterized, among other things, by the fact that in their context the participants take on roles that differ from those they play elsewhere.[18] Members of modern parliaments are expected to distinguish between their role as parliamentarians and other roles, for example as the owners of firms (making political decisions that benefit their firms and harm their competitors is frowned upon, to say the least). Modern parliamentary procedures are therefore autonomous. By contrast, we will see further down that the roles the estates played at imperial assemblies were closely bound to, and dependent on, their position in the wider social hierarchy and that no one expected them to ignore this link. Hence, procedures at imperial assemblies were not autonomous; rather, it was taken for granted that they would generate decisions which helped the estates in the roles they played outside the diets.

Finally, to allow for reaching legitimate decisions, procedures must be stable.[19] If they are not, that is, if they can be agreed ad hoc, it is likely that they are shaped in a way that makes it easier for some actors, whose position happens to be momentarily strong, to reach their aims than for others. The issue is highly relevant. Historians have focused on the ability of the constitution of the Holy Roman Empire to integrate ad hoc created ways of political decision-making mainly with regard to the fourteenth and fifteenth century—a period for which the medievalist Peter Moraw coined the term 'open constitution'.[20] At that time, the constitution was rudimentary enough to be seamlessly supplemented by institutions such as regional leagues of estates or ad hoc convened assemblies.[21] Part of this 'openness' was still present in the sixteenth century. It allowed experimenting with different types of assemblies or decision-making bodies, from a government that was to rule in the emperor's absence abroad to various forms of conferences or diets, some of which were essentially no more than committees of the imperial diet that met at a separate location and time.[22] There were procedural rules that structured decision-making, at which we are going to look later, but while they were broadly similar across different types of assemblies, not all of them were universally acknowledged, fixed, and unchangeable.[23] This did not only concern details but occasionally fundamental issues as well, as for example the question of whether it should be the imperial diet or a *Münztag*—a currency conference—that should make far-reaching decisions about monetary policies.

Problems like these have led scholars such as Barbara Stollberg-Rilinger to focus on an alternative mechanism that may have helped to bind the estates to centrally made decisions which went against their interests: on political rituals or ceremonies in the sense of complex, repeated, and symbolic sequences of acts.[24] Indeed, there was a period earlier in this century when many historians focused on such aspects of politics to an the extent that the main purpose of imperial diets appeared to have been staging rituals rather than making political decisions.[25] Still, there is no denying that rituals took up far more time than in modern politics and that we need to explain why contemporaries attached so much importance to them. Stollberg-Rilinger's core idea is that by participating in them, the imperial estates not only professed to belong to the Empire's political elite; they also reached (and demonstrated) agreement about the place of each member of the Empire within its political structure.[26] Imperial diets, especially, offered the chance to achieve this. At no other occasion would the emperor meet so many spiritual and temporal princes and lords, delegates of so many free and imperial cities, and envoys and observers from other European powers, be they kingdoms like France, republics like Venice, or the Papacy. It has been aptly said that it was a function of the diets to visibly embody and depict the Empire as a political entity capable of collective action.[27] At diets, conflicts would be brought out into the open and occasionally even settled; the hierarchy of the estates would be readjusted, and questions of status decided. Importantly, all this took place in a visible manner in front of spectators.

Stollberg-Rilinger claims that what the diet enacted in a ritualistic and symbolic way 'could not be undone',[28] though this does evidently not imply that everybody would feel bound to it. However, there is an additional argument. Each act within an early modern political ritual pointed symbolically to the rank that the actor held in the outside world, that is, in the wider context of the social hierarchy that reached from the emperor at the top, descending via princes of diverse rank and members of the lower nobility, to the common man at the bottom. As this hierarchy was imagined to be unchangeable, violating a decision that had been ritually enacted would mean violating the social order itself.[29] The argument is that this would make anyone interested in social stability reluctant to go against what had been symbolically enacted.

The approach that focuses on the binding power of ritual politics has several weaknesses. It plays down the fact that rituals may also serve entirely different purposes, for example helping people who take part in them to supress feelings of aggressiveness.[30] Early sixteenth-century Germany was a society that was only just emerging from an extremely violent past. Aggressiveness was widely accepted, and more than that: Showing aggression brought honour to men. If imperial assemblies were to work, any aggressive impulses of the attendants had to be reined in, and ceremonies may well have primarily served this purpose. Furthermore, when historians first stressed the binding power of rituals, the idea was that they symbolically enacted decisions made earlier in the political process. Thus, when the emperor ceremonially invested a prince with his fief, the decision to invest him had obviously been made beforehand. Analysing the ritual may help to explain why contemporaries felt the investiture to be valid, but not how the decision to invest a specific prince with the fief had been made in the first place. To overcome this weakness, historians have in recent years begun to combine both approaches, that is, the idea that following procedures may generate legitimacy and that participating in rituals may effectively bind the actors. The idea is now that premodern decision-making procedures had a strongly ritual component; an idea encapsulated in the term 'ceremonial procedures'.[31]

Selective incentives

Further down, we will explore in detail what this implied for how discussions at imperial diets and other assemblies of estates were structured. There is no doubt that keeping the ritual aspect of political procedures in mind allows us to draw a fuller picture of how decisions were made. However, the question remains whether any of the factors so far discussed was sufficient to bind the participants to the decisions reached with their help. To spell it out: feeling bound to a decision means being willing to observe and implement it even when it goes against one's interests. Did procedures and rituals produce this effect? That is doubtful. There was one problem of which contemporaries were aware (and that, at least where monetary policies were concerned, they solved in a remarkably effective way), which historians, however, have not explicitly addressed: the problem which social scientists discuss under the heading of 'collective action'.

Unsurprisingly, it was economists who first highlighted this problem. Economists traditionally tend to assume that people are self-interested utility maximizers, deceiving others, breaking laws, and violating agreements if the expected benefits of this behaviour outweigh the costs. As Mancur Olson demonstrated in a study whose publication in 1965 initiated a paradigm-shift,[32] from this perspective the time-honoured belief that people who have a common interest or aim—such as a stable a common currency—will work together to realize this aim looks unfounded. That is even more the case when the aim is something from which all can benefit regardless of whether they help to bring it about.[33] This is because cooperating with others is costly. It costs time and frequently other resources, too: personnel that could also be employed elsewhere, money and so on. Why spend these resources? Self-interested utility maximizers realize that they will benefit from the common aim being achieved but will benefit even more if it is the others who bear all the costs. The obvious snag is that if everybody thinks like this, no one will invest in reaching the aim, which will therefore remain elusive.

If this is the case, how is it possible to create and enforce laws that benefit everyone? After all, no ruler, not even an autocrat and least of all the emperor of the Holy Roman Empire, was able to design, implement, and enforce law on his own. Collective action was essential; hence the problem self-interest posed had to be solved. As Olson has shown, there are ways this can be done (even in the absence of legitimacy-generating procedures and rituals that help binding the participants). One of his fundamental early insights was that the number of people expected to cooperate matters. In a small group, whose members know each other and who interact regularly, the interest in their reputation may be sufficient to induce them to work together and to bind them to agreements they have reached even in cases where everyone realizes that violating the agreements would be in their short-term interest. But how about larger, more anonymous groups? In its original form, Olson's collective action theory argued that 'selective incentives' are essential, that is, incentives that apply only to those members who visibly cooperate (rewards) or cheat (punishments).[34] Modern behavioural research suggests that this strict form of collective action theory may go too far. Notions such as fairness have been shown to influence the willingness to cooperate,[35] and it is likely that whether a law or agreement is perceived as legitimate has a similar effect. Still, no one denies that selective incentives affect individual decisions about whether to engage in collective action or not.

The last few paragraphs have demonstrated that the monetary policy-situation in which the emperor and the estates found themselves in the first half of the sixteenth century matched the one that collective action-theory presupposes in several ways. First, the common currency, which most of the estates desired, would benefit them all but creating it required cooperation, and this was costly. As we will see below, attending a diet was costly. It was not only the desire to avoid becoming 'enmeshed' in procedures that prevented the estates from attending assemblies; costs mattered, too. Second, merely agreeing to a common currency bill at an imperial diet was not enough. Every single estate, small or large, faced incentives to undermine the currency once it had been established. After all, it was easy to increase one's revenues from the seignorage by covertly reducing the bullion content of the coins one produced. In a currency union, where one's money circulated at parity with that minted by one's neighbours, the temptation to do so was particularly strong; it would allow to use one's neighbours' coins as raw material in one's mint. However, if one estate did this, it would set off an avalanche. To protect the bullion supply of their mints, neighbouring estates would be forced to follow suit, and then their neighbours, and so on. Hence, every single imperial estate had the power to bring down the common currency. And finally, while selective incentives would reduce the likelihood that this would happen, providing such incentives was a further problem. Every estate might be interested in the detection of offenders who violated the rules on which the common currency rested, but each one would be reluctant to spend resources on checking the quality of the coins the others had issued. In addition to that, punishing offenders (or alternatively, providing some kind of reward for those who cooperated) would again be costly and would involve a collective action problem.

In Chapter 6, we will see that to bring about the collective action on which the functioning of the common currency depended, neither the emperor nor the estates placed their trust in procedures and rituals. Rather, they turned to selective incentives and found an ingenious and effective way to provide them. Incidentally, the mechanisms they designed betray what they thought of the motives governing the behaviour of their fellow-estates: They started out from the assumption that if left unconstrained, every one of their number would behave in exactly the way modern economists expect of ruthless, opportunistic utility-maximizers.

This chapter began with the story of the attempt of Elector Maurice of Saxony's envoy Abraham von Einsiedel to join the general assay in Nuremberg in May 1551, and with the question of why observing relatively obscure-looking rules and directives was so important. Evidently, part of the answer is that following rules generated legitimacy. If the assay had been performed in a way that went against what the imperial diet had decided, it would have been possible to call its results into question, for example by casting doubt on the impartiality of the assayers (they might have been accused of falsifying their results in the elector of Saxony's interest, for example). However, the economic approach to collective action suggests a further reason why following rules was so important. When it is difficult to cooperate because others suspect you are a devious utility-maximizer, signalling your reliability and establishing a reputation as rule-abiding helps.[36] If you observe rules, no matter how unimportant they look, the implication others will draw is that you will also adhere to agreements such as those on which cooperation is based. They will be more ready to work with you.

Having been snubbed by the emperor's commissioner at the assay in Nuremberg, Einsiedel turned to the next-highest ranking personage present: the chancellor of the elector of Mainz. His request was again turned down. The morning after he was back. This time he pleaded with Solms: Might he not at least have a copy of the assay results, so that his most gracious lord the elector had something to discuss with the delegates at his own regional diet? Charles V's commissioner seems to have betrayed some impatience: The day before Einsiedel had understood very well that, not having been sent by the imperial circle but by just one of the circle's estates, it would not do to admit him to the assay; far less appropriate would it be to let him have a copy of the proceedings. If he had been sent on the authority of the circle, in keeping with the ruling which the imperial diet had agreed, he would have been admitted; as that was not the case, the assay results would be sent to the emperor as soon as possible; but he, Solms, had no authority to let him, Einsiedel, or anyone else know what the assayers had found.[37] That was the end of the matter. Sticking to the rules was evidently really important.

The 'public enemy no. 1'

Overcoming distance

To the minds of contemporaries, the geographical extent of the Holy Roman Empire may have been vague, but no one doubted that it was vast. At the end of the Middle Ages, travelling from the foothills of the Alps to the coast of the North Sea took at least a month, depending on the season, one's means of transport, and a variety of other factors, most of which were linked to politics.[38] Some sixteenth-century Germans did not hold back with criticism when talk turned to this issue. In 1523 Christoph Furer, the Nuremberg metal merchant and author of several political memos we have met above, had this to say about the subject:

> While Germany is burdened more than other nations with large and heavy custom dues, road tolls, convoy service fees, and other impositions, which should be collected solely for the purpose of securing the roads and the common man, who pays them, there is no place in Christendom and probably among the heathens, too, where peace and law are enforced and maintained less than among the Germans. And this is unhidden to all who daily visit foreign realms, countries, and principalities; and it is more than obvious what mockery, scorn, and contempt it has so far caused among other nations.[39]

We need to take this with a pinch of salt. Furer directed his complaints to the government that had been formed to rule the Empire while Charles V was abroad. He wanted to convince that body that taxing trade any further was impossible.[40] This is why he did not only associate custom-dues paying merchants with the common man, but also had an obvious interest in sounding negative. Still, it is undeniable that he had a point. Overcoming the large distances across which the Empire stretched took time and money and was often unsafe. As we will see, this complicated formulating and pursuing coherent policies immensely—which is why Braudel called distance the 'public enemy no. 1' in sixteenth-century politics.[41]

As for safety, Charles V put tackling highway robberies on the agenda of his first imperial diet in 1521.[42] This showed goodwill, but noticeable effects were slow to materialize. To be sure, major princes of the Empire visiting imperial assemblies were safe enough. The landgrave of Hesse or the elector of Saxony, for example, might travel with retinues of between 200 and 300 armoured knights (there was a clear element of competition in this, with everyone trying to outdo the other), and in addition there were wagons for food, fodder and, last not least, the 'imperial chest', that is, a crate filled with a selection of documents that might come in handy during the negotiations. A Saxon ordinance of 1530 allowed each count and baron in the elector's retinue five horses, and each knight and counsellor three. One groom was needed for every three horses, and there were clerics, cooks, footmen, and tailors (who had to fit out the whole train uniformly in the Saxon colours of green, gold, and black), and in cases when the elector was joined by his wife, an additional court with servants and ladies-in-waiting. However, many estates could not or did not want to afford such a cavalcade. Imperial cities, for example, usually sent small delegations and sometimes only a single man.[43] A lone rider was exposed to all kinds of dangers. Not for nothing did the proverb claim 'far from home is close to harm'.[44]

The costs of travel did not only depend on the size and composition of the delegations that the estates sent to the diets, but also on the distance they had to cover between their place of residence and that where the assembly met. When the electoral Saxon delegation planned their journey to the diet of Regensburg in 1594, they expected to cover the distance of 220 miles in twelve days, including two days spent resting.[45] Nowhere did princely retinues go much faster. Queen Anne of Denmark, for example, achieved a maximum of 20 miles per day on her journey from Edinburgh to Windsor in 1603, once James I and his retinue had met her at Towcester.[46] All in all, Furer was certainly right that conditions were bad, but whether they were worse than elsewhere is a moot point.[47]

Low speed implied many overnight stays, and these obviously increased the costs—and not just those involved in reaching a diet. Short of sending a carrier pigeon, there was no way of transmitting information that did not require someone to travel. Even letters could therefore be excruciatingly expensive, and political correspondence particularly so. Between 1532 and 1562 the magistrate of Hamburg paid on average more than £12 to send a courier on foot to Speyer (which was about 320 miles away).[48] To put this in perspective: in Hamburg, a bricklayer received a daily wage of 3½ *Schillings* in 1530 and 4⅓ *Schillings* in 1550.[49] If he worked about 260 days a year (that is, five days a week), he had a yearly income of between £45 and £56. In other words, getting a letter (or a bundle of letters not heavier than a man could carry) delivered to Speyer cost the magistrate of Hamburg the equivalent of what a skilled craftsman earned in three months, provided he found regular employment. While cheaper options were probably available, the magistrate did not choose to entrust their political correspondence to just any traveller who happened to go in the right direction. They employed their own messengers—conspicuous in their livery of green, red, and grey[50]—and evidently thought they were paying a fair price for the certainty of their mail reaching its destination safely and unopened. The upshot of all this is that the quality of communications was abysmal: Travelling was dangerous and slow, and even something as basic as sending a letter was horrendously expensive.

The question is what the high costs and low speed of travelling and communication implied for how politics were made in the Empire, especially for its cohesion and for the ability and willingness of the estates to take part in decision-making. Historians have pointed out that in this as in almost any other respect, the country showed wide geographical variations. Following Peter Moraw's lead, they have constructed a model that distinguishes between parts of the Empire that were politically well integrated and open to the emperors' influence—next to Austria and the Low Countries, especially parts of Swabia and Franconia—and regions 'distant' from the emperors—the periphery, in particular the coasts of the North Sea and the Baltic.[51] Political decisions made by imperial diets and other assemblies tended to find much less acceptance in 'distant' regions—though it is claimed that these regions shrank in the first half of the sixteenth century, with at least the Northwest becoming for the first time fully integrated into imperial politics.[52]

The best place to hold a diet

Integrating the Empire's periphery was essential if the country was to be able act as a coherent whole. This required coming as close as possible to solving the first of the three interlinked collective action problems that the creation of a common currency involved and that we have examined above: As many estates as possible had to participate in decision-making, and hence the costs of attending a diet had to be minimized. The easiest way to achieve this was holding the assembly at a place that as many estates could reach at as low cost as possible. The emperor and the electors considered the issue carefully before each diet. From a purely geographical perspective, the Empire's centre was located somewhere between the village of Ostheim vor der Rhön and the town of Mellrichstadt close to the border of the county of Henneberg with the bishopric of Würzburg. Given the lack of precise maps and a clear idea of the extent of the country, it is unlikely any contemporaries were aware of this; moreover, an open field was not an appropriate site for an imperial assembly. What was needed was an imperial city, a town that was neither ruled by the Habsburgs nor by any of the princes of the Empire and that the most powerful actors could therefore consider neutral ground. The imperial city closest to the country's centre was Schweinfurt, and that is where a diet took place in 1532. However, this was the worst-attended diet during Charles V's reign, with few estates being represented and hardly any princes present in person (Figure 3.1).[53] While poor attendance had several causes—among others, the deepening religious rift caused by the Reformation—Schweinfurt was clearly not the best place to meet.

The problem with Schweinfurt was that the imperial estates were unevenly distributed across the country. Any political map of the sixteenth-century Empire shows three broad political zones: the east, which was dominated by a few relatively large principalities—from Pomerania in the north via Brandenburg, Saxony, and Bohemia to Austria in the south—the south-west, where there was a plethora of small territories—from Württemberg, which was still fairly large, to micro-estates such as the imperial nunnery of Rottenmünster—and finally the west and northwest, where most territories were medium-sized (Map 1.1). Imperial cities were located almost exclusively in Southwest and West Germany. This implies that the country's political centre of gravity diverged from its geographical centre: It was the imperial city that the largest number of estates could reach at the lowest total cost. Taking distance as a rough indicator of travel costs, it is possible to find this place. The basis is the imperial register compiled in 1521 and updated in 1545.[54] To be sure, the register contained inaccuracies and estates that were clearly not members of the Empire—remember Danzig (Gdańsk) and Elbing (Elbląg) or the 'duke of the Mase'. To some extent it was a wish list containing anyone whom its creators would have liked to belong to the Empire rather than a proper membership directory.[55] Still, we need no more than a rough guide indicating who would have been admitted to an imperial diet if he had shown up, and for that purpose the register serves well enough. As we also know the usual places of residence of most estates listed, we can compute the total distance they would have had to cover to reach any of the 86 imperial cities. If we do so, using the distance as the crow flies (unavoidably: in most cases we do not know which roads the estates would have chosen), we obtain a travel-distance optimality ranking, with the city that could be reached most easily being Wimpfen (today Bad Wimpfen).

We do not know how large Wimpfen was in the sixteenth century, but in about 1550 it had 350 inhabitants who enjoyed full citizen rights, that is, about as many as in the mid-nineteenth century, when the total number of inhabitants was smaller than 3,000.[56] An imperial assembly could be a huge affair. The diet of Worms in 1521, for example, attracted at least 10,000 visitors, the one of Augsburg in 1566 10–15,000. Such numbers were exceptional (the diet of Speyer in 1529 was visited by a mere 2–3,000 people),[57] but after all, before the meeting was underway no one could be sure of how many would come. A place like Wimpfen was clearly incapable of hosting a diet. Neighbouring Heilbronn and Schwäbisch Hall, at places 2 and 3 in the travel-distance ranking, were not large enough either. However, Speyer and Worms, at places 4 and 5, were a different proposition. For Speyer, the total distance the estates had to travel was only 2.5 per cent larger than for Wimpfen; for Worms it was 3 per cent larger. Both places were more populous than Heilbronn or Schwäbisch Hall. Speyer, with about 7,500 inhabitants in the first half of the sixteenth century, had the minimum size acceptable, while Worms had *c.*13,000 inhabitants, which put it in the group of the ten largest imperial cities.[58] During Charles V's reign, the emperor and estates met twice in Worms (in 1521 and 1545) and four times in Speyer (1526, 1529, 1542, and 1544). Without having access to modern maps or GIS tools, they were evidently able to find a place remarkably close to the optimum location of an imperial diet. Still, consider Map 3.1.

The map shows the Empire's geographical centre north-northwest of Schweinfurt, its political centre of gravity in Wimpfen, which from a travel-distance point of view was the optimal place to hold an imperial diet, and the cities where diets actually took place. For each of these cities, their position in the optimality ranking and the number of diets they hosted is indicated (for example, Worms, which holds place 5 in the ranking, hosted two diets). Neither Worms nor Speyer were the most

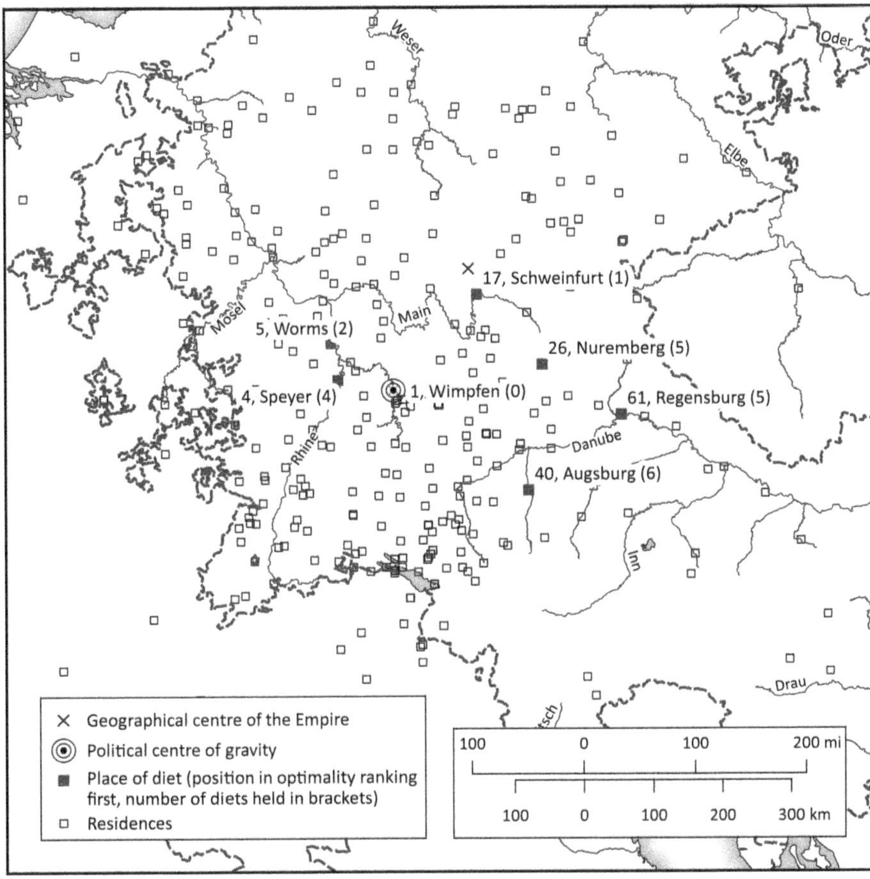

Map 3.1. Geographical and political centres of the Empire, 1521–59

Note: The position of an imperial city in the optimality ranking was computed based on the direct distance between the places of residence of the identifiable estates listed in the imperial register of 1521 and all imperial cities. The register is published in Wrede, *Reichstagsakten*, vol. 2, no. 56, pp. 424–42.

popular locations. Regensburg, Nuremberg, and Augsburg, all at positions much further down in the travel-distance ranking, hosted more diets, with Augsburg being the most favoured place. Evidently, there were other considerations apart from travel distances and costs that determined the choice of an imperial city.

In part, the focus on established, legitimacy-generating procedures played a role. One of the Empire's fundamental laws was Emperor Charles IV's 'Golden Bull' of 1356. The law determined how emperors were to be chosen and explained that since time out of mind,

> the solemn election of a Roman king and future emperor had taken place in the city of Frankfurt, the coronation in Aachen and the first imperial assembly in Nuremberg. We have therefore good reason to declare that unless there are serious impediments it shall henceforth be held like that, too.[59]

Nuremberg, located on the road that linked Charles IV's lands in Luxemburg and Bohemia, was thus a traditionally important location to hold a diet. Moreover, it was the city to which the imperial regalia were entrusted and was—by German standards—huge: In the first half of the sixteenth century, it housed about 37,000 inhabitants. And yet, Charles V chose another city for his first diet. A serious impediment had arisen: an epidemic, perhaps the bubonic plague that was endemic in Europe since the fourteenth century and whose unpredictable appearance kept forcing people to change plans at short notice. When the counsellors of the electors met in September 1520, Cologne's representative therefore suggested that there were no more suitable alternatives to Nuremberg than Frankfurt, Speyer, and Worms.[60] Probably in view of the masses of visitors expected to attend the new emperor's first diet, the choice fell on the largest of these cities, that is, on Worms. Nuremberg, though, remained a popular location despite its relatively low place in the travel-distance ranking. Its role as keeper of the regalia—a permanent feature, not a transient one like Frankfurt's as the city where emperors were elected—and its size that allowed it to host even well-attended diets relatively easily turned the scales. Moreover, for the Habsburgs, with their centres of power in Brussels and Vienna, Nuremberg was as well situated as an imperial city could possibly be.

How about the other two popular places, that is, Augsburg and Regensburg? From a purely Austrian perspective Regensburg was perfect: no other imperial city was closer. However, Augsburg had several advantages that Ferdinand I described to his son, the future Emperor Maximilian II, in 1563:

> As your grace knows very well for himself, its buildings, people, and many other circumstances make Augsburg a brighter, more charming, and jollier place than Regensburg, where moreover everybody can find better and more stately accommodation, and wine, fish, fruit, and other similar victuals are all to be obtained more easily than in Regensburg. We, in particular, are lodged better and can have much sport and diversion with hunting, falconry and the like.[61]

Augsburg was not only commercially more important than Regensburg; it was more modern in every respect, and this made hosting an imperial diet much easier. Besides, Augsburg had one more advantage which Ferdinand did not mention—in fact, none of the parties deciding about the location of a diet did—but which still may have played an important role: the emerging network of the imperial mail.[62] As we have seen, Hamburg's magistrate was willing to spend large sums to get its political correspondence delivered. By the time they did so, a cheaper, quicker, and more reliable way of transmitting information had already begun to develop. In 1516 the director of the imperial messenger service, Francesco de Tassis, discovered that the service, rather than losing money, could be made to pay for itself if the messengers were allowed to carry private mail for a fee.[63] The consequence was that soon, a network of relay posts began to spread across the Habsburg lands and the territories in between, with mounted couriers not only travelling regularly and according to predetermined schedules but also faster than ever before. Communications costs dropped precipitously: By 1577, sending a letter from Augsburg to Cologne—a distance of 260 miles—cost a mere 10 *Kreuzers*, that is, 3 *Kreuzers* less than what a bricklayer earned per day.[64] In other words, while in about 1560 Hamburg paid the equivalent of three monthly bricklayer wages to send a courier over the 320 miles to Speyer, in Augsburg in the 1570s it was possible to post a letter over a slightly smaller distance for less than a day's wage. While it is likely that Hamburg's couriers carried more than one letter each, it is evident that Europe's first modern mail service cut communication costs drastically. Its main route linked Brussels in the Habsburg Low Countries with Innsbruck in the Tyrol. It crossed the Rhine on a ferry close to Speyer, with Worms only one relay post away, and passed through Augsburg.[65] The historian Wolfgang Behringer has recently suggested that access to this route was a key factor influencing decisions about where to hold an imperial diet.[66]

The costs of making politics

How did travel and communications costs affect politics in the Empire? As for communication costs, we have good anecdotal evidence for a direct influence on the monetary policy-talks that concern us here. Some of the most important negotiations took place during two conferences in Speyer in 1549. During the talks, not only did the representatives of Charles V use the imperial mail; the envoys of the estates did so, too, if they could reach their masters in this way. Simultaneously, rulers such as Duke William IV of

Bavaria and the emperor used the mail to intervene in the talks.[67] However, with the Empire's postal network still in its infancy, not everybody had this chance. When in March 1549 the Austrian delegates argued against a prorogation of the talks, they suggested the delegates at the conference should rather use the mail to ask their masters for further instructions that would allow the conference to continue. They, the Austrians, offered to do so themselves; King Ferdinand's answer would likely arrive within ten or twelve days.[68] That might well have been the case, but while places such as Brussels, Vienna, and Munich could easily be reached by mail from Speyer, large parts of the Empire were not yet linked to the new network. Importantly, this applied to Saxony. In February 1549, the Saxon delegates at the meeting reported back to their home government that they kept thirteen horses in Speyer ('at what costs must be born in mind'); also, they could not tell which route through Hesse was most convenient for reaching Saxony. They asked Dresden for more detailed instructions but did not receive an answer before the conference broke up.[69]

While some were struggling with the problems of communication, others used them to gain tactical advantages. During the follow-up conference in Speyer in autumn 1549, for example, the envoys of the electors on the Rhine opposed a policy suggested by the representatives of the emperor. Their claim that their masters had given them no pertinent instructions may have been true, as was the argument that it would take time to reach at least some of the electors. However, five weeks later it turned out that they still had done nothing to inform their masters.[70] They apparently tried to prevent a decision by delaying the talks. This is even more likely as the electors, once their envoys had finally informed them, needed barely two and a half weeks to meet and draft a written rebuttal of the policy suggested by Charles V's representatives.[71] When Charles neglected to answer for several months, they took the chance to delay the talks at the meeting in Speyer until after the start of the next imperial diet, which made the conference redundant.[72]

While examining such anecdotal evidence gives us an idea of how important *communication* costs were, exploring the effects of *travel* costs requires a different approach. Travel costs are unlikely to have influenced the talks once the discussants were all gathered in one place. However, it is likely that the imperial estates took them into account when they decided whether they would participate. To analyse this, we need a series of events that may have been affected by travel costs to a different extent. Imperial

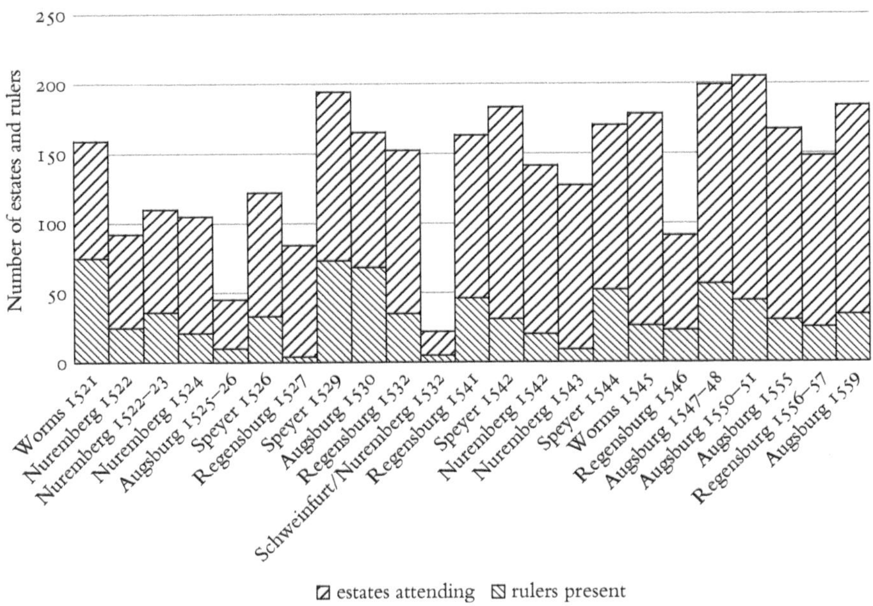

Figure 3.1. Attendance at imperial diets, 1521–59

Source: Aulinger and Schweinzer-Burian, 'Präsenz'; Leeb, Reichstag zu Regensburg 1556/57, vol. 2, no. 577, pp. 1406–08; ibid., Reichstag zu Augsburg 1559, vol. 3, no. 806, pp. 2033–47.

assemblies and their attendance serve this purpose perfectly: They were frequent, took place in different cities, and large numbers of people visited them. The question is therefore, did choosing a location that was suboptimal from a travel-cost point of view reduce attendance at diets (as the poor attendance of the diet of Schweinfurt in 1532 suggests)? Before answering this, and several other more detailed questions, let us briefly look at how attendance at imperial diets developed during the reigns of Charles V and Ferdinand I (Figure 3.1).

There were relatively large variations, but on average 139 estates were represented and 34 rulers—that is, spiritual and temporal electors and other princes, counts, barons, and abbots, and in the case of imperial cities burgomasters—attended in person. The question is, which factors determined whether an estate would come? We can provide an answer because for the period from the accession of Charles V to 1555, historians have gone through the sources and collected the relevant information; for the period thereafter, the concluding documents of the diets—the recesses or *Abschiede*—contain fairly reliable lists of the participants.[73] We therefore do not only know which rulers were personally present, but also how many counsellors they brought (or sent, if they decided not to come in person), who these counsellors were, whether they held a university degree, and whether they worked for only one estate or represented a whole group.

That travel distance mattered for many of these aspects characterizing the attendance at diets is highly plausible. Historians have shown this in a different context, finding that in late medieval and early modern Europe there was a clear and statistically significant link between the size of a country and the frequency of the meetings of its representative assembly: Assemblies met the more often, the smaller the territory was.[74] Our situation is different. We are looking at one polity only, and at a polity whose size did not much change over the time we are considering. However, if we relate the travel distance between the residences of the estates listed in the imperial register and the location of the imperial diets to what we know about actual attendance, a clear pattern emerges: Even among the few estates whose place of residence was within a radius of just 20 miles around the location of a diet, attendance was on average no higher than 63 per cent, and from then on it dropped almost consistently with every additional mile the delegations had to travel. The finding supports the idea that a country's size mattered for the effectiveness of premodern political assemblies. Still, we can do better than this. We can analyse statistically how strong the impact of distance was.[75] The result is significant in every respect. With every additional ten miles, the probability that any of the estates listed in the imperial register would attend dropped by about 0.9 per cent. In practice, this meant for example that if the diet took place in Augsburg, the likelihood of the imperial city of Straßburg (Strasbourg) being represented was about 10 per cent larger than that of someone from the city of Goslar attending. Similarly, if the diet took place in Nuremberg, the bishop of Augsburg was 10 per cent more likely to be represented than the duke of Pfalz-Simmern-Sponheim. If we ask how distance affected the presence of a ruler, we find that the effect was a little weaker: The probability that the ruler himself would come fell by 0.6 per cent for every ten additional miles. As personal presence was important (being involved in the procedures of the assembly lent the decisions legitimacy and made it harder to refuse to implement them) it follows that the more distant an estate was from the location of a diet, the lower the chance that what the emperor and Empire had decided would be executed. Holding a diet as close to the Empire's political point of gravity as was practically possible did really make a difference.

The size of delegations also shrank if the estate's residence was more distant. In fact, there was only a single countervailing effect of distance: The larger it was, the higher was the share of university-educated counsellors in an estate's delegation—a finding which suggests that princes and other estates who wanted to avoid the costs of coming themselves or sending large delegations used quality to make up for the lack of quantity. Typically, it was counsellors who held a university degree—generally a doctorate in law—who undertook most of the heavy lifting in the negotiations at imperial assemblies.[76] Still, there were other factors, which blurred the effect of distance. In part, traditional political bonds between emperors and estates still played a role: Estates located in regions historians identified as being 'close to the emperor' in the fifteenth century sent significantly larger delegations to diets in the sixteenth century. The effect was relatively weak, though, and regions 'distant from the emperor' had no significant effect at all. That Pomerania on the coast of the Baltic was very active on imperial assemblies that discussed the creation of a common currency in the middle of the sixteenth century is thus entirely in line with the results of the statistical analysis.[77]

Let us look at two further results of the analysis. First, it shows clear changes in attendance patterns over time. In the almost 40 years it covers, the probability of estates being represented at a diet increased significantly. With the fall-off in the personal attendance by princes that some historians have detected for this time[78] not yet being significant, and with both the size of delegations and the numbers of university-trained delegates increasing, the conclusion is that over the period considered here, the Empire became politically significantly better integrated. In fact, in about 1560 it was in better shape and closer to functioning like a multilayered, complex state than ever before.

Behind the scenes and in the open

The arrival

How did an imperial assembly begin? Not on time; that's for sure.[79] Precisely coordinating dozens and possibly hundreds of participants, who all wanted to avoid arriving early and spending money on lodgings and victuals before the talks had even begun was impossible; communications were far too poor.

For example, let us take the currency conference scheduled to begin on 2 February 1549 in Speyer. Charles V had invited the estates on 12 August 1548, a few weeks after the imperial diet held in Augsburg decided on such a meeting.[80] Relatively few estates—58, some of which sent joint delegates—answered the summons (Map 3.2),[81] among them electoral Saxony whose delegation was headed by Abraham von Einsiedel. This is what he reported to his home government in his first dispatch, sent ten days after his arrival:

> We cannot conceal from your graces and lords that we arrived here in Speyer on the Monday after St Scolastice's day, the eleventh of February, between 11 and 12 o'clock, and despite being somewhat late according to the decision made in Augsburg, the depth of the snow, the state of the roads, and the bad weather prevented us from ending our journey earlier, and thus we excused our delay to the imperial commissioners and to the counsellors of his royal Majesty [Ferdinand I, who was king of the Romans, of Bohemia and Hungary] and asked them to excuse our most gracious lord and hold him excused.[82]

Einsiedel was received by Reinhard von Solms, one of the two commissioners of Charles V at the coinage conference (the other was Philip von Flersheim, the bishop of Speyer). Having perused the Saxon counsellor's accreditation, Solms expressed his pleasure in seeing him and invited him to join the other delegates who had already arrived.[83] On imperial diets it was normally the chancellor of the elector of Mainz who welcomed the participants and checked their accreditations, but apart from this, the reception of the Saxon delegation at the coinage conference in February 1549 was unremarkable.[84]

Delegates arriving, like Einsiedel, nine days late was not remarkable either. For the follow-up currency conference that began in September 1549 we can trace their arrival day-by-day.[85] On the scheduled start date, 1 September 1549,[86] the counsellors of the elector of Mainz were the only ones who appeared, and this was despite having a longer journey than, for example, those of the elector Palatine, whose residence in Heidelberg was almost within sight of the tower of Speyer cathedral. On the day after, the delegates of King Ferdinand, the archbishop of Salzburg, and of the cities of Nuremberg, Augsburg, and Cologne arrived, on 3 September those of Ulm, Jülich-Cleves-Berg, and Münster, and so it went on (in the event the meeting turned out to be better attended than the one of February to March, with 111 imperial estates being represented: see Map 3.2).[87] The elector Palatine sent his envoys on 6 September. Evidently, he expected the beginning of the talks to be imminent, but in fact this took another few days.

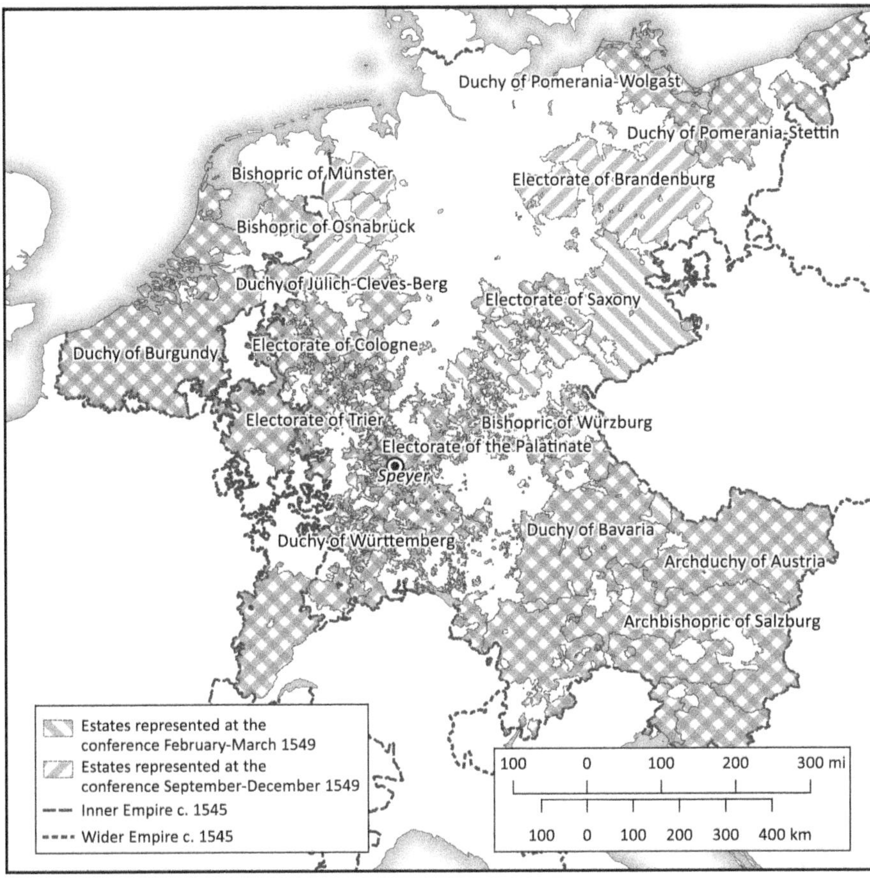

Map 3.2. Attendance at the currency conferences of Speyer 1549
Note: Volckart, *Währung*, no. 88, pp. LXXXVII–XCVIII.

Flersheim and Solms made the decision to open the assembly carefully. It is likely that Flersheim was responsible. As bishop of Speyer, he was a prince of the Church and ranked higher than Solms, who was a mere count. Born in 1481, Flersheim had studied law at Heidelberg, Paris, and Leuven, gained a doctorate and had years of experience as a princely and imperial counsellor. He had also attended almost all imperial diets since 1521, which meant that he did not only know everybody who was anybody in the Empire's politics but was also thoroughly familiar with the ins and outs of imperial assemblies. On top of that, he had a reputation as a careful manager, having done much to restore the prosperity of his bishopric, which had been ravaged in the Peasants' War and ruined by the profligacy of his predecessor as bishop.[88] By the end of the 1540s his health was failing, but to Charles V he must still have appeared perfect as commissioner.[89] Now, he and Solms decided to wait until the evening of 9 September before notifying the delegations, which had by then arrived, of the imminent beginning of the talks. At 8 o'clock on the morning after, they walked over from the bishop's palace, where Flersheim had invited Solms to lodge,[90] to the townhall a few hundred yards down the high street, where the counsellors and envoys of the estates were gathering. When all present in Speyer had arrived there, they opened the conference by reading out the agenda Charles V had set and the instructions he had given them.[91] Three days later on 13 September, when the estates had had a chance to prepare their responses to the points the emperor had raised, the talks began in earnest.[92]

Informal talks

In recent years, historians have reached a broad consensus about the functions of imperial diets and, by implication, of other assemblies including currency conferences like those which took place in 1549.[93] First, such occasions were a forum where formal political negotiations took place and decisions were made. This has always been recognized. Second, diets and, to a much lesser degree, other imperial assemblies were an occasion where the participants symbolically enacted the Empire, making it visible in the true sense of the word. This function has been stressed more recently, and most strongly by authors who focus on the ceremonial aspects of early modern political behaviour. Finally, diets served as a forum where the estates and their delegates could make informal contacts that they could use to defuse conflicts or exchange news and knowledge. Being related to each other, having friends in common, sharing religious convictions, or having made similar experiences—by attending the same university or previous diets, for example—was important; even more important was establishing a good working relationship with the counsellors or commissioners of Charles V and King Ferdinand.[94]

In his dispatches from the meeting in Speyer in February 1549, Einsiedel described how this worked. In line with the instructions he had received for the talks, he hurried on the evening of his arrival to approach Jacob Jonas, who headed King Ferdinand's delegation. Jonas had a distinguished career behind him: He had been chancellor of the bishop of Constance and of the archbishop of Mainz; as such, he had been responsible for the ecclesiastical oversight of many of the German bishoprics. He had been sent on diplomatic missions to Italy and had been present at all the imperial diets of the 1540s, variously acting as representative of the elector of Mainz, the archbishop of Magdeburg and Salzburg, the bishop of Halberstadt, and King Ferdinand. Since 1544 he was Austrian vice-chancellor, moreover, he was a member of the law faculty of the University of Vienna.[95] Einsiedel may have found him particularly accessible because Jonas knew Saxony: In the early 1520s he had been enrolled at the universities of Leipzig and Wittenberg; in spite of his strong Catholic leanings he had studied under Luther's colleague and collaborator Philipp Melanchthon and gained a bachelor degree.[96] Now, he treated Einsiedel with an affability that went beyond his usual obliging manner. He promised to inform King Ferdinand of the stance of the Saxon government and stressed that he himself had been instructed to contact the Saxon delegation as well. Like any skilful politician would, Einsiedel noted and interpreted every nuance of Jonas' behaviour:

> When there was a dispute between us about who should enter the room first, he explained that it did not behove him to take precedency because he was here as a representative of an archduke of Austria, whereas I represented an elector, and electors ranked higher than archdukes. This you might take to suggest that his royal Majesty does not mean to include the Bohemian lands in the common currency.[97]

Ferdinand I was king of Bohemia; hence the fact that he preferred to appear in his role of archduke of Austria at the currency conference might indeed be interpreted this way. If Einsiedel's presumption was right, he was supplying valuable information to the government of Saxony, which after all bordered on Bohemia. The case indicates that often, an estate's rank in the Empire's feudal hierarchy was ambiguous; there was enough freedom to stress different aspects, thereby signalling one's political intentions. If one wanted to do so, one had to get along well with the other delegates, and this was one reason why such talks behind the scenes were important. Few other eyewitness accounts have survived, but there is much indirect evidence. On one occasion in Spring 1549, for example, Austria and Salzburg must have coordinated their monetary policy-positions outside the official negotiations; they submitted a joint memorial in whose drafting other estates evidently had no part.[98] On another occasion in September, they were joined by the delegates of the counties of Henneberg and Mansfeld.[99] More generally, in the official negotiations during the monetary policy conference that began in September 1549, Austria and Bavaria conspicuously often made joint statements,[100] which is all the more remarkable considering their traditional rivalry: The Bavarian Wittelsbachs never accepted the idea that the Austrian Habsburgs were a cut above them.[101] One need not believe that informal talks were regularly used to sound out whether a formal consensus was within reach in order to recognize how important and frequent they were.[102] Behind the scenes encounters such as the one between Jonas and Einsiedel must have been commonplace at imperial diets just as well as at assemblies such as the currency conferences, whose records have yielded the examples used here.

Neither imperial diets nor other assemblies had a quorum. At diets, it was either the emperor or, if he was not present, the elector of Mainz—the German chancellor—who judged whether a sufficiently large number of participants had arrived to begin the formal discussions. At the currency conference of autumn 1549 we have seen the imperial commissioners make this decision. This was not easy. *Münztage* such as those in spring and autumn 1549 were significantly less well-attended than imperial diets, with smaller delegations and hardly any rulers being present in person (there was a significantly larger share of university-trained counsellors, though: see Table A.1). Still, introducing a quorum was never discussed. In fact, the estates seem not to have been interested in a rule that clearly determined how many of them had to be present to make a resolution legitimate and binding for those who were absent as well as those who opposed it. Some, at least, made tactical use of the lack of clarity: After all, if one disliked the outcome of the talks, one had the chance to claim that the meeting had been too poorly attended and that any decision was therefore null and void.[103] When this happened at the currency conference of autumn 1549, Charles V's counsellors argued that, 'as all estates have been suitably summoned and invited, it must be held for just in itself that despite some or even many failing to appear, the obedient ones who are present have the right to proceed with the transactions and to represent the absent ones'.[104] Flersheim and Solms added that it would violate all principles of justice and equity to stay away, let the estates that had come shoulder the costs of attending the meeting, and then reject its decisions.[105] Still, the issue would not go away. At the imperial diet of Augsburg a year later it was dragged up again. The elector of Trier's suggestion that the presence of 'several' electors, princes, and other estates should be necessary for monetary-policy decisions to be valid went unheeded.[106]

One reason why a simple, numerical quorum was never considered was the inequality among the imperial estates.[107] They were no more than the tip of the iceberg of a fundamentally unequal society (smallholders and cottagers, serfs and freeholders, domestic servants, craftsmen, merchants, patricians, and members of the lower nobility all enjoyed different rights and privileges that defined their position in the social hierarchy), and that they were all admitted to an imperial diet or a similar assembly does not mean that they all enjoyed the same rights. Among other things, the way they addressed each other reflected this. The emperor was 'his most illustrious highness', an elector 'his most gracious highness', a simple prince 'his gracious highness' and so on. A textbook that taught letter writing to secretaries working in the chancelleries of the estates listed 49 graded forms of address for spiritual personages, from cardinal to common priest, and 180 for temporal persons from emperor down to bailiff and cellarer (counting German recipients only). One-hundred and forty-two of these forms of address applied to imperial estates.[108] And of course, any communication directed towards someone higher up in the hierarchy had to be peppered with 'submissive', 'most submissive' (if the social distance was more than one rank) and similar expressions of deference. No wonder English travellers, used to a less-graded society, found the Germans 'ever tedious in their stiles or titles'.[109]

Colleges, hierarchies, power, and influence

As at all other late medieval and early modern representative assemblies, the attendants at imperial diets or similar assemblies—including the *Münztage* of 1549—sorted themselves into several groups. There were three of these councils or colleges: The first and highest ranking was the electors' college which was formed by the princes privileged to choose the emperor (except the king of Bohemia, who never attended). The second college was composed of the other princes, from archbishops and dukes down to the abbots of imperial abbeys and small counts and barons. The third, finally, represented the imperial cities. Defining an overarching quorum would have been impossible without at least implying that the estates were equals. It would have been correspondingly difficult to negotiate.

For the diet to pass a bill, the two higher colleges had to agree with each other. In this respect they were of equal weight, but as the electors' college had a mere six members, each elector had a much larger influence than any of the up to 280 members of the princes' council (in practice there was no occasion when all were present). As for the cities' college, the two others argued that it merely had a *votum consultativum*: They were prepared to let its members have their say but felt in no way bound to it. At the currency conference in Speyer in autumn 1549, the higher colleges regularly discussed matters jointly; the minutes show that they informed the delegates of the cities every few days of what they had decided.[110] They clearly despised their lower-ranking colleagues. On one occasion, a delegation of the cities' college approached the electors' envoys and handed over a memorial, asking 'to have it read and pass it on to the imperial commissioners'. When the electoral delegates discussed this during a joint meeting with the princes' college, the princely counsellors merely stated that it 'was neither customary nor ancient practice to accept something from the cities and pass it on to the commissioners; if they wanted to say something, they should do so themselves'.[111]

Despite the contempt of the higher colleges, the cities were strongly interested in attending imperial assemblies. Statistically, they were as likely to be represented as the higher estates, though burgomasters tended to come significantly less often than territorial rulers. Also, towns sent fewer delegates, among whom the share of university-trained counsellors was significantly smaller than in the delegations of electors and princes (Table A.1). The cities' college spent a lot of time and energy (and salaries for legal advisers) on redressing the imbalance in its position. However, it took them a full century to achieve a breakthrough, which was confirmed only in 1648.[112] Earlier sources reflect the disparity existing until then: When mentioning the participants of a diet, they talked of the 'electors, princes and common estates'.[113] Tellingly, the cities were not even mentioned.

While both princes in the narrow sense of the word and 'common estates' sat in the princes' college, the distinction was important. Over the decades of Charles V's reign, it became customary to reserve so-called *viril* votes for the higher-ranking spiritual and temporal rulers—archbishops, bishops, dukes, margraves, and landgraves—which meant that each of them was allowed to voice his opinion individually. By contrast, the lower-ranking members of the college—counts, barons, and prelates—sat on shared benches during the deliberations, with each bench having only one vote. From the 1540s, the idea gained ground that counts and barons from the same broad geographical regions—Franconia and Swabia on the one hand, the Wetterau district in modern Hesse on the other—should use the same benches.[114] The upshot was that all counts and barons had only two joint votes, and the prelates another two. As the imperial register listed 80 prelates and more than 120 counts and barons, the political weight of each count was one-sixtieth and that of each prelate one-fortieth of that of a prince with a *viril* vote. Attendance patterns reflect this imbalance. Statistical analyses show that princes holding a *viril* vote were significantly more likely to be represented at imperial diets. They also tended to have larger delegations, though they brought or sent fewer university-trained counsellors than other estates did (Table A.1). The implication is that they were more deeply enmeshed in the deliberations than the representatives of the other estates, and hence more likely to implement the decisions imperial diets made.

The colleges discussed the points on the diet's agenda among themselves, with the higher colleges using a peculiar and highly ceremonial way of structuring the talks that was based on the position each of the participants held in the Empire's feudal hierarchy. This was the main reason why procedures here were lacking autonomy (the role each member of the diet played corresponded to his role in wider society), and it is what historians who stress the importance of 'ceremonial procedures' have in mind when they discuss the importance of rituals in political decision-making. A report compiled by a member of the chancellery of the elector of Mainz in about 1570 shows how this worked.[115] In the electors' college, it was the task of the elector of Mainz to first call his chancellor who, in set and traditional phrases, would propose the topic to be discussed. This was a feature that gave the procedure a ceremonial or ritual character. Next, the elector of Mainz would ask the other electors in their order of rank to state their views: first Trier, then Cologne, the Palatinate, Saxony, and last Brandenburg. Finally, it was Saxony's privilege to ask Mainz for his opinion.[116] In the absence of unanimity, this process of 'questioning' or 'polling' was repeated until at least a majority agreed.[117] The princes' college followed an analogous procedure, and according to the report from Mainz the cities' college did so, too.[118] However, the minutes of the deliberations of this college show that its discussions were in fact more open and less formal than was claimed.[119]

One effect of structuring discussions in the manner followed by the two higher colleges was that it promoted consensus. This was first because while each member of one of the diet's colleges had the chance to express his views, lower-ranking members were discouraged from disagreeing with previous higher-ranking ones if they did not want to antagonize them.[120] Second, there is a common phenomenon whose effects have been observed in economic behaviour as well as in politics: People are the more likely to adopt an idea, the larger the proportion of earlier speakers is who have already expressed support of it. Where voting behaviour is concerned, social scientists have found that the desire to support a winner (or desert a loser) is a strong motive for jumping on a 'bandwagon', as the phenomenon is called. Alternatively, later voters may assume that earlier ones have information that they lack and so use earlier votes to update their judgement as to which policy is best.[121] Whatever the exact mechanism, the bandwagon-effect implies that, having listened to what those ahead of him had said, a member of one of the diet's colleges would tend to follow the preceding speakers even if this went against his own interests—or at least against what he had thought his own interests were before polling began.[122] This was the more likely, the more earlier speakers had shared this opinion. The discussions' structure thus promoted consensus primarily in the short term. In the medium and long term, it tended to cause problems. This was bound to happen when the participants in the decision-making process, once the pressure and example of their betters in the college was gone, realized that they had been talked into agreeing to something that went against their own best interest. The bandwagon-effect probably explains a good deal of the inconsistencies between the decisions diets and other imperial assemblies made and their implementation on the ground, including in the field of monetary policies. In Chapter 6, we will encounter a characteristic example of how this played out.[123]

Despite the inequality among the members of the respective colleges, over the sixteenth century the principle gained ground that decisions should be based on the majority vote of those present.[124] To see how this worked in monetary policies, let us look at the negotiations taking place in a committee the currency conference in Speyer formed on 5 October 1549 to discuss the draft of a currency bill. The committee was composed of representatives of all three colleges. Still, its members followed a procedure that closely resembles the one used within the individual colleges of the diets; this was possible because the colleges themselves were ranked. After a few days of preliminary talks, the chancellery of the elector of Mainz presented a rough draft of the ordinance. Then, normally one of the delegates from Mainz proposed the paragraph that was to be debated. Let us take an item that did not touch any of the fundamental interests of the participants and where agreement was therefore straightforward, for example the question of whether information on the total nominal value of coins made from one mark (about half a pound) of pure silver should be deleted from the draft. The issue was relevant because this so-called 'mint-equivalent'* made it possible to assess and compare the intrinsic value of the coins at a glance.[125] Electoral Trier voted first, with its delegate Otto von Lengenfeld arguing that it was better not to reveal the mint-equivalent in the final, published form of the bill. The delegates from electoral Cologne joined him, as did Hans Steinhauser, who represented the elector Palatine. With no one from Saxony being present, electoral Brandenburg was next in line. Its delegate Timotheus Jung, who evidently felt out of his depth and was often poorly prepared, suggested resurrecting a failed earlier currency bill. The minutes of the discussion do not register Mainz's vote. Austria joined the Palatinate, whereas Bavaria voted in favour of leaving the draft unchanged. This seems to have swayed the mood. Burgundy voted like Bavaria, and the delegates of Jülich-Cleves-Berg, of the Wetterau counts, and of the imperial cities of Nuremberg and Ulm did likewise. As Mainz did not vote and electoral Brandenburg did not address the issue at hand, the result was a six-to-four majority in favour of publishing the information in question.[126] The draft ordinance of the bill accordingly listed the total legal tender value of each type of coin minted from one mark of pure silver.[127]

All this sounds straightforward enough, and Charles V's counsellors claimed that the emperor was in principle prepared to accept what the majority of the colleges (and by implication of committees formed by the colleges) decided. Referring to the bimetallism-issue that caused many problems at the currency conference in autumn 1549, they argued that in this case

> his Majesty would no doubt have liked that, following ancient custom, both the electoral and princely colleges had agreed unanimously or at least by the majority, so that any further deliberation or resolution would have been unnecessary. His Majesty would certainly have approved of the decision made by the common estates and would have duly confirmed it with his imperial authority.[128]

Still, the majority principle was by no means universally accepted. In fact, the imperial diet had developed a formal mechanism that estates unhappy with majority decisions could use: the protestation.[129] Protestations owe their fame to the estates that rejected the decision of the majority of the diet of Speyer in 1529 to outlaw Luther (and who accordingly became known as Protestants),[130] but were used in monetary policy-matters, too. For example, Austria, Salzburg, Brandenburg-Kulmbach, Mansfeld, the Wetterau counts, and electoral Saxony lodged formal protests against the resolution of the majority of the estates to end the currency conference of Speyer in March 1549 and to reconvene in September.[131] Even the emperor did not always feel bound to majority decisions, as the electoral delegates in Speyer in autumn 1549 pointed out in order to explain why they were persisting in their views despite the opposition of the princes' college: 'It had indeed happened in former times that a majority decision had been presented to his imperial Majesty, and his Majesty still found and decided on a better solution, which thereafter all estates accepted and observed.'[132] Majority decisions were known but when push came to shove, it was not a given that they would be accepted: The rank of estates opposing or supporting them played a large role. We therefore need to know which factors determined this rank. To contemporaries, the answer was by no means obvious, and the case of King (or Archduke) Ferdinand shows, there were ambiguities. Universally valid and consistent rules that allowed determining the position each individual held in the ranking were not only absent; they were impossible to design.

While occasionally the parties involved referred to readily visible criteria to decide the issue—a prince's age relative to that of the others might turn the balance[133]—a systematic examination of the polling process yields further insights. This works best for the princes' college, as the electors' college had too few members to allow an analysis and in the cities' college, the detailed minutes we have from 1556 onwards show that discussions were relatively open. For the princes' college, accurate information is available from the mid-1550s onwards. If we consider a sample of seven rounds of polling that took place at the diets of Augsburg in 1555, Regensburg in 1556–7, and Augsburg in 1566,[134] we find first that the number of voters varied between 12 and 26, with 19 being the average. As we do not know how many counts and prelates attended (they did not cast individual votes), this merely gives us the minimum number of participants. Still, one thing is obvious: The diets of Charles V and Ferdinand I may normally have been attended by hundreds of representatives of the imperial estates, but that does not mean that huge numbers of people were involved in decision-making. In fact, the politics of the Empire were directed by a manageable number of persons (and their advisers): a few dozen, maybe, rather than hundreds, all three colleges counted. As for the polling order in the princes' college, Austria took first place in all but one case, where Salzburg presided. Bavaria invariably came second, and Salzburg normally third. Further down the ranking became more variable—interestingly, without this causing any quarrels that left traces in the sources. Thus, in the first of two rounds of questioning that took place on the same day in 1555, the duke of Württemberg spoke in the fourth place, whereas in the second round he came ninth.

Can we link the position in the polling order to any independent, outside factors? We can indeed. One such factor is the contribution each estate made to the fiscal needs of the Empire. In 1521, the estates had agreed to support Charles V's planned expedition to Rome, where he hoped the Pope would crown him emperor. Their contributions—called 'Roman Months' because they were supposed to be sufficient to maintain a specified number of troops for one month—were listed in the imperial register.[135] Subsequently, the list was used to compute each estate's contribution to the Empire's military requirements in general, and in order to simplify matters, the numbers of troops were converted into *Guldens* (with one foot soldier counting for four *Guldens*, and one cavalry man for twelve).[136] Interestingly, the values thus derived were expected to reflect economic prosperity. This was made explicit during their renegotiation in the 1540s, with the recess of the diet of Regensburg in 1541 stating that the contributions of some should be reduced 'because of their impoverishment' whereas others, 'whose wealth has obviously increased', should pay more.[137]

The statistical analysis of attendance patterns at the diets shows a clear and significant association with the Roman Months: For every additional 100 *Guldens* an estate contributed, the likelihood that this estate would attend a diet increased by 7 per cent (with the likelihood of the ruler himself being present increasing by 1.7 per cent, cf. Table A.1). Evidently, the more an estate was expected to contribute, the stronger was the incentive to be present when decisions were made that concerned payments and the use to which the money was put. The question is, did this also affect an estate's rank in the polling-process of the princes' college? To see how we can answer the question, let us first look at the briefing that Caspar Ber, one of the counsellors of young Duke Christoph of Württemberg, gave his lord ahead of his first imperial diet in 1550.[138] Ber ranked the estates of the princes' college from one (Austria) to 18 (Anhalt) according to their position in the polling order. As we have ranked values on the one side, we need ranked values on the other, too, if we want to detect a link between polling order and Roman Month contributions. We therefore convert the contributions (as given in the imperial register) into a ranking, with the estate listed with the highest contribution (Austria) receiving rank one and the one contributing the least (Braunschweig-Grubenhagen) rank 18. In Figure 3.2, a strong link between the estates' polling rank and their rank in the order of Roman Month contributions would be indicated by the markers, which symbolize each estate's position, being in close proximity to the diagonal trendline.

In fact, however, the markers are all over the place. If we believe Caspar Ber, therefore, the contributions an estate was expected to make to the military requirements of the Empire and its rank in the princes' college had as good as nothing to do with each other.[139]

In all fairness, Ber cannot have been a particularly competent counsellor, at least when it came to explaining how the imperial diet worked. That is no wonder. He had never attended a diet,[140] and the old minutes and other acts he submitted together with his briefing were not detailed

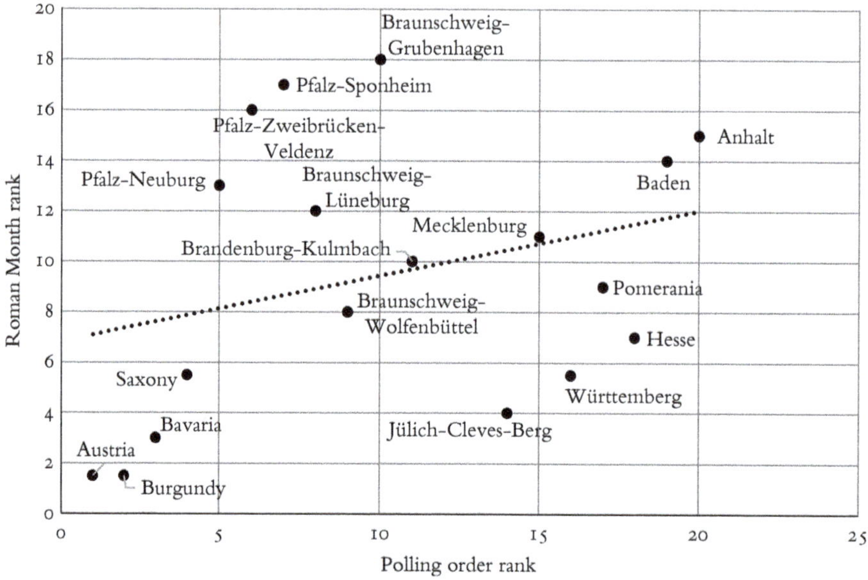

Figure 3.2. Polling order rank versus Roman Month rank, princes' college, according to Caspar Ber's briefing of Duke Christoph of Württemberg

Source: Neuhaus, 'Streit', p. 285.

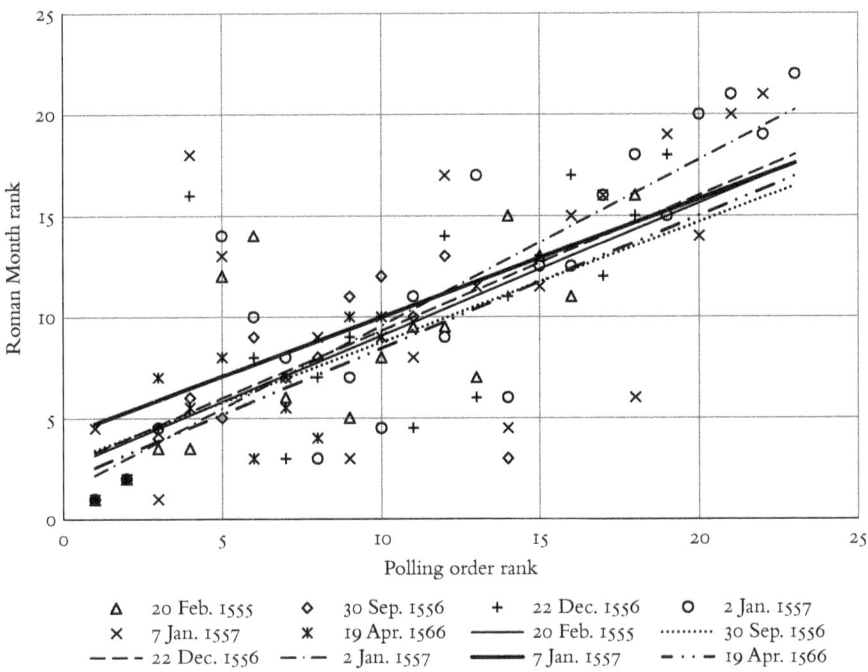

Figure 3.3. Polling order rank versus Roman Month rank, princes' college, actual polls 1555–66

Source: Aulinger, Eltz, and Machoczek, Reichstag zu Augsburg 1555, vol. 2, no. 145, p. 1274; Leeb, Reichstag zu Regensburg 1556/57, vol. 1, no. 122, pp. 450–2; no. 160, pp. 499–504; no. 167, pp. 509–12; no. 170, p. 515; Lanzinner and Heil, Reichstag zu Augsburg 1566, vol. 1, no. no. 86, pp. 578–9.

enough to allow him to check how polling was organized. We are therefore in a better position than he was if we want to examine this. The result differs strikingly from the picture he drew in 1550. The correlation between polling order and Roman Month rank was never perfect (it would have been if the markers in Figure 3.3 were all located exactly on the trendlines) but always much stronger than according to Ber's briefing in 1550.[141]

Figure 3.3 leaves no doubt that the princes' college followed a general rule: The more one had agreed to contribute to the Empire, the earlier one was allowed to vote (and the better were one's chances to sway the views of speakers lower down in the ranking). At this point, a caveat is in order. The analysis shows that an estate's Roman Month payment and its rank in the princes' college were closely correlated, but it does not necessarily point to a causal link. It does not imply, for example, that if an estate had promised to contribute more, its ruler would have moved up in the ranking. At present, we can therefore say no more than that the larger the estates' fiscal stake in the Empire was, the larger was their role in policymaking. Their likelihood of attending a diet was higher and their position in the princes' college more influential.

What light does all this shed on the effectiveness of policymaking at the level of the Empire? Evidently, historians who stress regional diversity are on the right track, though the importance of regions close to and distant from the emperor should not be over-rated. By the period that concerns us here, they had lost much of their traditional influence. However, purely geographical distance still mattered, though as the increasing attendance at diets indicates, its relevance declined. Nevertheless, it remained the strongest factor in deciding whether an estate would attend an imperial diet. Attending, especially attending in person, in turn 'enmeshed' rulers in the policymaking procedures in a way that lent decisions legitimacy and made it more likely that they would be implemented. Still, we should not over-rate the importance of this factor either. A bill's legitimacy did not guarantee its observance. We will see below that in the context of monetary policies, the emperor and the estates designed mechanisms that provided incentives to make sure that their decisions would be respected even by those who never took part in policymaking.

A second general conclusion concerns the importance of the estates' economic prosperity, which the size of their contributions to the Empire's military needs was supposed to reflect. At least in the princes' college it was this factor that decided an estate's position in the polling order. A high position gave a prince the chance to dominate discussions and to decisively influence their results, first, because lower-ranking members of the college were probably reluctant to antagonize their betters by contradicting them, and second, because bandwagon-effects tended to create an at least superficial unanimity. The downside was that there was a strong risk of the agreement falling apart once the assembly had dispersed.

What light does all this throw on the debate about whether the Holy Roman Empire functioned like a state, which was mentioned above? There is no denying that the Empire had dysfunctional features. For its complex system to work, the interplay between the imperial, the circle- and the estate-levels of authority had to work smoothly, and there were occasions when it did not. However, at least some of the obstacles that created frictions—mainly large distances and poor communications—became easier to overcome in the first half of the sixteenth century, with the consequence that the coordination of the levels of power improved. To judge by the attendance at imperial diets, by the 1550s the Empire was significantly better integrated politically than ever before.

Was that sufficient to make it a state, though? Decision-making procedures stayed dangerously ineffective. One such procedure was the polling system practiced at imperial assemblies. It was good at generating superficial agreement but was likely to cause problems in the medium and long term: Once individual estates realized they had jumped on a bandwagon that took a direction they disliked, they tended to go back on their word, which in practice meant that they failed to implement decisions to which they had agreed only a short time before.[142] Such events severely disturbed the interplay between the levels of authority that in the 'statist' interpretation of the Empire complemented each other. Emperors focusing on building consensus and agreeing compromises could mitigate the problem, but solving it would have required a fundamental reform of how the diet worked. Without this, coordination failures remained a feature of the system—failures more severe than any experienced in modern decentralized states. We will see an example of this in Chapter 6. As for other early modern polities (which are more appropriate comparisons for the Empire), it is true that law enforcement remained patchy everywhere.[143] Still, these countries do not seem to have suffered from the systematic decision-making problems endemic in the Empire. In sum, we should certainly not play down the differences between the sixteenth-century Empire and modern multilateral political systems (for example, the imperial estates fit into an established feudal hierarchy instead of being equals). However, understanding the Empire in terms of multilateralism captures more of its essential features than interpreting it as a state does.

In Chapters 4 to 6 below we will examine how the emperor and the imperial estates tried to solve a lower-level problem than that of the systematic inefficiencies which beset decision-making: the problem of monetary disorder. They did so against the background of, and often in close connection with, general political developments. When the seven electors chose Charles V as emperor in 1519, few would have guessed at the drama that would unfold over the coming decades. Charles' election ushered in one of the most tempestuous reigns of early modern history. It led him from Spain to the Empire, from the North-German plains to the African desert, and from triumphs over his enemies to defeat, the frustration of all his most cherished plans, and eventually his abdication and retirement in Spain.

Only two years before Charles' election, Martin Luther, a little-known professor at the newly founded university of Wittenberg in Saxony, had published 95 theses directed against what he considered abuses of the Church. Over the 1520s, Luther's ideas kept gaining ground not only among the common man—they strongly influenced the 'Peasants' War' of 1525—but among the imperial estates, too. When Charles' first imperial diet met in Worms in 1521, there was only one Lutheran estate (the imperial city of Reutlingen);[144] during the diet of Speyer eight years later there were 25, among them one elector (Saxony) and several important princes. As we will see, the diet was strongly aware of the tensions between its Lutheran and Catholic members and of the need to agree if not in religious matters, then at least on monetary policies. What was even more important for monetary policies at the level of the Empire were Charles V's frequent periods of absence abroad. He left shortly after the conclusion of the diet of Worms to deal with trouble in Spain, returned briefly in the early 1530s, and then for a longer period in 1541. From then on until the early 1550s, the imperial diet met almost yearly and regularly spent much time and energy on monetary-policy discussions.

In 1546–7, Charles waged a short and sharp war against the Lutheran estates united in the Schmalkaldic League. Charles won, intentionally misquoted Caesar (for him, it was not '*veni, vidi, vici*' but '*veni, vidi, Deus vixit*')[145] to make it clear that comparing him to ancient Rome's greatest military genius was entirely appropriate, and set about capitalizing on his new position of strength by punishing opponents and rewarding supporters. Most importantly, he stripped John Frederick 'the Magnanimous' of Saxony, who had been one of the leading figures of the Schmalkaldic League, of the Saxon electorship and transferred it to Duke Maurice of Saxony, who had been conspicuous among his backers in North Germany. Charles was also determined to use the occasion to finally solve the Empire's monetary problems. This was decided in principle at the diet of Augsburg of 1547–8—the 'diet-in-arms', so called because of the troops the emperor stationed in and around the city. The diet called the currency conference in Speyer which Flersheim and Solms chaired as imperial commissioners. It gave the meeting the most comprehensive mandate imaginable: The imperial estates should send fully authorized expert counsellors who should not only draft a bill for a currency valid in the whole Empire, but should independently pass this bill, which was to be binding without any further involvement of a diet.[146] As we will see in Chapters 4 and 5, the conference did indeed prove decisive. But let us begin at the beginning. Let us first look at what shaped the monetary-policy stance many of estates took in the discussions: the supply of precious metals, first and foremost of silver.

4
The age of silver

The mining boom

Bullion mining and its importance

In later centuries people liked to tell of a pedlar who lost his way in the wild woods that covered the Schneeberg, one of the mountains in the range that marks the border between Bohemia and Saxony. After much wandering Sebastian Romner—for that was his name—finally reached a footpath that led to a pit where iron ore was mined. He called out the foreman, shared his provisions with him, and asked for the road to Bohemia. When their talk turned to business, the foreman complained about the poor quality of the ore, which he and the other miners found, and finally exclaimed 'that they did not know why God punished them so—if things did not change, they would all have to leave the land'. Romner picked up a few lumps of ore, 'pretending he wanted to inquire in Steyr in Austria, where he bought his merchandise, for artisans who maybe knew help in the matter'. After the foreman had shown him the way, he escaped the woods and reached Bohemia. There—in the town of Görkau, today Jirkov—he met a group of gold prospectors from Italy to whom he showed the ore and who claimed it was 'almost half pure silver'. In Nuremberg, famous for its metal craft, Romner found experts who confirmed this; so he returned to Saxony to try his luck there. However, on the market in the town of Zwickau he got into a brawl, was taken to the bailiff and, half-drunk as he was, told something of 'knowing a treasure not far off that could make him a gentleman'. The bailiff investigated, discovered Romner was right and, being an honest man, decided to share the silver with him. This is supposed to have happened in about 1470.[1]

Whatever we make of the story, by the end of the 1470s the Schneeberg in Saxony was one of the world's richest silver mining districts that attracted thousands of miners.[2] In his dialogue *Bermannus*, published in 1530, the humanist and mineralogist Georg Bauer, who Latinized his name as Agricola, characterized these workers: 'We are all people who strive for money', he has one of them say, 'and we desire to become as rich as possible with little effort, with a minimum of labour and in the shortest possible time'.[3] This captures the aims and preferences of the miners accurately enough if we add a tendency to reckless aggressiveness, which the lawless and violent conditions on the Schneeberg of the 1470s suggest (there were reports of 'much murder and rioting').[4]

Stories of poor pedlars who found unexpected riches were popular with the common folk who had little hope of escaping poverty themselves. Still, we should not discount such anecdotes. They often reflect the atmosphere of a period and region more accurately than the usual dry and dusty records—for example of monetary-policy negotiations—do. Concerning Romner, we do not know anything definite, though his legend seems to have a basis in fact in much the same way the older legends about the discovery of silver in the Harz mountains in the tenth century have.[5] Pedlars like Romner were common everywhere, so much so, in fact, that established merchants, who were organized in guilds, approached the territorial authorities in order to lobby against them.[6] Moreover, a certain Martin Römer, who towards the end of the fifteenth century was considered the richest man in Saxony, did not only have a suspiciously similar name, but also a remarkably similar fate: Like Romner, Römer seems to have had contacts in Nuremberg where he had his ore samples tested, and like Romner he cooperated with members of the urban elite of Zwickau to finance his mining venture.[7] Finally, what Romner reputedly achieved—the discovery and exploitation of a deposit of silver ore—was typical of a development that in some places began about a generation earlier but that gathered pace at the time he was said to have been active. New ore deposits were found, known deposits began to be exploited, and mines that had lain dormant for generations reopened while others were newly set up. Conditions began to resemble those on the Schneeberg in many places. Freiberg, Annaberg and Marienberg in Upper and Goslar in Lower Saxony, Joachimstal (Jáchymov) in Bohemia, and Schwaz in the Tyrol were among the most important sites of large-scale excavating and processing silver ore. In Upper Hungary—from 1526 under the rule of Ferdinand of Austria—Neusohl

(Banská Bystrica) and Kremnitz (Kremnica) played in the same league. All these places grew quickly in size and wealth and developed into centres of innovation and culture once the wild conditions of the first years had been overcome.[8]

In an edict Charles V issued in 1525 to prevent the diet from passing a bill against the monopolies of large trading firms, the emperor stressed the importance of the mining sector. It was

> not only the large treasure, which is produced and obtained in gold, silver, copper, tin, quicksilver, lead, iron, and other metals and which amounts to about—and rather to more than to less than—twenty times 100,000 *Guldens* per year, but also that in the German lands several hundred thousand people—old and young, women and children, and many others, too—could not find their necessary livelihood except in mining, digging, and smelting; and moreover that the export of those same metals into many countries provides income to many other people, as carters, innkeepers, burghers, peasants, and common craftspeople everywhere on the roads, in villages and towns. Likewise, there is no other trade or business in the whole German nation and in the Holy Roman Empire by which princes and lords can as much increase and enlarge their revenues from taxes, custom dues, and tolls, so that the mines, their operation and good and stately maintenance must be strongly promoted by all ways and means that may prove useful.[9]

Charles had an obvious interest in the issue: His most important creditors were merchants who had invested heavily in mining and felt threatened by the planned antimonopoly legislation. He could not afford to alienate these men. Elector John Frederick of Saxony's view that 'the German nation receives not the least of its welfare from the mines' sounds no less partial, given that he himself controlled some of the most important silver ore deposits.[10] Still, modern research supports the gist of such remarks. It has found that in the early sixteenth century 10,000 miners were working in Schwaz in the Tyrol—no more than a village 100 years before—and that by the middle of the century in all Tyrol 40–50,000 people were employed in mining.[11] In the late 1530s, Annaberg and Marienberg in Saxony employed about 7,000 miners each; the mines of Freiberg and Schneeberg were of about the same size.[12] Most of the ore produced was silver or contained a high percentage of silver. Gold deposits, by contrast, were rare, with the only ones of any importance in the Empire being located in Salzburg and Bohemia.[13] While we do not know the weight of the mining sector in terms of its share in the total workforce or in the total output of the Empire's economy, there is no doubt that the 'Central European Mining Boom'—as John Munro has called the growth in silver mining between the 1470s and the 1540s—had huge economic importance.[14] A veritable age of silver had begun.

Its effects on the Empire's monetary policies in the sixteenth century were profound. Like the lack of currency borders, which allowed the trade in coinage to flourish and expand until the imperial estates began to regard it as a major threat, the silver boom was one of the core parameters shaping their monetary policy-outlook. If we want to explain why they made the decisions they did, we need to understand how the boom came about and whom it affected in which way. These are the questions addressed in this chapter.

Late medieval rulers were strongly interested in the production of precious metals, from which they hoped to benefit economically and politically. They therefore tried to regulate and control mining as closely as possible, which is why we are relatively well-informed about gold and silver mines. Still, accurate and consistent figures that allow drawing a clear picture of how output developed exist only for the period from the end of the fifteenth century onward. Scattered earlier evidence suggests that production of precious metals began to decline in the early fourteenth century. The big silver mine of Kutná Hora in Eastern Bohemia had yielded between 30 and 35 tons of pure silver per year in the first decades of the century. After *c.*1350 this fell to about 10 tons, and between 1420 and 1460 mining ground to a halt entirely.[15] Other silver mines, for example in the Harz mountains, suffered a similar fate.[16]

Historians used to argue that mining in general went into decline in the fourteenth century due to technological causes:[17] Mines had become so deep that it was impossible to exploit them any further before the problem of draining them of water had been solved. More recent research is pointing out that there were other mining sectors that continued or only began to flourish at this time (coal mining, for example), and that where there was a decline, it was for a whole complex of causes.[18] Given current concerns with the climate, it is perhaps no surprise that this factor has been brought in. When summers became cooler and shorter during the late Middle Ages, miners working relatively high up in the mountains were no longer able to grow food themselves. Instead, they had to be supplied from the lowlands, and this increased production costs.[19] Arguably, the Black Death—the bubonic plague that swept Europe from 1347 and killed about half of the population over the next four or five decades—had a similar effect as it reduced the labour supply and allowed workers to negotiate higher wages.[20] Again, it is probably not by accident that attention has turned to this factor in 2020. Political unrest in the fifteenth century made matters worse: Thus, the decline of Kutná Hora was closely linked to a religiously inspired uprising in Bohemia that began in 1419 and during which the place was sacked.[21] All these factors could be linked to the problem of water management that historians used to stress. The danger was leaving a mine derelict for even a short period of time, whether because of warfare or high wages. The deeper shafts and tunnels would soon drown, and while continually extracting small amounts of water might have been possible, draining a whole mine that was deep under water was technically difficult and financially demanding.[22] By the late fifteenth century, a solution—albeit a costly one—had been found: the so-called 'water art', which was able to drain water from mines even deeper than 70 metres.[23]

Another problem resulted from the quality and composition of the ore. In many places—for example in Schwaz in the Tyrol, Eisleben in the county of Mansfeld, and Neusohl (Banská Bystrica) in Upper Hungary—it contained a mixture of silver and copper or lead, which needed to be separated.[24] This was done with the help of a process called liquation, whose earliest traces historians used to locate in about 1430 in Nuremberg. Recent research has found that it was well known in many places by that time; where and when it was first used is apparently no longer possible to determine. What is beyond dispute is that it was from Nuremberg that the liquation process spread across Central Europe.[25] It relied on the strong chemical affinity of silver with lead and on the fact that lead melts at lower temperatures than copper (327° versus 1083°), which allows separating the two metals.[26] A contemporary described the process like this:

> The copper that has been mined is brought to the liquation works, where silver is being separated from copper and copper made ready and pure. One adds a quarter part of lead to the silver-bearing copper and places 24 such pieces in the liquation furnace; there the lead liquifies, and it and the silver drop down from the copper bars . . . The smoke rising from the liquation works is yellow or as green as a greenfinch . . . and he who is worst off and liquates most dies.[27]

This is a rare reference to how pollution caused by early modern industry put the life of the workers at risk. For liquating copper, the Thüringer Wald region halfway between Nuremberg and the mining district of the county of

Mansfeld was particularly suitable. Much of Thuringia was (and is) heavily wooded and mountainous; waterpower to drive the mills needed to crush the ore and charcoal for smelting it in the liquation works were therefore readily available. Charcoal especially was needed in huge quantities, as was lead, much of which came from the mines of the city of Goslar in the Harz mountains, while smaller quantities were imported from Poland and as far away as England—a line of business in which Thomas Gresham was involved.[28]

Buying stocks and granting loans

The problems of draining mines and of separating silver from copper had one thing in common: Solving them was costly. Between 1453 and 1456 the magistrate of the imperial city of Goslar, which controlled the drowned Rammelsberg mines in the Harz mountains, paid 3,000 Rhenish florins for the water arts of one Claus von Gotha to be installed, only to find that the engineer demanded another 1,000 *Guldens* to finish his work.[29] It is in this field where a crucial development got under way in the fifteenth century. To see what happened and how it helped mining, let us take a closer look at how the industry was organized.

By the fifteenth century, the imperial estates normally claimed a 'regal right' in all mineral deposits found in their lands, which in effect meant that they controlled who was allowed to open and operate a mine at which conditions. In Saxony, for example, anybody wanting to prospect for precious metals had to apply for permission from one of the ruler's officials (who had, for example, to make sure that claims were not too close to each other). This gave the prospector two weeks to sink a shaft. If he found ore, he would receive the new mine in the legal form of a fief, which meant that he held it in return for the 'tithe'—that is, a levy of 10 per cent of the precious metal output—that the Saxon electors and dukes reserved for themselves. The rulers also claimed pre-emptive rights in all silver the mine produced.[30]

Once invested with his claim, the miner would need to find capital to maintain and extend his venture. To do this, he divided his property into so-called *Kuxes* that he offered to investors. On this basis, a vibrant market developed, in fact, the first fully-fledged stock market in world history.[31] *Kuxes* could be traded at any price the buyer and seller agreed without the existing shareholders—who collectively formed a *Gewerkschaft*, that is, a joint-stock mining company—having a say.[32] They differed from modern stocks in that the buyers did not only acquire the right to a share in the profit, but also the duty to subsidize the mine if this should prove necessary.[33] *Kuxes* traded at the fairs in Leipzig were purchased by investors from, for example, Nuremberg, Erfurt, Magdeburg, Wittenberg, Berlin, and Dresden, that is, mostly from Northeast Germany. Investors from broadly this region seem to have dominated in Saxony in general, though occasionally others from further afield—Augsburg, Regensburg, Cologne, and Jülich near Aachen—appeared, for example among the buyers and sellers of *Kuxes* traded at the annual fairs of Frankfurt.[34]

Recent work done by Max-Stephan Schulze, David Chilosi, and myself has revealed that capital markets in fifteenth-and sixteenth-century Germany were relatively well developed. Most investors placed their capital within a 130- to 140-miles radius around their hometown. This was probably possible because medieval towns were largely autonomous and free to design their own legal codes. Many copied tried and tested institutions of not only neighbouring towns but also of more distant but commercially successful places.[35] When urban autonomy came under increasing threat from the late fifteenth century onward, town law was assimilated into the legal codes princes published within the framework of the Empire's *Policey*-legislation.[36] Despite the high degree of decentralization, private law that governed transactions on financial markets was therefore broadly similar, which implies that investments outside one's home town generally enjoyed a high degree of legal protection—at least under normal circumstances. Under such circumstances, *Kux*-prices depended on much the same factors that govern share prices today: supply and demand, with demand being affected for example by the availability of alternative investment opportunities and by the profits a venture made or was expected to make.[37] Prices were correspondingly volatile: 'Mining is a gamble', one eminent merchant from Leipzig quipped in 1536, 'and *Kuxes* can rise and fall overnight'.[38]

Politics could have a strong impact on demand, too. Abraham von Einsiedel, the electoral Saxon delegate at the coinage conference of Speyer in spring 1549, was instructed by his home government to use the occasion to complain about this to the representatives of King Ferdinand and Charles V. During the Schmalkaldic War, Charles had outlawed several Protestant investors and issued a mandate demanding that the Saxon government hand over their *Kuxes* (which the government apparently had done). In consequence, the market collapsed. During the quarter year before the meeting in Speyer more than 6,000 *Kuxes* were left on the shelf. Einsiedel was to request that his Majesty should 'henceforth most graciously spare the *Bergherren**'—the estates who controlled mining districts of their own—'further such mandates and confirm this in an official deed, which would be put up at the mines', where everyone could see it. In Speyer, Einsiedel was reluctant to raise the issue with Jacob Jonas and Thomas Behaim, the director of the Austrian mints who accompanied King Ferdinand's vice-chancellor. As he pointed out to the Saxon government, 'his royal Majesty had himself passed on, granted and given away several *Kuxes* that had belonged to outlaws',[39] presumably to reward followers. We do not know whether the emperor had done the same, but all-in-all it is unlikely that he complied with the Saxon request.

Gewerkschaften existed in all mining districts, but their structure and influence differed. Take the county of Mansfeld between Saxony and the Harz mountains, where there were rich deposits of copper shale that had a high content of silver. At the currency conference in Speyer in March 1549 the delegate of the counts claimed their masters faced a particularly difficult situation. This was because the mines the counts controlled

> were not, like the Saxon ones, managed and financed by common hands [that is, by a large number of small investors] but rather by only a few firms or merchants . . . And if there is a year when so little shale and ore is found that the profit does not cover the production costs, they withdraw their hands and shut down the mines, because they are not out for losses but have invested several hundred thousand of *Guldens*, which they would need to let lie idle when the mines yield no profits.[40]

The Saxon electors and dukes were thinking of cases like this when they prohibited individual *Gewerkschaften* from holding more than one mine.[41] They deliberately pushed back the influence of the shareholders, with their officials making managerial decisions in what was called a 'direction system'. By the mid-sixteenth century, the *Gewerken* had not yet been reduced to mere providers of capital who received dividends if things went well and had to subsidize mining if they did not (as would be the case by around 1600),[42] but already now *Gewerkschaften* had much less influence vis-à-vis the rulers than in nearby Mansfeld.

In the Habsburg-ruled Tyrol, too, *Gewerkschaften* were relatively weak, though for different reasons. At the bottom of the divergence were the rulers, whose decisions in this field were governed by their fiscal needs.

Whereas the Saxon electors and dukes never aspired to influencing politics at the European level (at least not before the end of the seventeenth century when Elector Augustus II became king of Poland) the interests of the Habsburgs spanned the whole continent. There were many occasions when they needed large sums at short notice, and this is why as soon as the mining boom started, they began using the mines they controlled as collateral for loans they took up to finance their policies. While their creditors did not necessarily join a *Gewerkschaft* straight away—not even the Fuggers did so—they still gained a strong influence on how the mines were run.[43]

By the middle of the sixteenth century, the mining interests of the Fuggers went back several generations. In 1487 Jacob Fugger had granted a 24,000 *Guldens* loan to Archduke Sigismund 'Rich-in-Coin' of the Tyrol, who despite his name was in constant need of cash. The *Gewerkschaften* of Schwaz stood surety, and in case the debt was not punctually serviced, the total silver output of their mines was to go to the Fuggers.[44] This had set the pattern for further contracts with the Habsburgs. In 1488, the Fuggers lent 150,000 *Guldens*, in return for which they received the total output of the Schwaz mines at a preferential price for the period until the loan was repaid, in 1496 122,000 *Guldens*, for which Maximilian I used the production of the Tyrolean copper mines as collateral.[45] In 1508 the Fuggers gained further rights in the copper and silver found there in return for a loan—this time 129,000 *Guldens*. Several other credits followed,[46] but all were overshadowed by the money they and some other firms mobilized in 1519 to finance the election of Charles V: 545,000 of the altogether more than 850,000 *Guldens* were lent by the Fuggers.[47] Once Charles had arrived in the Empire, the parties signed an agreement about the redemption of the imperial debts—by then *c.*600,000 *Guldens*. The Fuggers were assigned the Tyrolean silver and copper output for about two-thirds of the sum.[48]

The Fuggers were the largest creditors of the Habsburgs in the late fifteenth and early sixteenth century, but they were neither the earliest nor the only ones. The Meutings, for example, another trading firm from Augsburg, began lending to Archduke Sigismund in 1453; they were granted similar conditions as the Fuggers some decades later.[49] However, once the Fuggers had entered the market, there was little room for anybody else, as Heinrich Wolff from Nuremberg learnt to his cost. In 1494, he lent a 'tidy sum of money' to Maximilian I. In return he was promised that part of the Tyrolean silver output, which normally the mint in Hall was receiving, for a period of four years. But of course, Maximilian had already granted the total silver output to the Fuggers, who refused to let go of their collateral. Wolff was referred to Duke Ludovico Moro of Milan, Maximilian's father-in-law, who still owed him part of the dowry of his recently wed wife Bianca Maria. The duke refused to pay up, too, and to maintain his link with the Habsburgs and save his capital, Wolff, who by then must have been desperate, decided to grant further loans to Maximilian. He eventually lost all he had, and the fact that the emperor later ennobled his son and made him treasurer of the Austrian hereditary lands was no more than gesture.[50]

These kinds of policies were bound to have a strong impact on investment. If one's product could at any point be signed away as collateral for a loan taken by a ruler—and a ruler at that, whom one suspected of being financially not particularly prudent—why then would anyone buy mining shares? *Gewerkschaften* were therefore relatively uninfluential in mining districts under Habsburg control, though their importance grew in the 1540s when the many small firms joined up to share the costs of draining their mines.[51] Still, when other investment dried up the creditors of the Habsburgs themselves had to step in, as the Fuggers did in 1522.[52]

What mattered for monetary politics was the capital they and the *Gewerkschaften* invested in silver mining and the effects this had on the supply of the metal. It was this that allowed applying 'water arts' and the liquation process to an unprecedented extent. The result was a spectacular increase in the output of the mines from the Harz mountains over the Mansfeld district, the Saxon mountains, and Bohemia to the Alps. In the mines of Schwaz in the Tyrol and Eisleben in the county of Mansfeld, for example, 100 kilogrammes of ore yielded less than 800 grams of silver in 1480; once the new process of separating silver from copper was introduced in 1490, this rose to almost 1,400 grams, that is, by 75 per cent.[53] Beginning in the mid-nineteenth century, historians have spent a lot of time and effort on collecting the evidence on European mining output.[54] There were huge obstacles to overcome: apart from finding and piecing together the documents that contain the often fragmentary data, assessing how the production of copper was linked to that of silver was particularly difficult. Table 4.1[55] thus summarizes the work of generations of scholars. This does not mean it is exhaustive, though. There were more mining districts—in Salzburg, the Leber valley in Alsace, and in Sweden—but the evidence from there is too fragmentary. The total production given in the last column of the Table 4.1 is therefore the minimum of what was achieved in these decades.

Table 4.1 Silver production, 1471–1550, five-yearly means in tons

Period	Saxony	Goslar	Mansfeld	Joachimstal (Jáchymov)	Kutná Hora, Kašperské Hory	Neusohl (Banská Bystrica)	Kremnitz (Kremnica)	Schwaz	Total
1471–75	4.36				4.50			4.11	12.97
1476–80	10.32				4.25			7.35	21.92
1481–85	3.74				4.00		1.80	9.75	19.29
1486–90	2.77				3.75		3.52	12.75	22.79
1491–95	3.76				3.50	1.96	3.52	12.42	25.16
1496–00	4.64	0.99			3.25	1.96	3.80	12.09	26.73
1501–05	8.98	1.17			3.00	2.87	4.07	11.77	31.86
1506–10	7.42	1.00	4.63		2.75	3.99	4.34	11.44	35.56
1511–15	6.93	1.02	5.71		2.50	3.63	4.61	11.11	35.52
1516–20	5.19	1.01	6.08	3.97	2.25	1.98	4.89	10.78	36.15
1521–25	3.70	1.07	6.30	9.70	2.00	2.49	5.16	10.45	40.88
1526–30	3.43	0.53	7.89	13.80	2.00	2.27	5.43	10.13	45.47
1531–35	6.66		6.30	16.55	2.00	2.27	5.43	10.13	49.35
1536–40	14.97		5.73	13.25	3.95	2.24	5.43	10.13	55.70
1541–45	7.74		6.14	10.94	4.00	2.14	5.43	9.96	46.36
1545–50	4.13		6.58	10.94	0.70	2.14	5.43	9.96	39.88

In Schwaz, the output was normally highest and over time relatively stable, though a slight downward trend is evident. Saxony experienced more ups and downs. Its total production was in most periods smaller than that of the mines in the Tyrol but reached a spectacular peak in the second half of the 1530s. Joachimstal (Jáchymov), finally, was a latecomer. It grew rapidly and reached a peak a little earlier than the Saxon mines to the north—a peak that was short lived, but during which its output surpassed that of any other district.

New World silver

From the 1540s, the boom began to fade. By the beginning of the seventeenth century, the output of silver at almost all the chief mining districts of central Europe had dropped to anywhere between one-third and one-twentieth of its maximum.[56] While we will see that politics attributed this to rising production costs—but then, there was no period when the *Bergherren* did not complain about rising production costs—there was one other crucial factor: the New World, large parts of which were at this time conquered by Spanish adventurers. Having destroyed the Aztec Empire in Central America in the early 1520s and the Inca Empire in the Andes in the mid-1530s, the Spaniards initially focused on looting, melting down, and exporting the golden and silver treasures that had been amassed by the American cultures. The mining of silver in New Spain began in the early 1530s.[57] In 1537, the Fuggers bought a mine in Súltepec in Mexico and sent German miners, and from about that time output increased slowly but steadily.[58] However, when Juan de Tolosa struck upon silver in the lands of the Zacatecos Indians in 1546, an unprecedented boom began.[59] A mere thirteen years after their foundation, the Zacatecas mines in New Spain were producing 19 tons of silver per year—16 per cent more than Joachimstal (Jáchymov) at its peak in the first half of the 1530s. In 1560 to 1565, production grew to more than 27 tons per year; in 1571 to 1575 it stood at almost 36 tons.[60] No single European mining district had ever come close to this scale of production. The Potosí mines in Peru (today Bolivia) easily surpassed that output. Founded in 1545 on the site of earlier indigenous mining activities, they produced almost 65 tons of silver per year between 1561 and 1565. Maintaining this pace proved impossible, but with a yearly production of 56 tons in the first half of the 1560s and 36 tons in the first half of the 1570s,[61] Potosí was still larger than Zacatecas and any other rival worldwide, and as we have seen, there were more New World mines. Silver imports to Europe grew by leaps and bounds. We know this because all American treasure—not only silver, but also gold—that legally entered Europe passed through Spain where it was carefully registered. The Spanish government tried to supress smuggling, but as they were not always successful the official figures give us the lower bound for the imports of bullion.[62] In the 1530s these already exceeded on average 8 tons a year, and from then on until the 1580s the quantities doubled or trebled every decade.[63]

What effects this had in Europe is under dispute. We know all kinds of goods became more expensive over much of the sixteenth century, with the increase (on average maybe 1.5 per cent per year) affecting not only nominal prices but also the quantities of silver people paid. By the 1540s contemporaries were beginning to blame this on the growth in the quantity of money that outpaced any increase in the supply of commodities.[64] The argument was taken up by modern research, but what share American bullion had in the inflation is by no means obvious.[65] Still, one thing seems to be beyond dispute: With the arrival of bullion from Zacatecas and Potosí, profits made in the old mining districts in the Tyrol, Bohemia, and Saxony came under pressure—a fact that contributed to the decline of the mines.[66] Before then, however, access to silver ore deposits was one of the key factors that drove monetary policies both on the side of the *Bergherren* and on that of the other estates. We therefore next need to look at how it shaped the decisions they took.

The talks are stalling

The price of silver

On St Nicholas Day, 6 December 1526, one of the many monetary policy-meetings, at which we have looked in Chapter 3, took place in Nuremberg. Given the high profile of the participants, it is unlikely they gathered in a common inn or hostelry; rather, the magistrate would likely have provided a room in the town hall. Count Albert VII of Mansfeld was personally present, but the other attendants were acting on behalf of princes who were all a few steps higher than he in the social and political hierarchy—in fact, they were among the most important estates of the Empire. Hans Auslasser and Ambrosius Mornauer spoke for King Ferdinand, Friedrich von Thun and

Matthias Giech for Elector John 'the Steadfast' of Saxony. Archbishop Matthew Lang of Salzburg had sent Bernhard von Trennbeck, and Duke George of Saxony Dr Otto von Pack[67]—the same Pack who a couple of years later forged a document intended to convince Landgrave Philip of Hesse that an alliance of Catholic princes had been formed to eradicate Lutheranism. Philip immediately began to arm in defence, and the affair could have escalated to a full-blown war if Pack hand not been found out.[68] Leopold von Ranke, one of the founding fathers of history as an academic discipline, called him 'untrustworthy, treacherous' and 'a thoroughly bad man',[69] but in December 1526 none of this was in evidence. Pack seemed to fit the company in which he found himself—other princely counsellors and, in the case of Mornauer,[70] a smelting works manager—very well.

The recess of the meeting that summarized the results of the talks also identified their aim: 'In order to maintain a good common coinage', all participants agreed that 'nothing more beneficial and useful can be done than that first a stable and constant price of silver is agreed and imposed throughout all the Holy Empire'.[71] This was the main point around which the talks in Nuremberg revolved and around which further discussions would revolve until the late 1540s. We therefore need to examine first how the arguments developed in this context shaped the talks. Only then can we look at other issues that the participants brought up.

On the face of it, it seems evident why silver prices were relevant. Unlike most imperial estates, the *Bergherren* controlled their own deposits of precious ore. In consequence, they could acquire bullion at lower costs and gain higher revenues from the seignorage. The problem appeared so obvious that from the early 1970s onwards, when Fritz Blaich first stressed its importance, it shaped the dominant perspective from which historians considered monetary policies in the first half of the sixteenth century. Some scholars did point to the Empire's political structure in order to explain the course of politics, but even they agreed that is was disputes about the supply of bullion and the profits from minting—envy and resentment, to spell it out—which hindered an agreement on a common currency and which, once such a currency had been imposed from above, prevented its universal acceptance and brought it down in a matter of years once it had been implemented.[72]

In fact, the idea that the *Bergherren* would be able to set higher seignorage rates than other estates is flawed; it misunderstands how the value of money, the price of silver, and the costs and profits of minting were linked. We will look at the details a little further below. For the moment, suffice to say that historians were not the only ones baffled by the problem. Contemporaries were prone to similar errors. A committee the imperial diet of 1522 had formed to discuss monetary policies, for example, saw a direct link between the price of silver and the seignorage.[73] This would change only from the mid-1540s, when fundamental new insights on the technicalities of minting spread—insights that considering their consequences amounted to a paradigm shift in monetary policies.[74] To the extent that until then, contemporaries were making similar assumptions as the modern historians who examined their debates, the argument is valid that disputes about the supply of bullion made it hard to find common ground.

That in principle all agreed on the importance of the price of silver did not prevent dissent in detail, and this was one reason for the meagre result of the talks among the *Bergherren* in Nuremberg in December 1526. It was not the only reason, though. All present realized that whatever they decided would be preliminary in any case because there were more authorities with mines of their own who would have to be brought into the discussions: Dukes Philip and Henry of Braunschweig-Grubenhagen, Count Botho of Stolberg, and the imperial city of Goslar were mentioned, all neighbouring the Harz mountains.[75] More importantly, while the *Bergherren* represented in Nuremberg thought a uniform price of silver was crucial, they disagreed on what that price should be. In fact, in contrast to what Blaich and later historians have assumed,[76] they did not form a united pressure group at all (Map 4.1). If we want to understand why not, and how their disagreement affected monetary policies at the level of the Empire, we need to take a closer look at the arguments dominating the talks between the 1520s and 1540s.

This takes us to a first attempt to create an Empire-wide common currency in the years before the *Bergherren*-meeting in Nuremberg. That Charles V should address the Empire's currency problems was a demand the electors put to him even before they chose him over his rivals Francis I of France and Henry VIII of England in 1519. The occasion was the negotiation of a formal contract between him and the electors, a so-called electoral capitulation. The document summarized the fundamental laws of the Empire in sufficient detail to make it a 'Magna Carta of the German nation', to quote an eighteenth-century legal expert, or 'a written constitution *avant la lettre*', as the historian Wolfgang Burgdorf recently put it.[77] It also pinned down the emperor to policies agreed with the electors. One of the clauses to which Charles put his signature—probably inserted on the insistence of the

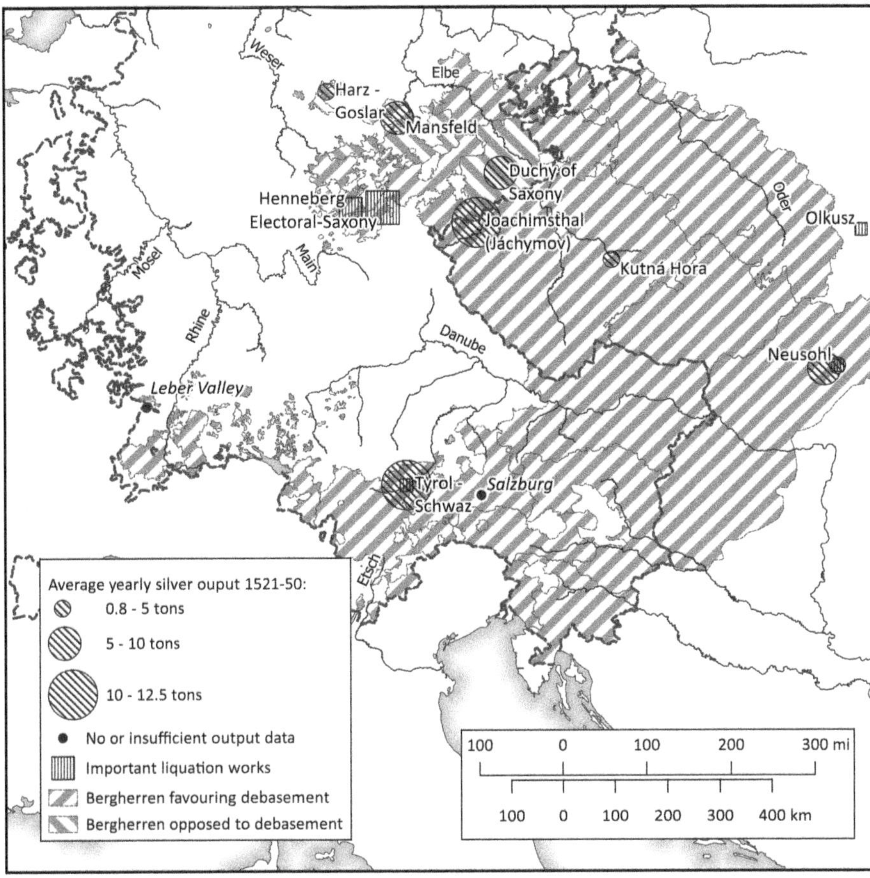

Map 4.1. *Bergherren* and average yearly silver output, 1471–1550

Note: Silver output: Munro, 'Monetary Origins', p. 8; Bingener, Bartels, and Fessner, 'Zeit des Silbers', p. 424; Westermann, 'Silber- und Kupferproduktion'. Political borders as of 1546.

electors on the Rhine, who were suffering from underweight imitations of their gold *Guldens*—concerned monetary politics. It stipulated that 'because in the Empire there were and still are many defects and deficiencies in the coinage', he would 'at the earliest opportunity and with the advice of the electors, princes and estates of the Empire remedy them and use all possible diligence to create stable and orderly conditions'.[78]

While the capitulation set the tone for Charles V's monetary policies, what initially turned out to be most important were his frequent periods of absence from Germany. This was expected; it was why the electors demanded that the emperor should establish an imperial governing council in which he and the estates would be represented.[79] That government, constituted with Charles' brother Ferdinand as his representative, soon tackled the reform of the coinage.[80] Like the wider public—remember Rösch's flysheet about the moneyer—its members considered anyone involved in the production of money an authority in all questions touching the monetary economy. In August 1522 they therefore convened a group of mint masters and assayers to form an expert panel.[81] What followed was a two-year period during which both the imperial diet and the government called various meetings where only one thing seems not to have been disputed: The new currency was to be based on gold and silver, with coins of both metals circulating in parallel and at fixed rates—in short, it was to be a bimetallic currency such as the English one at that time.[82] In 1524, the imperial diet finally instructed the government to use a memorial it had drafted as a basis for a last round of discussions with mint masters and assayers. Their decisions were then to be published as a universally valid currency law. Tellingly, the diet left a backdoor open for anyone unhappy with the result by adding that whatever the outcome of this process might be, it was not to compromise the liberties and privileges of electors, princes, and other estates.[83] The government accepted this risk. On 10 November 1524 it published a currency bill which became known as the 'Esslingen Coinage Ordinance' from the name of the city where the government had its seat.[84]

The ordinance envisaged an Empire-wide currency where the largest silver piece was to match the Saxon *Guldengroschen* and was to be the equivalent of a Rhenish florin that was to continue in use. *Guldengroschens* and gold *Guldens* were to be supplemented by a range of smaller silver coins down to a piece of the value of one-quarter *Groschen;* even smaller units such as *Pfennigs* and half-*Pfennigs* were to be minted according to the discretion of any authority privileged to issue coins (Table A.3). The government thus did not pursue complete, Empire-wide uniformity; harmonization concerned only the larger coins. There was no plan to withdraw the old money from circulation; the bill merely contained a list that determined the exchange rates of some of the more important coins in new money.

It quickly turned out that most imperial estates took advantage of the backdoor option: The ordinance was never adopted by more than 13 out of the about 90 authorities that were minting coins in 1525 and the years immediately thereafter.[85] When the representatives of the *Bergherren* met in Nuremberg two years after the publication of the bill, the only thing they had to say about it was that 'there were many good reasons why their masters thought it inconvenient'.[86] So what was wrong with it, in their eyes? Most historians argue that the ordinance failed because first, the planned new money contained too much pure silver and second, it exclusively served the interests of the estates without mines of their own.[87] Neither point seems particularly plausible. To be sure, the bill was published by the government which at that time was formed by delegates of Austria, Upper Germany, the Rhineland, and the Low Countries and advised by Upper German mint officials—that is, with the exception of Austria by estates that did not control silver deposits.[88] However, if the composition of the government had determined the type of the currency it adopted for the Empire, we might have expected it to choose that of the Rhenish Union. Instead, the Esslingen Ordinance drew on the coinage issued by the electors and dukes of Saxony, who were among the most important and influential *Bergherren*. The Austrian representative openly protested this but was over-ruled and was unable to alert Ferdinand in time to stop the publication of the bill—essentially a consequence of high communication costs.[89]

What about the other argument—the claim that the ordinance failed because the money it tried to introduce contained too much pure silver? There is some evidence that seems to back it. To see what it was, let us take a closer look at the reaction of the emperor and his brother to the currency law. Before the government published the Esslingen Ordinance in November 1524, it failed to inform not only Ferdinand, but also Charles V, who was at that time in Spain. When abroad, the emperor generally insisted on confirming—or rejecting—bills the diet or the government had agreed.[90] In the case of the Coinage Ordinance he did neither. He first ignored it and then undermined it by exempting Austria from having to observe the law.[91] His reasons were complex. For one thing, Charles was utterly convinced of his universal mission as the supreme ruler of Christendom.[92] As for the mindset with which he approached his imperial office, the Venetian ambassador Gasparo Contarini described him a few years after his election as

> gloomy, but not without temperament, and his whole disposition matches this attitude. He is very religious, free of all vices and not, like other young people, given to salaciousness; he does not know other diversions either. Occasionally, but rarely enough, he goes hunting; negotiations and attending council sessions are his pleasures, and there he is tenacious and spends most of his time. He is not affable and more tight-fisted than generous; therefore he is not particularly popular.[93]

Add to this Charles' fascination with warfare and his irritableness, which in later life increased due to his gout, and you have his character as modern biographers draw it, too.[94] Cancelling a law announced not only without his consent, but without his knowledge—in effect, behind his back—was certainly not beyond him. However, this was not just a question of Charles' character and of how he saw his office as emperor. What also mattered was that his brother Ferdinand had requested his intervention against the Esslingen Ordinance. Like Charles, he may have been offended at having been passed over, but he was a quite different character. Our old acquaintance from Pomerania, Bartholomäus Sastrow, met him at the imperial diet of Augsburg in 1547–8 and remembered later that Ferdinand

> was rarely without guests, was always splendidly entertained with all kinds of pastimes and magnificent dances. Had exceedingly fine, well-ordered *musicam, non solum instrumentalem, verum etiam vocalem* [not only instrumental but also vocal music]; in addition to other amusements, he had always a jester at his back with whom he exchanged witty repartees, and he had usually royal, electoral, and princely persons *utriusque sexus* [of both sexes] as company at table with whom he kept up entertaining conversation because his tongue was never still.[95]

It is unlikely that Ferdinand asked Charles to intervene against the Esslingen Ordinance merely because he felt the government had slighted him. What other fault did he find with the bill, then? The emperor's edict that exempted Austria from the law argued that if Ferdinand

> implemented the published ordinance, his Grace would not only suffer notable damage in the revenues from his demesnes, but would also in many ways harm his lands and people, all the Roman Empire and before anything else the German nation and the common labouring man, because in consequence of the ordinance many excellent mines in our and his principalities and lands would perish, and in the end nothing would follow but that the Holy Empire, which receives most of its silver from the Austrian lands, would suffer much scarcity of coin and silver.[96]

The clue is in the passage about the adverse effects of the planned new currency on the supply of silver in general and silver mining in particular. But why did the emperor argue monetary standards would affect mining?

Discord among the *Bergherren*

It was a view many *Bergherren* shared, and to understand why they did so, we must turn to a public debate that took place in the late 1520s and early 1530s in Saxony. There, the traditional monetary unity began to fragment when Elector John 'the Steadfast' decided that debasing the *Taler* made sense, whereas his cousin Duke George favoured maintaining the traditional standard on which the Esslingen Ordinance had been based. The dispute between them triggered the publication of a series of pamphlets that set out the arguments of both governments. The anonymous authors—evidently well-connected persons with an intimate knowledge of politics—discussed the links between monetary standards and trade, and this is the aspect that has interested historians most.[97] However, the issue of most interest here is mining. One of the pamphlets that appeared on the electoral side argued that while silver production was at its peak, the metal had been cheap, and the princes could mint high-value coins. In future, this would no longer be possible. As 'the costs of establishing and maintaining the mines were increasing by the year', a debasement was unavoidable.[98] In short, increasing production costs had to be offset by a lower pure silver content of the coinage.

The split in the Saxon coinage was healed a few years after Elector John Frederick 'the Magnanimous' succeeded John 'the Steadfast' in 1532, but the new elector later tried to return to his father's policies. A portly gentleman whom Lucas Cranach portrayed with a bland, sleepy face that belied the seriousness with which he approached his office as ruler, he tried to use the talks at the level of the Empire to marshal support for his policy. The instructions he gave his delegates at the diet of Worms in 1545 required them to point out that

> at present the situation of the mines of the electors and princes of Saxony—and no doubt that of other mines, too—was such that they had become very deep and had to be maintained and exploited at high and notable costs, which were increasing by the day. Moreover, timber and charcoal, lead, iron, tallow, and other things one must needs have at the mines are becoming the more expensive, the more time is passing.[99]

It was therefore crucial to resist any measure that might depress the price of silver. If the metal became cheaper, the princes would have to subsidize the mining companies, and if they did not, 'what follows would be that the *Gewerken* abandon the mines and let them lie idle'.[100] John Frederick's idea of how monetary standards would affect silver prices and the profitability of mining were shared by other *Bergherren*. At one of the coinage conferences in Speyer which the imperial diet had called for 1549, Austria and Salzburg argued that in former times, mining costs had been lower, silver could be purchased at lower prices and turned into coin more profitably. Now, the mines had become so deep and the quality of the ore so poor that the mining firms had to be subsidized 'and where previously one workman had been enough, now four or more are needed and must be paid much higher wages'. In consequence 'silver, as a noble and valuable commodity, has become—and is still becoming—more expensive, because if that did not happen the smelters and mining firms . . . could not continue in business and would have to abandon the mines. And because of this increase in the silver price, little has been minted according to the old standard of the coinage', which therefore could no longer be maintained.[101] In short, the silver price had to be stabilized at a high level to keep mining profitable. Prices in general fell if the bullion content of the coinage increased and rose when it declined, and as those of silver were no exception to this rule, a debasement was desirable. The Saxon *Guldengroschen* that the Esslingen Ordinance had adopted contained so much silver that it would make it impossible to keep the mines open; so this seems to have been why Ferdinand—like the *Bergherren* represented at the meeting in Nuremberg—rejected the common currency.

The argument was remarkably inconsistent. The mining princes shut their eyes to the fact that any debasement would offer at best temporary relief. Once merchants noticed the measure, they would raise prices in general; wages would go up as well, and the upshot was that nominal production costs at the mines would increase. When faced with this idea,[102] the line of defence of the *Bergherren* was that 'the argument is unfounded that debasements cause a rise in commodity prices. Within human memory the price of almost everything and especially real estate has increased twofold, while the coinage has been debased by less than one-quarter.'[103] That may have been not exactly correct, but in principle the observation that sixteenth-century inflation outpaced the decline in the bullion content of the coinage was accurate. We know today that factors the *Bergherren* did not consider—most importantly the increase in the quantity of money that was a direct consequence of first the mining boom and then the import of New World bullion—played an important role in inflation.[104] Still, if they argued that reducing the pure silver content of the coinage had no effect on prices, why did they expect it to increase the profitability of mining?

Such a lack of consistency is suspicious. It makes one doubt that Ferdinand and the other *Bergherren* in favour of debasement intended to depress mining costs at all, or at least that this was their main point. Unsurprisingly, therefore, there is evidence for another aim. In most talks with estates without mines of their own, the delegates of the mining princes proceeded with sufficient delicacy not to reveal what was on their minds. On one occasion, though, Austria and Salzburg issued a joint statement where they claimed that they had talked about mining costs often enough. Still,

> his royal Majesty and the archbishop of Salzburg have for years received serious and pitiful complaints about the praiseworthy, heavy coins of their forbears and predecessors being exported, melted and broken, in place of which many unequal, poor, and foreign coins are by and by imported, to the considerable damage and disadvantage of the German nation and the common man. They have therefore found that the extreme and urgent need requires to suppress this unbearable and self-interested traffic.[105]

Apparently, the mining-costs argument was, if not entirely sham, then at least in part specious. What seems to have been on the mind of Austria and its associates was a new strategy to deal with that perennial problem, the trade in coinage and its consequences. We have seen in Chapter 2 that many estates turned to defensive debasements; now, the *Bergherren* suffering from the export and reminting of their coins planned to take this policy one step forward: Instead of a defensive debasement, they were thinking of a pre-emptive one. We do not have any documentary evidence for Ferdinand of Austria having this in mind when he rejected the Esslingen Ordinance of 1524. However, given the inconsistency of the mining-costs argument it is likely that he thought along these lines. In sum, Ferdinand rejected the Esslingen Ordinance because he feared the common currency would end as raw material in the mints of his neighbours.

As we have seen, there was one currency that did not suffer from the trade in coinage: the *Taler*, which markets overvalued so far that melting and reminting it was no attractive proposition. Maurice, the duke and after the Schmalkaldic War of 1546 to 1547 elector of Saxony, therefore had good reasons to depart from the policies his cousin John Frederick pursued. A wiry man with a foxy disposition, nineteenth-century German historians credited him with 'coldly calculating ambition' and called him 'the no doubt most gifted, indeed, the only real politician among the German princes and statesmen of the time'.[106] This says perhaps more about a generation of scholars whose ideas of political sophistication were shaped by what they had read of Machiavelli and seen of Bismarck than about Maurice himself. The Saxon elector was by no means the Empire's only deft political actor. We will see, for example, that King Ferdinand developed into more than a society man; in fact, he turned his social skills to his political advantage, becoming what any successful emperor had to be: a dealmaker rather than an authoritarian. Still, Maurice of Saxony certainly was one of the most astute political operators of the Empire.

In opposing the debasement of the *Taler*, Maurice continued the policy of his father Duke George. During a *Bergherren*-conference King Ferdinand had called in June 1543 in Prague, he argued that lowering the standard would not help the *Gewerken*; they would gain nothing in terms of the intrinsic value of the money they were paid.[107] In Speyer in 1549, his envoys went into the details, explaining that

> if the coinage was debased, the *Gewerken* would have to purchase everything needed at the mines at higher costs . . . and the wages of workmen, miners and carters would also increase, because these people would need to buy all their sustenance with debased coins at higher prices than they paid before with better money and would therefore not be content with their previous, usual pay. And . . . as the *Gewerken* are not forced to maintain the mines but do what they do out of their own free will, desire, and inclination, they would abandon the mines, which would entirely perish if they were burdened with such additional costs. This would cause the decline, decay, and ruin not only of his electoral grace's lands and subjects but also of the neighbouring lands and the whole German nation.[108]

The Saxon delegates could not stress this last point strongly enough: If everything became more expensive and wages went up, it would not just be mining that would take a hit, but manufacturing and trade in general would be 'driven out'.[109] In the last resort, therefore, the *Bergherren* failed to agree on a currency because while most of them suffered from the breaking and reminting of their coins by neighbouring estates without mines of their own, there was one—Saxony—whose coinage was not subject to this kind of attrition. When push came to shove, Maurice of Saxony prioritized maintaining the overvalued *Taler* over agreeing on a common currency or even common monetary policies among the *Bergherren*.

The estates without mines of their own

The discord among the *Bergherren* did not hinder the other imperial estates to imagine all sorts of dangers which might threaten from that direction. That bullion mining was geographically restricted was something of which they were painfully aware.[110] A good example of how this shaped their approach to the problem of the silver supply is given by Duke William IV of Bavaria, who feared in 1549 that 'because the price of silver is not equal and cannot be harmonized . . . the right to mint coins might be restricted to a few estates that can then arbitrarily and for their own profit debase the coinage'.[111] Duke William and other estates like him were not interested in the costs and profits of mining. They desired monetary stability—or at least, that is what they said—and did not want to give up their privilege of minting, which was at least in part a matter of prestige.

In fact, there was little need to worry about the loss of minting rights. There were indeed some *Bergherren*—most prominently Maurice of Saxony—who called for a wholesale cancellation of the minting privileges many estates enjoyed. During the diet of Speyer in 1544 Maurice made the case that trying to create a common currency was futile

> as long as almost all estates of the Empire were minting, regardless of most having no mines, as it is noticeable and obvious that these same estates melt down the coins of other estates and turn them into baser money, which has caused the inequality and low value of the coinage of the German nation.[112]

The observation was correct, of course, and there were some who did not only share it but also agreed with Maurice's conclusion. That the right to mint was exercised by 'everybody, even nuns and monks' (a point made by Catholic Trier at a monetary policy-conference in the 1550s) was widely considered a grievance.[113] Maurice's cousin John Frederick, too, believed that electors, princes, and the most important counts and cities should be the only estates allowed to issue coins.[114] However, he urged caution. Forcing estates without mines of their own to give up their privilege would cause great discord in the Empire 'where there is more than enough discord as it is. And if, in addition to that, discord about the coinage would arise the total break-up and downfall of the Empire might follow.'[115] This was an alarmist position. Neither the emperor nor the diet—nor the two of them acting together—had any realistic chance of withdrawing privileges like the right to mint from hundreds of estates, some of which were among the most influential in the Empire.

While concerns about the loss of minting rights were unfounded, the estates without mines of their own also worried about the attempts of the *Bergherren* to unilaterally set the price of silver. In trying to fight off these attempts, they initially referred to ideas first voiced in the 1520s. Recall the 'Needs of the German Nation', the pamphlet that claimed to have been composed by Emperor Frederick III and that appeared in Saxony in 1523. The anonymous author called for the creation of a central imperial office—an 'imperial treasury' distinct from the emperor's privy purse—which would purchase all newly mined bullion at fixed prices and use it to produce a common, Empire-wide coinage.[116] Friedrich Weigandt's political programme for the insurgents of 1525 copied this idea word for word,[117] and apparently Christoph Furer, whom we have met as the author of a monetary policy-memorial submitted to the government about a year before the publication of the Esslingen Ordinance, had heard of it, too. Among other things, Furer suggested

> that those in whose principalities, lordships, or lands silver ore is found, agree and consent to the good of the Empire not to mint any of this silver, but rather to sell it to the Empire's mints for a period of ten years or longer at a specified price, that is, for about as much as it is worth now in Nuremberg or Frankfurt. In return, they should receive payment in cash, so that the princes and lords who now receive revenues from their silver mines are not harmed by this sale.[118]

Furer's aim was providing a source of income for the Empire that would allow it to avoid creating a common external customs border (in addition to the existing internal custom posts) which would harm trade. Instead, he advocated using the seignorage of five or six imperial mints, which were to turn the silver bought from the *Bergherren* into coins.[119] What is important is that the idea of a central imperial agency for the acquisition and distribution of precious metals, which we can trace back to the 'Needs of the German nation', appears to have become widely known in the 1520s. It is therefore no surprise that it resurfaced as soon as the discussions about a common currency gathered pace twenty years later.

The occasion was a *Tag* the members of the Swabian circle of the Empire convened in November 1543 to prepare the upcoming imperial diet. The *Tag* formed a committee to discuss the issue of the coinage. This committee drafted a report that placed the blame for all problems on the fact that the trade in silver had devolved from the 'heads' (which probably meant the *Bergherren*) to 'particular persons' (which was code for merchants and mining firms). As a remedy, the committee

> could think of no more convenient and better means than that the common estates of the Empire unanimously agree and decide to persuade their imperial and royal Majesties in seemly and fitting ways to take the mines and the silver trade out of the hands of the particular persons and to return them to the heads or, if possible, to the commonwealth, that is, into the Empire's hands.[120]

There was no prospect whatever of Ferdinand or any of the other *Bergherren* agreeing to the idea that their mines should be managed by 'the Empire's hands'. The suggestion was dead the moment it saw the light of day. It still is remarkable and important—not because it had any practical consequences, but because of the historical insights it opens up. What the Swabian estates suggested in 1543 allows linking their policies to the importance of following rules, which we discussed in Chapter 3, and taking the ideas we encountered there one step further. The proposal shows to what extent the estates argued based on law rather than power: If the law allowed to do something, they assumed it would be possible to do it. Such a stance may look naïve, but it is characteristic of a political outlook that kept gaining ground in the Holy Roman Empire not just in the sixteenth century, but over the rest of the early modern age: The Empire was seen as grounded in law. This implied that political differences tended to be approached like legal disputes, which made observing the rules that structured these conflicts all the more important.

At the turning point

A paradigm shift

If we survey the talks that intermittently took place between the early 1520s and the late 1540s, what is most striking is how haphazard and unfocused they were. There were several issues that the groups involved tried to push: the price of silver, the costs and profits of mining (at least in part a cover for a background problem, the trade in coinage and the effects of Gresham's Law), alternative ways to ensure the supply of silver, and the right to mint, for which at least some estates feared. In the last section, we have looked at these topics one by one, but such a perspective downplays how shambolic the talks were. They clearly lacked direction in both sense of the words:

No one bothered to direct them by setting an agenda and holding the estates to it, and instead of progressing towards a clear goal, the discussions were prone to moving down all kinds of rabbit holes that turned out to be fruitless to explore. All this would change at the end of the 1540s.

We will see there was no single cause of change. Rather, several factors came together, most importantly a new view of how the provision of mints with raw materials worked and a fundamentally different political climate. Petr Vorel has stressed an additional factor, pointing to the arrival of large quantities of New World silver in Europe. His argument is that this reduced the influence of the *Bergherren*; with American bullion becoming available, it no longer mattered whether one or the other ruler in the Empire controlled silver mines of his own.[121] In the long term—that is, over a course of the second half of the sixteenth century—this was very likely the case. However, there is reason to doubt that silver from the New World affected monetary policies in the Empire already in about 1550. To be sure, the Spanish government began shipping American silver to Antwerp in the 1530s, and chemical analyses of surviving sixteenth-century coins have shown that between 1570 and 1620 about 70 per cent of the raw material used by mints in Central Europe came from Potosí.[122] Still, if American bullion was ever mentioned in the talks about an Empire-wide common currency (whether at a diet or a coinage conference), this left no trace in the surviving sources. However, there is good evidence for another development: The way the estates thought about the supply of silver began to change. Here, the diet of Worms that began in December 1544 and continued to August 1545 was particularly important.

The starting point was a procedural decision of the diet. Shortly after opening, it delegated currency questions to a committee. This committee was remarkably diverse not just because electors, princes, and cities were represented, but also because its members came from practically all parts of the Empire, with *Bergherren* among them as well as estates without mines of their own. Moreover, both Catholic and Protestant estates were represented—a noteworthy fact at a time when the imperial diet had become so polarized that the two higher colleges had split into confessional subgroups that were barely on speaking terms.[123] As the colleges elected their representatives, Catholic princes must in this case have voted for Protestant committee members. Some time ago I argued that monetary policies remained free of confessional influences because the stance of the estates depended on whether they had access to silver ore deposits of their own. They could therefore not arbitrarily adapt their monetary policy positions to that held by their co-religionists, as they tended to do, for example, in disputes about territorial inheritances.[124] The argument is valid as far as it goes, but we have seen that economic geography does not explain everything: The *Bergherren* all controlled mining areas but were still not all on the same page.

For the work of the committee, this did not matter. Its two mining princes, Elector John Frederick and King Ferdinand, saw eye to eye when it came to debasements and their effect on the profits of mining. Still, as the committee made its decisions based on simple majorities, the views of the estates that did not control their own mines tended to prevail. Leaving aside contentious questions such as that of the price of silver, they were able to quickly draft a currency bill and a law intended to make sure it was correctly implemented.[125] They also exchanged several memorials and counter-memorials with the other *Bergherren* present at the diet, who had formed an informal monetary policy-pressure group. Both draft bills—especially the one that was to regulate how the new currency was to be implemented—were important; many of their paragraphs would appear in later laws, too. However, from a long-term perspective, the ideas exchanged between the committee and the *Bergherren* group were more relevant. It was here that the fundamental shift in the way the estates thought about the value of money and the costs of minting was prepared—a shift that eventually allowed moving on from the perennial question of the silver price harmonization and to agree on a range of common coins that were to be legal tender across the Empire.

The committee used the Esslingen Ordinance of 1524 as a starting point for the talks, where Ferdinand and John Frederick tried to push their usual agenda.[126] They stayed in close and regular contact with the other mining princes present at the diet, among whom Duke Maurice was conspicuously absent.[127] This allowed them to suggest a common monetary standard based on a uniform Empire-wide price of silver.[128] However, the majority of the committee had already moved on from this issue. One idea that was conceptually important and that they had included in the draft of the currency bill was that in future, coins should no longer be issued for profit, that is, that the seignorage was to be abolished.[129] In this, they adopted an idea which the envoys of the *Bergherren* had agreed at their meeting in Nuremberg almost twenty years before and against which the electors on the Rhine had argued in vain in the late 1520s.[130] What is relevant here is not so much the question of whether minting authorities were really willing to forego the seignorage; rather, the important point is that thinking about how the price of silver was linked to the standard of the coinage was easier once the seignorage was taken out of the equation. It must have been in early June 1545 when a committee member articulated a crucial insight:[131] Next to the cost of silver, the only other relevant factor that remained was the costs of producing the coins themselves, that is, the costs of base metals, charcoal for the furnace, tools, the mint building and its maintenance, and the wages of the moneyers and mint officials. The logical conclusion was that it was not necessary to agree on the silver price before defining the standard of the coinage. Rather, one merely had to determine

> which kind of silver *Gulden* was to be made and how it should be subdivided into smaller pieces. And only after agreeing on this [the price of silver] could be computed . . . in such a way that the silver contained in one mark is also found in the coins struck from that mark, minus that used to cover the regular costs of minting.[132]

The 'mark' meant here was the unit of weight (roughly half a pound) used to measure the weight of gold and silver. The argument was still relatively muddled, but further discussions helped clarify the issue. In late July, the committee countered the usual mining-costs arguments of the *Bergherren* by pointing out that

> silver is purchased with silver, so that when a *Bergherr* sells one mark of silver in one piece to a minting estate, this estate returns it in many pieces, that is, in the form of coins, and retains nothing except the proper minting costs . . . And though the *Bergherr* may have found the silver hard and costly to mine, one cannot pay him more than one mark for each mark he sells, and in the form of coins as much less as minting the silver has cost.[133]

To drive the point home, the committee explained what this implied for the costs of mining:

> For the mines it is neither here nor there whether one mints a light or a heavy silver *Gulden* because if one purchases a piece of pure silver, one returns exactly the same amount in many or in a few coins, retaining only the regular costs of minting.[134]

From our perspective, the way the *Bergherren* and the coinage committee at Worms in 1545 expressed their ideas in the memos they exchanged often seems convoluted and cumbersome. Still, there are two reasons why it is worth spending time on these documents. First, they offer a unique insight into how the people involved in shaping policies thought about issues that were among the technically most complex ones they faced. And second, the discussions show that manipulating the prices mints offered for silver (in gold) or gold (in silver)—a method many Western European mints used to attract one metal or the other—played no important role in the mid sixteenth-century Empire. Usually, mints used silver coin to purchase the silver they needed as raw material.

In order further to clarify the issue, let us look at it from a modern perspective. The upshot of the argument made by the coinage committee was that a coin would enter circulation at a value that matched its production costs (plus traditionally the seignorage, which the discussants in 1545 chose to ignore).[135] The production costs had two components: first the costs of the bullion which the coin contained, and second all other costs and wages the mint had to pay. In return for his raw bullion, a *Bergherr* would therefore receive less silver in the form of coins—less, because the difference had to cover the rest of the production costs.

For the talks about the creation of an Empire-wide common currency, the new insights into the value of money made all the difference. For twenty years, the price of silver had been the most contentious issue; now, it became evident that this had been a red herring. At first it was only the majority of the committee members who adopted the idea that it was

> not necessary first to determine the price of silver. Rather, once the standard of the coinage and the number of coins minted from one mark of pure silver have been agreed, silver prices follow of their own accord, so that anyone who sells silver receives in return as much silver in the form of coins as he has given away, the proper costs of minting alone having been deducted.[136]

By the end of the 1540s the *Bergherren* had come round to this view, and from then on, the memorials and reports submitted by the coinage committee in 1545 were treated as reference material. When the price of silver resurfaced briefly during negotiations in 1557, the representatives of the elector of Trier had merely to point to the argument raised by the committee at Worms twelve years earlier to close the matter.[137]

The power of Charles V

For the talks aimed at creating a common currency, the insight that silver prices could be safely neglected amounted to a change of paradigm. Still, there was a second factor that caused a far more stringent and expedient style of negotiations: the general change in the political climate after Charles V's victory in the Schmalkaldic War. Again, the effect was not immediate, but by 1549 it was obvious.

Consider Charles V's selection of commissioners at the two coinage conferences in Speyer in that year and at the general assay in Nuremberg in early 1551. There were obvious reasons why from his perspective not only Flersheim, but Solms was a good choice. In the Schmalkaldic War, Solms had been a leading commander on the emperor's side; later he had been responsible for disbanding the troops of Landgrave Philip of Hesse and for disarming the Hessian fortresses.[138] There is no direct evidence for Charles V taking this into account when choosing Solms, but we know the emperor was aware of how intimidating military personnel could be at imperial assemblies. He had played that card at the Diet-in-Arms in Augsburg in 1547–8, and it was certainly not beyond him to try playing it again. Solms' mere presence must have reminded the delegates of the estates of who wielded most power in the Empire.

It certainly seems both commissioners made a strong and successful effort to keep the talks in Speyer on track. They themselves rarely intervened in the negotiations, but they received and answered written communications from the delegates and signed off the recess that summarized the discussions. At the end of the first meeting in March 1549, they gave the delegates a list of topics their home governments should discuss before the talks resumed in September: whether the largest silver piece should match the value of a Rhenish florin or that of a *Usualgulden*, how it should be subdivided into smaller units, what weight and purity the coins should have, and how many of them should be minted from one mark of pure silver.[139] We know some governments failed to consider these questions over the summer,[140] but the minutes of the talks in Speyer that autumn show that the discussants were more focused and talks made more progress than in spring. In fact, it took the delegates only about two weeks to agree on each of the questions Flersheim and Solms hat put to them in March.[141]

Still, there were contentious issues—especially the question of whether the Empire should adopt a bimetallic currency—which moved to the foreground once the estates had agreed on the silver coins. When after weeks of discussions nerves began to fray and some delegations talked of leaving the conference, Flersheim changed tack. He pointed out that his co-commissioner had left for Brussels to notify Charles V of the bimetallism dispute, and that the emperor was 'a skilful and profound master who considers everything carefully'. The delegates should on no account leave the conference before he had declared his decision; after all,

> it had been found how dangerous it was to damage his Majesty's reputation, grandeur, etc., as had become quite evident during the late war, when his Majesty had not set himself so strongly against Saxony and Hesse because of reasons of religion but because of their lack of obedience.[142]

If this was a veiled threat, the veil was so transparent as to be practically non-existent. In any case, as a tactic in monetary policy negotiations it was unprecedented. The delegates at the *Tag* in Speyer may not have expected Charles V to go to war over bimetallism, but the emperor's displeasure was still not to be taken lightly. He used it strategically and often with success to discipline the estates. He would, for example, demonstrate his explicit preference for some while he ignored others, thereby unsettling them and generating compliance.[143]

The *Münztag* of the autumn of 1549 ended without agreeing on the bill that was to establish the common currency, so that the discussions continued at the next imperial diet. Flersheim and Solms, who in view of their failure to engineer an agreement in Speyer lived themselves under the shadow of the emperor's displeasure, now tightened the screws. Just before the diet opened in Augsburg in July 1550, they required the delegates of the estates who had resisted an agreement most strongly—those of the electors of Mainz, Trier, Cologne, and the Palatinate—to appear in their lodgings, forbade them to seek further council in monetary matters, set them a time limit, and then ordered them out of the room—all this in a tone that before the Schmalkaldic War would have been unthinkable between representatives of the Emperor and the highest-ranking estates of the Empire.[144] All in all, it is evident that Charles V's victory gave him the chance for the first time to rule in the authoritarian style he preferred. We will see that this worked, though it did so only until he overplayed his hand and triggered the emergence of an opposition far more effective than the Schmalkaldic League had ever been.

The two factors that allowed for progress in the negotiations of the years 1549 to 1551—the new thinking about how the standard of the coinage was related to the price of silver and the strengthened position of the emperor—thus had different effects. That of the paradigm shift, which began in the mid-1540s, was enduring. The old argument that debasements would help mining or prevent the breaking of coins never again played a role. Monetary policy talks at the level of the Empire thus offer a prime example of the fact that politics are not only shaped by the interests of the actors and the costs of decision-making, at which we looked in Chapter 3. Rather, the actors develop what the economists Arthur Denzau and Douglass North call 'mental models'—'myths, dogmas, ideologies and "half-baked" theories'—that help them making sense of their environment and deciding what to do.[145] The idea shared by most *Bergherren* that a debasement would increase the profits from mining and protect their coins against being used as raw material in their neighbours' mints was such a 'half-baked' theory—and considering that it contributed to bringing down the Empire's first law that was supposed to establish a common currency, it was not merely half-baked, it was calamitous. To change mental models, Denzau and North stress that feedback is needed—feedback given in a form that makes it obvious how relevant it is for the model.[146] This is what happened during the discussions between the members of the coinage committee and the mining princes at the diet of Worms in 1545, where the committee countered every memorial of the *Bergherren* with a carefully argued document of their own. As a result, the *Bergherren* eventually dropped their model.[147] Charles V's transient success, by contrast, underlines how important a consensus-oriented style of politics was, that is, a style that did not rely on threats and pressure to generate superficial agreement. It is time for us to examine this issue in more detail, and here one metal and one region of Germany at which we have so far looked only in passing become important: gold, and the territories along the river Rhine.

5
The Rhine gold

Caravans and caravels

Through the Sahara and over the ocean

The Rhine does carry some gold. Before the river was regulated in the mid-nineteenth century, gold washing used to yield a few hundred grams a year as a byproduct of the extraction of gravel and grit. In recent years, a firm in the town of Rheinzabern, a few miles south of Speyer, has revived the tradition. The business is profitable not because production costs are low, but because Rhenish gold can be sold at about twice the usual market rate.[1] The Rhine gold has this kind of reputation. It has been famous for centuries, if not millennia, and people are willing to pay a premium to get hold of it.

That is because ever since the Middle Ages, what people had in mind when they thought of gold and the river Rhine was emphatically not sifting through sand and gravel to find the occasional microscopic nugget. What they had in mind was a legendary hoard—a hoard of unimaginable wealth and beauty guarded by a dragon, won by a human hero, and concealed in the river by a murderer. The story is one of the oldest legends of Germany and according to *The Oxford Companion to German Literature* 'one of the most impressive, and certainly the most powerful, of the German epics of the Middle Ages'.[2] It has long been central to German culture and to the way Germans think about themselves and their country, not least because of how nationalist and national-socialist propaganda exploited it in the nineteenth and twentieth centuries.[3] It is, of course, the *Nibelungenlied* or the 'Lay of the Nibelungen'. The *Lied* had been composed in the thirteenth century; by the late sixteenth century, it had faded from memory. However, a shorter version of the legend—the *Lied vom Hürnen Seyfrid*

('Song of the Horn-Skinned Seyfrid')—appeared in print in 1530 at the latest and was turned into a play by Hans Sachs—like Kunz Haß a member of Nuremberg's guild of master singers—in 1557.[4] The story was widely known.

Understandably, people associated the Rhine with treasure, and they are still doing so despite the hoard never having been found (not for lack of trying).[5] So is the gold no more than a myth? Not quite: in the fifteenth century the river did literally carry gold—not tiny nuggets, but large quantities of solid metal in the form of coin and bullion. Commercial activity along the river carried so much of it that it allowed the princes whose territories straddled the Rhine—most importantly the electors of Mainz, Trier, Cologne, and the Palatinate—to supply the Empire and many of its neighbours with gold coins perfectly suited to large-scale commercial and political transactions.

Where did the gold come from that flowed along the Rhine in the late fifteenth and early sixteenth century? In the high Middle Ages, the most important European centre of production had been Hungary, whose gold output was an impressive three to four tons a year in the fourteenth century. Over the fifteenth century, it declined to just above a ton, and by the 1520s, Hungary produced maybe a quarter or half a ton of gold per year.[6] The amount mined within the Empire was far too small to make up this shortfall, and no other European country could do so either.

To identify the origin of the Rhine's association with gold, we must leave the Empire and its neighbourhood. We must turn towards the Mediterranean and the countries to its south, and here a famous late medieval map of the world can guide us (Plate 5.1). This map, known as the Catalan Atlas, was commissioned in the fourteenth century by King Pedro IV of Aragon as a diplomatic gift for Charles V of France. It shows the world from the perspective of Aragon, representing the Mediterranean and the countries around it with striking accuracy. The map is covered with crisscrossing 'rhumb lines' to aid navigation. Colourful little flags indicate which city belonged to which lord, and exquisitely painted vignettes show characteristic animals or activities typical for each part of the world. The lower edge of the map depicts the middle of the Sahara—nothing south of this is shown—and there, close to the edge, sits the figure of an African king, dressed in a flowing garment, crowned with a European-style golden crown, holding a sceptre in one hand and gazing at a massive ball of gold held aloft in the other.

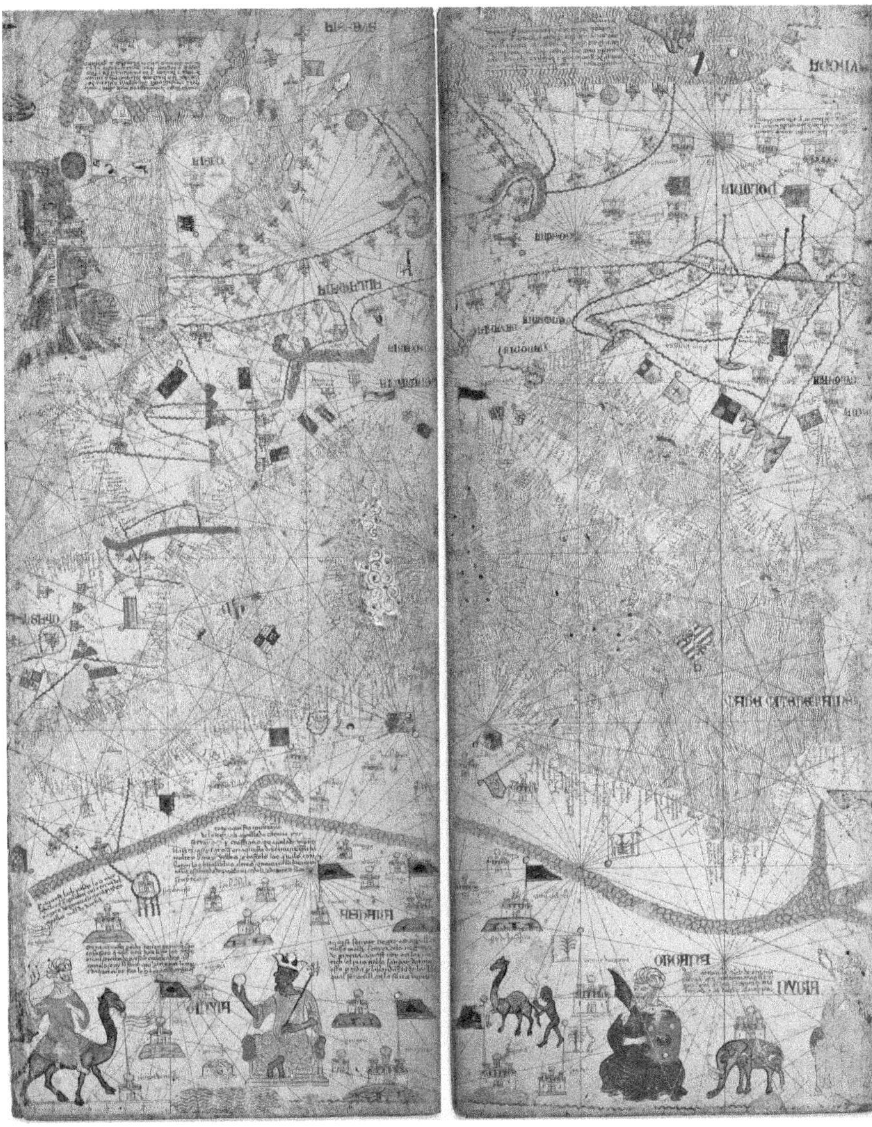

Plate 5.1. From Mali to the Rhine on the Catalan Atlas

Source: Public domain, https://commons.wikimedia.org/wiki/File:1375_Atlas_Catalan_Abraham_Cresques.jpg (accessed 20/02/2023).

This is Mansā Mūsā, emperor of Mali in the early fourteenth century and, as the caption next to him explains, 'the richest and most distinguished ruler of this whole region on account of the great quantity of gold found in his lands'. There is probably no other single object that illustrates more clearly than the Catalan Atlas how prominent sub-Saharan Africa was in the medieval world.[7] The Atlas also illustrates the ultimate origin of much of the gold the electors on the Rhine turned into Rhenish florins from the late fourteenth century onwards. The question is, how did the metal move from inner West Africa to Central Europe, and who carried it?

The 'golden trade of the Moors' has a long history.[8] Once the camel had been domesticated towards the beginning of the first millennium, trans-Saharan trade became a regular feature of life in West Africa. In the late Middle Ages, the caravan terminus south of the Sahara was Timbuktu, which Mansā Mūsā made part of his empire in the 1320s.[9] Ẉasan ibn Muḥammad al-Wazzān, the famed traveller, diplomat, and merchant who had been captured by pirates, sold into slavery in Italy, and christened as Giovanni Leone—he is better known as Leo Africanus—left one of the earliest first-hand descriptions to become known in sixteenth-century Europe.[10] In the land around Timbuktu, he noted that

> corne, cattle, milke and butter this region yeeldeth in great abundance: but salt is verie scarce here; for it is brought hither by land from Tegaza, which is fiue hundred miles distant. When I my selfe was here, I saw one camels loade of salt sold for 80. ducates. The rich king of Tombuto [Timbuktu] hath many plates and scepters of gold, some whereof weigh 1300 poundes: and he keepes a magnificent and well furnished court.[11]

Nowadays, Tegaza is little more than an abandoned salt mine about two-thirds of the way between the Mediterranean and Timbuktu. But in the Middle Ages, the mine was used by Arab and Berber merchants who would save transport costs by picking up their salt on their way south. The 80 ducats, which according to Leo Africanus Timbuktu merchants would pay for a camel-load of salt, were the equivalent of about 280 grams of pure gold,[12] though it seems that on occasion merchants could make more. Salt was so scarce in the Sudan—as all the lands along the southern edge of the Sahara were called—that it is said to have sometimes been exchanged for its weight in gold.[13]

Gold was by no means the only commodity merchants took back north. They also bought spices, ostrich feathers, ivory, and slaves, but gold was special. No other good was so valuable relative to its weight, and this made it profitable to use the long route through one of the parts of the globe most hostile to life. Once the gold had reached the shores of the Mediterranean, merchants from Aragon and Italy exchanged it for silver, much of which had been mined in the Holy Roman Empire. This made sense: In the early fifteenth century one could buy a given weight of gold for about 8 times its weight in silver in North Africa and Syria, whereas you could sell it in Italy and Germany for between 10 and 12 times its weight.[14] In short, Europe had a higher gold–silver ratio than the Orient, which allowed merchants to profit from arbitrage, buying cheap in one place and selling dear somewhere else.

When Leo Africanus visited Timbuktu in the early sixteenth century, the route through the Sahara was no longer the only one. A hundred years before, Portuguese navigators had begun to push south along the coast of Africa, with their caravels reaching the Senegal river in the 1440s. Their expeditions were initially no more than extensions of earlier plundering raids along the coast of Mauritania.[15] However, the resistance of the African kingdoms on the coast convinced them that peaceful commercial relations would work better. Establishing these took time,[16] but once it had been achieved the transport cost advantages of the seaborne trade over trans-Saharan caravans were brought to bear. The caravel was key to unlocking these advantages, as it had a far more favourable ratio of men to weight carried than earlier medieval vessels and could cover larger distances per day than the camel caravans.[17] The caravan trade continued mainly because the barrier of the forest and the lack of navigable rivers between the Sudan and the coast of West Africa insulated the inland areas. From Timbuktu, for example, reaching the Mediterranean via the Sahara was still easier than reaching the coast to the south and then taking ship towards Europe. However, by the fifteenth century, the main source of West African gold lay in the middle Volta region, much closer to the coast than Timbuktu. It was this gold that the Portuguese caravels carried to Europe from the middle of the century onwards—along with ivory, guinea pepper, and growing numbers of slaves.[18]

Two generations later, the Portuguese captain, explorer, and cartographer Duarte Pacheco Pereira dedicated a manuscript to King Manuel I of Portugal that was long kept secret and was believed to have been lost. There he claimed that from Timbuktu, 'every year a million gold ducats go . . . to Tunis, Tripoli of Soria and Tripoli of Barbery and to the kingdom of Boje and Feez and other parts', that is, to lands from Morocco in the west to Syria in the east. The Portuguese, by contrast, who offered 'brass bracelets, basins of the same metal, red and blue cloth, linen neither very coarse nor very fine, and "lanbens", that is, a kind of mantle made like the shawls of the Alentejo' to buyers along the African coast, took home about 200,000 dobras.[19] A million ducats was the equivalent of 3.5 tons of pure gold; 200,000 dobras equalled about 5.25 tons.[20] On the face of it, both quantities sound at least possible, and historians have tended to believe Pacheco Pereira's figures.[21] Depending on the temperature, the difficulty of the terrain and so on, a camel carries a load of about 180 kilogrammes, so to transport 3.5 tons of gold you would need no more than 19 or 20 animals—one small caravan if you took it all in one go. Caravels could transport much more—one, for example, which French pirates captured in 1495, carried about half a ton of gold.[22] However, if compared to modern estimates based on the production of gold in early colonial times, Pacheco Pereira's total of more than eight tons of gold that annually flowed out of West Africa sounds like a wild exaggeration. The Portuguese may have exported about 700 kilogrammes a year in the first two decades of the sixteenth century, and the yearly quantity transported by camel caravan across the Sahara probably never exceeded one ton.[23] All in all, it is unlikely that African gold was ever able to make up for the shortfall caused by the failure of the Hungarian mines in the late Middle Ages.

Where gold was concerned, the New World was neither in absolute nor in relative terms as important as for silver. Over the sixteenth century, nearly three-quarters of the world's silver came from America, but less than 40 per cent of the gold did so.[24] To be sure, most of the initial return on the investment the Spanish conquistadors made on the Caribbean islands and on the mainland consisted of gold looted from the indigenous populations. Over the first two decades of the sixteenth century, this amounted to a total of at most about 19 tons—less than one ton a year on average.[25] More circumspect Spanish invaders soon noticed that plunder was a short-term option and that supplies would quickly dry up if not replenished by mining. Once this got going, imports of American gold into Europe grew from about 1.5 tons a year in the 1530s to a peak of 4.3 tons in the 1550s. From then on and for the rest of the century they stagnated at on average 1.3 tons.[26] Thus, imports from the New World were generally of the same order of magnitude as those from West Africa, which implies that they may have roughly doubled the supply of gold to Europe.

Trade in gold, trade in silver

We have seen how the bullion reached Spain and the northern coast of the Mediterranean. But how did it get from there to the Holy Roman Empire? We cannot draw a map that shows the routes, but we can identify several commercial pathways that brought some of the African and American gold to Central Europe. What was relevant was the commodity trade, currency arbitrage, and the trade in coinage, which we have encountered above and which by no means took place only between the imperial estates, but affected the Empire's relations with its neighbours, too.

Taking the value of silver (in terms of gold) in the Empire and elsewhere in Europe into account was essential in long-distance trade. If we consider the exchange rate of commonly used gold coins in local silver money, we find that for example in the 1550s, one unit of weight of gold bought between 12 and 13 units of silver in Vienna and Augsburg and between 14 and 15 units in Hamburg, but only about 11 to 12 in London.[27] In Florence, 1 unit of gold bought about 10 units of silver from the late fourteenth century onwards and about 11 at the end of the 1560s.[28] Given such values, it made sense for merchants to use gold to purchase export commodities in the Empire: grain from Mecklenburg and Pomerania, fustian—a heavy cloth made of cotton and linen—from the region around Augsburg, wine from the Rhineland, and copper and silver from the Alps and Saxony.

Other metals were important, too. Most of the brass bracelets and basins that the Portuguese sold on the coast of Africa—and that West African artists turned into works of art which today are world famous—originated in the workshops of craftsmen in Nuremberg, Aachen, and Cologne.[29] The Corollary of the outflow of silver, which contemporaries noticed and explained as a consequence of the Empire's overall passive balance of trade, was, therefore, an inflow of gold—the more so, the more the mining boom of the first half of the sixteenth century added to the supply of silver in the German lands. In many cases, the gold stayed in circulation in the form of coins, which is why almost half of the types of gold coins tested by the assayers in Nuremberg in spring 1551 were from outside the Empire.

Commodity trade was not the only factor, though. Historians have shown to which extent merchants took differences between local gold–silver ratios into account to make a profit from currency arbitrage, using gold coins to purchase silver money where silver was cheap, and selling silver where the exchange rate of gold coins was low.[30] This did not require large spreads between the gold–silver ratios such as those existing between North Africa and Italy, rather, given that gold weighed so little relative to its value, minute deviations between local ratios were often enough to offer the chance of a deal. The chronicler Hermen Bote from Braunschweig described in about 1500 how this worked. According to him, in the mid-fifteenth century, the Rhenish florin had cost 21 *Schillings* in the city of Hildesheim,

> and in the cities by the sea [that is, in Hamburg, Lübeck and Wismar] the *Gulden* was to be had for 24 *Schillings*. Now here was a bargain that allowed people to look to their advantage and self-interest because with every *Gulden* 3 *Schillings* could be won, so that in these cities all *Schillings* were bought up and brought here to Braunschweig and Hildesheim. And many people got rich through this trade.[31]

This was no instance of the trade in coinage at which we have looked above and which aimed at breaking and reminting coins as base copies of the originals. Currency arbitrage was normally legal, though occasionally (and usually without success) local authorities tried to regulate it by fixing exchange rates. This kind of trade has so far been studied in the German context only.[32] However, we know that similar transactions that involved silver currencies only were going on across late medieval Northern Europe,[33] and it is safe to assume that gold–silver arbitrage was widespread, too. It linked the Empire with its neighbours and was in part responsible for the inflow of gold into the German lands.

Finally, contemporaries also suspected that the trade in coinage drove long-distance gold flows. A memorial Charles V sent Philip von Flersheim shortly before the start of the currency conference in Speyer in spring 1549 claimed that it was 'very likely that there are mint masters in Germany who break gold and silver coins to turn them into *Talers* and Crowns'.[34] *Taler* imitations need not concern us here; what is relevant is the gold, and here, the counsellors of the emperor were right. There were imperial estates who cashed in on the trade in gold in the way they had in mind. Hans Appenfelder, the mint master of the imperial city of Kaufbeuren who was at the bottom of the Augsburg coinage scandal of 1543, was involved in this. Appenfelder was in no way discouraged by the fine of 500 *Guldens* he had to pay his home magistrate on that occasion.[35] Only two years later he was back in business, producing imitations of Neapolitan gold crowns.[36] In Nuremberg in spring 1551, the assayers tested these pieces, finding that they contained 2 to 4 per cent less pure gold than genuine Italian crowns as minted for example by the dukes of Florence, Ferrara, and Urbino, the margrave of Montferrat, or the Pope.[37] One Italian ruler harmed by this practice was none other than Charles V, king of both Sicilies. Charles did not have to wait for the general assay in Nuremberg to learn what was going on. In December 1548, his chancellery wrote to the magistrate of Kaufbeuren, announcing that 'because of the manifold complaints brought before us because of your minting', the emperor was determined to make this an issue at the forthcoming currency conference in Speyer. There, 'ways and means were to be found' how Kaufbeuren could be made to pay for the damage it had caused.[38] Kaufbeuren's burgomaster and magistrates protested they were no worse than other estates and, though quite innocent, were willing to cease minting for the moment.[39] They sent Appenfelder to represent the city in Speyer and take the flak there,[40] but the imperial commissioners let the matter rest. When Charles' counsellors pictured German mint masters breaking golden coins and issuing imitation crowns, they had cases like Kaufbeuren in mind. What is important in our context is that such practices were aimed at pulling additional gold into the orbit of the imperial estates—additional to the bullion that entered the Empire in consequence of its external trade and currency arbitrage.

The lure of silver

Bimetallism

The central topic Appenfelder and the other delegates of the imperial estates discussed in Speyer during the second meeting, which began in September 1549, was bimetallism, that is, a system where gold and silver coins were not merely issued in parallel, but where coins made of both metals circulated at legally fixed and stable rates. Before the end of the 1540s, no one had ever considered anything else for the planned Empire-wide common currency. We have seen that the Esslingen Ordinance of 1524 tried to create a bimetallic currency; later talks, for example at the diet of Worms in 1545, envisaged the same kind of system.[41] Bimetallism was the undisputed reference point.

There can be little doubt that the attachment to this kind of currency was a consequence of the high value the imperial estates and everybody else placed on the concept of order.[42] Order, however, did not result from the spontaneous interaction of people; rather, it required the intervention of the appropriate political authorities. Where gold and silver coins were concerned, fluctuating exchange rates were a sign of disorder; the implication was that authorities had to take remedial action. Many had done so in the fifteenth century, giving rise to the use of the *Gulden* as a unit of account when the value ratio between gold and silver stayed stable for about two generations around 1500. This, apparently, was the order of which the imperial estates were thinking between the 1520s and 1550s and which they wanted to recreate—now, however, at the level of the Empire. 'What more honourable or fitting could be decreed in the coinage', asked the currency committee at the diet of Worms in 1545, 'than that one had everywhere in the Empire one and the same *Gulden* in gold and in silver, in large and small pieces etc. of the same value, so that one might know which money was current and much fraud and malpractices were avoided?'[43]

On the face of it, the consensus on the desirability of bimetallism was universal. The cities' college favoured such a system (it was the 'most useful, best, equitable, and correct' one),[44] and so did the princes whose delegates claimed in 1549 that it was 'the unequal and self-interest-serving increase of the value of the Rhenish gold and of many silver coins' that made it necessary to 'determine not only a common, equal, and seemly monetary standard of both the silver and the gold coinage, but also its fair value (which however it does not befit the local magistrates to set, far less private and commercial persons, but rather the high and regular authorities)'.[45] The counsellors of the Rhenish electors argued in a similar vein: It was 'well-known that the value of the coinage is not set according to the estimation of the subjects and private persons but to that of the high authorities entitled to decree it'. Interestingly, though, they admitted an exception:

> It must be born in mind that merchants and traders who do business in foreign parts pay attention to the assay of the coin and to its standard, which they can easily learn, regardless of which nominal value the authorities have given it, so that they know what they receive in return for their goods, and they must not be hindered to get their money's worth in this.[46]

The concern of the electoral delegates for the welfare of long-distance commerce does not sound particularly credible given how princes and their advisers were normally thinking about merchants, and we will see a little further below that they were really pursuing quite different aims. For the moment, what is relevant is that the façade of unanimity evidently concealed some potential for conflict.

At the end of September 1549—and seemingly out of the blue—bimetallism became hotly contentious. The trigger was a move by the imperial commissioners Flersheim and Solms at the second coinage conference of Speyer that turned out to be a serious tactical blunder. It threw the talks into confusion, prevented an agreement, and crucially contributed to the problems from which the implementation of the new currency was to suffer.

What happened was this: Until the last week of September, the talks in Speyer had been far more constructive and focused than during the preceding meeting in spring. Early on, the *Bergherren*—minus electoral Saxony and the sons of the demoted former Saxon elector John Frederick, who had not sent any envoys—agreed on the standard of the new coinage, defining the total nominal value of the coins to be minted from one mark of pure silver. They did so in *Guldens* of account of 60 *Kreuzers*, thus adopting the established Austrian–South German system. The delegates of the other princes quickly joined them. The electors' college raised some objections and made a countersuggestion but gave in once a committee the conference had formed to examine the question came out in favour of the silver content on which the princes' college had agreed.[47]

Agreeing on a standard was only the first step, though. What had to be decided next was the structure of the currency: What was to be the legal value of the largest silver coin, which smaller coins should supplement it, and what type of small change was to be issued? After some days of fruitless discussions, the delegates of the electors and princes submitted a memorial to the imperial commissioners where they set out their differences and

> most submissively requested that their princely grace and grace [the proper way to address Flersheim as a bishop and Solms as a count] would graciously disclose their discretion to the attending counsellors and envoys of the estates in order to promote the common weal, which they were without any doubt desirous to do, and help to bring about an agreement in this matter.[48]

In a later report to the counsellors of Charles V, where Flersheim and Solms explained there reaction, they tried to cover their backs by stressing that they acted on the advice of 'several coinage experts to whom his imperial Majesty had pointed them'.[49] We know of only one such expert: Hans Steinhauser, one of the treasurers of the electoral Palatinate, praise of whose 'particular knowledge and dexterity in matters of coinage' had reached the emperor.[50] It was likely on his advice that the two commissioners decided to do what the envoys of the estates had requested and submitted a memorial of their own where they set out the structure of the new currency from the smallest up to the largest silver unit. They suggested that this should be a 72-*Kreuzers*-piece and the equivalent of a Rhenish florin (which was to be maintained). Crucially, the commissioners stressed that 'everyone entitled to receive gold should be bound to accept this piece with no refusal in place of a Rhenish gold *Gulden*'.[51]

At first sight, all this seemed to make sense and to be uncontroversial. A 72-*Kreuzers*-piece—six times twelve—worked well within the duodecimal structure everyone preferred. As Flersheim and Solms pointed out, it allowed 'whole, correct, orderly and good payments, and one piece fits the other in an orderly fashion with no remainders and no need to use fractions in payments'—in modern parlance, it reduced transaction costs.[52] In addition, 72 *Kreuzers* was the legal value that King Ferdinand had given the Rhenish florin in 1542 and that the Bohemian estates and the city of Augsburg had adopted in the years thereafter.[53] Having a silver coin that embodied this value would therefore minimize the changes introducing the new currency involved and would thus smooth the process.

Despite this, Flersheim and Solms' intervention caused—or rather, brought to light—a deep rift between the estates. The princes' college enthusiastically accepted their suggestion, whereas the cities' college and, more importantly, the delegates of the electors vehemently opposed it. In the absence of Saxony, the group was dominated by the electors on the Rhine, whose delegates fought the core concept of bimetallism—silver should be accepted in place of gold—tooth and nail, using every argument and every trick out of the procedural book to delay and prevent a decision.

But why? So far, everyone had been happy with the idea of a bimetallic currency. Moreover, earlier monetary-policy talks had already touched on the issue Flersheim and Solms now brought up. The first coinage ordinance draft that the currency committee at the diet of Worms had submitted four years before had contained a provision very similar to the one they suggested: It had determined that the 'common imperial silver coins shall be spent and accepted by everyone in the Empire in purchases and sales and all other payments in place of gold'.[54] A revised draft had added the qualification that 'payments which previously contractually had to be effected in gold, likewise those that in future are being agreed and contracted to be paid in gold, and other payments which according to ancient custom are made in gold shall not be affected but shall always be treated as exceptions'.[55] Now, by contrast, the imperial commissioners suggested that their 72-*Kreuzers*-piece was to be legal tender in every respect and all situations, with no one being allowed to reject it. From the perspective of the electors on the Rhine, this made all the difference. We will see why that was the case, but let us first look at why the idea of the commissioners was so enthusiastically received by the princes' college.

Golden fetters

In fact, the delegates of the princes could hardly contain their acclaim for 'his imperial Majesty, our most gracious lord's praiseworthy commissioners',[56] declaring that they

> could come to no other conclusion than that it was to the Holy Empire's highest, obvious, and common good that a permanent ratio of silver and gold coins was determined, decreed, and imposed here in Speyer without any further delay and deferment and regardless of the fact that not all imperial estates have sent delegations to this conference, also regardless of anything else that might be brought forward in order prevent or delay this good work.[57]

During a meeting with the electoral delegates, they explained that Flersheim and Solm's suggestion would 'serve the common weal and would in particular help to finally create a stable order and still the complaints of the common man, who would like to pay silver in place of gold but was coerced to surrender gold pure and simple'.[58]

The princely delegates may have believed that a reference to the common man—in whose interest policies were supposed to be—would be irrefutable. In this case, however, the counsellors of the electors could point out with some justification that 'the common man had little to do or to trade with gold, or to conclude contracts in gold; hence his complaints were not that serious or important'.[59] The envoy of Duke William 'the Rich' of Jülich-Cleves-Berg then tried to be more specific, mentioning the 'great grievances of the poor man . . . that he cannot obtain gold to pay the tolls or had to purchase it at too high rates',[60] and at this point, the tactic of the delegates of the princes began to unravel. It was now obvious that they were thinking not of honest peasants or craftsmen—the people everyone had in mind when the common man was mentioned—but of merchants. Merchants, however, were almost universally despised and mistrusted, and arguing that a policy would help the common weal because it made life easier for them was anything but credible.

In fact, the delegates of the princes were thinking along entirely different lines. To see what was really on their minds, we need to take a step back and consider wider financial practices in early sixteenth-century Germany. Let us begin with an example from Erfurt in Thuringia, at that time an autonomous city under the nominal rule of the archbishop of Mainz and surrounded by the lands of the elector of Saxony. There, on 5 August 1519, the magistrate signed a contract with abbot Valentine and the convent of Lehnin Abbey about 130 miles to the northeast in Brandenburg. The contract noted that in return for 2,000 Rhenish florins, which Lehnin had some time ago made available to the city's magistrate, Erfurt had 'sold' the abbey a yearly rent of 120 Rhenish florins. Unfortunately, Erfurt had failed to pay some of the yearly installments, which was why the contract had to be renegotiated. Lehnin Abbey now agreed that Erfurt would

> henceforth, beginning from the date of this letter, pay and deliver with no refusal every year on a specified day, that is at Michaelmas [29 September] here in our city of Erfurt, in our treasury, 80 florins of current coin, counting 21 *Groschens*, each 12 *Pfennigs* worth, for every florin, towards said 2,000 florins.[61]

In Germany transactions like this are attested from the late thirteenth century onward. 'Selling a rent' essentially meant taking up a loan from a person or organization—like the 2,000 florins Erfurt borrowed from Lehnin Abbey—in return for a yearly interest payment.[62] The loan was secured with a piece of tangible and income yielding property—typically land or other real estate. The income was used to pay the interest, which was called rent. This was essential. Medieval theologians condemned lending at interest as a mortal sin but accepted receiving a rental income on property like land, and that income could very well be transferred to someone else.[63]

By the sixteenth century, 'selling rents' had become immensely popular. In 1542 almost a quarter of the 438 burghers of the small town of Frankenhausen 30 miles north of Erfurt had done so, having borrowed money for which they were paying a yearly interest to their creditors. Among the lenders, the friaries and abbeys in Frankenhausen and its neighbourhood were most popular, and not just among the local burghers: 36 per cent of the loans they had granted and for which they were receiving rents in 1542 had gone to other ecclesiastical institutions and 17 per cent to peasants.[64] In the first half of the sixteenth century, peasants were regularly active on the market for rents. In Württemberg, they needed the permission of their manorial lords (they could often buy this for a one-off payment).[65] From elsewhere—for example from near Zürich and Straßburg (Strasbourg)—there is evidence that the need to pay rents burdened peasants to an extent that forced them to abandon their land holdings.[66] This happened despite relatively low and falling interest rates. Erfurt had originally agreed to 6 per cent—paying 120 florins a year in return for the loan of 2,000 florins—but when the contract was renegotiated in 1519, the rate was reduced to 4 per cent, and rates around 5 per cent were common in the Empire all through the sixteenth century. Still, peasants selling rents got into trouble so often that the matter was raised in popular flysheets.[67]

Among urban governments, selling rents had by the sixteenth century emerged as the dominant form of deficit finance. There were few towns and cities, large or small, imperial or under the rule of a prince, that did not cover part of their expenses in this way.[68] As we have seen, territorial governments were in debt, too. *Bergherren* used the output of their mines as collateral for loans they took from firms like the Fuggers; imperial estates without mines of their own used other assets. From the fourteenth century onward, parts of their lands, towns, castles, markets, villages and individual demesnes, forests and vineyards, gardens and fishponds, hunting rights and the income from mills, mints, tolls, courts of law, or specific taxes served to secure credits—it was a political system where literally anything could be turned into capital.[69] This could take extreme forms: In return for a 36-year loan of 154,000 *Guldens,* Count-Palatine Ottheinrich of Neuburg—a splinter-territory of Bavaria formed at the beginning of the sixteenth century and centred on the town of Neuburg on the Danube—transferred three of the districts of his small principality to the city of Nuremberg, while Elector Joachim II of Brandenburg used a whole county—Ruppin, which Brandenburg had acquired only a few years before—as collateral for the money he had borrowed from the Loitz trading firm from Stettin (Szczecin). For the duration of the contract, the firm received all revenues Ruppin yielded.[70]

Territorial governments were selling rents, too. Take for example Philip von Flersheim. We are relatively well-informed about his finances because in 1541 he ordered his chief fiscal official Conrad Jung to put together a summary of his revenues and expenses over the last decade.[71] According to Jung's calculation, Flersheim received revenues of not quite 12,000 *Guldens* a year. He took over a debt of almost 11,300 *Guldens* from his predecessor bishop George, a younger son of the elector Palatine, and added another 5,600 *Guldens* during the ten years covered by the source. The earliest credit he incurred himself was 500 *Guldens* borrowed from one Hans Zolf von Grumbach, who received a yearly rent of 50 *Guldens* in return. Ten per cent was expensive. Later loans Flersheim took during his first decade as bishop of Speyer were cheaper, with the interest rate being on average 4.3 per cent per annum.[72]

At the imperial diet of Speyer in 1544, the electoral Saxon delegation presented a memorial claiming that there were hardly any princes of the Empire—particularly secular ones—who were not burdened with debts; few had yearly revenues above 100,000 *Guldens*, 'and more than one with an income of barely 50,000 *Guldens* must pay 20- or 30,000 *Guldens* . . . a year to service his debts and stop the usurer's mouth'.[73] Apart from showing how representatives of the German high nobility talked of their creditors behind their backs, the statement begs the question of whether the Saxons were at least broadly correct. After all, they aimed at demonstrating that the princes were unable to pay higher contributions to the Empire and were accordingly biased. Historians have done much to allow us to assess how valid the claim was. There are several reasons why this work was extraordinarily complex. Most estates did not have a central treasury, but rather a number of offices that received different types of revenues, often without any coherent form of book-keeping and accounting.[74] The problem was aggravated if the lands of a ruler were geographically dispersed and heterogeneous, with Charles V's situation as emperor, king of Spain, and ruler of diverse other territories that spanned much of Europe and indeed the globe being the most difficult.[75] Moreover, all imperial estates received part of their revenues not in money but in kind,[76] which means that we need much information about local prices to compute their monetary values—information that in many cases we are still lacking. While there are several territories about which we are informed in detail—electoral Saxony, for example, and Hesse—we are not yet in a position that allows drawing a comprehensive picture of the revenues and debts of the imperial estates.[77] Table 5.1[78] summarizes the essence of what we know.

Table 5.1. Revenues and debts of imperial estates, *c.*1510s to 1570s

Estate	period	total yearly revenues	debt stock	yearly debt service
		all sums rounded to thousands		
Emperor Charles V	1519–31		6,407,000 dc.	
	1532–41		10,596,000 dc.	
	1542–51		11,325,000 dc.	
	1552–56		11,044,000 dc.	
Emperor Ferdinand I	1564	870,000 fl.	12,300,000 fl.	
Emperor Maximilian II	1573		7,000,000 fl.	
Elector Jacob III of Trier	1567		470,000 fl.	
Elector John Frederick of Saxony	1532–43			94,000 fl.
	1535/36	103,000 fl.		6,000 fl.
	1538/39	144,000 fl.		8,000 fl.
	1543			9,000 fl.
	1543/44	116,000 fl.		13,000 fl.
Elector Maurice of Saxony	1550	433,000 fl.	829,000 fl.	
Elector Joachim II of Brandenburg	1540		1,000,000 fl.	
	1549		2,000,000 fl.	
	1564		2,930,000 fl.	
Bishop Otto von Waldburg of Augsburg	1540	33,000 fl.		
Bishop Weigand von Redwitz of Bamberg	1541–50	17,000 fl.		
	1553		200,000 fl.	
Bishop Veit II. von Würtzburg of Bamberg	1567		806,000 fl.	
Bishop Ernest of Freising	1577	9,000 fl.		
Bishop Burkhard von Oberg of Hildesheim	1560		230,000 fl.	
	1565			60,000 fl.
Bishop George of Speyer	1529		11,000 fl.	
Bishop Philip von Flersheim of Speyer	1529–41	12,000 fl.		9,000 fl.
Dukes William IV/Louis X of Bavaria	1511–13	162,000 fl.	488,000 fl.	22,000 fl.
	1514		742,000 fl.	
Duke William IV of Bavaria	1550		1,200,000 fl.	
Duke Albert V of Bavaria	1551–56	105,000 fl.		
	1557		1,230,000 fl.	
	1566–75	192,000 fl.		

Continued

Table 5.1. *Continued*

Estate	period	total yearly revenues	debt stock	yearly debt service
		all sums rounded to thousands		
Duke Julius of Braunschweig-Wolfenbüttel	1579/80	150,000 fl.		
Duke William of Jülich-Cleves-Berg	1543	247,000 fl.		
Duke Wolfgang of Pfalz-Zweibrücken	1568	26,000 fl.	700,000 fl.	35,000 fl.
Duke John Frederick of Saxony	1549	104,000 fl.		
Duke John William of Saxe-Weimar	1567	132,000 fl.	700,000 fl.	
Duke Christoph of Württemberg	1552	124,000 fl.	1,700,000 fl.	9,000 fl.
Landgrave Philip of Hesse	1510–19	28,000 fl.		
	1520–29	52,000 fl.	159,000 fl.	
	1530–39	85,000 fl.	610,000 fl.	26,000 fl.
	1540–49	116,000 fl.	833,000 fl.	
	1550–59	156,000 fl.	992,000 fl.	
	1560–68	163,000 fl.	895,000 fl.	53,000 fl.
Count-Palatine Ottheinrich of Neuburg	1508–44	27,000 fl.		
	1535		348,000 fl.	
	1542		962,000 gl.	
	1544		1,138,000 fl.	
Count-Palatine Wolfgang of Neuburg	1568	60,000 fl.	80,000 fl.	4,000 fl.
Margrave Casimir of Brandenburg-Kulmbach	1515		171,000 fl.	9,000 fl.
Margrave George of Brandenburg-Ansbach-Kulmbach	1527		458,000 fl.	
	1528	64,000 fl.		25,000 fl.
	1535	173,000 fl.		48,000 fl.
	1536	173,000 fl.		42,000 fl.

The sums listed in Table 5.1 must be taken with a pinch of salt. Most are given in *Guldens* of account, a unit whose value changed over time and varied between places. Moreover, as large and wealthy imperial estates tend to be better documented than small and poor ones, we know more about the fiscal situation of electors and important dukes than about that of, for example, minor bishops or counts. The picture emerging from Table 5.1 is therefore distorted to an extent which is impossible to assess.

Still, there is no doubt that many of the most important estates were heavily in debt, with several—for example, the count-palatine of Neuburg in the mid-1540s, the duke of Württemberg in about 1550, the duke of Bavaria a few years later, and the duke of Pfalz-Zweibrücken at the end of the 1560s—having obligations that exceeded their yearly revenues by a factor of more than ten. This was a lot by international standards. In 1550 the English Crown, for example, collected revenues of about £553,000 (*c.*1.15 million Austrian–South German *Guldens* of account).[79] At the same time, it carried a debt burden of £350,000, which implies a revenue-to-debt ratio of about 1 to 0.6. This grew to 1 to 0.8 at the death of Edward VI in 1553 and to 1 to 0.9 at the accession of Elizabeth I in 1558.[80] English monarchs were in a comfortable position because they could easily tax foreign trade that had to pass through a few ports where traffic could be controlled at low costs. There, they could also extort forced loans from merchants by prohibiting exports—a strategy devised by Thomas Gresham and practised by Somerset as lord protector during the minority of Edward VI as well as by Elizabeth I.[81] By contrast, most princes of the Empire were still expected to live off the income from their demesnes, supplemented by a few taxes.[82] If a prince needed more—to pay for attending a diet, to finance his court, to send and maintain envoys to other princes or to the emperor, to cover the costs of lawsuits and occasionally of armaments, if a conflict threatened to get out of hand—he had to beg and cajole his territorial estates that might or might not grant an additional tax. If this proved insufficient, taking up a loan was often the easiest way forward.[83]

On the plus side were the favourable rates at which the princes of the Empire could borrow. Landgrave Philip of Hesse paid 4 to 5 per cent per year, as did Landgrave Louis Henry of Leuchtenberg, Count Louis Casimir of Hohenlohe, and Bishop Philip von Flersheim of Speyer. In 1554, Bishop Melchior Zobel of Würzburg took up a loan from Götz von Berlichingen (Goethe's 'Knight of the Iron Hand', who never let his career as trouble-maker stand in the way of business) at 2.5 per cent. King Ferdinand had to pay 6.3 per cent.[84] The English Crown, by contrast, borrowed from the Fuggers, Tuchers, and other banking houses at punitive rates of 12 to 14 per cent.[85] But then, Edward VI or Elizabeth I never considered signing over

Kent or Sussex to their creditors, as Elector Joachim II did with the county of Ruppin.

As we have seen, the princes of the Empire stood by no means alone in their dependence on deficit finance. With the likely exception of vagrants and paupers, there were no social groups in Germany whose members did not borrow money, from the peasantry upwards to the electors and the emperor himself.[86] They often did so in much the same way and for similar purposes, for example selling rents in order to bridge periods when they lacked cash—a fact that is obscured when one contrasts a culture based on aristocratic values of obligation centred on exchanging gifts with one based on urban and commercial activities centred on making a profit, as historians have recently done.[87] What this implies is that where the consequences of a common currency for the servicing of obligations were concerned, the indebted imperial estates were on the same side as much of the rest of the population. What affected them would affect many thousands of others in the same way.

How to pay your debts

Why should bimetallism or the opportunity to pay in silver instead of gold have been a problem? In the last resort, this was because of the influence of the thirteenth-century theologian and philosopher Thomas Aquinas. Aquinas was intensely interested in usury and in whether and when lending was sinful. In this context, he drew a distinction between fungible and non-fungible goods. Goods that were indistinguishable from others in their group by some specific defining characteristic were fungible: sheaves of wheat, for example, or jars of olive oil, or coins. Aquinas argued that if a person lent such goods to somebody else, the lender lost them in much the same way as if they had been destroyed. Repayment, therefore, had to be made with other, but identical units, that is, with the same quantity of wheat or oil or coin—coin, that is, of exactly the same type as that which the borrower had received.[88] According to this so-called 'realist' school of medieval thought, loans taken in gold, therefore, had to be serviced in gold and those taken in silver in silver.

The principle was widely acknowledged. Take for example Hildesheim. In 1542, the local magistrate published an ordinance that regulated how debts were to be serviced. 'One truly knows', the law asserted, 'that many usurers take more than 28 Guldens a year as usury from 100 Guldens, and many are even more evil, having practiced usury and demanded large and heavy sums two or three times a year'. Taking up short-term loans was much more expensive than selling long-term rents: From Augsburg, we have evidence for people paying rates of 10 per cent *per week* on small-scale loans. There, the magistrate intervened on a case-by-case basis.[89] In Hildesheim, the decision was that 'one Christian should pay another one—spiritual or temporal—5 *Guldens* in gold for 100 gold *Guldens*, and 5 *Guldens* in silver coin for 100 *Guldens* in coin' per year.[90] What is relevant here is not that the ordinance addressed Christians (to Jews, other rules applied) or that it determined a specific interest rate. Rather, what matters is that while the rate the magistrate set was the same regardless of whether the debt had been incurred in gold or in silver, both metals were listed separately—an echo of Aquinas' approach to usury and interest. Flersheim and Solms' suggestion to require creditors to accept silver in place of gold thus broke with a long-established and widely accepted norm.

It is now becoming clearer why the delegates of the princes were so delighted with the idea. In a long memorial they submitted to the imperial commissioners two days after these had presented their own position paper, they warned of dire consequences if Flersheim and Solms' suggestion was rejected. It is the description of these consequences that betrays why they were so pleased:

> Because for many years no or few gold *Guldens* have been minted on the Rhine, so that they are very difficult to obtain, what would follow would be that many people of high and low status, who must pay interest or tolls, redeem securities or repay old debts in gold, had to purchase this gold at much higher and more expensive rates than their forebears, who borrowed the money, and their descendants and inheritors had ever enjoyed. In consequence, the descendants and inheritors of the original creditors would enrich themselves at the expense of the descendants and inheritors of the debtors, and the debtors' inheritors and descendants would be severely harmed and ruined despite being blameless, without having defaulted, and for no good reason.[91]

The central issue was paying interest, redeeming securities, and servicing debts denominated in gold. Here, the envoys of the princes claimed, a fixed legal ratio between gold and silver coins would help.

It is hardly possible to overstate how important this was for most of the imperial estates, especially for those represented in the princes' college. Table 5.2[92] summarizes what we know of the exchange rate of the Rhenish florin in some major markets of the Empire during the reigns of Charles V

Table 5.2. Market exchange rates of the Rhenish florin in local silver, 1519–64

period	Hamburg (*Schillings*)	Cologne (White *Pfennigs*)	Nuremberg (*Schillings*)	Vienna (*Kreuzers*)	Augsburg (*Kreuzers*)
1520–24	25.01	28.25			
1525–29	27.50	32.60	11.17	64.00	64.00
1530–34	27.90	37.10		64.33	66.00
1535–39	30.42	39.50	11.88	69.67	
1540–44	32.00	44.60		70.00	65.00
1545–49		50.30			67.83
1550–54	32.48	52.10	13.13		72.96
1555–59	34.00	55.10	13.13		74.57
1560–64	35.42	57.90			

and Ferdinand I. The table shows rates that resulted from contracts concluded on these markets, leaving politically imposed rates such as those Ferdinand decreed in 1542 out of account. It was data like these that the delegates of the princes at the coinage conference in Speyer in 1549 had in mind when they claimed that anyone who had to service long-term liabilities in Rhenish florins had to purchase the gold at higher rates than at the date when he had incurred the debt.

Evidently, there was something to the argument of the princely delegates. By the end of the 1540s, the Rhenish florin cost between 8 and 70 per cent more than it had done in the 1520s. Given the silver mining boom—which peaked during these decades—and the Empire's dependence on imported gold, it is obvious why the florin appreciated. And it was not only nominal exchange rates that were going up; the value ratio of raw silver to gold did so, too.[93] We are therefore not merely observing the result of the debasement of local silver currencies as, for example, Duke William IV of Bavaria believed.[94] Gold did genuinely become more expensive in terms of silver.

No wonder Conrad Jung's summary of Flersheim's revenues and expenses carefully noted next to each loan he had taken whether he had incurred the debt in gold.[95] During the talks in Speyer in late September 1549, Flersheim made it quite clear where the problem lay: As bishop of Speyer, he had to 'purchase the gold he needed to service his obligations from merchants, and this with growing difficulties, high costs and insufferable fees'. Rhenish florins were impossible to obtain, and this was why it was necessary to mint a silver piece that could be used instead.[96] Evidently, Flersheim and

Solms were also acting in the interest of the emperor. The more than 2.25 million ducats Charles V owed in 1546 were denominated in gold, and German merchants and banking firms were prominent among his creditors.[97] An anonymous memorial found in the Habsburg archives in Vienna among the papers relating to the coinage conferences in Speyer in 1549 looked at the issue from another angle:

> One also needs to consider that if someone has sold—and is bound to pay—a rent, and the contract is expressed in gold or gold coins and determined an interest rate of 5 per cent at the time it was concluded, and the gold now continues to rise, and debts made in gold must be paid in gold, this causes great hardship for those who must have and obtain gold. It could very well follow that in the end the debtor must give 8 or 10 per cent, and it is easy to compute what great advantage and profit those who receive rents would then gain.[98]

In 1519, when Erfurt renegotiated its contract with Lehnin Abbey, gold had not yet appreciated so much; the *Gulden* of account still matched the Rhenish florin. The abbey, therefore, allowed Erfurt's magistrate to pay the rent in 'current coin, reckoning 21 *Groschens*, each 12 *Pfennigs* worth, for every florin', that is, in Saxon silver money. By the middle of the sixteenth century, something like this would have been unacceptable—unless a bimetallic currency was introduced where silver was unlimited legal tender.

Still, bimetallism would favour debtors only under specific conditions: On the one hand, they had to be able to purchase the coins they needed to service their obligations at exchange rates close to the market price of raw gold and silver, on the other, to compel their creditors to accept these coins at their legal value. Daily experience taught that official exchange rates were impossible to enforce in the markets of the Empire.[99] At the same time, princes would be able to force their creditors to respect imperial law, including a law that determined the official ratio of gold and silver coins. To service their gold-denominated debts, they would thus have the chance always to choose the metal whose market price was lower than its official value determined in 1549. It is obvious why the delegates of the princes were delighted with this prospect.

While their enthusiasm was justified, it is a different question whether it helped the negotiations. So far, the reform process had been driven by the desire of the estates to prevent the trade in coinage, the breaking of their coins, and the harm this did to their revenues and prestige. These had been aims on which all could agree. Now, the commissioners went back on what had been discussed at the diet of Worms a few years before, where several exceptions to bimetallism had been defined: Contracts which said payments had to be made in gold should stand, and payments that according to ancient customs were made in gold should remain unaffected. From now on, the enticing prospect of servicing gold-denominated debts and other obligations with silver overshadowed the original aim of the reform. How divisive this idea was is something Flersheim and Solms would soon find out—though it would take some years for the scale of their blunder to become fully obvious.

The gold of the electors

Opposition and obstruction

Burghers of imperial cities—first and foremost the commercial elites—were prominent among the creditors of princes. Count-Palatine Ottheinrich owed most of his money to Protestant merchants from Augsburg and Nuremberg, and Nuremberg and Ulm had lent large sums to the Habsburgs.[100] It was these cities whose envoys played a leading role among the urban delegates at the conference of autumn 1549,[101] and accordingly, the cities' college opposed bimetallism. In this, the cities stood shoulder to shoulder with the electors on the Rhine. In a long talk Flersheim and Solms had on 30 September with Hans Steinhauser and Christoph Mathias,[102] the two representatives of the electors' college failed to explain what exactly they disliked about the idea that the silver 72-*Kreuzers*-piece should be used in place of the Rhenish florin. The imperial commissioners were clearly puzzled: They 'knew full well that the electors had incurred debts in gold just as well as other estates and were lying sick of the same disease, of which they and the others now had a chance to be cured with no risk of future harm and damage'. Flersheim and Solms also tried to drive a wedge between electors and cities: 'If all electors, princes, and other estates considered to whom most debts, pensions and yearly rents are owed and must be paid . . . they would have to admit that these are the big cities and communes'[103]—to no avail.

During a joint meeting of the princes' and electors' colleges, the envoys of Mainz, Trier, Cologne, and the Palatinate did become more specific. First, they called 'all *novae leges periculosae*', that is, all new laws perilous (a Latin phrase or two would always suggest you were making a well-founded legal argument), and this law, in particular, gave cause for concern. As creditors would not allow themselves to be forced to depart from the letter of their contracts and accept silver in place of gold, 'insufferable confusion, strife, excuses and other inconveniences would follow, grow, and result'.[104] Without referring to Aquinas, the counsellors of the electors were evidently thinking along the traditional lines: Debts had to be repaid in the type of coin in which they had been contracted. However, this was not their only argument. They also feared that if the Rhenish florin was treated as the equivalent of a 72 *Kreuzers* silver coin, 'gold . . . will in its entirety be exported from the German nation'.[105] Why they expected this was left unexplained, but their concern was well founded. When King Ferdinand, the Bohemian estates and Augsburg had valued the Rhenish florin at 72 *Kreuzers*, this applied to coins of the Austrian–Upper German standard of 1535. The standard on which the delegates had agreed at the beginning of the talks in Speyer was lower. Equating the Rhenish florin with such coins meant depressing the official value of gold far below its rate in neighbouring countries, no matter whether you used the planned 72-*Kreuzers*-piece or small change. Table 5.3[106] lists the relevant ratios.

Table 5.3. Official gold–silver ratios 1535–49

Law/planned law	Gold coin type	Pure gold in grams	Silver equivalent	Pure silver in grams	Gold-silver ratio
Ordinance of 1535	Rhenish florin	2.527	72 Austrian–Upper German *Kreuzers*	29.928	1:11.84
Ordinance of 1535	Rhenish florin	2.527	1.2 Austrian–Upper German 60-*Kreuzers*-pieces	30.843	1:12.21
Planned in Speyer 1549	Rhenish florin	2.527	72 imperial *Kreuzers*	26.886	1:10.64
Planned in Speyer 1549	Rhenish florin	2.527	1 imperial 72-*Kreuzers*-piece	27.497	1:10.88
French ordinance of 1549	*Écu effigie*	3.176	4.1 silver *Testons*	37.094	1:11.68

If the Rhenish florin was equated to 72 *Kreuzers* of the standard agreed in Speyer in 1549, one could buy one unit of weight of gold for 10.6 to 10.9 units of silver in Vienna, Augsburg, Frankfurt, or Cologne, and sell it for 11.7 units in Paris. The difference amounted to about 9 per cent. This would probably have covered the costs of exporting the metal from the Empire.

The envoys of the electors at the coinage conference thus did have a good reason to reject Flersheim and Solms' suggestion that everybody should have to accept the silver 72-*Kreuzers*-piece in place of a Rhenish florin. Still, it is striking that during the meeting in Speyer they were focusing on procedural problems rather than on these points. They explained that personally, they were perfectly willing to agree with the delegates of the princes and the imperial commissioners, but unfortunately, their masters had given them no instructions that concerned the interchangeability of silver and gold. Moreover, too few imperial estates had sent envoys to Speyer for the *Münztag* to be able to decide on such a fundamentally new law.[107] When the delegates of the princes suggested they should ask the electors for the necessary instructions, their discomfort was palpable: They admitted this was 'not a bad idea', but excused themselves with the slow speed and high costs of communications: Some electors, who lived nearby, could be reached easily, but others were so distant that receiving their answer would take time. As an afterthought, they added that in any case, none of the electors on the Rhine would make a decision without having consulted the others.[108] This was their last word.

The conference finished the draft of the currency ordinance less than two weeks later, leaving the disputed paragraph open.[109] From then on, Flersheim kept the delegates kicking their heels in Speyer, waiting for the return of Solms who had gone to Brussels to inform Charles V and obtain his resolution. Predictably, the emperor came out in favour of what his commissioners had suggested and the princely delegates enthusiastically accepted.[110] When this was announced and it turned out that the electoral delegates still had not informed their principals, the imperial commissioners adjourned the meeting for three weeks, declaring that they 'expected and asked graciously and friendly' that upon their return the envoys of Mainz, Trier, Cologne, and the Palatinate would 'announce an answer of their most gracious lords, the electors, which allows to bring these negotiations to a real agreement and conclusion in accordance with the imperial resolution'.[111]

Instead of instructing their envoys as requested, the Rhenish electors decided to bypass the currency conference by turning directly to

Charles V.[112] It is the memorial they submitted to Brussels that contains the fullest account of why they objected to the fungibility of gold and silver. They elaborated the arguments put forward by their delegates a few weeks before, warning of feuds and riots if creditors were forced to accept silver in place of gold and explaining more carefully why they feared gold would be driven out of the Empire.[113] In addition, they stressed two further points: the wishes of their regional diets that insisted on maintaining established practices, and the vagaries of mining that caused changes in the value of gold and silver. A permanent value ratio between both precious metals was therefore impossible to achieve, so that the planned currency bill would soon be outdated and invalid.[114]

With their last argument, the electors anticipated a view that would dominate research on bimetallic currencies for a long time. Changes in the relative price of raw gold and silver were considered the Achilles heel of such systems. Historians believed that given a legally fixed value ratio between coins minted from both metals, consumers would immediately react to an increase in the market price of one of the metals: They would withdraw the coins made from it from circulation, melt them, and sell the metal. In consequence, bimetallism would constantly tend to revert to monometallism, that is, to a currency where only one precious metal was used.[115] More recently, it has become evident that bimetallic currencies can be stable. Culling coins whose intrinsic value has increased becomes profitable only if the difference between the legal and the market value ratios between gold and silver is large enough to cover the costs involved in melting the coins and in selling their metal.[116] However, even then shifts in the relative prices of gold and silver do not necessarily cause the disappearance of one of the metals from circulation. This is the case only if political authorities are strong and well-organized enough to force consumers to use coins at their legal value. If that is not the case—and in sixteenth-century Germany, it was not—consumers do not withdraw coins whose intrinsic value goes up from circulation; rather, they use them at a premium.[117] That this might happen is something which the delegates of the electors had suggested early in the talks in Speyer in September 1549.[118]

That they raised this point several weeks before Flersheim and Solms started their ill-fated initiative begs a question: Why did they focus on procedural problems—the absence of many estates at the conference and their lack of instructions—rather than on this and their other substantive arguments to convince the imperial commissioners and the envoys of the princes? The answer is that Flersheim and Solms' suggestion spelt trouble for the electors—trouble of a kind their delegates did not want to mention during the talks at Speyer. To see why, we need to take a closer look at the role the electoral lands played in fifteenth- and early sixteenth-century trade—particularly in the gold trade.

The Rhine trade and its perks

As a silver-rich country whose authorities were not above turning to sharp practice when it came to attracting gold, the Empire experienced an inflow of the metal. However, remember that the Rhine especially had long been associated with gold and that in the fifteenth century, the myths had a basis in fact. This was a result of an important change in the routes merchants used at that time—a change that was a consequence of political and economic geography in Renaissance Europe. What was relevant were war and unrest on the one hand, and the location of economic activity on the other.

Mentioning the Renaissance already suggests part of the answer: Italy, that is, the part of Europe from where the movement originated, which contemporaries involved in it perceived as the rebirth of the culture of Antiquity. Next to the Low Countries, at which we have looked above, Italy was one of the most densely urbanized parts of Europe, with up to 17 per cent of the population living in towns with more than 10,000 inhabitants.[119] As a high degree of urbanization indicates prosperity, this implies that the Low Countries and Italy were the two poles of economic activity in Renaissance Europe. Their wealth concerned the Rhineland because from about 1400 onward, commerce began to recover from its late fourteenth-century depression. The revival took place by following new routes secure from the turmoil of the Hundred Years' War that France and England fought mostly on French soil.[120] To evade the widespread devastation, trade sought the least costly alternative to the traditional route that led along the Rhône and Saône—always preferring waterways to roads as water transport was far more cost-effective.[121] This was why Genoese and Venetian galleys now firmly established the sea route through the Strait of Gibraltar that they had pioneered in the thirteenth century.[122] In addition, a new transcontinental route emerged that was longer than the old one but took less time than travelling around Spain and Portugal. It led from Verona at the foot of the Alps over the Brenner Pass to reach Innsbruck in the Tyrol, from there through Bavaria or Swabia, and then down the Rhine to

Cologne, and ultimately to the Low Countries.[123] The big river thus became the most important transcontinental artery of trade in Europe. English cloth and textiles made from Spanish wool woven in Flanders flowed south; in the opposite direction, Italian merchants sent Chinese silk and Persian tapestries, cotton fabrics from India, perfumes like incense and musk, ivory, dyes, and spices such as cinnamon, saffron, and cloves. They also took gold that the commercial centres of Italy imported from Africa and minted not only to satisfy domestic demand, but especially for export.[124] Their trade had a profound effect on the territories on the banks of the Rhine, and most importantly on the electorates of Mainz, Trier, Cologne, and the Palatinate. It also played a crucial role in the monetary policies the electors pursued at the level of the Empire—a role of which historians have only recently become aware.[125] There was a simple link: Trade was taxed, the taxes affected the fiscal position and interests of the authorities collecting them, and this shaped their monetary-policy outlook. How exactly did this work?

Since gothic best-seller author Ann Radcliffe pioneered what became the Rhine romanticism of the nineteenth century, British tourists have followed her lead in admiring how mountains, rivers, and castles combine to create the unique scenery between Mainz and Koblenz:

> The Rhine no where, perhaps, presents grander objects either of nature or of art, than in the northern perspective from St. Goar. There, expanding with a bold sweep, the river exhibits, at one coup d'œil, on its mountainous shores, six fortresses or towns, many of them placed in the most wild and tremendous situations; their antient and gloomy structures giving ideas of the sullen tyranny of former times.[126]

This is how Radcliffe saw the middle Rhine in 1794, and what concerns us here is her 'sullen tyranny of former times'. From the early thirteenth century onward, St Goar was a customs post—not an electoral but a Hessian one—[127] a few miles upstream lay Kaub and Bacharach, which belonged to the Elector Palatine, and Ehrenfels, a toll of the elector of Mainz. A little downriver, once you passed Boppard—another toll of the landgrave of Hesse—you reached Lahnstein, again a toll of Mainz. And so it went on. There were about 30 toll posts on the middle and lower Rhine in 1500, 14 of which belonged to the electors of Mainz, Trier, Cologne, and the Palatinate (Map 5.1).

Modern research is rejecting the nineteenth-century idea—based on the self-justification of the authorities collecting the dues along the Rhine—that

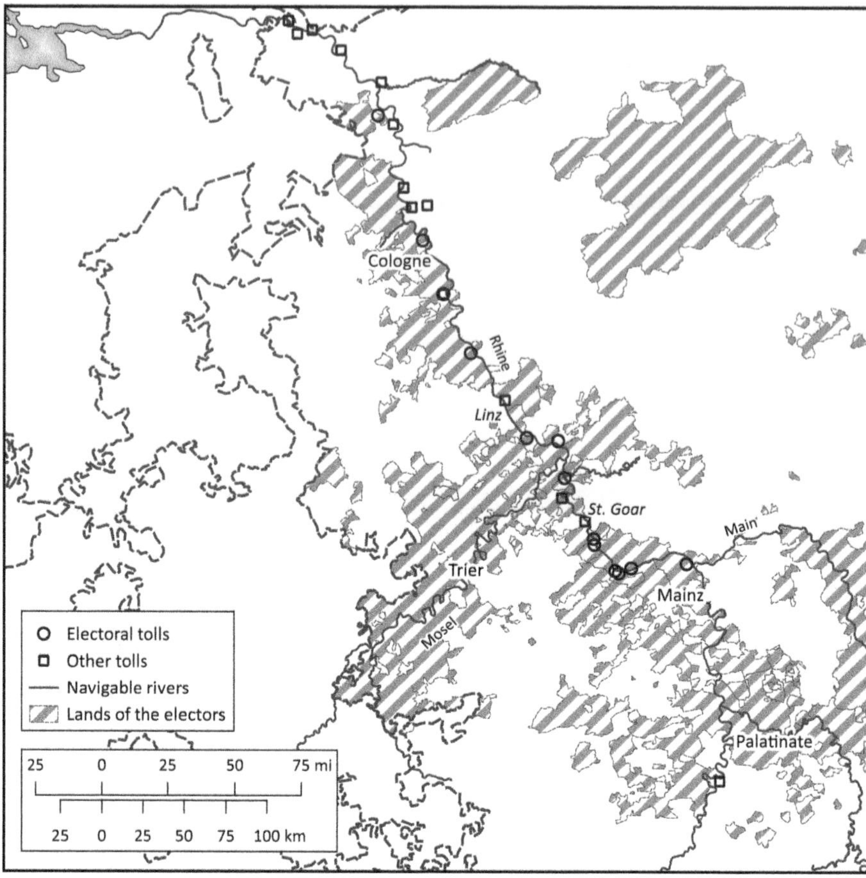

Map 5.1. Tolls on the Middle and Lower Rhine *c.*1500
Note: Pfeiffer, *Transitzölle*, pp. 191–321.

the tolls were originally and essentially fees merchants paid for protection and the maintenance of infrastructure such as the towpaths along the river. What early historians acknowledged for the late Middle Ages is now considered to have been valid throughout: 'From the perspective of the rulers collecting the tolls, the sole and only function of the river Rhine was filling their coffers.'[128] The electors claimed a right of political oversight over practically the whole length of the river. In 1492, they concluded a treaty, promising that

> in case anyone, whoever he may be, with no exception, obtains, accepts, creates, or makes a new toll, which has not existed before the date of this document, on the river Rhine from Basel down to Rees [a toll in the county

> of Cleves north of Cologne, close to where the Rhine split into several arms] and collects it contrary to established practice ... or harasses and harms merchants, bargemen, and others, who use and travel the Rhine up- and downriver, with convoy service fees or other impositions, regardless of how they are called ... each and every one of us shall individually or jointly, if he is summoned by the others, diligently help prevent this so that we support each other and do not cease to do so until such abuses have been abolished and brought to an end.[129]

Long-established tolls owned by other authorities had to be accepted, but new ones were forbidden. This was no empty threat. For example, in the late fifteenth century the electors took drastic action to shut down a toll Emperor Frederick III had granted to the imperial city of Cologne in 1475. They closed the Rhine to all downriver transport and to all barges from Cologne that went upriver, forcing merchants to take the costly detour overland. In 1490 Maximilian I mediated a settlement that allowed the urban toll to continue to operate for a few more years in exchange for a hefty fee the city had to pay the electors.[130] Methods became less rough once legal due process gained ground in the Empire and especially after Charles V had agreed in his electoral capitulation not to permit any new tolls without electoral consent.[131]

In the years around 1550, what counted for monetary-policy—especially for the attempt to create an Empire-wide common currency—was that the electors (and the other estates on the banks of the Rhine) did not merely tax trade in any way that occurred to them. Rather, they had one very specific interest: the gold that merchants carried between Italy and the Low Countries. Therefore, they defined and demanded custom dues in gold.[132] In the fifteenth century, obtaining the metal does not seem to have been a problem; enough gold was flowing along the Rhine. The electors were therefore in an unusual and enviable situation. Other rulers without gold or silver mines of their own needed a positive balance of trade to attract specie to their territories or had to manipulate the prices their mints offered for gold and silver to draw in one or the other metal. Sitting astride the most important transcontinental trade route of Europe, the archbishops of Mainz, Trier, and Cologne, and the count Palatine did not need to do so. They taxed trade up to a level that equalled the costs the merchants would have to bear if they used alternative routes,[133] raking in a treasure in every respect comparable to the one the Nibelungen *Lied* located at the bottom of the Rhine. Their mints turned much of the gold expropriated from merchants into Rhenish florins.[134] It almost goes without saying that the custom dues dominated their revenues, too.[135] By late fifteenth-century standards, the electors were wealthy, with Venetian observers estimating Trier's yearly revenues at 40,000, Mainz's at 60,000 and the elector Palatine's at 80,000 *Guldens*. In the case of electoral Cologne earlier in the century, between half and three-quarters of the income was derived from the tolls.[136] When a fifteenth-century poet rhymed that, 'had I the tolls on the Rhine, who next to me would shine?', he hit the nail on the head.[137]

Trade shifts to the Atlantic

It was not to last. During the first half of the sixteenth century, the Empire, in general, kept attracting gold—its growing supply of silver made sure of that—but the river of gold that the Rhine had been in the preceding period seems to have dried up to a trickle. Both the appreciation of gold in Cologne (Table 5.2) and complaints about how hard it was to pay the custom dues in gold suggest that the fifteenth-century abundance was gone, never to return.[138]

To see why this was the case, we must again leave the Empire and consider developments in the wider world. Ultimately, it was the ongoing voyages of Portuguese explorers and the evolving patterns of trade in the Indian Ocean in about 1500 that changed the fiscal position and determined the monetary-policy stance of the electors on the Rhine. After reaching the Gold Coast on the Gulf of Guinea in West Africa, Portuguese navigators kept pushing on. In 1488, Bartolomeu Dias reached the Cape of Good Hope. A decade later Vasco da Gama rounded it and went on to India. Using firearms and pirate tactics, the Portuguese muscled their way into the long-established trading networks that spanned the Indian Ocean from Zanzibar to Singapore and from the Persian Gulf to Bali. They had already begun to import African spices to Europe; now, they added cinnamon and cloves, pepper and nutmeg—that is, goods for which so far Venetians, who bought them in Alexandria or Beirut from Arab merchants, had enjoyed a monopoly. In 1501, the first spice-laden ship from Lisbon dropped anchor in Antwerp. From 1503, re-exports of Asian spices from Lisbon to the Low Countries were large and regular.[139] The Venetian Girolamo Priuli expressed widely shared fears when he noted in his diary that because of the Portuguese competition, 'the spices in the Venetian galleys must lessen and also the merchants. And when this traffic and merchandise is lessened in

Venice, it can be considered that the milk and nutriment of Venice are lessened . . . Some very wise people are inclined to believe that this thing may be the beginning of the ruin of the Venetian state.'[140] In fact, the collapse of the Venetian trade was only temporary. Arab merchants were able to rebuild part of their network, avoiding those sections of the Indian Ocean dominated by the Portuguese. From the 1530s, spices and other oriental goods—raw silk, luxury fabrics, precious stones, and gems—again entered Europe via the Mediterranean.[141] However, the Venetian spice monopoly was gone, and so was the Venetian spice trade as a whole once the Dutch took over commerce in the Indian Ocean in the early seventeenth century.[142] From then on, Atlantic trade ruled.

The effects of the global trade route change on the Rhine tolls were becoming obvious from the middle of the sixteenth century. Electoral custom officials were apparently widely suspected of exploiting the situation. An anonymous report claimed that

> when a boatman arrives at a toll post and complains about his lack of gold, and does not know where to obtain any, the customs official knows how to advise him where to find it, and it may very well be that he, the official, is involved in this trade and has gold himself.[143]

It is likely that demanding a premium in silver from merchants unable to pay the rates of duty in gold was what the Rhenish electors had in mind. An Empire-wide bimetallic currency based on a fixed gold–silver ratio would have made this illegal.

In any case, the consequences of the decline in the Rhine trade between Italy and the Low Countries and in the income from the tolls cannot be overstated. The electors found it hard to develop other sources of revenue. Their lands were less consolidated than the territories of many other major imperial estates, with small pieces of territory scattered over relatively large parts of the Rhineland and beyond. This made it difficult to establish bureaucracies needed to effectively tax the population. To be sure, on occasion some Rhenish electors still played important political roles. Mainz, especially, could take advantage of his office as arch-chancellor of Germany.[144] However, in the long term, the shift of trans-European trade from the Rhine route to the Atlantic contributed to the decline of influence that the Rhenish electors experienced. In the shorter term, they marshalled whatever power and influence they had to block any monetary-policy decisions which they expected to further undermine their standing.

This was the main reason why they were so fiercely opposed to the idea that a fixed legal ratio of gold to silver coins should be established and that everybody was to accept silver at this rate and in place of gold.

Admittedly, neither they themselves nor their delegates at the Speyer conference of autumn 1549 raised this point, and why should they have done so? It would have exposed them to being accused of acting out of self-interest. As we have seen, given the focus on the common weal, this was the most damning indictment possible. Others saw through their stance, though. Elector John Frederick of Saxony had already in 1545 pointed out that 'as the tolls on the Rhine are set in gold, the electors will suffer noticeably if the rate of the Rhenish florin declines and the appreciation of gold ceases'.[145] Now, in Speyer, Flersheim spelt out the implications in the most direct way imaginable: Not only were 'the tolls themselves illegitimate', but if his and Solms' suggestion was not accepted and the delegates of the electors failed to agree with those of the princes, 'no one but their most gracious lords would be made responsible, who valued their tolls and self-interest so highly and ignored the common weal'.[146]

While the *Münztag* of Speyer that had begun so auspiciously in September 1549 failed to pass the common-currency bill, it did make several fundamental decisions. Importantly, the participants determined the official value and bullion content of the silver coins that were to be used throughout the Empire as legal tender. Another decision—one that was as characteristic as important in the long term—concerned the structure of the planned currency. The *Tag* decided to supplement the common money with a range of regional small-change systems. These were composed of coins up to the value of 6 *Kreuzers* and were to be used in the lands of the electors on the Rhine, in those of the electors and dukes of Saxony and in the Franconian circle, in electoral Brandenburg, in the Habsburg Low Countries, and in the Lower Saxon circle. In addition, the delegates in Speyer agreed on a much wider range of regional *Pfennig* and ½-*Pfennig* types that they wanted to retain.[147]

While there were some who spoke out in favour of complete monetary uniformity,[148] this was never the aim of most estates when they set about creating a common currency. It made sense to show consideration for the higher ranking and more influential princes, whose support for the common currency was needed and part of whose prestige had for centuries rested on having their own coinage. That is why in Speyer, the delegate of Elector Joachim II of Brandenburg insisted on Brandenburg being treated in the same way as electoral Saxony where regional small change was concerned.[149] Still, the planned bill had to be accepted not only by the imperial estates, but by the common man, too. The currency committee at the diet of Worms in 1545 had explained how important it was that 'it should be possible to easily conclude future contracts, purchases and sales and other matters in such a way that goods down to the penny-bread'—the generic term used for all low-price goods—'do not become dearer or more expensive, because local small change will everywhere be retained'.[150] This was the position the *Münztag* in Speyer adopted, though it also followed the Pomeranian delegates who stressed the need to avoid having to convert relatively small sums that had to be paid regularly—for example the rents peasants owed to their landlords—into new money.[151] Both points were valid and important. With the vast majority of people being illiterate, it would have been impossible to inform them of the correct conversion rates in sufficient detail to prevent abuses—whether by members of the nobility, who would have had every chance to illicitly increase the rents and other dues their peasants paid, or by merchants, who could use the new common currency to drive up prices.[152] The suggestion to introduce Empire-wide larger coins but to retain regional small change was thus a pragmatic compromise that took both the wishes of some of the imperial estates and the needs of the common man into account.

The so-called 'Probation Ordinance—'probation'was the term used for the metallurgical analysis of coins—on which the *Münztag* agreed was equally important. The delegates in Speyer drafted it based on the law first discussed in Worms four years before. The Probation Ordinance contained detailed provisions designed to prevent the estates from undermining the common currency.[153] Finally, the *Tag* suggested that the bill should come into force only after the value of the old money current in the Empire had been determined. For that purpose, a general assay was to be held that mint officials and other metal experts sent by the imperial circles were to attend.[154]

Despite all decisions and the undeniable progress that had been made, the bimetallism dispute remained unresolved. However, the next imperial diet, which took place from June 1550 to February 1551 in Augsburg, adopted the draft currency bill drawn up the year before almost without changes, and left the Probation Ordinance entirely unchanged. It also approved the plan to hold a general assay and asked Charles V to publish the bill immediately after this had finished and its results had been made available.[155] As we have seen, the assay took place in Nuremberg in the spring of 1551: The report the assayers submitted at the end of May was our guide through the jungle of currencies used in the Empire. The emperor received the report a little later, and on 28 July 1551, he did as the diet had requested and signed the bill.[156] To Charles, its publication by the Augsburg printer Philipp Ulhart must have appeared as one of the big legislative successes of his reign, at least on a par with the ratification of the common criminal law code by the diet of Regensburg in 1532.[157] In fact, the 'Augsburg Coinage Ordinance', as it became known, marked one of the high points, if not the high point, of his power.

Like its predecessor, the Esslingen Ordinance 27 years before, the Augsburg Ordinance created a bimetallic currency (Table A.4). The largest silver coin, the 72-*Kreuzers*-piece, was the equivalent of the established Rhenish florin; both coins were to be used in parallel as legal tender. They were supplemented by a range of smaller units down to the *Kreuzer*. The bill permitted the regional small change planned in Speyer and integrated the long catalogue of old coins and their values that the assayers in Nuremberg had put together, determining that these old coins should be gradually phased out.[158] This included the Saxon *Taler*, which was provisionally allowed to circulate as a 68-*Kreuzers*-piece, but whose further production was prohibited. The Probation Ordinance, which was to make sure that the estates issued the new money correctly and in accordance with the bill, was the necessary corollary of the Augsburg Coinage Ordinance. Finally, the Empire had got its common currency. Or so it seemed.

6

The new money

The mirage of success

The Empire at work

For some months, it seemed as if all problems had been solved. Not that there were no glitches. The idea was to make the ten imperial circles responsible for publicizing the currency bill and Probation Ordinance. The directors of each circle—one spiritual and one temporal prince—were to be sent copies of the new laws to make them known among the other estates of their respective circles. But who were the directors? If this had ever been formally decided, the imperial secretariat had failed to keep a record. Accordingly, Johann Obernburger, who headed that office, requested the relevant information from the secretariat of Archbishop Sebastian von Heusenstamm, the elector of Mainz. Heusenstamm was the arch-chancellor of Germany and therefore responsible for keeping the minutes and the rest of the paperwork of the imperial assemblies. The head of Heusenstamm's chancellery complied and sent the information, but not without covering his back: He pointed out that he was unable to provide more than an 'approximate register of which princes should, in his opinion, receive copies of the bills'.[1] Naturally, this took time. Moreover, it turned out that the list Mainz sent was at least in part incorrect. The bishop of Augsburg, Cardinal Otto von Waldburg—the same to whom Silvester Raid had tried to pass on the '*Kreuzers*' from Hildesheim a couple of years before—had to inform the emperor that neither he nor the margrave of Baden were the directors of the Swabian circle—they were the bishop of Constance and the duke of Württemberg.[2] This took more time.

Still, most circle directors reported back to the emperor as requested, notifying him of the measures they had taken to make the currency bill and the Probation Ordinance known among the other estates of their circle (Map 6.1). For example, Duke John II of Pfalz-Simmern wrote that he and his cousin Bishop Henry of Worms, who together chaired the Upper Rhenish circle, had called a circle-level *Tag* for 25 April 1552 to announce the laws.[3] Similar responses arrived from other circles, with the bishop of Münster and the duke of Jülich-Cleves-Berg (from the Lower Rhenish Westphalian circle) reporting that they already had informed their circle's estates of the currency and probation bills. The Westphalian estates had agreed

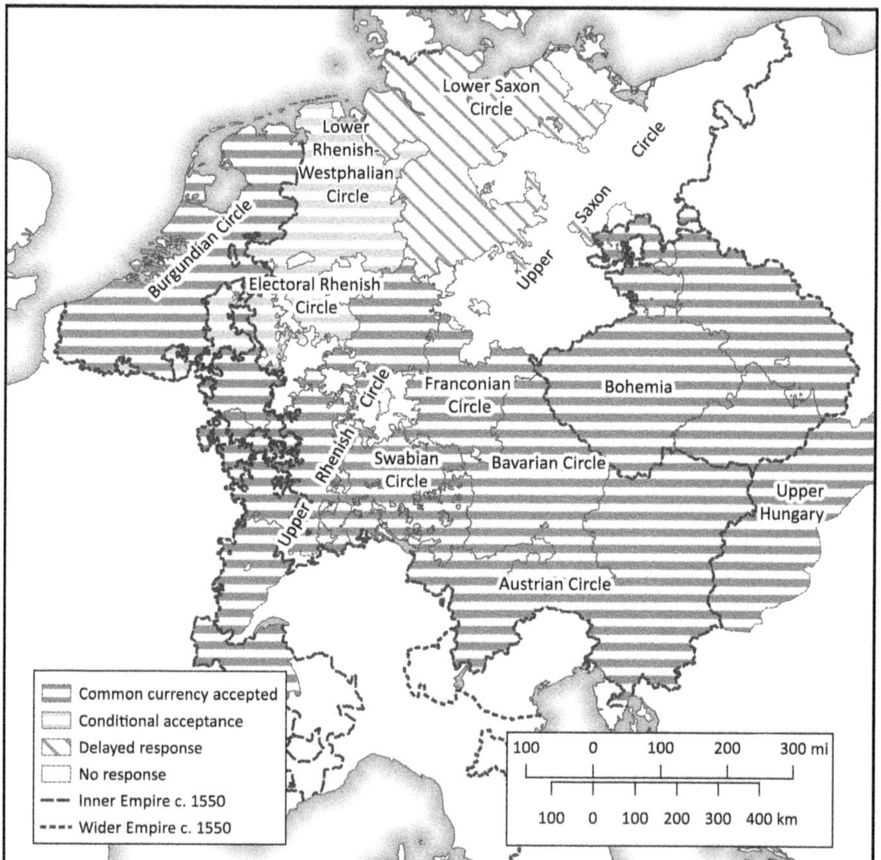

Map 6.1. The common currency-zone as of early 1552

> to publish and announce said ordinances to their subjects on the Monday after *Quasimodo Geniti* [25th of April 1552] and if such bills are likewise being accepted and obeyed by the neighbouring circles and in your Majesty's Lower Hereditary Lands, that is, in the Burgundian circle (as they did not doubt), that they would then employ all their resolve and industry to ensure that the currency bill is being observed among their subjects, too. Because if that is not the case, they fear that obeying the law will hardly be possible.[4]

The news from the Lower Saxon circle—none of whose members had attended the meetings in Speyer in 1549—was less good. Duke Henry of Braunschweig-Wolfenbüttel reported in March that only three estates had followed his summons to the circle-*Tag*. The delegates professed themselves insufficiently authorized to accept the Coinage and Probation Ordinances on behalf of their masters but agreed at least to reconvene in early April.[5] As it turned out, events were about to overtake them.

The process shows perfectly how the Empire was working in the mid-sixteenth century—and where it was not. Ideally, each of its interlocking levels of authority played its part in decision-making and implementing what had been decided, with the reaction of the Westphalian estates underlining the importance of a universal buy-in to the policy. There were frictions—typically caused by poor record keeping and lacking information—but by early modern standards and considering the complexity of the system it went into action reasonably smoothly in seven out of ten circles. The Lower Saxon circle was one exception, along with the Electoral Rhenish and Upper Saxon circles. From the latter two, Charles V's secretariat never registered responses. We will see further down why that was the case.

The bishop of Münster and the Duke of Jülich-Cleves-Berg had been quick to react, but some estates sprang into action even quicker. In late February 1551—when the general assay in Nuremberg had not even begun, and more than half a year before Charles V signed the currency bill—King Ferdinand issued an edict to his subjects in Bohemia. He announced that at the planned assay, 'it will probably be the case and happen that the better *Talers* so far minted will be valued at no more than 17 *Batzens* or 68 *Kreuzers* of the new common coinage', and warned his subjects to 'accept and spend the *Talers* . . . in such a way that after the end of the assay, and when the coins have been officially valued and the currency bill has been published, you will the better avoid and prevent harm and damage to yourselves'.[6] That sounded innocuous enough. In 1542, when the imperial diet had granted financial support for the defence of the Empire's south-eastern border against the

Ottoman Turks, Ferdinand had already valued the *Talers* sent by some estates at 68 *Kreuzers*;[7] so it might seem as if he now intended no more than to ease the introduction of the new common currency by minimizing the change this involved.

However, matters were more complicated. Ferdinand's edict failed to mention that the new common-currency *Kreuzers* contained less pure silver than the traditional Austrian *Kreuzers*. Based on bullion parity, Saxon *Talers* should not have been rated 68, but more than 70 new *Kreuzers*. It therefore seems likely that the edict was directed less at Ferdinand's Bohemian subjects than at the assayers about to gather in Nuremberg, and that the aim was to make sure they undervalued the *Taler*. The assayers took the hint: The report they submitted to the emperor at the end of May suggested to rate the *Taler* at 68 *Kreuzers*. The currency bill published in July adopted that value,[8] presenting consumers with a choice: For large transactions they could either use *Talers* or new imperial 72-*Kreuzers*-pieces. The incentives were clear: They would prefer the new pieces and melt *Talers*—whose value as bullion was higher than their legal value as coins—or sell them to a mint. From Charles V's perspective this was highly advantageous. To produce the new common coinage, raw material was needed, and *Talers* were made of high-quality silver that easily lent itself to that purpose. Still, there was another reason why their demise suited the emperor.

The background was that Maurice of Saxony was increasingly unhappy with the position in which he found himself since the Schmalkaldic War. To be sure, Charles V had transferred the Saxon electorship from John Frederick the Magnanimous to him and he had also got a good chunk of his cousin's lands. He had thereby not only advanced in rank among the imperial estates but had also strengthened his resource base. The downside was that by supporting the emperor against the Schmalkaldic League, he had ruined his reputation among the other Protestant estates of the Empire. That Charles refused to release Maurice's father-in-law Landgrave Philip of Hesse from captivity added insult to injury.[9] Finally, the new elector does not seem to have relished his role as the emperor's enforcer in North Germany either. He was thoroughly displeased—as were many other princes.

At the Diet-in-Arms in 1547–8, Charles V had tried to reform the Empire's constitution, aiming at strengthening his own role. This had failed, but with his Spanish troops, Spanish advisers, and at-best-halting German no one doubted his intention to finally teach the Germans how obedience was spelled in Spanish. His plan was now to replace King Ferdinand, who was his designated successor, with his son Philip. As emperor, the future Philip II of Spain would be able to draw on far more resources than Ferdinand—resources he could use to rein in the imperial estates. Philip spent part of 1550 and 1551 on a goodwill tour of the Empire, but as he drank no beer and was useless at jousting, the impression he left with the German princes was decidedly mixed. When Charles tried to force Maurice to back the 'Spanish Succession' by threatening to reinstate John Frederick as elector, he merely estranged his ally further.[10]

Margrave John of Brandenburg-Küstrin—another of the Protestant supporters of Charles from the Schmalkaldic War who was having second thoughts—began to look about for allies already in early 1550. The dukes of Mecklenburg and of Prussia—the latter outside the Empire and a Polish vassal, but with close cultural and family ties especially to Protestant Germany—proved willing.[11] Maurice was still on the emperor's side. However, he prepared his defection. In the winter of 1550–1, he contacted King Henry II of France to make sure of his backing. At the same time, he was recruiting troops and negotiating with mercenary leaders whom Charles had outlawed because they had fought on the Protestant side in the Schmalkaldic War. This could hardly be kept a secret. In fact, the emperor was soon warned, among others by his brother, of what was going on.[12]

Given the growing tensions between him and the elector of Saxony, it seems likely that undervaluing *Talers* served a second purpose besides providing the raw material for the new common currency. After all, *Talers* were the most prestigious product of the Saxon mints; they made a weighty contribution to Maurice's revenues. The seignorage probably accounted for between 10 and 20 per cent of his total income.[13] As we have seen, *Talers* were also the basis of Saxony's commercial prosperity and helped maintain its large non-peasant population. Driving them out of circulation would therefore not only politically damage the new elector's reputation but also weaken him economically. The surviving sources do not allow us to determine whether undervaluing the *Talers* contributed to the falling-out of the emperor and the Saxon elector, or whether Ferdinand—with Charles V in the background—manipulated the value of the *Talers* in response to this estrangement and to put pressure on Maurice. Still, there is no doubt that the emperor's monetary policy decisions in early 1551 made a rapprochement between him and the elector harder. The process of estrangement concluded in May 1551, when Maurice entered a formal alliance with the princes opposing Charles V—among them Albert Alcibiades of Brandenburg-Kulmbach, whose pillage master Silvester Raid would become.[14]

In March 1552, Maurice and his allies revolted. Charles, who had thrown all warnings to the wind, was caught unawares. When the 'War Princes' invaded the Tyrol, he fled across the Alps to Carinthia. The rebellion shook his rule to the core. It also threw the reform of the Empires' currencies into disarray. King Ferdinand, for example, who had meanwhile persuaded the territorial estates of Bohemia and Hungary to join the common-currency zone,[15] had prepared everything: The edict that was to announce the introduction of the new money was drafted to be published on 2 April 1552, and the bill itself, dated 1 April, was printed and ready for distribution.[16] With the revolt in full swing, none of this happened, all the more so as the emperor left negotiating a settlement with the rebels to his brother.

Ferdinand did this with great skill and foresight. Importantly, by 1552 his religious outlook had changed. Unlike his brother, he felt no longer bound to the heresy laws of Church and Empire and was therefore able to establish a fundamental political consensus not only with the majority of the estates but also the War Princes. This consensus allowed a provisional agreement in June 1552 where Protestants and Catholics accepted their respective vested rights and promised not to harass or make war on each other.[17] The next imperial diet in Augsburg 1555 amended and formalized the treaty as the 'Religious Peace of Augsburg' that became one of the fundamental laws of the Empire, an essential part of its constitution, and a safeguarded of its political stability. It allowed two generations of Catholics and Protestants to get along peacefully—in stark contrast to Western Europe, much of which became embroiled in wars over religion, sovereignty, or both.[18] Eventually, the provisions of the peace proved instrumental in keeping the Empire afloat for another 250 years. Charles V, however, would have none of this. Humiliated by having been put to flight, disgusted with Ferdinand's willingness to compromise, and having failed in all his religious and constitutional projects, he abdicated as emperor, renounced his other titles, and withdrew to a monastery in Spain.[19]

There were estates that had started minting the common currency before the Peace of Augsburg: Elector Joachim II of Brandenburg, Dukes Albert V of Bavaria and Christoph of Württemberg, the sons of John Frederick the Magnanimous (who may still have hoped that their branch of the family would regain the Saxon electorship), the bishops of Würzburg, Regensburg, and Chur, a number of imperial cities (mostly in Swabia), and, surprisingly, some of the towns of the Swiss Confederacy that had in no way been involved in decision-making (we will see further below why they did so). However, most estates bided their time. Some more adopted the common currency soon after 1555, but there were never more than 20 who did so.[20] Why not? After all, the currency bill had enjoyed wide support at the diet of 1550–1; so why was it not implemented everywhere once the princes' revolt was over and lasting peace had been established?

The causes of failure

King Ferdinand's experiences suggest part of the answer. The currency ordinance whose publication he had planned for April 1552 finally appeared four years later.[21] However, once that had happened it quickly became obvious that crying down the *Talers* to 68 *Kreuzers* did not work. An edict Ferdinand published in May 1556 conceded as much:

> Because the good golden and silver coins in our lands are bought up by foreigners at the value given them in the ordinance and are exported to neighbouring lands, where the currency bill and valuation are not yet in force, and are spent there with much profit, whilst conversely our subjects are forced to buy dearly abroad, but have to sell to their disadvantage at much lower prices within our lands: because of these and other important reasons we have been moved to suspend the said valuation until further notice.[22]

In Austria, *Talers* disappeared from circulation as intended, but they left the country rather than ending in the Austrian mints to be turned into 72-*Kreuzers*. Essentially, Ferdinand's edict admitted that the uncoordinated introduction of Charles V's common currency had failed.

Moreover, coordination failures had already beset the way the bill was designed. The currency conference in Speyer in 1549 had not managed to pass the bill on its own, but that was not a problem: The imperial diet could take over—and so it did. However, the diet of 1550–1 experienced a catastrophic failure of coordination that showed the Empire at its most dysfunctional. If we want to understand how this was possible, we must take a closer look at how the imperial estates who in Speyer had objected to the planned currency came to agree to the diet's decision to ask Charles V to publish the currency bill once the general assay in Nuremberg had finished.

These estates were Saxony, that had expressed its opposition to the project during the first meeting in spring 1549, and the Rhenish electors, who had done so at the second meeting in autumn.

There seem to be three reasons for this. For one thing, there was the pressure applied by Flersheim and Solms. Recall how the commissioners slammed the delegates of the Rhenish electors shortly before the opening of the diet of Augsburg in July 1550. This was effective; at the diet, opposition to the law drafted by the *Münztag* in Speyer immediately crumbled. Only two days after the talks had begun, the envoys of the elector Palatine declared that they were happy with the planned currency bill, while Trier stated that the draft prepared in Speyer should stand.[23]

Still, if the pressure under which the electoral delegates found themselves contributed to their change of mind, it is unlikely to have been the only reason. There were probably more systematic factors, one of which the Austrian delegates had mentioned already at the currency conference of spring 1549. There, Jacob Jonas and Thomas Behaim had warned against deferring the talks: Leaving without an agreement and reconvening later would do more harm than good because 'usually the matter is then taken up by new and mostly insufficiently experienced counsellors and delegates who are poorly informed about the issues at hand'.[24] This is what happened in 1550. Only two of the delegates of the Rhenish electors who had rejected the plan of a bimetallic currency in Speyer were also present at the diet of Augsburg: One accompanied the archbishop of Mainz, the other the one of Cologne—and these were the electors who stuck to their guns. By contrast, the electors of Trier and of the Palatinate were represented at the diet by counsellors new to monetary policies, inexperienced, and very likely poorly informed of what had been discussed in Speyer.[25] That they gave in more readily might have been expected.

Finally, the way decision-making was organized at imperial assemblies played a role. As we have seen in Chapter 3, the polling process used by the higher colleges (and by committees formed by members of several colleges) was good at generating agreement. It encouraged lower-ranking members to consent to suggestions made by higher-ranking earlier speakers whom they did not want to antagonize. Moreover, the bandwagon effect caused speakers to agree to measures the more readily, the larger the number of earlier speakers was who had already given their consent. If we want to see how this worked, the case of the Saxon delegates at the diet of Augsburg provides an excellent example. Elector Maurice had instructed his envoys—Drs Melchior von Ossa and Joachim von Kneutling, Magister Franciscus Kram, and the bailiff of the district of Leipzig Asmus von Könneritz—to reject the common currency.[26] That is what they did during the first meeting of the electors' college on 7 August. Ten days later (days filled with intensive discussions and some joint meetings with the princes' college) the Saxons had been brought round so far that they declared 'if the others thought it necessary, they would willingly promote what was pleasing to the emperor'. From then on, we see them constructively discussing the currency bill alongside the other delegates, asserting on 27 November that they 'did not want to distance themselves from the majority'.[27] Finally, on 14 February 1551, they put their signatures to the recess of the diet that instructed Charles V to publish the currency ordinance immediately after the planned general assay in Nuremberg.[28] The bandwagon had rolled its course.

The upshot was that the diet placed the emperor in an impossible position. Trier and the Palatinate may have been—at least for the moment—genuinely resigned to the bimetallic currency he favoured. To be sure, not only their delegates but also those of Mainz and Cologne explicitly agreed to asking the emperor to publish the currency bill.[29] Like electoral Saxony, they must have jumped on the bandwagon. Still, they seem to have continued to offer at least some resistance to bimetallism. This is the most likely reason why the version of the bill drafted at the diet of Augsburg in 1550 omitted the paragraph that concerned the equal value of Rhenish florin and silver 72-*Kreuzers*-piece, which the text discussed in Speyer in 1549 had contained.[30] The recess of the diet that summarized the results of the talks and instructed the emperor to publish the bill left the question open, too.

What was Charles supposed to do? If he did not want to directly go against the wishes of the diet, he had to publish the bill within a reasonably short period of time after the old and foreign money had been tested at Nuremberg. He could not do this without using his discretion to resolve the issue the diet had left open. He was aware of the pro-bimetallism position of the princes' college, along with the fact that at least some of the Rhenish electors opposed such a system.[31] Whichever choice he made, he must have known he would antagonize important estates. More than that: his decision would be his own and no one else's. Given the political setup of the Empire, this exposed it to being seen as illegitimate. After all, legitimate decisions required those expected to implement them to have been enmeshed in the procedures that governed how they were made. To what extent Charles was aware of this is doubtful. His advisers certainly argued that in

> cases of discord in the common affairs of the Holy Empire, when the estates fail to agree despite all their diligence, it is held that his Majesty as the head [of the Empire] is necessarily burdened with resolving the issue . . . Because otherwise it could not be known how or by whom those affairs and tasks of the Holy Empire that cannot bear a delay or deferral should be finally decided.[32]

In the end, Charles took the risk. He came out in favour of the option he himself and the princes' college preferred: bimetallism. The bill he published in July 1551 determined that silver coins from the 72- down to the 6-*Kreuzers*-piece were to be 'given and taken by everyone in sales, purchases and other transactions as legal tender in place of gold'.[33]

We have seen above that once a decision influenced by the bandwagon-effect has been made, the participants tend to realize that they have been talked into agreeing to something that goes against their own best interest. This is what happened after Charles V had published the Augsburg Coinage Ordinance of 1551. It explains why neither the Upper Saxon circle of the Empire (which was dominated by electoral Saxony) nor the Electoral Rheish circle responded to his request to report back to him on what they had done to publicize the ordinance among the estates of their circle. Following their lead, other estates that had always had their doubts about the bill refused to accept it, too, reducing Charles to pleading with them to put it into effect.[34] Hence, the bill did not merely fail because its implementation had been insufficiently coordinated (though this factor did indeed play a role, as King Ferdinand learnt in Austria). It also failed because the agreement reached at the diet of Augsburg in 1550–1 was incomplete (leaving an essential issue to the discretionary decision of the emperor, which undermined the bill's legitimacy) and superficial (being based on important estates jumping on the bandwagon, which meant that they agreed to decisions they were likely to rue later). By the time the imperial diet met in Regensburg in July 1556—not quite a year after the one in Augsburg that had passed the Religious Peace had closed—it was obvious that a new start was needed.

Compromise and consensus

Ferdinand I signals his willingness to compromise

It is no surprise that the diet returned to the currency issue—only to delegate it to another conference in Speyer that was to begin in June 1557.[35]

This meeting had a far more limited remit than the earlier ones. In 1549, the *Münztag* was expected not only to discuss a currency bill but to pass it without any further involvement of the imperial diet. This had not worked in the first place. Moreover, experiences with the implementation of the bill in the Lower Saxon, Electoral Rhenish, and Upper Saxon circles had driven home how important universal consent was. To achieve it, an assembly less well attended than an imperial diet would not be enough. Accordingly, at Regensburg the estates decided that the planned meeting in Speyer should merely discuss which mistakes had been made in 1549 and 1551, and how to avoid these in future. Also, estates unhappy with the currency bill should bring their concerns to the attention of the commissioners of King Ferdinand (who had not yet been raised as emperor). The results of the deliberations would then be made available to the next imperial diet.[36]

The conference duly convened in Speyer in June 1557. It proved to be relatively well attended, with 140 imperial estates having either sent their own delegations or authorized others to speak in their name.[37] At the first meeting the sparks flew. Minutes do not survive, but according to the report the electoral Saxon delegation sent home, 'the other envoys were initially minded upholding the currency bill' Charles V had published six years before. However, first the Saxons and the deputies of electoral Cologne and the Palatinate flatly denied that their masters had ever agreed to the bill. Then the chancellor of the elector of Mainz stated that the publication of the ordinance had never been authorized; it remained to be seen who had sent it to the publisher, 'but the chancellery of Mainz was inculpable in this'. The Saxon report claims this was the cue for almost all other deputies: They had not realized that the bill had not been passed unanimously; if they had known, their masters would not have agreed to it either, nor would they have started to issue coins in accordance with its regulations, 'and all confessed and stated that it would have been much better if this currency law and ordinance had never existed'.[38]

So much for the electoral Saxon view of what was going on. Other attendants had a more favourable impression. King Ferdinand, for example, had sent two new commissioners. Flersheim had died in 1552, and Ferdinand probably did not want to employ Solms, whom the estates associated with what they thought had been an attempt by Charles V to dominate the Empire militarily. Instead, he selected two of his counsellors, with his choice reflecting the more restricted remit of the meeting in Speyer: Hans Philipp Schad, who was responsible for the royal silverware, and Johann Ulrich

Zasius, a university-trained lawyer who, like Flersheim, was well connected, having attended many imperial diets of the later part of Charles V's reign.[39] The report Schad and Zasius sent home emphasized the constructive atmosphere in Speyer. They praised 'with what even-mindedness even those estates' had joined the talks, 'who at the recent imperial diet had sharply and with bitterness cried out about the bill and law and had emphasized the serious complaints they held against it'.[40]

The background to this were the discussions at the diet of 1555 that passed the Religious Peace of Augsburg. Back then, the Rhenish electors had argued that while Charles V's Augsburg Coinage Ordinance had been published, the electors had never 'accepted, affirmed, or confirmed it', 'wherefore said Coinage Ordinance was still defective and could not be considered a universally valid law of the Empire'. The electors also tried to put pressure on Ferdinand: If he did not accept the exceptions to bimetallism discussed in Worms in 1545—gold should have to be paid where either ancient custom or contractual clauses required payments in this metal—they were not authorized to get involved in any further talks.[41] In Speyer in 1549, about ten days after Flersheim and Solms had spelled out the implications of bimetallism, the envoys of the electors had reminded the conference of the idea discussed at the diet of Worms.[42] At that time, neither the princes' college nor the imperial commissioners had shown any interest in it. Now, however, after six years and much political turmoil, things had changed. Ferdinand was adamant that the currency bill of 1551 was valid law,[43] but showed himself open to compromise in the detail. After all, his imperial Majesty had authorized him to modify the bill:

> Considering the damage with which this disorder [in the monetary economy] threatened the whole German nation and the common man and the fact that even good coins would eventually be brought down by the import of poor foreign ones if the ordinance established *in anno* '51 was not actually implemented, he was willing to make use of his imperial Majesty's authority and accept that the diet's recess should note that the ordinance should stand, but with the clarification that in those cases listed by the electors one should not be bound to accept silver in place of gold.[44]

Nota bene, this was in September 1555, about half a year *before* Ferdinand published Charles V's ordinance in Austria—only for the king to learn within weeks that *Talers* were being exported rather than sold to the mint to be turned into 72-*Kreuzers*. When the diet of Regensburg met in the following summer, no one had the slightest reason to doubt his willingness to compromise. There, the need to approve further financial aids for the defence against the Ottomans and fruitless talks about religion delayed the discussion of the currency bill to the last week of the diet. By that point, it was obvious that an immediate decision would not be possible and that another coinage conference was needed.[45] The princes' college suggested that every imperial circle should send two representatives, but the electors prevailed with their idea to combine the planned conference with the audit of the imperial chamber court in Speyer that was due in the summer—a cost-saving measure, as Mainz pointed out in the electors' college.[46]

Abandoning bimetallism

Given this history, why did the delegates at the conference in Speyer in Summer 1557 act so surprised when they learnt that electoral Saxony and the Rhenish electors rejected Charles V's currency bill? At the diets of 1555 and 1556–7, the electors had made their stance clear enough, yet most attendants at the coinage conference of summer 1557 seem not to have been aware of this. The answer is probably again—like in the case of the capitulation of the electors of Trier and the Palatinate at the beginning of the diet of Augsburg in summer 1551—the lack of continuity among the delegates. The only attendants at the conference of 1557 who had also been present at one of the preceding diets were Jobst Tetzel and Johann Rudolf Ehinger. Tetzel—who had also been at the meetings in Speyer in 1549—represented Nuremberg. He had a lot to go for him: Being an entrepreneur who owned shares in a copper smelting works in Cuba he was familiar with trade and had an international outlook.[47] However, as an urban delegate he was kept out of most discussions and was relatively poorly informed. Ehinger had been joint delegate of several Swabian counts at the diet of Regensburg in 1556–7;[48] now, in Speyer, he represented all counts and barons on the imperial register.[49] As counts did not have a *viril* vote in the princes' college, we cannot be sure if he was present at the monetary policy discussions of the diet. All other delegates in Speyer were new, if not to monetary policy, then at least to the situation after King Ferdinand had signalled his willingness to compromise. Such a lack of continuity was a systematic weakness of policymaking in the Empire; its effects were evident at the start of the meeting in June 1557.

In any case, the conference was poorly prepared. The diet had invited all imperial estates unhappy with Charles V's coinage ordinance to submit their complaints beforehand, but none had done so. Improvising, the delegates decided to discuss the weak points of the ordinance based on its text, which at least some of them had brought with them (you can read their handwritten marginal notes on the copy of the Bavarian envoys).[50] What was apparently not improvised was the way discussions were arranged. Organizationally, the coinage conferences that had taken place in 1549 had mirrored an imperial diet, with the attendants sorting themselves into the three colleges of electors, princes, and cities. Now all talks took place in plenary sessions that were arranged like the meetings of the committees formed by many imperial assemblies in the preceding decades to prepare decisions concerning particularly tricky problems. That the colleges should not convene in 1557 had probably been agreed beforehand—at least, that is what Elector Augustus of Saxony (Maurice's brother and successor) implied when he called the conference a 'deputation or committee' in the instructions he gave his delegation. Of course, this does not mean that the discussions lacked structure. The polling process worked as usual, with Augustus telling his envoys that they and their colleagues from Mainz should take turns leading the questioning of the other delegates.[51]

In the discussions, the Rhenish electors maintained their previous stance. The delegates from electoral Saxony declared their master was willing to join the common currency if the nominal sum minted from one mark of pure silver was at least equal to the one now produced by the Saxon mints: a hardly veiled demand to adopt the Saxon *Taler*.[52] So far, nothing had changed. However, despite their outcry at the beginning of the talks, most delegates were still in favour of Charles V's currency bill if one condition was met: Everybody had to implement it. Obviously, Gresham's Law still spooked everyone, with the big fear being individual estates might undercut the new money and use it as raw material to produce their own debased copies. There were some strong and outspoken supporters of the bill, too: Electoral Brandenburg, which is no surprise given the sums Joachim II owed his creditors, and Bavaria and Württemberg—both likewise deep in dept—that were prominent among the princes (Table 5.1).[53] Once the conference got going, the delegates of the two duchies submitted memorials that made their stance plain. The texts also made the point explicit to which the majority had merely alluded: the need to prevent the trade in coinage and the breaking of coins. Obviously, the original motive that had fuelled the reform process had been overshadowed for some time by the aim of making it easier to service gold-denominated debts, but had survived in the background and still counted. In addition, both Bavaria and Württemberg pointed out they had spent a lot of resources minting the new money—investments that would be lost if there was another reform.[54]

Speaking of all who had not yet begun minting Charles V's common currency, the Bavarian memorial argued that, 'as his Roman royal Majesty [King Ferdinand] has graciously agreed to mitigate the bill and allow several exceptions, the Bavarian envoys opine that said electors, princes, and estates for their part may now approve the law like other obedient estates'.[55] This referred to the exceptions to bimetallism the electors demanded—and Ferdinand accepted—during the diet of Augsburg in 1555 to signal his willingness to compromise: Where ancient custom or explicit contractual clauses demanded payments in gold, it should not be possible to use the silver 72-*Kreuzers*-piece in place of the Rhenish florin. The Bavarians had a point. Ferdinand had offered to fulfil the demand of the electors; so why did not that settle the currency question once and for all?

In fact, the conference did recommend that the next imperial diet should amend the currency bill as suggested. Schad and Zasius received a summary of the discussions and of the content of the memorials Bavaria, Württemberg, and several other estates had submitted, and countered this with a report of their own where they stated that 'they agreed with the opinion of the deputies, counsellors, and envoys of the electors and other princes'.[56] However, the discussions brought to light a few other areas of disagreement that needed to be resolved. Most importantly, while most of the delegates were happy with the range of coins defined in the bill of 1551—a position the royal commissioners shared—a minority had other ideas. Some merely suggested that the 72-*Kreuzers*-piece should be subdivided into smaller units in a different way, others wanted to abandon this piece altogether and replace it with one whose value matched that of the *Usualgulden* or *Gulden* of account of 60 *Kreuzers*.[57] Probably because the latter point had been raised by the delegates of an elector—that of the Palatinate—Schad and Zasius felt they could not simply join the majority of the deputies at the conference. They decided to leave this issue to the next imperial diet.[58]

This was a wise decision; after all, the majority principle did not reign unchallenged. In fact, the topic had only recently gained new relevance. To speed up decision-making at the level of the Empire, the imperial diet of

1555 had created a new type of assembly called 'deputation diet', composed of the deputies of 16 estates: all six electors, eight princes, and two representatives of the cities. What the imperial diet had left open was whether deputation diets should form three colleges or rather plenary sessions. Predictably, when the new assembly first met in 1564 the issue became hotly contested.[59] On earlier occasions—for example during the coinage conference in autumn 1549—majority decisions made by cross-college committees had been accepted.[60] However, this had concerned questions like, for example, whether the Saxon small change should be adopted at the level of the Empire, where the electoral delegates had voted with the majority. Events since 1551 had made abundantly clear what happened when their masters opposed a decision the emperor had made based on a simple majority of the estates. Obviously, Schad and Zasius did not want to run the risk of something like this happening again.

Taken together with Ferdinand's willingness to compromise, the decisions his commissioners made in Speyer in 1557 let us glimpse the outlines of a new approach to monetary policies. Clearly this was at least in part the result of a learning process. Ferdinand had first-hand experience of his brother's political style and had had enough opportunities to watch its consequences unfold. If he was to succeed where Charles had failed it was essential to avoid undermining the legitimacy of the future currency during its planning stage. This required first, to leave contentious decisions to the appropriate forum where they were made in the time-honoured way, that is, to the imperial diet that made decisions within its three colleges. Second, unlike Charles V, Ferdinand realized that he had to achieve as broad a buy-in to the common currency project as possible, even if this meant that he could not have it all his way. For him, making politics meant reaching compromises. At the next diet, his strategy would pay off.

The new currency

At that diet—Augsburg again, from early March to mid-August 1559—Ferdinand, who by now was Emperor, and his counsellors made a valiant last stand for bimetallism. They argued that without clearly defining the value of coins made from both gold and silver—a matter 'on which this whole coinage issue rests'—it would be impossible to establish a stable currency.[61] In addition, the imperial counsellors raised a new point, turning one of the principal substantive arguments of the opponents of bimetallism—that depressing the value of gold would cause an outflow of the metal from the Empire—on its head:

> If one allows the Rhenish gold florin to appreciate freely and arbitrarily, other gold coins as for example ducats, crowns, and common gold guldens will certainly appreciate, too . . . Foreign rulers do not have silver mines but import silver or silver coin from Germany into their countries, in return exporting their gold . . . into the Empire. If they gain large and high values in the sale of their gold, they bring the more of it into Germany and export the good silver coin, all under the pretence of trade. In this way . . . the Empire is stripped of its good coinage. However, if one devalues gold, they will keep their gold or at least import less of it, or merchants will reexport it to purchase goods, and the good coin is left in the Empire.[62]

Ferdinand's counsellors may have expected this argument to resonate with a public used to treatises like Eberlin von Günzburg's, which we have examined in Chapter 2. The fear that the country would be denuded of coin was widespread. However, the fear concerned gold and silver alike—not for nothing did Luther call the imperial city of Frankfurt with its huge annual international fairs the hole through which Germany was drained of its silver *and* gold.[63] The imperial counsellors tried to persuade the attendants of the diet that silver was the more important metal—most debts were in silver, most tolls had to be paid in silver, and most money invested was silver—but this was a moot point.[64] In the absence of statistical data there was no way to tell if they were right. Their argument therefore fell flat, and the princes' college, that initially had wanted to maintain the fixed ratio between gold and silver, eventually joined the electors.[65]

The princes went further, not only abandoning bimetallism, but also the 72-*Kreuzers*-piece. Their college now adopted the position of the delegates of the elector Palatine wholesale: They favoured a silver *Gulden* of 60-*Kreuzers* and suggested a matching range of smaller denominations.[66] While minutes of the meetings of the colleges have survived, they are lacking in detail. We therefore do not know why the princes took this decision. Historians have speculated that it was a matter of convenience: After all, other countries had replaced their traditional top unit of account with a coin; like England in 1489, when the golden Sovereign, whose value matched £1 Sterling, was first minted. Other scholars referred to the interests of Emperor Ferdinand: By 1559, the Austrian–Upper German currency union had issued 60-*Kreuzers*-coins for some decades, so having a similarly structured Empire-wide currency would be an advantage. A further point was that replacing the 72- with a 60-*Kreuzers*-piece would make a bimetallic system look less obvious than if the top gold and silver units had the same initial nominal value.[67]

All these motives sound plausible. However, there is a further reason that historians have not considered. At the coinage conference in Speyer, the envoys of the Palatinate had argued that coins appreciated more easily the larger they were, and that 60 *Kreuzers* was a high enough value for the largest piece.[68] They may have thought of the *Taler* that was commonly traded at a high premium, but there is no reason why this would necessarily apply to other, similarly large coins. Why, for example, should a 72-*Kreuzers*-piece have circulated at a premium? Or if it did—maybe because the imperial estates issued a too large quantity of small change—why should the 36-, 12- and 6-*Kreuzers*-coins not have also appreciated, given that they contained proportionally as much pure silver as the largest unit? Still, it is possible that the committee at the diet of 1559 was convinced by the argument put forward by the delegates of the Palatinate. If that was the case, their interest in preserving order prevailed—as we have seen, in monetary affairs order meant that coins were used at the value the authorities had given them, rather than at that established on the market. 'Whole, correct, orderly, and good payments' of the kind the imperial commissioners had tried to make possible in 1549—payments where 'one piece fits the other in an orderly fashion with no rests and no need to use fractions'[69]—would be impossible when the values of coins of the same currency were shifting. Having a currency where the numerical ratio between the several units was fixed reduced the costs—for example, the time—needed to agree on sales and purchases; in modern terms, it reduced transaction costs, and this was a crucial advantage.

In any case, a cross-college committee that the diet constituted accepted the suggestions the princes' college had made. The committee also came out in favour of maintaining the monetary standard enshrined in Charles V's coinage ordinance: The total nominal value of coins to be struck from one mark of pure silver was to remain unchanged. Considering that since 1551 some estates had invested a lot in producing the new coinage, this was seen as an important advantage. As for the value of gold, the committee tried to strike a compromise between what the coinage conference of 1557 had recommended and what the imperial counsellors wished. They admitted only one exception to the legal tender-function of silver coin: Debts denominated in gold should be serviced in gold 'unless someone willingly agrees to accept silver coin in place of gold. This is what the majority decided.'[70] There is no evidence for why they retained this exception rather than retaining the one that referred to the payment of gold in accordance with ancient custom, which would have allowed the electors on the Rhine to continue collecting their tolls in gold (or to demand a premium if traders paid silver). We are so poorly informed about the discussions within the committee that we cannot even tell why they recommended a fixed value of the Rhenish florin of 75 *Kreuzers* in the same paragraph where they argued that this should be the maximum value.[71]

What we know is that the diet eventually decided on a new compromise. On the one hand, the currency bill on which it agreed defined a maximum value of the Rhenish florin—which was to be slightly debased—of 75 *Kreuzers*, clearly stating that everybody was free to give or take it at a lower rate.[72] This took the further appreciation of the florin since 1551 into account (towards the end of the 1550s it was occasionally traded at 75 *Kreuzers*),[73] at the same time making it more profitable to produce, so that more florins would enter circulation. On the other hand, the diet determined that the imperial silver coins, ranging from the 60-*Kreuzers*-piece called the silver *Gulden* down to the individual *Kreuzer*, should be Empire-wide legal tender (Plate 6.1). 'However, payments that have been denominated on gold, likewise those that in future will be denominated in gold and are agreed and contracted accordingly, and other payments that according to ancient custom are made in gold are not affected but reserved.'[74] In most other respects, the 'Second Augsburg Coinage Ordinance', as the currency bill of 1559 became known, closely resembled its forerunner of 1551. It allowed fewer regional small-change types that were to supplement the Empire-wide larger coins, but contained the same list of old and foreign coins which it rated at the same values—values the general assay in Nuremberg in spring 1551 had originally established. It also again valued the Saxon *Taler* at 68 *Kreuzers* and again declared that it should no longer be minted.[75]

The electors on the Rhine had won—in a way. They could continue to define the custom dues in gold, but if they collected them in silver, the exchange rate to which they could drive up the Rhenish florin was capped at 75 *Kreuzers*. If the electors were the winners of the whole tortuous political process, or at least came close to winning, who were the losers? The

Plate 6.1. Imperial silver *Gulden* (60 *Kreuzers*), Augsburg 1574
© Fritz Rudolf Künker GmbH & Co. KG, Osnabrück (with kind permission).

indebted princes had to give up their dream of using a bimetallic currency to make servicing their obligations easier. However, this had never been their original aim. It had been an argument of the imperial commissioners at the coinage conference of autumn 1549 that the princes found attractive and that for some time may have helped to convince waverers of the utility of the common currency. However, in the background the original aim—preventing the trade in coinage, the breaking of coins, and the proliferation of underweight side-strikes, in short, avoiding the effects of Gresham's Law—had continued to exert its influence. This was the aim on which all estates could agree and the motive that eventually prevailed.

Ferdinand's compromise was widely accepted. This was not only because it was a compromise, that is, a solution that went a long way towards satisfying several interest groups without giving anyone everything they had asked for; it was also because he proceeded more cautiously than his brother had done in the early 1550s. He did not just ask the estates to pass a draft of the currency bill whose legitimacy some questioned because, allegedly, too few estates had been involved in discussing it. Neither did he make any decisions that were not explicitly backed by the imperial diet, as Charles V had done when he overruled the objections of some electors and adopted a bimetallic system, evidently pursuing motives unrelated to the need to deal with the consequences of Gresham's Law. Rather, Ferdinand focused on as broad a consensus as possible, and to make sure that there were no objections he had the new ordinance published at the seat of the highest-ranking elector, the archbishop of Mainz. Five weeks after the end of the diet of Augsburg in July 1559, the bill appeared in print.[76]

There were some objections, though. Elector Augustus of Saxony registered his formal protest against the Second Augsburg Ordinance with the Empire's chancellery, claiming (as usual) that adopting the common coinage implied a debasement that would harm Saxony's silver mines and that the Saxon regional diet would reject.[77] However, during the discussions at the diet that passed the ordinance, the Rhenish electors had already signalled that they were expecting Saxony to give in once the bill was implemented.[78] In fact, Augustus had already begun to work towards a face-saving solution. In September 1558, he had slightly debased the *Taler* so that its intrinsic value came closer to its official value of 68 *Kreuzers*.[79] Then, in 1566, the imperial diet made Augustus an offer he could not reject. In an amendment to the bill of 1559, the diet no longer demanded that *Talers* should be demonetized. Rather, its recess stated that 'experience has shown that because in many places and lands of the German nation contracts and agreements are concluded in the said *Talers*, present conditions do not allow excluding them from the range of other common coins of the Holy Empire'. *Talers* should accordingly become part of the common currency next to the silver *Gulden*, if Elector Augustus agreed to make one final concession: a further small debasement.[80]

This he did—although, he had little choice. The *Taler*-standard the imperial diet adopted in 1566 matched the one other imperial estates (for example, the duke of Braunschweig-Lünburg) had used in the years before 1559.[81] This standard was now acknowledged and enshrined in imperial law. If Augustus did not follow suit, the consequences would be obvious: His own *Talers* would end up in the melting pots of other estates, to be used as raw material for what were in effect base imitations of his originals—but imitations that enjoyed all legitimacy the Empire was able to bestow on them. In short, having learnt all there was to learn about the trade in coinage, the breaking of coins, and the minting of side-strikes, the imperial diet

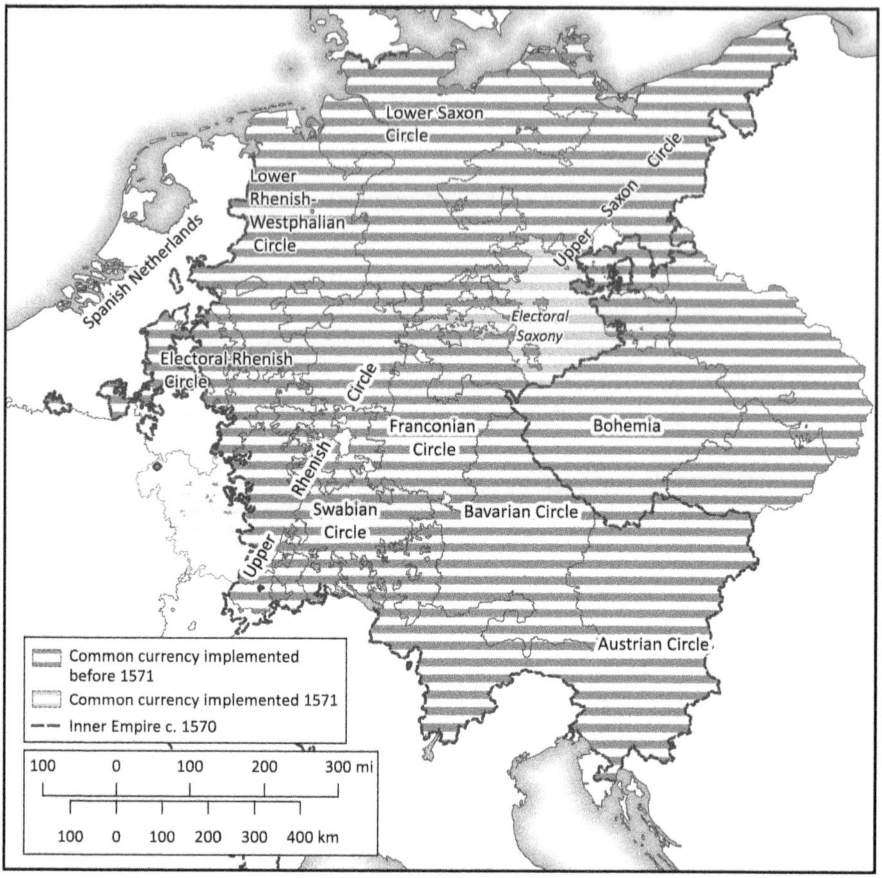

Map 6.2. The common currency-zone in 1571

weaponized Gresham's Law to force dissenters into line. This worked. Without great fanfare the Saxon elector capitulated and adopted the common coinage in 1571 (Map 6.2).[82]

The new money in practice

New rules and their enforcement

Contemporaries and later observers praised this outcome. In 1571, an anonymous author noted that Ferdinand's bill and its amendment of 1566 were 'imposing and well considered' and could 'hardly be improved'; twenty years later, another admitted that while they had met some opposition ('like all good proposals'), they took all relevant circumstances into account and were 'highly useful measures'.[83] There were weak points: For example, the integration of the Habsburg Low Countries that the estates had repeatedly demanded failed.[84] This caused problems we will look at further along. Still, in monetary terms, the Empire had never been as coherent and unified as it was after the reforms of 1559 and 1566.

In 1560, almost 150 authorities within the Empire were minting: about 110 imperial estates from the large electorates of Brandenburg and the duchies of Bavaria, down to the tiny imperial abbeys of Corvey and cities like Isny. This was along with 37 other entities: from important towns like Braunschweig and Erfurt to backwaters like Berlin.[85] For the common currency to work, all of these authorities had to cooperate, maintaining the imperial standard. This required solving the collective action problem examined in Chapter 3: After all, each individual authority faced incentives to increase its revenues by issuing underweight money, but if one did so, there was the risk that the trade in coinage with all its unpleasant consequences would restart—consequences that included rounds of competitive debasements such as those seen during the first half of the sixteenth century among the rulers and towns that minted *Batzens* and *Maria Groschens*. The question was, how could this be avoided?

To explain why no government has ever relied solely on force to make sure that people obey its laws and directives, historians stress the importance of legitimacy, and when it comes to premodern rule the binding power of rituals and ceremonies. Both are valid points. Many of the imperial estates issuing money in the 1560s had been directly enmeshed in the procedures that governed how the diet drafted and passed the Coinage Ordinance of 1559 and its amendment seven years later, and many of these procedures did have a ceremonial or ritual component. These estates would certainly not deny the legitimacy of the bills. However, emperor and estates did not solely rely on this factor when implementing the laws. Rather, they started out from the assumption that if left unconstrained, minting authorities would give in to the temptation to undercut the imperial standard, and that constraints would therefore have to be introduced. If such constraints were not to be dead letters, they had to be supplemented by selective incentives—specifically by penalties for rule breakers. Both the Coinage

Ordinance itself and the Probation Ordinance that supplemented it provided such incentives.

One fundamental issue was the way the production of coins was financed. In the late Middle Ages, rulers often outsourced their mints. For example, the French government saved the initial outlay needed to run a mint by auctioning off the right to issue coins of a prescribed standard to the highest bidder; this was normally done for a year at a time. In fifteenth-century Germany, four to six years were common.[86] Often, the successful bidders—the mint farmers—seem to have been the mint masters themselves who had a hand in the trade with precious metals. Charles V's currency bill of 1551 prohibited the practice; this was one of the complaints the delegates of the elector of Trier raised against the ordinance during the conference in Speyer in 1557.[87] On that occasion, the envoys of Württemberg summarized the common objections to mint farming: They considered it 'most harmful and serving to nothing but to allow the mint masters to look to their self-interest and hinder the common weal, as daily experience has—with all due respect—shown almost everywhere'.[88] Mint farmers were obviously tempted to debase the coinage without the government's knowledge, thereby increasing their share in the profit. Calling a practice 'self-interested', as the Württembergers did, was typically sufficient to close the matter, and that was also the case here. Ferdinand's amended currency bill of 1559 prohibited outsourcing mints just as its predecessor had done.[89]

A mint's financial autonomy, implied by the practice of mint farming, made governmental supervision harder. However, in principle, mint masters working as government officials faced the same incentives as mint farmers. Their wage consisted of a share of the coins they produced, and this could be increased by clandestinely debasing the coinage. In the late Middle Ages, rulers had begun to realize that supervising mints was necessary and had begun to appoint officials tasked with checking their mint-masters' work: assayers like those employed by large commercial centres such as Augsburg.[90] However, not every ruler had done so. Most were struggling to make do with their regular revenues, and having to pay the salary of another official was something that particularly poor ones tried to avoid.[91] Now, the Probation Ordinance made having a technical supervisor mandatory; moreover, it closely regulated what this official had to do. An essential part was checking that the alloy that the mint master prepared contained the correct proportion of pure gold, silver, and base metal, and that the coins minted from it had the correct weight.[92]

So far, the two ordinances did not deviate from tried and tested practices. However, the emperor and estates realized that this was not enough. After all, mint masters and their supervisors faced incentives to collude: They could agree on a debasement, share the profits, and no one would be the wiser. The Probation Ordinance prohibited this,[93] but how could it be prevented? It was this problem to which the imperial diet found a solution that was not only innovative and effective, but ideally suited to a decentralized polity like the Empire. It would shape its monetary policies for centuries. Phrased in the ceremonial language of the time, the relevant paragraph of Ferdinand's bill read:

> So that Our and the Holy Empire's Coinage Ordinance is obeyed and observed the more strictly, the minting authorities in each of the Holy Empire's circles shall ordain that common probation diets and tests of the common imperial coins shall be held twice every year... for which reason we have ordered a particular Probation Ordinance to be set up. We also wish that soon after this imperial edict has been published, each circle's minting authorities agree on a common place to meet where the first probation shall be held on the first day of May and the second on the following first of October, as defined in said our Probation Ordinance.[94]

Making the circles responsible for supervising the coinage was a master stroke. As we have seen, they had been created at the beginning of the sixteenth century to help with the enforcement of internal peace, and there had been earlier attempts to utilize them in the context of monetary policies: Charles V drew on the circles to implement the Ordinances of 1551, and we have seen that this worked reasonably well. The Probation Ordinance of 1559 ordered every imperial estate issuing coins to send one or two counsellors experienced in monetary politics together with its mint master and assayer to the probation diet of its circle; estates that failed to do so three times were to forfeit their right to mint.[95] Later imperial assemblies added a few more provisions: Each circle was to shut down all except three or four mints, and neighbouring circles were to 'correspond', that is, to cooperate in currency questions, holding, for example, joint probation diets.[96] The assayers of the estates had to bring samples of every batch of coins minted since the last meeting—samples marked with the date they had been produced. These were then analysed in the presence of all counsellors, mint masters, and other assayers. If they did not bring specimens of coins they had produced, this would likely be noticed. The crucial provision was that estates which were not minting were required to attend the probation diets, too.[97] This was essential: After all, minting estates could try to conceal debased coins that they had issued from the probation diet. However, estates that did not mint—that entirely depended on the money produced by their neighbours—faced strong incentives to report the producers of underweight coins to the circle authorities and to make sure that the sanctions defined by the Coinage and Probation Ordinances were applied. As a solution to the problem of providing selective incentives, requiring estates that did not mint to attend the probation diets was nothing short of brilliant.

In recent years, historians have begun to examine in detail how well the circles performed. The Lower Saxon circle has received special attention—it was the only one not represented at either of the two currency conferences in Speyer in 1549 (Map 3.2), and we have seen that the Lower Saxon estates hesitated when summoned to implement the Coinage Ordinance in early 1552. After the imperial diet had passed the bills of 1559, there was also trouble. Like seven years before, the emperor employed the circles to make the content of the bill known among the estates (including those that had not attended the diet) and the wider population.[98] Where the Lower Saxon circle was concerned, the process suffered from the same problems as in 1551 and 1552: The imperial chancellery did not know who the directors of the circle were and sent copies of the bills to Archbishop George of Bremen instead of Archbishop Sigmund of Magdeburg.[99] This was a minor glitch. What was more important was that once the circle diet convened, the Lower Saxon estates refused to implement the Coinage and Probation Ordinances. In 1564, the emperor insisted again, but to no avail. This changed only once the imperial diet had accepted the *Taler* as part of the Empire-wide common currency. In 1568, the Lower Saxon estates agreed to implement the amended version of the laws passed nine years before.[100] From then on, the common currency was as well managed in Lower Saxony as it was further south, for example in Bavaria, Franconia, or Swabia.

Probation diets did not hesitate to censure the estates if deficiencies came to light. For example, at an Upper Saxon diet held in December 1571 in Jüterbog (close to the border between electoral Brandenburg and Saxony) it was noted that

> a mint master expelled from the Lower Saxon circle is operating an illicit mint on behalf of counts Volrath and Charles of Mansfeld, where good coins are being melted and turned into bad and poor ones, so that at that place the Imperial Coinage Ordinance is being violated in many ways.[101]

The probation diet decided not only to notify Emperor Maximilian II—Ferdinand's son and successor—but also to call on the director of the Upper Saxon circle, Elector Augustus of Saxony, to intervene.[102] In 1572, Saxon officials destroyed the illicit mint and arrested its staff.[103] Moreover, when the circle implemented the decision of the imperial diet to shut down all except three or four of its mints, they chose Leipzig, Berlin, and Stettin (Szczecin), leaving the counts of Mansfeld empty-handed—despite the counts controlling one of the most important silver mining districts of the Empire.[104] Other circles proceeded in a similar way, with the Lower Rhenish Westphalian one choosing Cologne, Aachen, Münster, and Emden—later supplemented by Cambrai—as their common mints. The Franconian circle chose Würzburg, Schwabach, Wertheim, and Nuremberg, and so on.[105]

Foreign money

As we have seen, the common currency enjoyed wide approval and esteem, but this does not mean that people were unaware of its shortcomings. In the early 1570s an anonymous author complained about the continued export of coin from the Empire,[106] and an equally anonymous memorial suggested that the 'foremost main cause of all troubles that at the present time arise in the coinage' was that 'the low-value and regional coins are minted much and in too large numbers whereas the good large species are being broken and reminted as *Pfennigs* and similar lowly types'.[107] In short, it seemed nothing much had changed. Or had it?

The Empire's passive balance of trade meant that there was no alternative to exporting money. Unless the country began selling greater quantities or higher values of goods abroad (or conversely, reduced its imports) this would not change. Bullionists who equated their country's prosperity with its stock of precious metal may have worried, but there was no reason why an outflow of the Empire's money in exchange for imported goods should have destabilized its currency. However, there was more to it. The Netherlands with their growing dependence on the import of grain, cattle, and other food turned out to be a serious problem.

During the run-up to the publication of the imperial coinage ordinances, many estates had repeatedly demanded the integration of the Burgundian circle of the Empire. At the meeting in Speyer in autumn 1549, the Burgundian envoys had been positive about this and accordingly, Charles V's ordinance of 1551 applied to the Netherlands too, granting them one of the regional small-change systems tied to common currency.[108] However, by the end of the 1550s the situation had changed. Charles V had abdicated and died. His son Philip had inherited the Netherlands together with Spain and the Italian possessions of the Habsburgs. He ruled them in an uneasy relationship with the emperor, his uncle Ferdinand. This complicated the issue so much that the Coinage Ordinance of 1559 omitted the Burgundian circle, though this was no more than a pragmatic decision intended to get the bill over the line. No one assumed that it would be the last word. During the imperial diet of 1566—the one that decided to legalize the *Taler*—the envoys of Burgundy declared they were willing to mint 'in accordance' with Ferdinand's currency bill and that they would contact the Lower Rhenish Westphalian circle to make the necessary arrangements. They never did.[109]

In previous decades, the Low Countries had covered part of their balance of trade deficit by using underweight imitations of the Rhenish florin to purchase the imports on which they depended. Now, the imperial currency offered an alternative. Like the German lands, the Low Countries used the *Gulden* (*guilder*) as a unit of account, and like Austria and the estates joined to it in a currency union since 1535, they began minting their *Gulden* as a coin. The problem was that this Burgundian Carolus-*guilder*—named in honour of Charles V—contained roughly 16 per cent less pure silver than its counterpart introduced by Ferdinand's bill of 1559 (Table A.2). From the perspective of the Netherlands, the 60-*Kreuzers*-piece was perfectly suited as raw material for Carolus-*guilders*, which could then be used to purchase goods in the Empire. Once the *Taler* was made part of the common currency in 1566, the Netherlands also began imitating it. The *Krujsrijksdaalder* (*Circle Imperial Taler*—the name referred to the Burgundian circle) introduced in 1567 contained almost 7 per cent less pure silver than genuine Imperial *Talers*, while the *Staten-Daalder*—minted ten years later by some of the provinces that rebelled against Spain—contained 12 per cent less silver.[110] The imperial circle harmed most by these practices was the Lower Rhenish Westphalian one—the direct eastern neighbour of the Netherlands. The circle had formally adopted the imperial currency in 1566,[111] but neither its diet nor any other imperial assembly ever succeeded in persuading the Spanish Netherlands—and far less the anti-Spanish rebels in the northern provinces—to cooperate in monetary policies.[112]

The question was, of course, what the Empire could do about this. As the archbishop of Salzburg had pointed out in 1559, monitoring the borders was impossible.[113] Given the Empire's decentralized constitution this seems obvious, but it is likely that a strong central authority would have been no more effective in keeping foreign money out of circulation. This, at least, is what a comparison with other countries of the time would suggest. England, for example, fared no better, as a report probably authored by William Smith, secretary to Lord Protector Somerset, in 1549 shows. The report complained about foreign merchants and

> coine made beyond the seas, like in all thinges to oure coine, which they brought ouer in heapes; and whan they see that esteemede as siluer, thei bringe that for oure commodities . . . And the stuffe is good cheape that they make yt off.[114]

In France in the 1560s foreign coins proved so popular that they generally circulated at a premium.[115] When in 1640–2, the French crown ordered Spanish, English, Dutch, German, and Italian coins to be withdrawn and reissued as French money, they collected gold to a value of 45 million *livres*. This alone matched 20 per cent of the total French quantity of money, and we do not know how much foreign silver was not reminted.[116] Monitoring cross-border circulation required resources that even rulers such as the kings of England and France did not have or want to spend. The Empire could not do so either.

Small change

The other problem contemporaries identified was the minting of large quantities of small change and the appreciation of the larger pieces that began to circulate at a premium.[117] Despite being one of the earliest currencies that used coins marked with their face values in Arabic numerals—from the silver *Gulden*, that showed '60' (60 *Kreuzers*) as its value, down to the 1-*Kreuzer*-piece, that showed a '1' (Plate 6.1)—neither the silver *Gulden* nor the *Taler* were consistently traded at their defined values (Table 6.1[118]).

Similar things had happened before. You recall that the Saxon *Taler* was minted as a 21-*Groschens*-piece but was typically traded at 24 *Groschens*. The Austrian silver *Gulden* appreciated, too, though less strongly. Like its successor, the imperial silver *Gulden*, it was supposed to be a 60-*Kreuzers*-piece; by

Table 6.1. *Taler* and *Gulden* rates in small change, 1565–1619

	Taler				*Gulden*		
	White *Pfennig*	*Groschen*	*Kreuzer*	*Schilling*	White *Pfennig*	*Groschen*	*Kreuzer*
1565–69			69.0	29.1		21.0	60.0
1570–74		24.0	67.0	30.9	27.0	21.0	
1575–79			72.2	31.0			
1580–84	32.6		70.7	32.0			
1585–89	34.0		71.4	34.0			60.0
1590–94	35.5		72.0	37.0	27.0		62.0
1595–99	36.3		73.4	38.0			64.0
1600–04	37.3	25.0	75.0	39.0			64.4
1605–09	39.4	27.1	79.1	38.6			68.4
1610–14	38.1	29.9	85.4	38.8		22.5	75.1
1615–19	41.1	32.1	89.9	42.6			80.1

the late 1530s people traded it at 64 *Kreuzers*.[119] The cause of the rising rates seems to have been a strong demand for a reliable alternative to the Rhenish florin; the consequence was an increase in the costs consumers faced when they negotiated purchases and sales: Rather than being able to rely on specific monetary units having stable values, everyone had to collect information on the current 'exchange rates' between *Talers*, *Guldens*, and their subunits before being able to conclude a contract.

Next to strong demand, one other factor drove the rates of *Talers* and *Guldens* up—a factor of which sixteenth-century coinage experts were well aware and that has received much attention from modern historians and economists.[120] The issue is straightforward. Relative to the total nominal value minted, the costs of producing small change and large coins differed, with the wages paid to the mint personnel playing the decisive role. Take the 2-*Kreuzers*-piece introduced by Emperor Ferdinand's bill of 1559. The amount of work needed to produce one such coin was practically the same as that needed to mint a silver *Gulden* whose official value was 60 *Kreuzers*. In other words: if you focused on issuing *Guldens* rather than 2-*Kreuzers*, you could produce 30 times as much money using broadly the same effort and bearing the same labour costs. The problem was that most minting authorities left it to their mints—which in practice meant, to their mint masters—to decide which coins they wanted to issue, and the mint masters often followed a simple calculus: As the Protestant poet Burkhard Waldis, who was also a metal expert, put it in a memorandum on monetary policies he compiled in 1532: 'Whenever they may mint more than one type of coin, they mint that one most which allows them to make the best profit.'[121]

Under such circumstances, mints faced no incentives to supply the market with small coins. This explains why, for example, Elizabethan England was permanently suffering from a shortage of small change.[122] Unlike the English crown, most authorities addressed the problem by reducing the pure silver content of small coins. Their aim was offsetting the higher labour costs of minting them with lower costs for the bullion needed as raw material. This turned small coins into official tokens—coins that were far more overvalued relative to their bullion content than the larger pieces of their currency. In the Empire, both the Coinage Ordinances of 1551 and its successor of 1559 applied this principle. In 1551, the line between full-bodied coins and small-change was drawn between the 6- and 3-*Kreuzers*-pieces, while eight years later anything below the value of 5 *Kreuzers* was a token. Such a policy was a balancing act, though. If you failed to lower the pure silver content of small change sufficiently, producing it was still so expensive that your mint would focus on issuing the larger pieces; if you reduced it too much, the markets would be swamped with small change.

During the meeting in Speyer in June and July 1557 some participants complained about the large numbers of 3-*Kreuzers* that had entered circulation mostly from Austria, but also from the Swiss Confederacy. The delegates from Württemberg even claimed that large pieces such as the 72-*Kreuzers* were being broken to be turned into this type of small change.[123] Evidently, the Ordinance of 1551 missed the correct balance of labour and silver costs, overvaluing small change too much relative to its bullion content. The Swiss cantons seem to have viewed this as an excellent chance to make a profit, producing 3-*Kreuzers* to buy up high-value 72-*Kreuzers* that they could use as raw material for yet more small change. As for Austria, King Ferdinand's commissioners in Speyer claimed he had never minted more 3-*Kreuzers* than necessary to pay the troops defending the country against 'the hereditary enemy of Christianity, the Turk'—but who was to tell if that was true?[124]

If the imperial estates had been able to force consumers to use coins at their face value, the consequence of the flood of 3-*Kreuzers* would have been that everybody would have used them for all transactions, withholding the larger coins. This would have happened as soon as the overvaluation of small change became known. However, no authority in the Empire was able to monitor markets closely enough to achieve this. What happened was rather that consumers began trading large, full-bodied coins at a premium.[125] This development was mirrored by that of the decades after 1559: not, however, because the Ordinance passed in that year overvalued small change too much. On the contrary. The currency committee convened at the diet of that year specifically recommended that the pure silver content of coins below the value of 5 *Kreuzers* should be set so high that no one would be tempted to issue small change only.[126] As it turned out, they missed the mark again. We can see this clearly because both the ordinance of 1551 and the one of 1559 permitted minting regional small-change types that were to circulate next to the Empire-wide coins, so that there is a broad range of overvalued token coins.

Figure 6.1 shows that coins were the more strongly overvalued the smaller they were. This helped covering the relatively higher labour costs their production involved. The trend lines also show a clear difference between the two bills, with the one of 1551 overvaluing small change too much and that of 1559 not enough. This explains why estates such as electoral Saxony (once it had joined the common currency zone in 1571), hardly minted any small change at all.[127] Elsewhere—for example, in the Lower Rhineland and

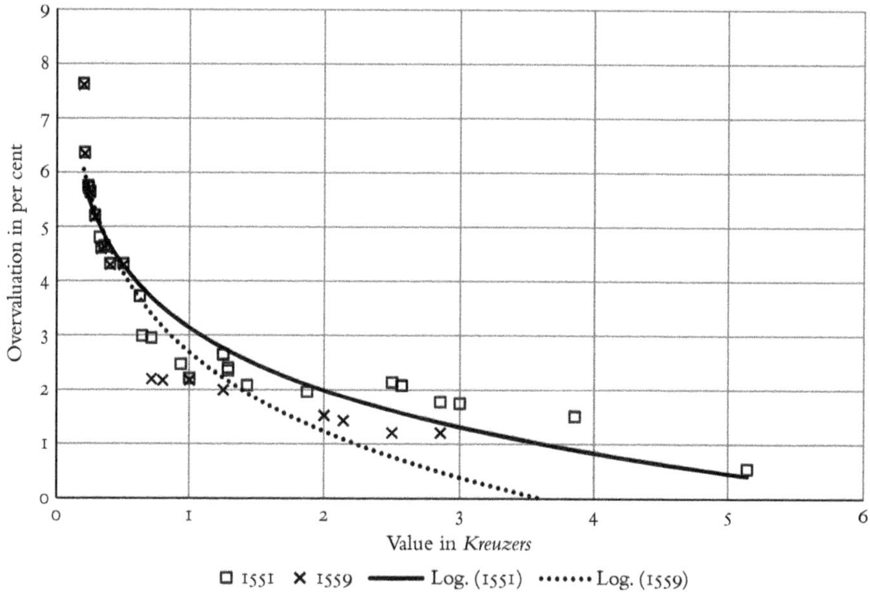

Figure 6.1. Overvaluation of small change relative to the large coins, 1551 and 1559

Westphalia—the imperial circles coordinated the response, agreeing on a concerted debasement of their regional small change.[128] This policy fuelled the appreciation of the imperial *Taler* and silver *Gulden*.[129]

All this happened despite the estates having been aware of the problem and thought about solutions for decades. In 1539, for example, Thomas Behaim, the director of the Austrian mints who accompanied King Ferdinand's vice-chancellor Jacob Jonas to the currency conferences in Speyer ten years later, recommended corporal punishments and fines to stabilize the value of the Upper-German silver *Gulden* in small change.[130] In Speyer, he and the other delegates agreed to a better thought-through measure. Following the example of a law issued in 1528 in Nuremberg, they tried to prevent the appreciation of the 72-*Kreuzers*-piece they were planning by restricting the legal tender function of overvalued small change.[131] The bill of 1551 determined that consumers needed to accept *Pfennigs* only in payments up to a value of 10 *Guldens* of account; for all larger sums they could insist on being paid in large coin.[132] Why this concerned *Pfennigs* only is a mystery. At any rate, the ordinance of 1559 was more precise: There, the provision applied to all coins below the value of 5 *Kreuzers*, which consumers had to accept in payments up to a maximum of 25 *Guldens*.[133]

As the economist Gustav Schmoller stressed 120 years ago, this was one of the earliest instances of a modern small-change policy (modern by nineteenth-century standards, when money was still based on precious metal).[134] Such a policy aimed at giving merchants, who sold raw materials to a mint, an incentive to insist on being paid in large, full-bodied coins. The hope was mints would then restrict their small-change output, and as a result large coins would no longer appreciate. This all sounded sensible and achievable. Still, it did not work.

Another point Schmoller raised helps to explain why it did not. If the Empire's currency bill of 1559 restricted the legal tender-function of small change to payments up to a certain amount, it should just as well have been possible to issue coins below 5 *Kreuzers* as coppers—that is, without any admixture of silver at all.[135] This would have drastically reduced the costs of producing small change, while larger coins would still have entered circulation in sufficient numbers. This is because no merchant would have been willing to supply any mint with raw material in exchange for coppers only. Also, the 'exchange rate' between small change and full-bodied large coins would have remained stable. However, if copper small change was viable, the debasement of smaller coins implemented, for example, by the Lower

Rhenish Westphalian circle towards the end of the sixteenth century should have been no problem. It should not have caused the 'exchange rates' of *Talers* and *Guldens* to rise.

That this still happened was probably due to two factors: first, the way the population perceived the currency bill and second, the limit up to which small change was legal tender. We have seen in Chapter 2 that the emperor and estates took for granted that their decisions would become known to merchants and the common man. In fact, the Empire's politics were characterized by a relatively high degree of transparency. The recesses of imperial diets, which summarized the results of the discussions, appeared in print as well as the full texts of the Empire's Coinage Ordinances, including the paragraphs about monetary standards. Western European governments treated such details of monetary policy as political arcana, informing the public merely of the names of the coins and their target values.[136]

The question is, though, how many consumers were able to access the information that seemed so readily available? Over the sixteenth century, the share of the population able to read and understand complex texts may have grown to above 5 per cent.[137] The Coinage Ordinances were *very* complex texts: pages upon pages of highly technical details that concerned, for example, the composition of the alloys or the way coins were to be produced. People able to read all this and take it in were never more than a tiny minority. To be sure, cities like Straßburg (Strasbourg) published lists of which coins were to be used as legal tender and at what value. Other major trading centres used printed posters to inform consumers about the basic features of the new money.[138] Relevant information will also have spread by word of mouth. Still, it is likely that most consumers—people for whom small change was particularly important: those who were less educated, less experienced in trade, and less wealthy than the 'coin traders' about whom the imperial counsellors worried—were poorly informed about the details of the Empire's currency legislation. Moreover, some estates seem not to have been aware of the importance of the provision that limited the legal tender function of small change. Tellingly, Straßburg's list of coins whose use the Imperial Coinage Ordinance permitted failed to mention this point. If such details were dropped so easily it is likely that most people were not aware of them. In other cases, it was the authorities themselves who undermined the law when they encountered better-informed consumers. In 1573, a joint probation diet of the Swabian, Franconian, and Bavarian circles stated that they had received complaints about

> several places in these circles where half-*Batzens* are being spent in large sums and where people are even being told that they had to accept half-*Batzens* in large payments, which is in explicit contravention of the Coinage Ordinance and seriously harms the common weal. Hence it is herewith decided . . . that no prince, estate, or local authority shall . . . urge or *imperio magistratus* [ex officio] oblige anybody to accept half-*Batzens* in large payments for more than 25 *Guldens*.[139]

Still, uneven, or lacking, information did not only affect consumers. The estates and their envoys were struggling with related problems when they made decisions concerning monetary politics. Let us take a brief look at how they had agreed on the sum up to which small change was to be legal tender. This was discussed at the currency conference in Speyer in early October 1549, that is, a few days after Charles V's commissioners made their ill-fated intervention on bimetallism. Faced with the dispute about this issue, the conference decided to constitute a committee to finalize the less controversial aspects of the planned bill. The chancellor of the elector of Mainz, who chaired the discussion, put the small change question on the agenda. Trier, first in the polling order, suggested leaving it to the individual imperial estates to decide the limit up to which *Pfennigs* had to be accepted. Electoral Cologne voted for 5 or 10 Guldens 'at most'; the Palatinate agreed with the previous speaker, and electoral Brandenburg, Mainz, Austria, Bavaria, Burgundy, and Jülich-Cleves-Berg voted for 10 *Guldens*. The joint delegate of the counts of the Wetterau district in modern Hesse argued that 10 *Guldens* were too much and that 5 were better—5 *Guldens* had been the limit imposed by Nuremberg's law of 1528, which was the earliest to restrict the legal tender function of small change in Germany.[140] The minutes of the meeting do not indicate whether or how the attendants backed up their views.

When the diet of Augsburg in 1559 took up the question again, this is no clearer. All we know is that the electors' college initially favoured supplementing the 10 *Guldens*-limit for *Pfennigs* with a 50 *Guldens*-limit for coins between *Pfennigs* and 5-*Kreuzers*-pieces, and that the princes' college thought this required further discussion.[141] The 25 *Guldens*-limit on which the diet finally agreed was a compromise that simplified the rule, but our sources do not tell why that sum was chosen. It is likely that the estates took prices paid on the markets of the Empire into account (you recall that the *Bergherren* used rising prices as an argument why mining was becoming less profitable than it used to be). If so, they betrayed how out of touch they were.

Table 6.2. Grain prices and maximum quantities payable with regional small change, 1560–9

Place	Average price in regional *Pfennigs*	per local measure	= bushels	Regional *Pfennigs* per *Gulden*	bushels one could buy for 25 *Guldens*
Altenburg (wheat)	924	*Scheffel*	3.9	252	26.4
Augsburg (rye)	991	*Schaff*	12.1	210	64.0
Erfurt (wheat)	2,285	*Malter*	18.6	252	51.2
Frankfurt (wheat)	408	*Achtel*	3.0	210	38.2
Lübeck (wheat)	144	*Scheffel*	0.9	288	45.9
Lüneburg (wheat)	106	*Himten*	0.9	288	58.1
Munich (wheat)	950	*Scheffel*	6.1	210	33.9
Vienna (wheat)	137	*Metze*	1.7	240	74.1

Average grain prices in the decade following the publication of Ferdinand's Coinage Ordinance of 1559 (Table 6.2[142]) show what the 25-*Guldens*-limit, up to which one could pay with small change, meant in practice.

Depending on the type of regional small change the Ordinance permitted, you could purchase up to about 74 bushels of wheat with coins below the value of 5 *Kreuzers*. This was a lot: roughly as much as what a mid-sixteenth-century English peasant could expect to harvest on five acres of land.[143] As a bushel of wheat yields about 87,000 kilocalories and the average person at around this time consumed *c.*2,100 kilocalories a day, the amount would be sufficient to feed you for about six weeks (if you ate nothing but wheaten bread, which is of course unrealistic).[144] Compare this with France, where a similar currency law achieved the desired result. In 1577, the French government restricted the legal tender-function of small change to payments up to 5 *livres*.[145] For that sum and at prices common in Paris and Lyon from 1578–87, you could buy only 2.2 bushels of wheat—about 4½ per cent of the maximum quantity imperial law allowed you to purchase.[146] The upshot is that if you could use small change to buy as large quantities of an essential commodity—and grain was *the* staple—as in the Empire, merchants supplying mints with raw materials faced no incentives to insist on being paid in newly struck imperial *Talers* or silver *Guldens*. Hence, too much small change kept entering circulation, driving up the rates at which the larger, full-bodied coins were traded.

If the currency committee at the imperial diet of 1559 did take prices into account when deciding about the legal tender-limit of small change, why did they get it so wrong? There is one likely cause: the side-lining of one important group of estates represented at assemblies, that is, the cities. To be sure, on one occasion the chancellor of the elector of Mainz called upon them to present ideas on how the excessive minting of small change could be prevented. At that point, the only suggestion they came up with was that its bullion content should be made proportional to that of the large coins.[147] However, it seems likely that if they had been more closely integrated into the debates, they would have realized that the important point was the chancellor's hint that 'small coins . . . were heaped up and often used in large payments',[148] and would have drawn on their expertise in trade and markets to respond to this issue. On balance, it seems likely that the two higher colleges did not listen when they chose the 25 *Gulden*-limit. This was a value that defeated the purpose of the provision.

If the common currency of the Holy Roman Empire was characterized by a weak link between small and large denominations, it was by no means the only one. Take the English Pound Sterling, that suffered from the same problem once the government had given up the idea of issuing full-bodied silver small change. A late-seventeenth-century report complained that

> [i]n Consequence of the Vitiating, Diminishing and Counterfeiting of the Currant Moneys, it is come to pass, That great Contentions do daily arise amongst the King's Subjects . . . about the Passing or Refusing of the same . . . Persons before they conclude in any Bargains, are necessitated first to settle the Price or Value of the very Money they are to Receive for their Good.[149]

Fundamentally, the Pound Sterling of the years after the Glorious Revolution was not so different from the common currency of the Empire a hundred years before, and neither were the currencies of France (where coins circulated at a premium if their edges had *not* been cut off by people illegally collecting gold or silver) and the Low Countries (where the value of the Carolus-*guilder* rose from 20 *stuivers* in 1544 to 30 *stuivers* in 1581).[150] Everywhere consumers had to first learn about the current 'exchange rate' of large coins in smaller units before they were able to conclude transactions. In sum, it turns out that both main weaknesses of the common currency that contemporaries identified and on which modern research has focused[151]—the circulation of foreign money next to domestic coins, and the weak link between large and small units—were shared by many other early modern monetary systems.

Epilogue

At the ripe age of 51, Fynes Moryson of Cadeby in Lincolnshire published an account of his travels. In 1591, at twenty-five and driven by his 'great desire to see forraine Countries',[1] he had set out for the European continent where he wandered widely for the next four years. The Holy Roman Empire, or most of it, had by now become a well-governed country. Moryson found the roads safer than in England or France, the local magistrates everywhere commendably polite and helpful, the inns frequent, and coaches or horses readily available for rent.[2] Things only got dangerous near the border of the Netherlands, where the Dutch war of independence spilled over into the Lower Rhenish Westphalian circle.[3] Nevertheless, the country had come a long way since the days of Johannes Sastrow and Silvester Raid.

For the convenience and benefit of his readers, Moryson prefaced his book with a 'briefe Table to understand in the First Part the expences in small Coynes most commonly spent'. This is not really what we would call a table. There are no rows and columns; rather, he provided a simple list. The entry for Germany reads:

> The Reichs Doller of Germany is worth foure shillings foure pence, and the silver Gulden is accounted three shillings foure pence English. Twenty Misen silver Groshen, 32 Lubecke shillings, 45 Embden stivers, foure Copstucks and a halfe, 55 groates, 36 Maria grosh, 18 spitz-grosh, 18 Batz, make a Reichs Doller. Two seslings make a Lubecke shilling: foure Drier a silver grosh: two dreyhellers a Drier: two schwerd-grosh a schneberger: foure creitzers a batz: foure pfenning a creitzer.[4]

In part, Moryson used terms that have so far not appeared in this book. Some are easy to guess (the 'Reichs Doller' is the imperial *Taler*), others are obscure (for example, 'Misen silver Groshen' are Meißen *Groschens*, named after the town of Meißen in Saxony, which are here simply called Saxon *Groschens;* 'schwerd-groshs' and 'schnebergers' are their multiples). 'Spitz-grosh' is evidently a regional name for what elsewhere was called 'batz' (*Batzen*), and a 'Maria grosh' was nothing but a ½-*Batzen*- or 2-*Kreuzers*-piece. Some of the diversity was in name rather than in fact. Also, Moryson's 'table' is not too long. In the 1907 edition of his book, it takes up ten lines of text; the entry for the British Isles is not much shorter (eight lines). The one for Italy takes up 17 lines. Granted, Moryson focused on the 'Coynes most commonly spent'. Still, remember the assay at Nuremberg in 1551, when the coinage experts whom the imperial circles had sent tested almost 340 different types of coins, about 200 of which had been minted in the German lands—and this despite the assayers having excluded everything smaller than a *Kreuzer* or issued by the currency unions already existing within the Empire. The Coinage Ordinance of 1559 had radically done away with the old monetary disorder we got to know in Chapter 1.

But what about the regional small change permitted by Ferdinand I's bill? Like its predecessor of 1551, the Ordinance defined two distinct types of these coins: a small number of pieces whose value lay between that of 1 and 5 *Kreuzers*, and a larger number of regional *Pfennigs* and half-*Pfennigs* with a value below 1 *Kreuzer* and a lower content of pure silver. Moryson did not list these coins in his table but discussed them in a later section of his account that is peppered with good advice for other travellers. In Germany, he said, the lands of princes were small, 'and each of these Princes doth coyne small pieces of brasse money'. He cautioned:

> It behooveth the passenger to take heede, that he spend each Princes brasse moneys within his Territory, or else that upon the confines hee change them into brasse moneys currant in the next Territory; which if hee neglect, the subjects of the new Prince . . . will not receive them without great gaine, they being of themselves little worth, and onely by the prerogative of each Prince, currant among their owne subjects.[5]

By the 1590s, when Moryson travelled through the Empire, the estates had debased regional *Pfennigs* to 'brass', which no one outside their home territories was willing to accept (at least not 'without great gaine'). Such coins were fiat money—money people used because they trusted in the integrity of the authority issuing it and knew they would be able to exchange them for silver. This trust was likely rooted in the continued observance of the legal standard of the larger coins that were valid throughout the Empire, primarily of silver *Guldens* and *Talers*.

Many small territories, each with its own small change that could be used nowhere else: from a modern perspective, this sounds like a nightmare.

However, Moryson found it not so bad. He contrasted it with the conditions in England, where the mint very effectively and reliably supplied 'great moneys of silver'. However, 'not having small coynes or brasse monies to pay for small matters, these things (I say) in this great plenty make us poore, and greatly increase the prices of all things'.[6] Moryson was strongly aware of how people were struggling under the chronic scarcity of small change in Elizabethan England—a consequence of the government's stubborn refusal to compensate for the higher labour costs that its production involved by reducing its bullion content.[7] While the situation in the German lands certainly did not seem perfect to him, he was willing to look on the bright side.

Conditions in the late sixteenth-century Empire did not only differ from those elsewhere but also from those of the times of Charles V and his predecessors. Recall the case of Carinthia, where the common man had been deceived with underweight 2-*Pfennig*-pieces from distant Henneberg, or the ordinance of the dukes and electors of Saxony of 1511: The Saxon subjects were expected to learn to recognize 37 different types of small change below the value of a *Groschen* alone—and not merely to recognize them, but also to use them at the value the Saxon governments had determined. Back then, even very small change circulated widely, creating uncertainty and complicating transactions. This had changed. Now, for example, consumers in the landgraviate of Leuchtenberg in the Bavarian circle used the copper half-*Pfennigs* and *Pfennigs* that the landgrave's mint produced for small purchases, the *Kreuzers* current in Leuchtenberg (as well as anywhere else in South Germany) to pay higher prices (for example, for a meal and wine at an inn), and *Talers* or silver *Guldens* for very large transactions.[8] For most people, conditions had become much simpler and clearer than they had been for their grandparents. Paradoxically, this was in part the result of the violation of the letter of Ferdinand's coinage ordinance, which determined the standard of the permitted regional *Pfennig*-types and defined the minimum pure silver content of half-*Pfennigs* (Table A.5). It was the fact that by the 1590s, the estates had debased such pieces to what Moryson called 'brass'—that they were fiat money—which prevented their wider circulation. This contributed to simplifying monetary conditions at the regional level, especially for the common man, who depended on small change more than merchants or members of the nobility. Still, like pretty much anything else the Empire did, historians traditionally considered the creation of its common currency either a failure or, at best, a partial success. This consensus has only recently begun to break up,[9] but to what extent the new money succeeded is still not clear. Let us briefly review the situation. Most importantly, we need to be aware of three points.

First, the aim of the talks about the creation of a common currency was never complete uniformity. Everyone always took for granted that Empire-wide legal tender would be supplemented by regional small change. This was an entirely pragmatic approach: On the one hand, it helped bring influential estates on board—estates whose prestige had for centuries been linked to having their own coinage. On the other hand, acting in what policymakers perceived to be the interest of the common man was crucial to make sure that legislation would be accepted; in this case, it meant protecting the common man against better-informed and socially superior (and therefore more powerful) merchants and members of the nobility who might try to use the introduction of new currency to drive up prices or rents.

Second, the common currency project was among the most complex pieces of legislation the Empire ever tackled. It was complex in several ways: The matter was highly technical—for example, an extreme degree of precision was required in the definition of the monetary standards—and it had ramifications that were complicated in themselves. When the Esslingen Coinage Ordinance was designed in 1524, no one gave much thought to whether the existing money should be withdrawn, and if so, at what rates it should continue to circulate until that was possible, or how debts and fixed obligations should be serviced in new money. Twenty-five or 30 years later, discussing and solving these problems took up much of the time and energy of the people involved in designing the currency laws. Moreover, monetary legislation was complex for political reasons. There was hardly any other topic where the universal consent of the imperial estates was as crucial, with even the weakest members of the Empire being able to undermine the currency once it had been created. Building consensus was the big political test which Charles V failed and Ferdinand I passed.

The third important point is that the currency bill (including its amendment of 1566) was a compromise. In this, it was typical of how the Holy Roman Empire worked. Whether the estates settled the amounts that every one of them was expected to contribute to defence or the maintenance of the imperial chamber court, whether they agreed on a *Policey*-ordinance or an Empire-wide criminal law code, the result had to be a compromise that allowed as many members of the Empire as possible to agree to the new policy. Making the result of any less pragmatic approach work involved costs that were so high as to be prohibitive. This applied to the coinage, too; in fact, Charles V's bill of 1551 is a perfect example of how an attempt to push through a policy that favoured one interest group over another could come to grief. However, what is equally typical is that the compromise did not mean the parties were meeting each other halfway. The Empire was neither a modern federal state nor a federation of states whose members are equal; rather, it retained many features of its feudal origin, among them the lack of equality among its members.[10] Some—the electors, in particular—did not only enjoy a higher status but also more power than others, and the result was that the common currency bill agreed in 1559 went a long way in accommodating the concerns the Rhenish electors had voiced in the years before. Importantly, it abandoned the long-cherished ideal of bimetallism. However, this did not make it any less of a compromise. Ferdinand's Ordinance did not just extend the currency of the Rhenish Union to the rest of the Empire but adopted the basic structure of the one which the Austrian–Upper German Union had issued since the middle of the 1530s: Its top unit was the silver *Gulden*, its lower denominations were valued in *Kreuzers*. Likewise, the amendment of 1566 did not merely legalize what was the general practice (as historians have sometimes argued).[11] Instead of caving in to the Saxon demands, the diet struck a balance by adopting the *Taler* as part of the common currency while requiring the elector to agree to a debasement. The amendment was a compromise, too.

Recently, an argument related to the culturalist interpretation of the Empire—the approach that stresses the importance of political rituals practically to the exclusion of the analysis of substantive policies—has been put forward. It is claimed that to count as a success, the Empire's Coinage Ordinances did not actually need to be implemented. The mere fact that the estates came together to discuss policies at the imperial level and achieved a kind of formal agreement in principle was enough to make it a success.[12] The argument resembles the idea that the point of early modern legislation, whether in the Empire or elsewhere, was not to change how people acted. Rather, rulers who published laws gave expression to their status as rulers—a kind of ostentation aimed at their subjects as well as at other rulers. In addition, being active in legislation underpinned their legitimacy.[13]

In our context, none of this sounds particularly convincing. Sources too often mention the need to 'really' bring the negotiations to a conclusion and 'really' enforce and implement the currency bills.[14] Addressing the futility of earlier talks, the counsellors of Charles V pointed out in 1549 that the common currency had been discussed at 'many and almost all imperial diets, especially during his Majesty's reign, but that a fruitful agreement, far less its good execution had never been achieved'.[15] They, at least, did not believe that talking to each other, finding an agreement in principle, and publishing it was enough. It was a necessary first step, but what had to follow was the 'good execution' of what the emperor and estates had agreed. This did not happen in the years after 1551, whereas it did so after 1559—at least to a certain extent. Was this sufficient to make the Ordinance a success?

By contemporary standards, it was. The purpose of the law for whose execution the imperial counsellors called was to cut the ground from under the trade in coinage and its unpleasant consequence—that is, to create conditions where Gresham's Law was no longer a problem. This was not achieved as far as relations with the Empire's neighbours were concerned. Most important among them were the Netherlands, which were economically close but politically increasingly distant. Of this, the emperor's counsellors were aware. In 1571, a memorial that the imperial *Pfennig*-master—the official tasked with collecting the contributions the estates made to the upkeep of the imperial chamber court—Georg Ilsung submitted lauded the Coinage Ordinance; the problem was that local authorities, in particular in the border regions of the Empire, did not put a stop to the import of base foreign coins.[16] Ilsung was certainly right, but what were local authorities supposed to do? There was no practicable way of keeping foreign money out. The Empire would continue to suffer from its circulation for the rest of its existence—but so did all other early modern countries, among them, as we have seen, England. It is too rarely realized that territorial currency monopolies are a nineteenth-century creation.[17] Before then, the money supply was in effect international, with most currencies dominating in some regions but, in principle, all currencies being acceptable everywhere.

However, within the Empire, the aim of preventing the trade in coinage, and the breaking and reminting of coins was largely achieved—at least for some decades. This, too, has been disputed. The argument is that the imperial circles failed to ensure monetary stability, with the rates at which small change was traded against larger coins being as open to negotiation among consumers as before.[18] We have seen that this is a valid point.

However, in this respect too, the common currency of the Empire functioned just as others of the time did: The French and Dutch money of the sixteenth century were no different, and the Pound Sterling suffered from the same problem once the government had decided to issue overvalued small change.

Problems evidently remained. Still, within the Empire, stability had increased markedly since the early sixteenth century. In Hamburg, the Rhenish florin appreciated by 10 per cent between 1520–4 and 1525–9, and by 9 per cent between 1530–4 and 1535–9. In Cologne, its exchange rate went up more than 15 per cent in the second half of the 1520 and by almost 14 per cent in the first half of the 1530s. On average, it appreciated by 9.5 per cent every five years between 1520 and 1564 (Table 5.2). By contrast, the rate of the imperial *Taler* in *Schillings* did increase by more than 8 per cent between 1585–9 and 1590–4, but this was exceptional. It was only in the immediate run-up to the Thirty Years War (1618–48) that debasement gripped the larger of the regional coins. Then, monetary instability increased so far that it resembled that of the first half of the sixteenth century (Table 6.1). This opened the door to a revival of the trade in coinage, the breaking of coins, the return of 'defensive' debasements and everything this entailed. Early in the Thirty Years War, the system spun completely out of control, causing a period of extreme instability and inflation. Until then, the common currency worked—not flawlessly, but considering the circumstances it functioned reasonably well. In this, too, it was typical of the Empire.

Of course, this was not the end of the story. In a way that so far no historian has explored in detail, the common currency was largely restored after its collapse in the early phase of the Thirty Years War. However, the damage had been done, and it was immense. Whereas peasants and merchants had the chance to offset the debasement of the coinage by increasing prices, all who depended on monetary incomes fixed in nominal terms suffered terribly—burghers who had bought rents just as well as parish priests, schoolteachers, public officials, servants, and farm hands.[19] Moreover, after the restauration of the currency, a return to the relative stability of the decades after 1559/66 proved elusive. In 1667, electoral Saxony and Brandenburg openly abandoned the imperial standard that had been agreed upon 100 years before; other estates followed.[20] In 1750, and without coordinating its policies with other estates, Brandenburg (now 'Brandenburg-Prussia' and Austria's big antagonist in the Empire) introduced a radically debased

Taler-standard.[21] At about the same time, Austria also abandoned the provisions of the ancient Currency Ordinance, but its so-called 'convention-standard' found relatively wide approval in the Empire (in stark contrast to Prussia's system). After the Seven Years War of 1756–63, many estates in South and West Germany joined it spontaneously.[22] Still, by now any semblance of Empire-wide unity was gone, never to be restored. The Mark, which Imperial Germany created as its common currency in 1873, was something entirely new. Not only was its area of circulation far smaller than that of the currency of 300 years before; but it was also based on gold (like many other countries of the time, Germany adopted the gold standard), with silver being relegated to the role of overvalued fiat money. Also, by now state capacities had developed so far that foreign money could be excluded from circulation;[23] it was moreover possible to maintain fixed relations between small change and larger units. The Mark—rather than the imperial currency of 1559/66—was Germany's first modern money. It was, however, the creation of a modern federal state rather than that of a system of multilateralism such as the Holy Roman Empire—a system that had its limitations but that during the period covered by this book served the people living within its framework remarkably well.

Appendix

TIMELINE

Year	*Monetary history of the Holy Roman Empire*	*General history of the Holy Roman Empire*	*Wider history*
1519	The electoral capitulation requires Charles V to solve the Empire's monetary problems (3 July)	Charles signes the Electoral capitulation (3 July)	The Spanish begin the conquest of the Aztec Empire in Mexico (April)
1520	The counts of Schlick begin issuing *Talers* in Joachimstal (Jáchymov)	Charles V crowned King of the Romans (23 Oct.)	Revolt begins in Spain (May)
1521	Johann Eberlin von Günzburg calls for an Empire-wide common currency	Diet of Worms (28 Jan. to 26 May)	Spanish rebels defeated (23 April)
1522	The government convenes an expert panel to advise it on the planned common currency (18 Aug.); the panel submits its report (8 Oct.)	Charles V leaves the Empire for Spain (26 May)	
1523	The anonymous 'Needs of the German Nation' calls for an Empire-wide common currency		
1524	Esslingen Coinage Ordinance (10 Nov.)	Beginning of the Peasants' War (June)	
1525	Friedrich Weigandt's plan of a reform of the constitution of the	End of the Peasants' War (Sep.)	

Continued

Year	Monetary history of the Holy Roman Empire	General history of the Holy Roman Empire	Wider history
	Empire adopts the ideas of the 'Needs of the German Nation' (before 18 May)		
1526	*Bergherren*-meeting in Nuremberg (6 Dec.)		Sultan Suleyman I defeats the Hungarians at Mohács, death of King Louis II of Hungary (29 Aug.); Ferdinand of Austria inherits Hungary and Bohemia with their precious metal deposits
1530	Electoral Saxony debases the *Taler* (the duchy of Saxony maintains the old standard) (3 April)	Charles V returns to Germany (2 May)	
1531		Ferdinand I is elected King of the Romans (5 Jan.); the landgrave of Hesse and the elector of Saxony form the Schmalkaldic League (27 Feb.)	The Spanish begin the conquest of the Inca Empire in Peru (April)
1532		Charles V leaves Germany for Italy (May)	
1534	The electorate and the duchy of Saxony reestablish a common *Taler*-standard (20 Jan.)		
1535	Many estates between Austria and Alsace form the Upper-German currency union		
1540		Charles V returns to the Empire (Feb.)	
1543	*Bergherren*-meeting in Prague (June); the Augsburg coinage scandal breaks (Oct.)		
1544		Diet of Worms begins (15 Dec.)	

1545	The diet of Worms forms a cross-college currency committee (12 Jan.); first draft of an Imperial coinage ordinance (15. Jan.); revised draft (6 Feb.); the currency committee argues that there is no need to harmonize the price of silver (5 June)	Diet of Worms ends (4 Aug.)	Diego Huallpa discovers silver ore at Potosí, Bolivia
1546		Schmalkaldic War begins (Aug.)	Juan de Tolosa discovers silver ore at Zacatecas, Mexico
1547		Charles V captures Elector John Frederick of Saxony in the battle of Mühlberg (24 April) and transfers the Saxon electorship to Maurice of Saxony (19 May); Landgrave Philip of Hesse surrenders (19 June) and is kept prisoner; 'Diet-in-Arms,' Augsburg, begins (1 Sep.)	Henry VIII dies (28 Jan.); Francis I dies (31 March)
1548	The 'Diet-in-Arms' calls a currency conference in Speyer for 2 Feb. 1549 (15 June)	'Diet-in-Arms' ends (30 June)	
1549	Currency conference, Speyer (12 Feb. to 16 March); follow-up conference opens (10 Sep.); agreement on a common silver standard (21 Sep.); the imperial commissioners suggest making silver unlimited legal tender (28 Sep.); agreement on the drafts of a currency bill and a probation ordinance (11 Oct.); meeting adjourned to 27 Nov. (5 Nov.)		

Continued

Year	*Monetary history of the Holy Roman Empire*	*General history of the Holy Roman Empire*	*Wider history*
1550	The currency conference of Speyer ends (15 Aug.); the imperial diet adopts the currency bill drafted in Speyer (6 Dec.)	Diet of Augsburg begins (26 July); Charles V plans replacing Ferdinand with his son Philip as successor	
1551	The diet asks Charles V to publish the currency bill once the planned assay in Nuremberg has ended (14 Feb.); Nuremberg assay (5 April to 27 May); Augsburg Coinage Ordinance (28 July); Charles V sends copies of the Coinage and Probation Ordinances to the circle directors (Nov. to Dec.)	Diet of Augsburg ends (14 Feb.); a group of Protestant princes led by Maurice of Saxony concludes an alliance with Henry II of France (5 Oct.)	
1552	Most circle directors convene circle-level diets to publicize the bills (Feb. to March)	Princes' Revolt (March to June)	
1553			Edward VI dies (6 July)
1555	Ferdinand signals his willingness to compromise on bimetallism (20 Sep.)	Diet of Augsburg (5 Feb. to 29 Sep.); Religious Peace of Augsburg (25 Sep.); Charles V transfers the rule of the Netherlands to Philip (25 Oct.)	
1556	Ferdinand publishes the currency bill of 1551 in Austria, suspends the devaluation of the *Taler* (30 May)	Diet of Regensburg begins (13 July); Charles V abdicates (3 Aug.)	
1557	The imperial diet calls a currency conference at Speyer for 13 June (16 March); currency conference takes place (28 June to 20 July)	Diet of Regensburg ends (16 March)	

1558	Electoral Saxony debases the *Taler* (27 Sep.)	The estates accept Ferdinand I as emperor (3 May)	Mary Tudor dies (17 Nov.)
1559	The Second Augsburg Coinage Ordinance abandons bimetallism (19 Aug.)	Diet of Augsburg (3 March to 19 Aug.)	Henry II (France) dies (10 July)
1562		Maximilian II elected as king of the Romans (24 Nov.)	
1564		Ferdinand I dies (25 July)	
1566	The imperial diet adopts a debased *Taler*-variant as part of the common currency (30 May)	Diet of Augsburg (23 March to 30 May)	
1571	Electoral Saxony joins the common currency (8 April)		

ATTENDANCE PATTERNS AT IMPERIAL DIETS AND CURRENCY CONFERENCES

Table A.1[1] presents the results of four regression analyses. The data are structured as a panel; the ID of each estate and that of each imperial assembly are the panel variables. The variables to be explained are 'represented?' (col. 2, a binary variable that takes the value of 1 if an imperial estate listed in the registers of 1521 or 1545 was represented at a diet, and else is 0), 'ruler present?' (col. 3, likewise a binary variable that indicates whether a ruler was personally present at a diet), 'no. of delegates' (col. 4, the size of the delegation, a natural number) and 'share of academics' (col. 5, a value between 0 and 1). The explanatory variables are listed in col. 1. 'Dist. residence—assembly' is the distance (as the crow flies) between an estate's usual place of residence and the location of the diet or coinage conference. 'Time' is a time trend that counts the years from 1521 (Charles V's first imperial diet). 'Diets attended' is the number of diets an estate had already attended, 'Roman Month' the sum the estate was expected to contribute to the defence of the Empire. 'Coinage conference' is a binary variable that takes the value of 1 if the assembly was one of the *Münztage* in Speyer in 1549 and 1557 and else is 0; 'Regions close to emperor' takes 1 if an estate's place of residence was located in Bavaria, Franconia, or Swabia (else 0); 'distant to emperor' is 1 of a place of residence was located in territories touching the coast of the North Sea or the Baltic. '*Viril* vote', 'Spiritual prince', 'Cities' college, and Protestant are further binary variables that take the value of 1 if

Table A.1. Attendance patterns at imperial diets and currency conferences, 1521–59

(1)	(2)	(3)	(4)	(5)
VARIABLES	(Panel logit) Represented?	(Panel logit) Ruler present?	(Panel) No. of delegates	(GLM) Share of academics
Dist. residence—assembly	−0.863***	−0.0808***	−1.319***	0.182***
	(0.0926)	(0.0291)	(0.107)	(0.0676)
Time	0.0510***	0.0101***	−0.00354	0.0123***
	(0.00382)	(0.00122)	(0.00507)	(0.00373)
Diets attended	0.00233	−0.00469***	−0.00847	0.00746*
	(0.00476)	(0.00159)	(0.00677)	(0.00381)
Roman Month	0.556***	0.219***	0.425***	−0.131***
	(0.0887)	(0.0303)	(0.0955)	(0.0413)
Coinage conference	−1.605***	−0.396***	−3.960***	1.902***
	(0.123)	(0.0396)	(0.568)	(0.177)
Regions close to emperor	0.112	−0.0891	0.387*	−0.387***
	(0.200)	(0.0683)	(0.201)	(0.0877)
Distant to emperor	−0.486	−0.257	0.0680	−0.175
	(0.450)	(0.160)	(0.461)	(0.193)
Viril vote	0.213	0.262***	1.167***	0.106
	(0.256)	(0.0911)	(0.281)	(0.122)
Spiritual prince	0.237	−0.153**	−0.723***	0.502***
	(0.208)	(0.0740)	(0.220)	(0.0950)
Cities' college	3.746***	−0.387***	4.719***	−1.534***
	(0.651)	(0.137)	(0.626)	(0.263)
Protestant	0.655***	0.160***	0.100	0.121
	(0.147)	(0.0484)	(0.196)	(0.112)
Constant	−0.0931	−0.440**	1.641**	−1.317***
	(0.608)	(0.204)	(0.670)	(0.384)
Observations	5,445	5,445	5,445	2,388
Number of imp. estates	257	257	257	

Robust standard errors in parentheses
*** p < 0.01, ** p < 0.05, * p < 0.1

an estate held a *viril* vote, was a spiritual prince, sat in the cities' college, or was Protestant.

MONETARY STANDARDS

In Table A.2,[2] the Date is the date the ordinance or bill was published. 'Type' is the type of coin that was to be struck. The Target value is the value at which the minting authority wished the coin to circulate.[3] The Basic weight is the unit of weight the mint used to measure precious metals, with the mark (m.) of Cologne being *c.*233.82 grams, the mark of Erfurt the same, the mark of Troyes 244.753 grams, and the Mark of Vienna 290.90 grams.[4] The Taille is the number of coins that were to be struck from 1 mark of alloy; the Finesses gives the purity of that alloy, and the Bullion content the content of pure gold or silver of each coin (if the legal standard was maintained). The Mint equivalent is the total nominal value of the coins made from one mark of pure silver.

Table A.2. Monetary standards

Date	Type	Target value	Basic weight	Taille	Fineness	Bullion content (grams)	Mint equivalent
Austria (from 1535: Upper German currency union)							
14/08/1510	¼-*Gulden*	15 *kr.*	m. of Vienna	38.50	0.938	6.840 Ag.	10.27 *fl.*
15/02/1524	Silver *Gulden*	60 *kr.*	m. of Vienna	9.75	0.895	25.772 Ag.	10.90 *fl.*
01/02/1535	Silver *Gulden*	60 *kr.*	m. of Vienna	9.75	0.895	25.772 Ag.	10.90 *fl.*
14/08/1510	*Kreuzer*	1 *kr.*	m. of Vienna	280.00	0.469	0.470 Ag.	9.96 *fl.*
15/02/1524	*Kreuzer*	1 *kr.*	m. of Vienna	585.00	0.895	0.430 Ag.	10.90 *fl.*
01/02/1535	*Kreuzer*	1 *kr.*	m. of Vienna	294.50	0.438	0.417 Ag.	11.22 *fl.*
Electoral Saxony							
17/05/1500	*Guldengroschen*	21 *gr.*	m. of Erfurt	8.00	0.938	27.402 Ag.	8.53 *fl.*
03/04/1530	*Taler*	21 *gr.*	m. of Erfurt	8.00	0.875	25.575 Ag.	9.14 *fl.*
20/01/1534	*Taler*	22 *gr.*	m. of Erfurt	8.00	0.903	26.387 Ag.	9.28 *fl.*

Continued

Table A.2. *Continued*

Date	Type	Target value	Basic weight	Taille	Fineness	Bullion content (grams)	Mint equivalent
27/03/1549	*Taler*	24 *gr.*	m. of Erfurt	8.00	0.903	26.387 Ag.	10.13 *fl.*
27/09/1558	*Taler*	24 *gr.*	Reduced m. of Erfurt[1]	8.00	0.903	26.181 Ag.	10.13 *fl.*
17/05/1500	*Groschen*	1 *gr.*	m. of Erfurt	88.00	0.483	1.282 Ag.	8.68 *fl.*
03/04/1530	*Groschen*	1 *gr.*	m. of Erfurt	88.00	0.458	1.218 Ag.	9.14 *fl.*
20/01/1534	*Groschen*	1 *gr.*	m. of Erfurt	88.00	0.469	1.246 Ag.	8.94 *fl.*
27/03/1549	*Groschen*	1 *gr.*	m. of Erfurt	88.00	0.455	1.209 Ag.	9.21 *fl.*
27/09/1558	*Groschen*	1 *gr.*	Reduced m. of Erfurt	88.00	0.406	1.079 Ag.	10.32 *fl.*
Electors on the Rhine							
12/03/1493	Rhenish florin	24 *alb.*	m. of Cologne	71.33	0.771	2.527 Au.	92.50 *fl.*
12/03/1493	White *Pfennig*	1 *alb.*	m. of Cologne	114.00	0.583	1.197 Ag.	8.14 *fl.*
Burgundy/Netherlands							
21/02/1543	*Carolus guilder*	20 *st.*	m. of Troyes	10.71	0.833	19.051 Ag.	12.85 *fl.*
01/04/1553	*Carolus guilder*	21 *st.*	m. of Troyes	10.71	0.833	19.051 Ag.	13.49 *fl.*
04/06/1567	*Krujsrijksdaalder*	32 *st.*	m. of Troyes	8.41	0.833	24.260 Ag.	16.13 *fl.*
1578	*Statendaalder*	32 *st.*	m. of Troyes	8.03	0.743	22.644 Ag.	17.28 *fl.*
21/02/1543	*Grote*	½ *st.*	m. of Troyes	134.00	0.292	0.533 Ag.	11.48 *fl.*

IMPERIAL COINAGE ORDINANCES

The Target value is the value at which the authority minting it wished the coin to circulate.[5] The Mint equivalent is the total nominal value of the coins struck from one Cologne mark of pure silver (Tables A.3,[6] A.4,[7] and A.5[8]).

Table A.3. Esslingen Coinage Ordinance, 10 November 1524

Type	Target value	Mint equivalent
Rhenish florin	21 *gr.* = 1 *fl.*	(97.09 *fl.* per m. pure gold)
Silver *Gulden*	21 *gr.* = 1 *fl.*	
½ silver *Gulden*	10½ *gr.* = ½ *fl.*	8 *fl.* 10 *s.* 8 *h.* (= 8.53 *fl.* per m. pure silver)
Ort (¼ silver *Gulden*)	5¼ *gr.* = ¼ *fl.*	
Zehner	1/10 *fl.* = 1/10 *fl.*	
Groschen	1 *gr.* = 1/21 *fl.*	8 *fl.* 12 *s.* 8 *h.* (= 8.63 *fl.* per m. pure silver)
½ *Groschen*	½ *gr.* = 1/42 *fl.*	
Gröschlein	¼ *gr.* = 1/84 *fl.*	8 *fl.* 15 *s.* (= 8.75 *fl.* per m. pure silver)
Pfennig	Not defined	≤ 9 *fl.* per m. pure silver
Heller (½ *Pfennig*)		

Maximum fee for the exchange of gold and silver: 1 *Gröschlein* per Rhenish florin.

Table A.4. First Augsburg Coinage Ordinance, 28 July 1551

Type	Target value			Mint equivalent
Empire-wide coinage				
Rhenish florin	72	*kr.*	= 1⅕ *fl.*	(111.07 *fl.* per m. pure gold)
Guldiner	72	*kr.*	= 1⅕ *fl.*	
½ *Guldiner*	36	*kr.*	= ⅗ *fl.*	
20-*Kreuzer*	20	*kr.*	= ⅓ *fl.*	10 *fl.* 12. *kr.* 1 *d.* (= 10.21 *fl.* per m. pure silver)
12-*Kreuzer*	12	*kr.*	= ⅕ *fl.*	
10-*Kreuzer*	10	*kr.*	= ⅙ *fl.*	
6-*Kreuzer*	6	*kr.*	= 1/10 *fl.*	
3-*Kreuzer*	3	*kr.*	= 1/20 *fl.*	10 *fl.* 23 *kr.* 1 *d.* (= 10.39 *fl.* per m. pure silver)
Kreuzer	1	*kr.*	= 1/60 *fl.*	10 *fl.* 26 *kr.* 3 *d.* (= 10.44 *fl.* per m. pure silver)
Coinage of the electors on the Rhine and their associates				
White *Pfennig*			1/28 *fl.*	10 *fl.* 25 *kr.* 1½ *d.* (= 10.42 *fl.* per m. pure silver)
½ white *Pfennig*			1/56 *fl.*	10 *fl.* $27\frac{3}{7}$ *kr.* (= 10.45 *fl.* per m. pure silver)
Rhenish *Pfennig*			1/224 *fl.*	10 *fl.* 43 *kr.* 1 *d.* (= 10.72 *fl.* per m. pure silver)

Continued

Table A.4. *Continued*

Type	Target value	Mint equivalent
Coinage of the Upper Saxon and Franconian circles		
Groschen	1/21 *fl.*	10 *fl.* 23 *kr.* $1^{23}/_{34}$ *d.* (= 10.39 *fl.* per m. pure silver)
½ *Groschen*	1/42 *fl.*	10 *fl.* 25 *kr.* 1½ *d.* (= 10.42 *fl.* per m. pure silver)
Gröschlein	1/84 *fl.*	10 *fl.* 31 *kr.* (= 10.52 *fl.* per m. pure silver)
Electoral Brandenburg's coinage		
¼ *Gulden*	15 *kr.* = ¼ *fl.*	10 *fl.* 12 *kr.* $1^{17}/_{127}$ *d.* (= 10.20 *fl.* per m. pure silver)
Markish *Groschen*	1/32 *fl.*	10 *fl.* 24 *kr.* 2½ *d.* (= 10.41 *fl.* per m. pure silver)
Markish ½ *Groschen*	1/64 *fl.*	10 *fl.* 27 *kr.* 3½ *d.* (= 10.46 *fl.* per m. pure silver)
Markish *Pfennig*	1/256 *fl.*	10 *fl.* 49 *kr.* 3 *d.* (= 10.83 *fl.* per m. pure silver)
Coinage of the Habsburg Low Countries		
4-Stieber	1/21 72-*kr.*	10 *fl.* 15. *kr.* 3 *d.* (= 10.26 *fl.* per m. pure silver)
3-Stieber	1/28 72-*kr.*	10 *fl.* 12. *kr.* 1 *d.* (= 10.20 *fl.* per m. pure silver)
2-Stieber	1/42 72-*kr.*	10 *fl.* 15. *kr.* 3 *d.* (= 10.26 *fl.* per m. pure silver)
1½-Stieber	1/56 72-*kr.*	10 *fl.* 21. *kr.* 3 *d.* (= 10.36 *fl.* per m. pure silver)
Stieber	1/84 72-*kr.*	10 *fl.* 25 *kr.* 1½ *d.* (= 10.42 *fl.* per m. pure silver)
½ *Stieber*	1/168 72-*kr.*	10 *fl.* $27^{3}/_{7}$ *kr.* (= 10.46 *fl.* per m. pure silver)
¼ *Stieber*	1/336 72-*kr.*	10 *fl.* 31 *kr.* 1 *d.* (= 10.52 *fl.* per m. pure silver)
Coinage of the Lower Saxon circle		
Schilling of Lübeck	1/24 *fl.*	10 fl. 25 *kr.* 3 *d.* (= 10.43 *fl.* per m. pure silver)
Sechsling of Lübeck = *Schilling* of Stralsund	1/48 *fl.*	10 fl. 29 *kr.* (= 10.48 *fl.* per m. pure silver)
Dreiling of Lübeck = *Witten* of Stralsund	1/96 *fl.*	10 fl. 36 *kr.* (= 10.60 *fl.* per m. pure silver)
Pfennig of Lübeck	1/228 *fl.*	10 fl. 54 *kr.* (= 10.90 *fl.* per m. pure silver)
Traditional regional *Pfennigs*		
Pfennig of the Tyrol	1/300 *fl.*	11 fl. 3 *kr.* (= 11.05 *fl.* per m. pure silver)
Franconian *Pfennig*	1/252 *fl.*	10 fl. 49 *kr.* 2 *d.* (= 10.83 *fl.* per m. pure silver)
Austrian *Pfennig*	1/240 *fl.*	10 fl. 49 *kr.* (= 10.82 *fl.* per m. pure silver)
Bavarian *Pfennig*	1/210 *fl.*	10 fl. 46 *kr.* (= 10.77 *fl.* per m. pure silver)

Pfennig of Schwäbisch Hall and Constance	$^{1}/_{180}$ *fl.*	10 fl. 42 *kr.* (= 10.70 *fl.* per m. pure silver)
Pfennig of Württemberg and Baden	$^{1}/_{168}$ *fl.*	10 fl. 42 *kr.* $^{4}/_{5}$ *d.* (= 10.70 *fl.* per m. pure silver)
Rappen *Pfennig*	$^{1}/_{150}$ *fl.*	10 fl. 40 *kr.* (= 10.67 *fl.* per m. pure silver)
Straßburg *Pfennig*	$^{1}/_{120}$ *fl.*	10 fl. 40 *kr.* (= 10.67 *fl.* per m. pure silver)
Heller (½ *Pfennig*)	Not defined	≤ 11 *fl.* per m. pure silver

Table A.5. Second Augsburg Coinage Ordinance, 19 August 1559

Type	Target value	Mint equivalent
Empire-wide coinage		
Ducat	≤ 104 *kr.*	
Rhenish florin	≤ 75 *kr.* ≤ 1¼ *fl.*	(≤ 116.76 *fl.* per m. pure gold)
Silver *Gulden*	60 *kr.* = 1 *fl.*	10 *fl.* 12 *kr.* $2^{1}/_{133.5}$ *d.* (= 10.21 *fl.* per m. pure silver)
½ *Gulden*	30 *kr.* = ½ *fl.*	
10-*Kreuzer*	10 *kr.* = ⅕ *fl.*	
5-*Kreuzer*	5 *kr.* = $^{1}/_{12}$ *fl.*	
Imperial *Groschen*	1 *gr.* = $^{1}/_{21}$ *fl.*	10 *fl.* 20 *kr.* (= 10.33 *fl.* per m. pure silver)
2½-*Kreuzer*	2½ *kr.* = $^{1}/_{24}$ *fl.*	10 *fl.* 20 *kr.* (= 10.33 *fl.* per m. pure silver)
2-*Kreuzer*	2 *kr.* = $^{1}/_{30}$ *fl.*	10 *fl.* 22 *kr.* (= 10.37 *fl.* per m. pure silver)
Kreuzer	1 *kr.* = $^{1}/_{60}$ *fl.*	10 *fl.* $26^{1}/_{7}$ *kr.* (= 10.44 *fl.* per m. pure silver)
Regional small change		
Schilling of Würzburg, Württemberg and Baden	$^{1}/_{28}$ *fl.*	10 *fl.* $21^{3}/_{7}$ *kr.* (= 10.36 *fl.* per m. pure silver)
Sechsling of Stralsund	$^{1}/_{48}$ *fl.*	10 fl. 25 *kr.* (= 10.42 *fl.* per m. pure silver)
Rappenvierer	$^{1}/_{75}$ *fl.*	10 fl. $26^{2}/_{15}$ *kr.* (= 10.44 *fl.* per m. pure silver)
Gröschlein	$^{1}/_{84}$ *fl.*	10 *fl.* $26^{2}/_{7}$ *kr.* (= 10.44 *fl.* per m. pure silver)
Traditional regional *Pfennigs*		
Pfennig of the Tyrol	$^{1}/_{300}$ *fl.*	11 fl. 3 *kr.* (= 11.05 *fl.* per m. pure silver)
Pfennig of Lübeck	$^{1}/_{248}$ *fl.*	10 fl. 54 *kr.* (= 10.90 *fl.* per m. pure silver)

Continued

Table A.5. *Continued*

Type	Target value	Mint equivalent
Franconian *Pfennig*	1/252 *fl.*	10 fl. 49 *kr.* 2 *d.* (= 10.83 *fl.* per m. pure silver)
Austrian *Pfennig*	1/240 *fl.*	10 fl. 49 *kr.* (= 10.82 *fl.* per m. pure silver)
Rhenish, Bavarian, and Swabian *Pfennig*	1/210 *fl.*	10 fl. 46 *kr.* (= 10.77 *fl.* per m. pure silver)
Pfennig of Schwäbisch Hall and Constance	1/180 *fl.*	10 fl. 42 *kr.* (= 10.70 *fl.* per m. pure silver)
Pfennig of Würzburg, Württemberg and Baden	1/168 *fl.*	10 fl. 42 *kr.* 4/5 *d.* (= 10.70 *fl.* per m. pure silver)
Rappen *Pfennig*	1/150 *fl.*	10 fl. 40 *kr.* (= 10.67 *fl.* per m. pure silver)
Straßburg *Pfennig*	1/120 *fl.*	10 fl. 40 *kr.* (= 10.67 *fl.* per m. pure silver)
Pfennig of Pomerania and Mecklenburg	1/576 *fl.*	≤ 11 fl. 15 *kr.* (= 11.25 *fl.* per m. pure silver)
Heller (½ Pfennig)	Not defined	≤ 11 *fl.* 5 *kr.* (= 11.08 *fl.* per m. pure silver)

GLOSSARY

Assayer	Official tasked with checking the intrinsic value and metallic composition of coins.
Bergherr	Literally 'lord of the mountain'; an imperial estate that controlled a mining district.
Bimetallism	A monetary system where coins made of gold and silver circulate side-by-side at legally determined rates and are unlimited legal tender.
Breaking coins	'Does not mean, in the literal sense, to break apart a coin, but rather to place one or more types of coin in a crucible, melt them and process the metal illegally and with the aim of making a profit.'[9]
Debasement	A reduction of the ratio between intrinsic and nominal value of a coin. Either the intrinsic value would be left unchanged and the nominal value increased, or the intrinsic value would be reduced while the nominal value was left stable.

Gresham's Law	Named after Thomas Gresham, financial adviser of Queen Elizabeth I of England. The law states that bad money drives out good, with the bad money being the one that is overvalued more than the good money → Overvaluation.
Gulden	(a) generic name of any gold coin, often short for Rhenish florin; (b) a unit of account of, for example, 60 *Kreuzers* (Austria) or 21 *Groschens* (Saxony); (c) a coin, minted in the Tyrol since 1486, whose value was intended to match the *Gulden* of account (60 *Kreuzers*).
Guldengroschen	Silver coin whose value was intended to match that of 1 gold *Gulden*, minted in Saxony since 1500.
Mark	(a) A unit of weight used to measure precious metal, roughly half a pound; (b) a unit of account and, since the early sixteenth century, a coin used in some places in North Germany.
Overvaluation	The degree by which the nominal value of a coin exceeds its intrinsic value.
Seignorage	The profit a minting authority makes; a function of the difference between a coin's production costs and the value at which it enters circulation.
Side-strike	In German, *Beischlag*. A poor imitation of a better coin; no forgery because the design differs (more or less subtly) from that of the original.
Taler	→ *Gulden*groschen.

Notes

INTRODUCTION

1. Magnus Ulrich Ferber, *Augsburg im 16. Jahrhundert* (Munich: Volk Verlag, 2012), p. 7.
2. Rosemarie Aulinger, ed., *Deutsche Reichstagsakten unter Kaiser Karl V.: Der Reichstag zu Worms 1545*, vol. 2 (Munich: Oldenbourg, 2003), no. 113B, pp. 1084–98.
3. Marcus Welser, Achilles Pirmin Gasser, and Engelbert Werlich, *Chronica der weitberüempten keyserlichen freyen und deß H. Reichs Statt Augspurg in Schwaben von derselben altem Ursprung, schöne gelegene zierliche Gebäwen unnd namhafften gedenckwürdigen Geschichten*, vol. 3 (Basel: Egenolff, 1596), p. 46; Achilles Pirminius Gasser, 'Annales civitatis ac reipublicae Augsburgensis', in *Scriptores rerum germanicarum, praecipue saxonicarum*, ed. Johannes Burkhard Mencke (Leipzig: Johann Christian Martin, 1728), col. 1824; Paul von Stetten, *Geschichte Der Heil. Röm. Reichs Freyen Stadt Augspurg: Aus bewährten Jahr-Büchern und Tüchtigen Urkunden gezogen, Und an das Licht gegeben* (Frankfurt: Merz und Mayer, 1743), p. 370.
4. Terms explained in the glossary (Appendix) are marked with an asterisk at their first appearance.
5. StAA, Ratsprotokolle 17/II (1543), fol. 45v.
6. Johann Christoph Hirsch, *Eröfnetes Geheimnus der practischen Münz-Wissenschafft samt beygefügter Tariffa, über Gold und Silber* (Nuremberg: Adam Jonathan Felßeckers seel. Erben, 1762), p. 123.
7. StAA, Ratsprotokolle 17/II (1543), fol. 47r.
8. StAA, Ratsprotokolle 17/II (1543), fol. 105v.; StAA, Bestand: Reichsstadt, Strafamt Nr. 96.1 (Strafbuch 1543–1553), fols. 14r–15r.
9. Mark Häberlein, *Brüder, Freunde und Betrüger: Soziale Beziehungen, Normen und Konflikte in der Augsburger Kaufmannschaft um die Mitte des 16. Jahrhunderts* (Berlin: Akademie Verlag, 1998), p. 320; Mark Häberlein and Christina Dalhede, 'Kraffter (Craffter, Krafter), Kaufmannsfamilie', in *Augsburger Stadtlexikon*, ed. Günther Grünsteudel, Günter Hägele, and Rudolf Frankenberger (Augsburg: Wißner-Verlag, 2010) (online: https://www.wissner.com/stadtlexikon-augsburg/artikel/stadtlexikon/kraffter/4475, accessed 17/02/2023).
10. StAA Ratsprotokolle 17/II (1543), fol. 105r. StAA, Strafamt Nr. 96.1 (Strafbuch 1543–1553), fols. 14v.–16v.

11. For the term 'trade in coinage' (*kauffmanschafft in der muntz*) see, e.g., Oliver Volckart, ed., *Eine Währung für das Reich: Die Akten der Münztage zu Speyer 1549 und 1557* (Stuttgart: Steiner, 2017), no. 37, p. 129.
12. See, e.g., Cornelis Rattmann, 'Die Mark kam aus Hamburg', *Welt am Sonntag*, 09/12/2001, online at https://www.welt.de/print-wams/article617965/Die-Mark-kam-aus-Hamburg.html (accessed 17/02/2023). Cf. Friedrich Frhr. von Schrötter, 'Das Münzwesen des deutschen Reichs von 1500–1566, Teil II', *Schmollers Jahrbuch für Gesetzgebung, Verwaltung und Volkswirtschaft* 36, no. 1 (1912), pp. 99–100; Peter Lennartz, 'Die Probationstage und Probationsregister des niederländisch-westfälischen Kreises', *Numismatische Zeitschrift* 46 (1913), p. 1; Johann Kamann, 'Der Nürnberger Patrizier Christoph Fürer der Ältere und seine Denkwürdigkeiten 1479–1537', *Mitteilungen des Vereins für Geschichte der Stadt Nürnberg* 28 (1928), p. 259; Fritz Blaich, *Die Wirtschaftspolitik des Reichstags im Heiligen Römischen Reich: Ein Beitrag zur Problemgeschichte wirtschaftlichen Gestaltens* (Stuttgart: Fischer, 1970), p. 15; Günther Probszt, *Österreichische Münz- und Geldgeschichte von den Anfängen bis 1918* (Vienna, Cologne, Graz: Hermann Böhlaus Nachf., 1973), p. 397; Gerhard Schön, 'Die Münzprobationstage im Alten Reich', *Abhandlungen der Braunschweigischen Wissenschaftlichen Gesellschaft* 61 (2008), p. 467.
13. Marc Flandreau, 'The Economics and Politics of Monetary Unions: A Reassessment of the Latin Monetary Union, 1865–71', *Financial History Review* 7, no. 1 (2000).
14. See Georg Schmidt, 'Das frühneuzeitliche Reich—Sonderweg und Modell für Europa oder Staat der deutschen Nation?', in *Imperium Romanum—irregulare corpus—Teutscher Reichs-Staat*, ed. Matthias Schnettger (Mainz: Philipp von Zabern, 2002); Joachim Whaley, 'The Old Reich in Modern Memory: Recent Controversies Concering the "Relevance" of Early Modern German History', in *German Literature, History and the Nation: Papers from the Conference 'The Fragile Tradition', Cambridge 2002*, ed. Christian Emden and David Midgley (Oxford: Peter lang, 2004), p. 34; 'The Holy Roman Empire: European Disunion done Right', *The Economist*, 22 December, 2012; Brendan Simms, 'The Ghosts of Europe Past', *The New York Times* 9 June 2013; Henry Kissinger, *World Order: Reflections on the Character of Nations and the Course of History* (s.l.: Penguin, 2015), p. 92; Peter H. Wilson, 'The Holy Roman Empire Can Help Inspire a Different European Union', *Financial Times*, 20 Jan. 2016; Dalibor Rohac, 'The Holy Roman Union', *The American Interest* (Washington, DC), 7 May 2019; Timothy Garton Ash, 'Since Reunification, Germany Has Had its Best 30 Years: The Next 30 Will Be Harder', *The Guardian*, 20 Sep. 2020; Johannes Burkhardt, 'Europäischer Nachzügler oder institutioneller Vorreiter? Plädoyer für einen neuen Entwicklungsdiskurs zur konstruktiven Doppelstaatlichkeit des frühmodernen Reiches', in *Imperium Romanum—irregulare corpus—Teutscher Reichs-Staat: Das Alte Reich im Verständnis der Zeitgenossen und der Historiographie*, ed. Matthias Schnettger (Mainz: Zabern, 2002), p. 316; Peter Claus

Hartmann, *Das Heilige Römische Reich deutscher Nation in der Neuzeit 1486–1806* (Stuttgart: Reclam, 2005), p. 9; David Pan, 'European Union and Holy Roman Empire', *Telos: Critical Theory of the Contemporary* 176 (2016), p. 207; Marlene Wind, 'The European Union as a Polycentric Polity: Returning to a Neo-Medieval Europe?', in *European Constitutionalism Beyond the State*, ed. J.H.H. Weiler (Cambridge: Cambridge University Press 2004), pp. 124–7. Also see Peter Haldén, *Stability Without Statehood: Lessons From Europe's History Before the Sovereign State* (London: Palgrave Macmillan, 2011), pp. 51–67.

15. Geoffrey R.D. Underhill, 'Multilateralism', in *A Concise Oxford Dictionary of Politics and International Relations*, ed. Garrett W. Brown, Iain McLean, and Alistair McMillan (Oxford: Oxford University Press, 2018).
16. Volckart, *Währung*.
17. Philipp Robinson Rössner, *Deflation—Devaluation—Rebellion: Geld im Zeitalter der Reformation* (Stuttgart: Steiner, 2012).
18. Friedrich Frhr. von Schrötter, 'Das Münzwesen des deutschen Reichs von 1500–1566, Teil I', *Schmollers Jahrbuch für Gesetzgebung, Verwaltung und Volkswirtschaft* 35, no. 4 (1911); ibid., 'Münzwesen, Teil II'; ibid., 'Der Speierer Reichsmünztag von 1557', *Zeitschrift für Numismatik* 29 (1912); Blaich, *Wirtschaftspolitik*.
19. Petr Vorel, *Monetary Circulation in Central Europe at the Beginning of the Early Modern Age: Attempts to Establish a Shared Currency as an Aspect of the Political Culture of the 16th Century (1524–1573)* (Pardubice: Univerziteta Pardubice, 2006).
20. Rössner, *Deflation*.
21. Hans-Jürgen Gerhard, 'Ursachen und Folgen der Wandlungen im Währungssystem des Deutschen Reiches 1500–1625: Eine Studie zu den Hintergründen der sogenannten Preisrevolution', in *Geld und Währung vom 16. Jahrhundert bis zur Gegenwart*, ed. Eckart Schremmer (Stuttgart: Steiner, 1993); ibid., 'Ein schöner Garten ohne Zaun: Die währungspolitische Situation des Deutschen Reiches um 1600', *Vierteljahrschrift für Sozial- und Wirtschaftsgeschichte* 81, no. 2 (1994); ibid., 'Neuere deutsche Forschungen zur Geld- und Währungsgeschichte der Frühen Neuzeit: Fragen – Ansätze – Ergebnisse', *Vierteljahrschrift für Sozial- und Wirtschaftsgeschichte* 83, no. 2 (1996); Michael North, 'Münzpolitik in der ersten Hälfte des 16. Jahrhunderts: Das Heilige Römische Reich und Sachsen im europäischen Kontext', in *Die drei Flugschriften über den Münzstreit der sächsischen Albertiner und Ernestiner*, ed. Bertram Schefold (Düsseldorf: 2000); ibid., 'Reich und Reichstag im 16. Jahrhundert: Der Blick aus der angeblichen Reichsferne', in *Der Reichstag 1486–1613: Kommunikation—Wahrnehmung—Öffentlichkeiten*, ed. Maximilian Lanzinner and Arno Strohmeyer (Göttingen: Vandenhoeck & Ruprecht, 2006); ibid., 'Geld- und Ordnungspolitik im Alten Reich', in *Geld, Handel, Wirtschaft: Höchste Gerichte im Alten Reich als Spruchkörper und Institution*, ed. Anja Amend-Traut, Albrecht Cordes, and Wolfgang Sellert (Berlin, Boston: de Gruyter, 2013); ibid., 'The Reception of Imperial Monetary Reforms in 16th-century Northern Germany',

in *Money and Finance in Central Europe During the Later Middle Ages*, ed. Roman Zaoral (London: Palgrave Macmillan, 2016).

22. Gustav Schmoller, 'Über die Ausbildung einer richtigen Scheidemünzpolitik vom 14. bis 19. Jahrhundert', *Jahrbuch für Gesetzgebung, Verwaltung und Volkswirtschaft im Deutschen Reich* 24 (1900); Thomas J. Sargent and François R. Velde, 'The Big Problem of Small Change', *Journal of Money, Credit and Banking* 31, no. 2 (1999); Thomas J. Sargent and François R. Velde, *The Big Problem of Small Change* (Princeton, Oxford: Princeton University Press, 2002).
23. Angela Redish, *Bimetallism: An Economic and Historical Analysis* (Cambridge, New York: Cambridge University Press, 2000).
24. Joachim Whaley, *Germany and the Holy Roman Empire*, vol. I: From Maximilian I to the Peace of Westphalia 1493–1648 (Oxford: Oxford University Press, 2012), p. xi.
25. Georg Büchmann, *Geflügelte Worte: Der Zitatenschatz des deutschen Volkes* (Cologne: Atlas-Verlag, 1956), p. 329.
26. Fynes Moryson, *An Itinerary Containing His Ten Yeeres Travell through the Twelve Dominions of Germany, Bohmer-land, Sweitzerland, Netherland, Denmarke, Poland, Italy, Turky, France, England, Scotland & Ireland*, vol. 2 (Glasgow: Glasgow University Press, 1617/1907), p. 163.

CHAPTER I

1. StAA, 00084 Urgichten 1549 VI 18 Silvester Raid: 1549.06.18, Donauwörth. Anna Raid an Rat Augsburg.
2. StAA 00084 Urgichten, 1549.VI.18., Silvester Raid: 1553.04.25, Donauwörth. Silvester Raid an Stadt Augsburg.
3. Joseph Kohler and Willy Scheel, eds., *Die Peinliche Gerichtsordnung Kaiser Karls V.: Constitutio Criminalis Carolina* (Halle: Verlag der Buchhandlung des Waisenhauses, 1900), § 111, p. 51; Klaus Geppert, 'Die Peinliche Halsgerichtsordnung Karls V. (die "Carolina")', *JURA—Juristische Ausbildung* 37, no. 2 (2015), p. 151.
4. StAA 00084 Urgichten, 1549.VI.18., Silvester Raid: 1553.IV.25, Donauwörth. Silvester Raid an Stadt Augsburg.
5. The surviving paperwork: StAA 00084, Urgichten 1549.VI.18.
6. Johannes Voigt, 'Musikliebhaberei des Herzogs Albrecht von Preußen', Allgemeines Archiv für die Geschichtskunde des preußischen Staates 2 (1830), pp. 73–5; Friedrich Roth, 'Silvester Raid, der Brand-, Proviant- und spätere Rentmeister des Markgrafen Albrecht Alcibiades von Brandenburg-Kulmbach, und Georg Fröhlich, Verfasser der "Historia belli Schmalcaldici"', *Archiv für Reformationsgeschichte* 9 (1911–12), p. 4; Häberlein, *Brüder*, pp. 208–9; ibid., *Die Fugger: Geschichte einer Augsburger Familie (1367–1650)* (Stuttgart: Kohlhammer, 2006), pp. 136–7. Raid's mine is mentioned in Paul Hektor Mair's chronicle of Augsburg: Friedrich Roth, ed., *Die Chroniken der schwäbischen Städte: Augsburg*, vol. 7 (Leipzig: Hirzel, 1917), p. 183.

7. Ibid., 'Silvester Raid', p. 7.
8. Häberlein, *Brüder*, p. 211; StAA 00084 Urgichten, 1549.VI.18., Silvester Raid: 1553.IV.25, Donauwörth. Silvester Raid an Stadt Augsburg.
9. The daily wage was 28 *Hellers*, with the *Kreuzer* being a 3½-*Heller* piece. Moritz J. Elsas, *Umriss einer Geschichte der Preise und Löhne in Deutschland vom ausgehenden Mittelalter bis zum Beginn des neunzehnten Jahrhunderts*, vol. 1 (Leiden: A.W. Sijthoff's Uitgeversmaatschappij, 1936), p. 731.
10. Häberlein, *Brüder*, pp. 208, 210.
11. StAA 00084 Urgichten 1549.VI.18, Silvester Raid: 1549.VII.16, Verhörprotokoll.
12. Schrötter, 'Münzwesen, Teil I', pp. 163–4.
13. Roth, *Augsburg*, vol. 7, p. 182.
14. StAA 00084 Urgichten 1549.VI.18, Silvester Raid: 1549.VII.16, Verhörprotokoll.
15. Roth, *Augsburg*, vol. 7, p. 183 with FN 2.
16. StAA 00084, Urgichten 1549.VI.18., Silvester Raid: No date, articles for the interrogation of Raid.
17. In an article published in 1996 a group of prominent economists wondered why merchants would be prepared to sell bullion to a mint in return for debased coins if they were aware of the debasement. They called this phenomenon the 'debasement puzzle'. Arthur J. Rolnick, François R. Velde, and Warren E. Weber, 'The Debasement Puzzle: An Essay on Medieval Monetary History', *The Journal of Economic History* 56, no. 4 (1996). Here is the solution to the puzzle.
18. Cf. John H. Munro, *Wool, Cloth, and Gold: The Struggle for Bullion in Anglo-Burgundian Trade, 1340–1478* (Brussels, Toronto: University of Toronto Press, 1972), p. 33.
19. Rössner, *Deflation*, pp. 486, 513, 553.
20. Henry Dunning Macleod, *The Elements of Political Economy* (London: Longman, Brown, Green, Lonqmaus and Roberts, 1858), p. 477; cf. John Guy, *Gresham's Law: The Life and World of Queen Elizabeth I's Banker* (London: Profile Books, 2020), p. 102–3.
21. Heinrich Buck and Max von Bahrfeld, *Die Münzen der Stadt Hildesheim* (Hildesheim, Leipzig: Lax, 1937), pp. 1, 65–6.
22. Buck and Bahrfeld, *Hildesheim*, p. 109.
23. Gustav Freytag, *Pictures of German Life in the Fifteenth, Sixteenth and Seventeenth Centuries*, vol. 1 (London: Chapman and Hall, 1862), p. 175.
24. Theodor Pyl, 'Sastrow, Bartholomäus', in *Allgemeine Deutsche Biographie*, ed. Historische Commission bei der Königlichen Akademie der Wissenschaften (Leipzig: Duncker & Humblot, 1890); Karl-Reinhart Trauner, *Identität in der frühen Neuzeit: Die Autobiographie des Bartholomäus Sastrow* (Münster: Aschendorf, 2004).
25. Bartholomäus Sastrow and Gottlieb Mohnike, *Bartholomäi Sastrowen Herkommen, Geburt und Lauff seines gantzen Lebens auch was sich in dem Denckwerdiges zugetragen, so er mehrentheils selbst gesehen und gegenwärtig mit angehöret hat*, vol. 1 (Greifswald: Universitäts-Buchhandlung, 1823), pp. 195–7.

26. Georg Gaebel, ed., *Des Thomas Kantzow Chronik von Pommern in hochdeutscher Mundart*, vol. 1: Letzte Bearbeitung (Stettin: Paul Niekammer, 1897), p. 346.
27. Ibid., *Des Thomas Kantzow Chronik*, vol. 1: Letzte Bearbeitung, p. 266.
28. Friedrich Zarncke, ed., *Sebastian Brants Narrenschiff* (Hannover: Georg Olms, 1854/1961), p. 97.
29. Kunz Haß, *Hierin vindet mon die vrsach wodurch alle hendel yetz in der welt verkert und verderbt werden* (Nuremberg: no publisher, *c.*1500), fols. 3v.–4r.; for similar complaints see for instance Albert Krantz, *Wandalia* (Cologne: no publisher, 1519), lib. 12, cap. 38; Urbanus Rhegius, *Der XV. Psalm Davids* (Magdeburg: Lotther, 1538), (unpaginated, p. 43); Karl Euling, ed., *Chronik des Johan Oldecop* (Tübingen: Litterarischer Verein in Stuttgart, 1891), p. 380.
30. Jürgen Bollandt, ed., *Hamburgische Burspraken 1346 bis 1594 mit Nachträgen bis 1699*, vol. 2: Bursprakentexte (Hamburg: Hans Christians Druckerei und Verlag, 1960), p. 322.
31. AHL, Altes Senatsarchiv, Interna 22,782 (ASA Interna—Münzwesen - 23/5).
32. ÖStA, HHStA Wien, Reichshofrat, Miscellanea Münzwesen 2: Münzwesen im Reich, 1551–1564, fol. 443r.
33. Precisely 28.6 per cent of that of a *Kreuzer*. ÖStA, HHStA Wien, Reichshofrat, Miscellanea Münzwesen 2, fol. 462r.
34. Erwein Eltz, ed., *Deutsche Reichstagsakten unter Kaiser Karl V.: Der Speyrer Reichstag von 1544*, vol. 1 (Göttingen: Vandenhoeck & Ruprecht, 2001), no. 70, p. 341; cf. Eduard Šimek, 'Die Zusammenhänge zwischen Währung und Handel im Böhmen des 16. Jahrhunderts', in *Der Außenhandel Ostmitteleuropas 1450–1650: Die ostmitteleuropäischen Volkswirtschaften in ihren Beziehungen zu Mitteleuropa*, ed. Ingomar Bog (Cologne, Vienna: Böhlau, 1971), p. 244.
35. Oliver Volckart, 'Money and its Technologies: The "Principles of Minting" in the Middle Ages', in *A Cultural History of Money in the Medieval Age*, ed. Rory Naismith (London, New York, Oxford, New Delhi, Sydney: Bloomsbury Academic, 2019), p. 25.
36. Munro, *Wool, Cloth, and Gold*, pp. 29–30; ibid., 'Bullion Flows and Monetary Contraction in Late-Medieval England and the Low Countries', in *Precious Metals in the Later Medieval and Early Modern Worlds*, ed. J.F. Richards (Durham/NC: Carolina Academic Press, 1983), p. 110.
37. Joachim Schüttenhelm, 'Zur Münzprägung und Silberversorgung süddeutscher Münzstätten im frühen 16. Jahrhundert', in *Der Anschnitt: Zeischrift für Kunst und Kultur im Bergbau. Beiheft 2: Montanwirtschaft Mitteleuropas vom 12. bis 17. Jahrhundert. Stand, Wege und Aufgaben der Forschung*, ed. Werner Kroker (Bochum: Deutsches Bergbau-Museum, 1984), p. 165.
38. See, for example, the Saxon currency bill of 1534 that warned of such 'Beischläge'. Des Chürfürsten vnd Hertzog Georgen zu Sachssen etc. Muntz Ordenung (s.l.: no publisher, 1534), unpaginated (p. 8).

39. David Chilosi and Oliver Volckart, 'Money, States and Empire: Financial Integration and Institutional Change in Central Europe, 1400–1520', *The Journal of Economic History* 71, no. 3 (2011).
40. Josef Leeb, ed., *Der Kurfürstentag zu Frankfurt 1558 und der Reichstag zu Augsburg 1559*, vol. 3 (Göttingen: Vandenhoeck & Ruprecht, 1999), no. 661, p. 1721.
41. E.g., Şevket Pamuk and K. Kıvanç Karaman, 'Different Paths to the Modern State in Europe: The Interaction Between Warfare, Economic Structure, and Political Regime', *American Political Science Review* 107, no. 3 (2013). Apart from lacking 'state capacity', the German principalities were not sovereign (being subject to the emperor), which makes using the term state all the more problematic. Whaley, *Germany*, I, p. 486.
42. StAA, Bestand: Reichsstadt, Strafamt Nr. 96.1 (Strafbuch 1543–1553).
43. StAA, Bestand: Reichsstadt, Strafamt Nr. 96.1 (Strafbuch 1543–1553), fols. 12v., 13v.
44. StAA, Bestand: Reichsstadt, Strafamt Nr. 96.1 (Strafbuch 1543–1553), fols. 14r.–16v.
45. Ulf Dirlmeier, *Untersuchungen zu Einkommensverhältnissen und Lebenshaltungskosten in oberdeutschen Städten des Spätmittelalters (Mitte 14. bis Anfang 16. Jahrhundert)* (Heidelberg: Carl Winter Universitätsverlag, 1978), p. 129.
46. StAA 00084 Urgichten, 1549.VI.18., Silvester Raid: 1553.IV.25, Donauwörth. Silvester Raid an Stadt Augsburg.
47. Roth, 'Silvester Raid', p. 9. For the office of 'pillage master' see Leonhard Fronsberger, *Von Kayserlichem Kriegßrechten, Malefitz vnd Schuldhändlen, Ordnung vnd Regiment* (Frankfurt: Feyerabend, 1564), fol. LXXXIIII v.
48. Roth, 'Silvester Raid', p. 14.
49. Luca Scholz, *Borders and Freedom of Movement in the Holy Roman Empire* (Oxford: Oxford University Press, 2020), p. 32.
50. Kaiser Karl des fünfften Newe Müntzordnung, Sampt Valuierung der Gulden vnd Silberin Müntzen, Vnd darauff eruolgtem Kaiserlichen Edict, zu Augspurg alles im Jar M.D.LI. aufgericht und außgangen, (Augsburg: Philipp Ulhart, 1551), p. 4 (original not foliated).
51. Heinz Thomas, 'Julius Caesar und die Deutschen: Zu Ursprung und Gehalt eines deutschen Geschichtsbewußtseins in der Zeit Gregors VII. und Heinrichs IV.', in *Die Salier und das Reich*, ed. Stefan Weinfurter (Sigmaringen: Thorbecke, 1991); Len Scales, *The Shaping of German Identity: Authority and Crisis, 1245–1414* (Cambridge: Cambridge University Press, 2012), p. 279; Peter H. Wilson, *The Holy Roman Empire: A Thousand Years of Europe's History* (London: Allen Lane, 2016), pp. 38–9.
52. Whaley, *Germany*, I, p. 17; Wilson, *Empire*, pp. 19, 32; Peter Moraw, *Von offener Verfassung zu gestalteter Verdichtung: Das Reich im Späten Mittelalter 1250 bis 1490* (Frankfurt, Berlin: Propyläen, 1989), p. 149; Heike Johanna Mierau, 'Das Reich, politische Theorien und die Heilsgeschichte: Zur Ausbildung eines

Reichsbewußtseins durch die Papst-Kaiser-Chroniken des Spätmittelalters', *Zeitschrift für Historische Forschung* 32, no. 4 (2005), pp. 543–4; Albrecht Luttenberger, 'Kirchenadvokatie und Religionsfriede: Kaiseridee und kaiserliche Reichsidee im 16. und 17. Jahrhundert', in *Legitimation und Funktion des Herrschers: Vom ägyptischen Pharao zum neuzeitlichen Diktator*, ed. Rolf Gundlach and Hermann Weber (Stuttgart: Steiner, 1992), pp. 185–8; cf. Ulrich Nonn, 'Heiliges Römisches Reich Deutscher Nation: Zum Nationen-Begriff im 15. Jahrhundert', *Zeitschrift für historische Forschung* 9, no. 2 (1982), pp. 130, 142; for a discussion of the relation between Germany and the Empire see Scales, *German Identity*, pp. 155–82.

53. Hartmut Boockmann, *Stauferzeit und spätes Mittelalter: Deutschland 1125–1517*, 4 ed. (Berlin: Siedler, 1994), pp. 8–9; Hans Boldt, *Deutsche Verfassungsgeschichte*, 2 ed., vol. 1: Von den Anfängen bis zum Ende des älteren deutschen Reiches 1806 (Munich: dtv, 1990), pp. 133, 136; Scales, *German Identity*, pp. 65–9.
54. Peter Heather, *The Restauration of Rome: Barbarian Popes and Imperial Pretenders* (London: Pan Books, 2013), pp. 286–7.
55. Scales, *German Identity*, pp. 73–4; Johann Friedrich Böhmer, *Regesta Imperii*, vol. V. Jüngere Staufer 1198–1272. Die Regesten des Kaiserreichs unter Philipp, Otto IV, Friedrich II, Heinrich (VII), Conrad IV, Heinrich Raspe, Wilhelm und Richard. 1198–1272, V. 1 (Innsbruck: Wagner'sche Universitäts-Buchhandlung, 1881), no. 672, p. 175; Ernst Schubert, 'Franken als königsnahe Landschaft unter Karl IV.', *Blätter für deutsche Landesgeschichte N.F.* 114 (1978), p. 874; Moraw, *Von offener Verfassung*, p. 157; Eberhard Isenmann, 'The Holy Roman Empire in the Middle Ages', in *The Rise of the Fiscal State in Europe c.1200–1815*, ed. Richard Bonney (Oxford: Oxford University Press, 1999), p. 252.
56. Götz Landwehr, 'Mobilisierung und Konsolidierung der Herrschaftsordnung im 14. Jahrhundert', in *Der deutsche Territorialstaat im 14. Jahrhundert*, ed. Hans Patze (Sigmaringen: Thorbecke, 1971/86), p. 494.
57. Timothy Reuter, 'The "Imperial Church System" of the Ottonian and Salian Rulers: A Reconsideration', *The Journal of Ecclesiastical History* 33, no. 3 (1982).
58. Peter Classen, 'Das Wormser Konkordat in der deutschen Verfassungsgeschichte', in *Investiturstreit und Reichsverfassung*, ed. Josef Fleckenstein (Sigmaringen: Thorbecke, 1973), p. 412.
59. Wilson, *Empire*, pp. 87–94; Whaley, *Germany*, I, p. 274.
60. Hendrik Spruyt, *The Sovereign State and Its Competitors: An Analysis of Systems Change* (Princeton/NJ: Princeton University Press, 1994), pp. 89–98; Michel Cassan, 'Die Krone und die Städte unter Karl IX. und Ludwig XIII.', in *Staatsbildung als kultureller Prozess: Strukturwandel und Legitimation von Herrschaft in der Frühen Neuzeit*, ed. Ronald G. Asch and Dagmar Freist (Cologne, Weimar, Vienna: Böhlau, 2005), pp. 135, 148.
61. Fernand Braudel, *The Mediterranean and the Mediterranean World in the Age of Philip II*, 5 ed., vol. 1 (Glasgow: Fontana, 1949/86), p. 55.

62. Thomas Szabó, 'Die Straßen in Deutschland und Italien im Mittelalter', in *Straßen- und Verkehrswesen im hohen und späten Mittelalter*, ed. Rainer Christoph Schwinges (Sigmaringen: Thorbecke, 2007), pp. 78–80.
63. Scales, *German Identity*, p. 80.
64. Evamaria Engel, *Die deutsche Stadt im Mittelalter* (Düsseldorf: Patmos Verlag, 1993/2005), p. 280.
65. Paul Bairoch, Jean Batou, and Pierre Chèvre, *La population des villes européennes: banque de données et analyse sommaire des résultats; 800–1850 (The population of European cities)* (Genève: Droz, 1988), pp. 253–4.
66. Cf. Robert L. Carneiro, 'A Theory of the Origin of the State', *Science* 169, no. 3947 (1970); ibid., 'The Circumscription Theory: A Clarification, Amplification, and Reformulation', *Social Evolution & History* 11, no. 2 (2012). Note that I am not following the strong version of 'constriction theory', which argues that the difficulty of leaving a region is a general factor in state formation.
67. Fritz Backhaus, '"Das größte Siedelwerk des deutschen Volkes": Zur Erforschung der Germania Slavica in Deutschland', in *Struktur und Wandel im Früh- und Hochmittelalter: Eine Bestandsaufnahme aktueller Forschungen zur Germania Slavica*, ed. Christian Lübke (Stuttgart: Steiner, 1998); Scales, *German Identity*, pp. 398–402.
68. Manuel Eisner, 'Modernization, Self-Control and Lethal Violence: The Long-term Dynamics of European Homicide Rates in Theoretical Perspective', *British Journal of Criminology* 41 (2001), p. 625.
69. Peter Moraw, 'Versuch über die Entstehung des Reichstags', in *Politische Ordnungen und soziale Kräfte im Alten Reich*, ed. Hermann Weber (Wiesbaden: Steiner, 1980), pp. 14–18, 24.
70. Ibid., 'Versuch', p. 31; Wilson, *Empire*, pp. 323–5.
71. Cologne: Erich Keyser, ed., *Deutsches Städtebuch*, vol. 3,3: Rheinisches Städtebuch (Stuttgart: Kohlhammer, 1956), p. 255; Paul Bairoch, 'Urbanization and the Economy in Preindustrial Societies: The Findings of Two Decades of Research', *Journal of European Economic History* 18 (1989), p. 6. Nuremberg: Erich Keyser and Heinz Stoob, eds., *Deutsches Städtebuch*, vol. 5,1: Bayern (Stuttgart, Berlin, Cologne, Mainz: Kohlhammer, 1971), pp. 391–3. Weil der Stadt had about 200 citizens in the sixteenth century; the number of inhabitants was larger. Isny had 1743 inhabitants in 1810. Erich Keyser, ed., *Deutsches Städtebuch*, vol. 4, 2: Württemberg (Stuttgart: Kohlhammer, 1962), pp. 296, 370.
72. Adolf Wrede, ed., *Deutsche Reichstagsakten unter Kaiser Karl V.*, vol. 2 (Gotha: Friedrich Andreas Perthes, 1896), no. 56, pp. 424–43. Gerhard Oestreich identified the 'duke of the Mase' as the duke of Bar on the border to France. Gerhard Oestreich, *Verfassungsgeschichte vom Ende des Mittelalters bis zum Ende des alten Reiches* (Munich: dtv, 1982), p. 139. Rosemarie Aulinger thinks of the duke of Mazovia in Poland. Aulinger, *Reichstag zu Worms 1545*, vol. 2, p. 1088 with FN 4.

73. Siegfried Fitte, *Das staatsrechtliche Verhältnis des Herzogtums Lothringen zum deutschen Reich seit dem Jahr 1542* (Strassburg: Heitz & Mündel, 1891), pp. 12–27.
74. Nicolette Mout, 'Die Niederlande und das Reich im 16. Jahrhundert', in *Alternativen zur Reichsverfassung in der Frühen Neuzeit?*, ed. Volker Press and Dieter Stievermann (Munich: Oldenbourg, 1995), p. 147.
75. Ibid., 'Die Niederlande', pp. 153–5.
76. Alexander Begert, *Böhmen, die böhmische Kur und das Reich vom Hochmittelalter bis zum Ende des Alten Reiches: Studien zur Kurwürde und staatsrechtlichen Stellung Böhmens* (Husum: Matthiesen, 2003), p. 311.
77. Cf. Georg Schmidt, *Geschichte des Alten Reiches: Staat und Nation in der Frühen Neuzeit 1495–1806* (Munich: Beck, 1999), pp. 10–7; ibid., 'The State and Nation of the Germans', in *The Holy Roman Empire: 1495–1806*, ed. Robert John Weston Evans, Michael Schaich, and Peter H. Wilson (Oxford: Oxford University Press, 2011), p. 46.
78. Thomas Christmann, *Das Bemühen von Kaiser und Reich um die Vereinheitlichung des Münzwesens: zugleich ein Beitrag zum Rechtssetzungsverfahren im Heiligen Römischen Reich nach dem Westfälischen Frieden* (Berlin: Duncker & Humblot, 1988), pp. 20–1. The dukes and electors of Saxony always minted without the formal consent of the emperors. Walter Schwinkowski, 'Das Geld- und Münzwesen Sachsens', *Neues Archiv für sächsische Geschichte* 38 (1917), pp. 141, 144; Bernd Sprenger, *Das Geld der Deutschen: Geldgeschichte Deutschlands von den Anfängen bis zur Gegenwart*, 3 ed. (Paderborn, Munich, Vienna, Zürich: Schöningh, 2002), p. 60.
79. Rössner, *Deflation*, pp. 564–8; cf. Eric Helleiner, *The Making of National Money: Territorial Currencies in Historical Perspective* (Ithaca, London: Cornell University Press, 2003), p. 21.
80. E.g., ÖStA, HHStA Wien, Reichshofrat, Miscellanea Münzwesen 2: Münzwesen im Reich, 1551–1564, fol. 99v., 450r., 455r.; Aulinger, *Reichstag zu Worms 1545*, vol. 2, no. 67, p. 889; ÖStA HHStA Wien, Reichshofrat, Miscellanea Münzwesen 1: Münzwesen im Reich (2. Konvolut), fol. 231 r.; Volckart, *Währung*, no. 34, p. 99, no. 83, p. 280, no. 84, pp. 292, 298–300, no. 86, pp. 304–5, 309–10. 'Confusion and disorder': ibid., *Währung*, no. 86, p. 309.
81. Winfried Dotzauer, *Die deutschen Reichskreise in der Verfassung des Alten Reiches und ihr Eigenleben (1500–1806)* (Darmstadt: Wissenschaftliche Buchgesellschaft, 1989), pp. 8–10.
82. Erwein Eltz, ed., *Deutsche Reichstagsakten unter Kaiser Karl V.: Der Reichstag zu Augsburg 1550/51*, vol. 2 (Munich: Oldenbourg, 2005), no. 305, p. 1589; Volckart, *Währung*, no. 88, pp. 318–42.
83. Hubert Emmerig, 'Der Münzbetrieb in Mittelalter und früher Neuzeit: Personal, Ausrüstung, Tätigkeiten', *Vorträge zur Geldgeschichte* 3 (2006), p. 8.
84. Sprenger, *Geld*, p. 81.
85. Cf. e.g., Oliver Volckart, *Die Münzpolitik im Deutschordensland und Herzogtum Preußen von 1370 bis 1550* (Wiesbaden: Harrassowitz, 1996), no. 10, pp. 409–11.

86. Wolfgang Schulten, *Deutsche Münzen aus der Zeit Kaiser Karls V.: Typenkatalog der Gepräge zwischen dem Beginn der Talerprägung (1484) und der dritten Reichsmünzordnung (1559)* (Frankfurt: Numismatischer Verlag P.N. Schulten, 1974); Volckart, *Währung*, no. 89, pp. 343–4.
87. Ibid., *Währung*, no. 88, p. 334.
88. Cf. Peter Spufford, *Money and its Use in Medieval Europe* (Cambridge, New York, Port Chester, Melbourne, Sydney: Cambridge University Press, 1991), pp. 321–3.
89. Volckart, *Währung*, no. 88, pp. 318–42; Bernhard Prokisch, *Grunddaten zur europäischen Münzprägung der Neuzeit ca. 1500–1990* (Vienna: Verlag Fassbaender, 1993), pp. 1–244.
90. Christian Binder and Julius Ebner, *Württembergische Münz- und Medaillenkunde*, vol. 1 (Stuttgart: Kohlhammer, 1910), p. 9.
91. Hans Krusy, *Gegenstempel auf Münzen des Spätmittelalters* (Frankfurt: Numismatischer Verlag P. N. Schulten, 1974); Karel Castelin, *Grossus Pragensis: Der Prager Groschen und seine Teilstücke; 1300–1547*, 2 ed. (Braunschweig: Klinkhardt & Biermann, 1973), pp. 74–9; Hubert Emmerig, 'Zur Datierung der Gegenstempelung von Prager Groschen in Süddeutschland', in *Nummi Docent! Münzen—Schätze—Funde. Festschrift für Peter Ilisch zum 65. Geburtstag*, ed. Gerd Dethlefs, Arent Pol, and Stefan Wittenbrink (Osnabrück: Numismatischer Verlag der Münzhandlung Fritz Rudolf Künker, 2012), p. 221.
92. Wilhelm Jesse, *Der Wendische Münzverein* (Lübeck: Hansischer Geschichtsverein, 1928).
93. Cf. Rössner, *Deflation*, p. 377.
94. Hansheiner Eichhorn, *Der Strukturwandel im Geldumlauf Frankens zwischen 1437 und 1610: Ein Beitrag zur Methodologie der Geldgeschichte* (Wiesbaden: Franz Steiner Verlag, 1973), pp. 12, 49–80; Johann Christoph Hirsch, *Des Teutschen Reichs Münz-Archiv*, vol. 1 (Nuremberg: Adam Jonathan Felßeckers seel. Erben, 1756), no. CLXXXV, pp. 273–5.
95. Heinrich Günter, *Das Münzwesen in der Grafschaft Württemberg* (Stuttgart: Kohlhammer, 1897), pp. 69–71, 108–10.
96. Peter Berghaus, 'Umlauf und Nachprägung des Florentiner Guldens nördlich der Alpen', in *Congresso Internazionale di Numismatica, Roma 11–16 settembre 1961* (Rome: Commision Internationale de Numismatique, 1965), p. 602.
97. Elisabeth Nau, 'Münzumlauf im ländlichen Bereich mit besonderer Berücksichtigung Südwest-Deutschlands', in *Die Grundherrschaft im späten Mittelalter*, ed. Hans Patze (Sigmaringen: Thorbecke, 1983), pp. 132–56; Chilosi and Volckart, 'Money', pp. 764–6.
98. Karl Weisenstein, *Das Kurtriersche Münz- und Geldwesen vom Beginn des 14. bis zum Ende des 16. Jahrhunderts: Auch ein Beitrag zur Geschichte des Rheinischen Münzvereins* (Koblenz: Numismatischer Verlag, 1995), pp. 71, 74–5.
99. Volckart, *Währung*, no. 88, p. 324; cf. Konrad Schneider, 'Norm und Wirklichkeit der rheinischen Goldgulden', *Jahrbuch für westdeutsche Landesgeschichte* 40 (2014), pp. 62–6.

100. Volckart, *Währung*, no. 88, pp. 319–26.
101. Ibid., *Währung*, no. 84, p. 292.
102. Weisenstein, *Geldwesen*, pp. 176 (composition of coin hoards), 264–269 (mint output, electorate of Trier).
103. Karl Moeser and Fritz Dworschak, *Die große Münzreform unter Erzherzog Sigmund von Tirol (Die ersten großen Silber- und deutschen Bildnismünzen aus der Münzstätte Hall im Inntal)* (Vienna: Verlag Dr Eduard Stepan, 1936).
104. Paul Arnold, 'Die sächsische Talerwährung von 1500 bis 1763', *Schweizerische Numismatische Rundschau* 59 (1980), p. 56–7.
105. Cf. Nathan Sussman and Joseph Zeira, 'Commodity Money Inflation: Theory and Evidence from France in 1350–1436', *Journal of Monetary Economics* 50 (2003), p. 1776.
106. Aulinger, *Reichstag zu Worms 1545*, vol. 2, no. 85, p. 943.
107. Volckart, 'Money and its Technologies', p. 31; Redish, *Bimetallism*, p. 22.
108. Philipp Robinson Rössner, 'Monetary Instability, Lack of Integration, and the Curse of a Commodity Money Standard: The German Lands, *c.*1400–1900 A.D.', *Credit and Capital Markets – Kredit und Kapital* 47, no. 2 (2014), p. 303.
109. Valentin Groebner, *Ökonomie ohne Haus: Zum Wirtschaften armer Leute in Nürnberg am Ende des 15. Jahrhunderts* (Göttingen: Vandenhoeck & Ruprecht, 1993), p. 48.
110. Bjørn Poulsen, 'Die ältesten Bauernanschreibebücher: Schleswigsche Anschreibebücher des 16. und 17. Jahrhunderts', in *Bäuerliche Anschreibebücher als Quellen zur Wirtschaftsgeschichte*, ed. Klaus Joachim Lorenzen-Schmidt and Bjørn Poulsen (Neumünster: Wachholtz, 1992), p. 93; Wieland Held, 'Geldwirtschaftliche und marktwirtschaftliche Aspekte der Stadt-Land-Beziehungen in Thüringen im 16. Jahrhundert', *Jahrbuch für Wirtschaftsgeschichte* 3 (1983), p. 110.
111. Sina Westphal, ed., *Die Korrespondenz zwischen Kurfürst Friedrich dem Weisen von Sachsen und der Reichsstadt Nürnberg* (Frankfurt, Berlin, Bern: Peter Lang, 2009), pp. 114–17.
112. Ibid., *Die Korrespondenz zwischen Kurfürst Friedrich dem Weisen von Sachsen und der Reichsstadt Nürnberg*, no. 447.7, p. 611.
113. Arnold, 'Talerwährung', p. 64; Volckart, *Währung*, p. LXX.
114. Rebecca R. Darley, 'Money, Art, and Representation: The Powerful and Pragmatic Faces of Medieval Coinage', in *A Cultural History of Money in The Middle Ages*, ed. Rory Naismith (London: Bloomsbury Academic, 2019), *passim*; cf. Heinrich Rüthing, 'Zur Geschichte des Mariengroschens', in *Mundus in imagine: Bildersprache und Lebenswelten im Mittelalter. Festgabe für Klaus Schreiner*, ed. Andrea Löther, Ulrich Meier, and Norbert Schnitzler (Munich: Fink, 1996), p. 36.
115. Karel Castelin, 'Zur Entstehung der ältesten "Joachimstaler"', *Numismatische Zeitschrift* 80 (1963), p. 72.

116. Joachim Schüttenhelm, 'Problems of Quantifying the Volume of Money in Early Modern Times: A Preliminary Survey', in *Precious Metals, Coinage and the Changes of Monetary Structures in Latin-America, Europe and Asia (Late Middle Ages—Early Modern Times)*, ed. Eddy Van Cauwenberghe (Leuven: Leuven University Press, 1989), pp. 90–4.
117. Volckart, *Währung*, no. 88, pp. 319–26.
118. Lübeck: Goswin Frhr. von der Ropp, ed., *Hanserecesse von 1431–1476*, vol. 1 (2. Abt.) (Leipzig: Duncker & Humblot, 1876), p. 107; Constance: Julius Cahn, *Münz- und Geldgeschichte von Konstanz und des Bodenseegebietes im Mittelalter bis zum Reichsmünzgesetz von 1559* (Heidelberg: Carl Winter's Universitätsbuchhandlung, 1911), p. 265; Saxony: Schwinkowski, 'Münzwesen', p. 160; Württemberg: Hermann Grote, *Münzstudien*, vol. 6, Heft 1 (Graz: Akademische Druck- u. Verlagsanstalt, 1857–77/1969), p. 117; Vienna: Carl Schalk, 'Die österreichischen Goldgulden im 15. Jahrhundert', *Numismatische Zeitschrift* 11 (1879), pp. 274–5.
119. Harry A. Miskimin, 'The Enforcement of Gresham's Law', in *Cash, Credit and Crisis in Europe, 1300–1600*, ed. Harry Miskimin (London: Variorum Reprints, 1985/89), p. IX, 149; Schwinkowski, 'Münzwesen', p. 160; Arnold, 'Talerwährung', p. 55.
120. Lacking enforcement: Miskimin, 'The Enforcement of Gresham's Law', p. IX, 147. Schalk, 'Goldgulden', pp. 274–7; ibid., 'Der Wiener Münzverkehr im 16. Jahrhundert', *Numismatische Zeitschrift* 13 (1881), pp. 260–2; ibid., 'Der Wiener Münzverkehr im XVI. Jahrhundert', *Numismatische Zeitschrift* 16 (1884), pp. 90–2; Volckart, *Währung*, p. LVIII.
121. E.g., Milan: Carlo Maria Cipolla, *Money, Prices and Civilization in the Mediterranean World, Fifth to Seventeenth Century* (New York: Gordian Press, 1956), pp. 46–7.
122. Chilosi and Volckart, 'Money'.
123. Rhineland white *Pfennigs* (legal pure silver content 1515): Weisenstein, *Geldwesen*, p. 235, Schneider, 'Norm und Wirklichkeit der rheinischen Goldgulden', p. 60; Franconian *Zwölfer* (legal pure silver content 1536): Ernst Scholler, *Das Münzwesen der Reichsstadt Nürnberg im 16. Jahrhundert: Ein Beitrag zur reichsstädtischen Wirtschaftsgeschichte* (Nürnberg: Benedikt Hilz, 1912), pp. 35–6, 72; Saxon *Groschens* (legal pure silver content 1534): Arnold, 'Talerwährung', p. 67; Upper German/Austrian *Kreuzers* (legal pure silver content 1535): Hirsch, *Münz-Archiv*, 1, no. CLXXXIII, p. 269; Upper German *Batzens* (mean of eight variants tested in Munich 1539): Johann Georg von Lori, *Sammlung des baierischen Münzrechts*, vol. 1 (s.l.: no publisher, 1768), no. CXC, p. 217; Burgundian *Grotes*: Gottfried Pusch, *Staatliche Münz- und Geldpolitik in den Niederlanden unter den burgundischen und habsburgischen Herrschern besonders unter Kaiser Karl V.* (Munich: Val. Höfling, 1932), pp. 9, 86; Markish *Groschens* (as tested in Nuremberg 1551), Pomeranian *Schillings*

(as tested in Nuremberg 1551), *Maria Groschens* (mean of ten variants tested in Nuremberg 1551): Volckart, *Währung*, no. 88, pp. 334–5.

124. Aulinger, *Reichstag zu Worms 1545*, vol. 2, no. 86, p. 951.
125. Ibid., *Reichstag zu Worms 1545*, vol. 2, no. 86, p. 950.
126. Volckart, *Währung*, no. 76, pp. 267–8.

CHAPTER 2

1. *Ein Frag an eynen Müntzer/wahin doch souil Geltz/kumme das man alltag müntzet* (Augsburg: Wolfgang Rösch, 1530); research survey: Daniel Bellingradt, 'Die vergessenen Quellen des Alten Reiches: Ein Forschungsüberblick zu frühneuzeitlicher Flugpublizistik im Heiligen Römischen Reich deutscher Nation', in *Presse und Geschichte: Leistungen und Perspektiven der historischen Presseforschung*, ed. Astrid Blome and Holger Böning (Bremen: edition lumière, 2008).
2. Johannes Burkhardt, *Das Reformationsjahrhundert: Deutsche Geschichte zwischen Medienrevolution und Institutionenbildung, 1517–1617* (Stuttgart: Kohlhammer, 2002), p. 25–30.
3. Robert W. Scribner, *Popular Culture and Popular Movements in Reformation Germany* (London: Bloomsbury Academic, 1987), p. 49.
4. Robert W. Scribner, 'Flugblatt und Analphabetentum: Wie kam der gemeine Mann zu reformatorischen Ideen?', in *Flugschriften als Massenmedium der Reformationszeit: Beiträge zum Tübinger Symposion 1980*, ed. Hans-Joachim Köhler (Stuttgart: Klett-Cotta, 1981), pp. 66–7, 69.
5. Pia F. Cuneo, 'Constructing the Boundaries of Community: Nationalism, Protestantism, and Economics in a Sixteenth-Century Broadsheet', in *Infinite Boundaries: Order, Disorder, and Reorder in Early Modern German Culture*, ed. Max Reinhart (Kirksville, MI: Sixteenth Century Journal Publishers, 1998), pp. 175–6.
6. Philipp Robinson Rössner, ed., *Martin Luther: On Commerce and Usury (1524)* (London: Anthem Press, 2015), pp. 121–3; Philipp Robinson Rössner, 'Monetary Theory and Cameralist Economic Management, *c.*1500–1900 A.D', *Journal of the History of Economic Thought* 40, no. 1 (2018), p. 110. Luther had not been the first either. Over 300 years earlier, Walther von der Vogelweide had complained about the Pope duping the Germans: 'Their wealth will all be mine, their German silver flows into my Roman shrine.' Walter Alison Phillips, *Selected Poems of Walther von der Vogelweide the Minnesinger* (London: Smith, Elder & Co., 1896), p. 110.
7. Walter Bauernfeind, Michael Diefenbacher, and Christine Sauer, eds., *Bilderpracht und Seelenheil: Illuminierte Urkunden aus Nürnberger Archiven und Sammlungen. Begleitband zur gleichnamigen Ausstellung in der Stadtbibliothek im Bildungscampus Nürnberg vom 13. Februar – 4. Mai 2019* (Nuremberg: Verlag Ph. C.W. Schmidt, 2019), p. 213.

8. Scribner, *Popular Culture*, pp. 49–69; Burkhardt, *Reformationsjahrhundert*, pp. 48–76. The relevant research is reviewed in Dagmar Freist, 'Öffentlichkeit und Herrschaftslegitimation in der Frühen Neuzeit: Deutschland und England im Vergleich', in *Staatsbildung als kultureller Prozess: Strukturwandel und Legitimation von Herrschaft in der Frühen Neuzeit*, ed. Ronald G. Asch and Dagmar Freist (Cologne, Weimar, Vienna: Böhlau, 2005), pp. 321–30.
9. For the problems that a top-down interpretation of premodern legislation involves see Achim Landwehr, '"Normdurchsetzung" in der Frühen Neuzeit? Kritik eines Begriffs', *Zeitschrift für Geschichtswissenschaft* 48 (2000), pp. 155–6.
10. Volckart, *Währung*, no. 37, p. 130; no. 52, pp. 199 f.; no. 84, p. 294.
11. Ibid., *Währung*, no. 21, p. 70.
12. Cf. e.g., Aulinger, *Reichstag zu Worms 1545*, vol. 2, no. 86, pp. 955–6, where the use of *Usualguldens* by merchants is being criticized.
13. Stefan Brakensiek, 'Akzeptanzorientierte Herrschaft: Überlegungen zur politischen Kultur der Frühen Neuzeit', in *Die Frühe Neuzeit als Epoche*, ed. Helmut Neuhaus (Munich: Oldenbourg, 2009), p. 400.
14. Volckart, *Währung*, no. 82, p. 279.
15. Brakensiek, 'Herrschaft', p. 400.
16. Werner Rösener, 'Die wirtschaftlichen Ressourcen der Fürstenhöfe: Die schwindende Bedeutung der Einnahmen aus den Kammergütern', in *Hofwirtschaft: Ein ökonomischer Blick auf Hof und Residenz in Spätmittelalter und Früher Neuzeit*, ed. Gerhard Fouquet, Jan Hirschbiegel, and Werner Paravicini (Sigmaringen: Thorbecke, 2008), p. 326.
17. Brakensiek, 'Herrschaft', p. 400; cf. Volker Press, 'Formen des Ständewesens in den deutschen Territorien des 16. und 17. Jahrhunderts', in *Ständetum und Staatsbildung in Brandenburg-Preußen: Ergebnisse einer internationalen Fachtagung*, ed. Peter Baumgart (Berlin, New York: de Gruyter, 1983), p. 289.
18. Brakensiek, 'Herrschaft', p. 401; cf. Achim Landwehr, *Policey im Alltag: Die Implementation frühneuzeitlicher Policeyordnungen in Leonberg* (Frankfurt: Vittorio Klostermann, 2000), pp. 10–38, 277–83; Steve Hindle, 'Law, Law Enforcement and State Formation in Early Modern England', in *Staatsbildung als kultureller Prozess: Strukturwandel und Legitimation von Herrschaft in der Frühen Neuzeit*, ed. Ronald G. Asch and Dagmar Freist (Cologne, Weimar, Vienna: Böhlau, 2005), pp. 228–9.
19. Scribner, *Popular Culture*, pp. 63–4.
20. Ernst Schubert, '"bauerngeschrey": Zum Problem der öffentlichen Meinung im spätmittelalterlichen Franken', *Jahrbuch für fränkische Landesforschung* 34/35 (1975), pp. 889–90.
21. Scribner, *Popular Culture*, pp. 50, 56–7.
22. Ibid., *Popular Culture*, p. 53.
23. Rainer Wohlfeil and Trudl Wohlfeil, 'Verbildlichungen ständischer Gesellschaft: Bartholomäus Bruyn d.Ä.—Petrarcameister (mit Exkursen von Marlies Minuth und Heike Talkenberger)', in *Ständische Gesellschaft und soziale*

Mobilität, ed. Winfried Schulze and Helmut Gabel (Munich: Oldenbourg, 1988), p. 299; J.M. Jacobs, ed., *Works of Martin Luther with Introduction and Notes*, vol. II (Philadelphia: A.J. Holman, 1916), p. 100.

24. Robert Hermann Lutz, *Wer war der gemeine Mann? Der dritte Stand in der Krise des Spätmittelalters* (Munich: Oldenbourg, 1979).
25. Lyndal Roper, '"The Common Man", "The Common Good", "Common Women": Gender and Meaning in the German Reformation Commune', *Social History* 12, no. 1 (1987), p. 2; Sheilagh Ogilvie, 'Married Women, Work and the Law: Evidence from Early Modern Germany', in *Married Women and the Law in Premodern Northwest Europe*, ed. Cordelia Beattie and Matthew Frank Stevens (Woodbridge: Boydell & Brewer 2013), pp. 216, 219–20; Jan Bloemendal and Arjan van Dixhoorn, 'Early Modern Literary Cultures and Public Opinion: An Epilogue in the Form of a Discussion', in *Literary Cultures and Public Opinion in the Low Countries, 1450–1650*, ed. Jan Bloemendal, Arjan van Dixhoorn, and Elsa Strietman (Leiden: Brill, 2011), p. 275.
26. E.g., Rudolf Bentzinger, ed., *Die Wahrheit muß ans Licht: Dialoge aus der Zeit der Reformation* (Frankfurt: Röderberg, 1983), pp. 261–9; cf. Ludwig Enders, ed., *Johann Eberlin von Günzburg: Sämtliche Schriften*, vol. 3 (Halle: Max Niemeyer, 1902), pp. 147–9.
27. Rudolf Endres, 'Zur sozialökonomischen Lage und sozialpsychologischen Einstellungen des "Gemeinen Mannes": Der Kloster- und Burgensturm in Franken 1525', *Geschichte und Gesellschaft: Sonderheft* 1 (1975); Margret Wensky, 'Städtische Führungsschichten im Spätmittelalter', in *Sozialer Aufstieg: Funktionseliten im Spätmittelalter und in der frühen Neuzeit*, ed. Günther Schulz (Munich: Harald Boldt, 2002), p. 19; Peter Blickle, *Der Bauernkrieg: Die Revolution des Gemeinen Mannes* (Munich: Beck, 2002), p. 43.
28. Werner O. Packull, 'The Image of the "Common Man" in the Early Pamphlets of the Reformation (1520–1525)', *Historical Reflections/Réflexions Historiques* 12, no. 2 (1985), p. 257.
29. Aulinger, *Reichstag zu Worms 1545*, vol. 2, no. 86, p. 955.
30. Oliver Volckart, 'The Dear Old Holy Roman Realm: How Does it Hold Together? Monetary Policies, Cross-cutting Cleavages and Political Cohesion in the Age of Reformation', *German History* 38, no. 4 (2020), p. 378.
31. Ibid., *Währung*, no. 99, p. 399.
32. Ibid., *Währung*, no. 19, pp. 62, 66–7, 399.
33. Ibid., *Währung*, no. 39, p. 179; no. 40, p. 181; cf. Peter Blickle, 'Der Gemeine Nutzen: Ein kommunaler Wert und seine politische Karriere', in *Gemeinwohl und Gemeinsinn: Historische Semantiken politischer Leitbegriffe*, ed. Herfried Münkler and Harald Bluhm (Berlin: Akademie Verlag, 2001), pp. 85–6, 99.
34. The monetary policy discussions at the imperial diets and a series of currency conferences held between 1544 and 1559 yield a sample of 69 references to the 'common man'. The term was used 43 times without any adjective. It was paired with 'poor' 18 times, with 'ignorant' five times, 'simple' twice, and

'innocent' once. Eltz, *Reichstag von 1544*, vol. 1, nos. 67–70, pp. 331–42; Aulinger, *Reichstag zu Worms 1545*, vol. 2, nos. 81–9, pp. 932–75; Ursula Machoczek, ed., *Deutsche Reichstagsakten unter Kaiser Karl V.: Der Reichstag zu Augsburg 1547/48*, vol. 3 (Munich: Oldenbourg, 2006), no. 224, p. 2018; Erwein Eltz, ed., *Deutsche Reichstagsakten unter Kaiser Karl V.: Der Reichstag zu Augsburg 1550/51*, vol. 1 (Munich: Oldenbourg, 2005), no. 73, p. 233; ibid., *Reichstag zu Augsburg 1550/51*, vol. 2, nos. 121–305, pp. 868–1597; Leeb, *Reichstag zu Augsburg 1559*, vol. 3, nos. 557–804, pp. 1380–965; Volckart, Währung, nos. 2–101, pp. 10–411; ÖStA, HHStA Wien, Reichshofrat, Miscellanea Münzwesen 1: Münzwesen im Reich (1. Konvolut), fol. 37v., (2. Konvolut), fol. 233v.–235v. Monetary-policy talks at the Augsburg- (1555) and Regensburg- (1556–7) diets yielded no results. Rosemarie Aulinger, Erwein Eltz, and Ursula Machoczek, eds., *Deutsche Reichstagsakten unter Kaiser Karl V.: Der Reichstag zu Augsburg 1555*, vol. 2 (Munich: Oldenbourg, 2009); ibid., eds., *Deutsche Reichstagsakten unter Kaiser Karl V.: Der Reichstag zu Augsburg 1555*, vol. 4 (Munich: Oldenbourg, 2009); Josef Leeb, ed., *Der Reichstag zu Regensburg 1556/57*, vol. 1 (Munich: Oldenbourg, 2013); ibid., ed., *Der Reichstag zu Regensburg 1556/57*, vol. 2 (Munich: Oldenbourg, 2013).

35. Volckart, *Währung*, no. 2, p. 10; cf. no. 92, p. 379.

36. Blickle, *Der Bauernkrieg*, pp. 68, 103; ibid., *Die Revolution von 1525* (Munich: Oldenbourg, 1981), pp. 36–89; cf. Tom Scott, 'The German Peasants' War and the "Crisis of Feudalism": Reflections On a Neglected Theme', *Journal of Early Modern History* 6, no. 3 (2002).

37. Horst Buszello, 'Gemeinde, Territorium und Reich in den politischen Programmen des Deutschen Bauernkrieges 1524/25', *Geschichte und Gesellschaft: Sonderheft* 1 (1975), *passim*; Günter Vogler, 'Reichsvorstellungen im Umkreis des Bauernkrieges', in *Alternativen zur Reichsverfassung in der Frühen Neuzeit?*, ed. Volker Press and Dieter Stievermann (Munich: Oldenbourg, 1995), p. 41; Peter Blickle, *Unruhen in der ständischen Gesellschaft 1300–1800*, 3 ed. (Munich: Oldenbourg, 2012), p. 74.

38. Helgard Ulmschneider, *Götz von Berlichingen: Ein adeliges Leben der deutschen Renaissance* (Sigmaringen: Thorbecke, 1974), p. 163; Blickle, *Die Revolution von 1525*; ibid., *Der Bauernkrieg*.

39. Heinz Angermeier, 'Die Vorstellung des gemeinen Mannes von Staat und Reich im deutschen Bauernkrieg', *Vierteljahrschrift für Sozial- und Wirtschaftsgeschichte* 53, no. 3 (1966), p. 340; Klaus Arnold, 'damit der arm man vnnd gemainer nutz iren furgang haben . . . : Zum deutschen "Bauernkrieg" als politischer Bewegung: Wendel Hiplers und Friedrich Weygandts Pläne einer "Reformation" des Reiches', *Zeitschrift für Historische Forschung* 9, no. 3 (1982), p. 286.

40. Buszello, 'Gemeinde, Territorium und Reich in den politischen Programmen des Deutschen Bauernkrieges 1524/25', p. 126.

41. Arnold, 'damit der arm man vnnd gemainer nutz iren furgang haben', pp. 258–9.

42. Ibid., 'damit der arm man vnnd gemainer nutz iren furgang haben', p. 304; translation: Tom Scott and Bob Scribner, eds., *The German Peasants' War: A History in Documents* (New Jersey, London: Humanities Press, 1991), no. 127, pp. 262–3.
43. Blickle, *Unruhen*, pp. 58–9.
44. Ferdinand Friedrich Oechsle, *Beiträge zur Geschichte des Bauernkrieges in den schwäbisch-fränkischen Grenzlanden* (Heilbronn: Carl Drechsler, 1830), no. 22, p. 289; Arnold, 'damit der arm man vnnd gemainer nutz iren furgang haben', p. 304; translation: Scott and Scribner, *Peasants' War*, no. 127, p. 263.
45. *Teütscher Nation Notturfft: Die Ordnung vnd Reformation aller Stendt ym Römischen Reych. Durch Kayser Fridrich den dritten Gott zu lob/der gantzen Christenheyt zu nutz vnd säligkeyt fürgenommen*, (Zwickau: Gastel, 1523).
46. *Teütscher Nation Notturfft*, pp. 22–5 (original not paginated).
47. Arnold, 'damit der arm man vnnd gemainer nutz iren furgang haben', p. 265.
48. Scribner, *Popular Culture*, pp. 50, 66–7.
49. Rössner, *Deflation*, pp. 381–6.
50. Cf. Whaley, *Germany*, I, p. 190.
51. Johann Eberlin von Günzburg, *15 Bundsgenossen, bearb. und eingerichtet von Michael Holzinger* (Berlin: Holzinger, 1521/2013), pp. 77, 80; Susan Groag Bell, 'Johan Eberlin von Günzburg's Wolfaria: The First Protestant Utopia', *Church History* 36, no. 2 (1967), p. 132.
52. Schubert, 'bauerngeschrey', pp. 889–90.
53. Aulinger, *Reichstag zu Worms 1545*, vol. 2, no. 83, p. 938; cf. ibid., *Reichstag zu Worms 1545*, vol. 2, no. 86, p. 959; Volckart, *Währung*, no. 37, p. 162.
54. Eltz, *Reichstag zu Augsburg 1550/51*, vol. 1, no. 82, p. 297 with footnote f.
55. Volckart, *Währung*, no. 37, p. 107; no. 86, p. 303.
56. ÖStA, HHStA Wien, Reichshofrat, Miscellanea Münzwesen 2: Münzwesen im Reich, 1551–1564, fol. 539r.–539v.
57. Poulsen, 'Bauernanschreibebücher', p. 93; Fritz Kiener, 'Zur Vorgeschichte des Bauernkriegs am Oberrhein', *Zeitschrift für die Geschichte des Oberrheins* 58 (1904), p. 496; Held, 'Stadt-Land-Beziehungen', p. 110; Govind Sreenivasan, *The Peasants of Ottobeuren, 1487–1726: A Rural Society in Early Modern Europe* (Cambridge: Cambridge University Press, 2004), pp. 89–91; Jochen Richter, 'Ländliches Kreditwesen in Mecklenburg 16./17. Jahrhundert', *Jahrbuch für Wirtschaftsgeschichte* 1 (1986), p. 134.
58. Friedrich-Wilhelm Henning, 'Ländliche Sozialstruktur und soziale Mobilität im Mittelalter', in *Struktur und Dimension. Festschrift für Karl Heinrich Kaufhold zum 65. Geburtstag*, ed. Hans-Jürgen Gerhard (Stuttgart: Steiner, 1997), p. 219.
59. Whaley, *Germany*, I, p. 543.
60. Franz Quarthal, 'Verfassung und Verwaltung in südwestdeutschen Städten der Frühen Neuzeit', in *Recht, Verfassung und Verwaltung in der frühneuzeitlichen Stadt*, ed. Michael Stolleis (Cologne: Böhlau, 1991), p. 219; Rudolf Endres, 'Adel und Patriziat in Oberdeutschland', in *Ständische Gesellschaft und soziale Mobilität*, ed. Winfried Schulze (Munich: Oldenbourg, 1988), p. 223.

61. Peter Blickle, 'Beschwerden und Polizeien: Die Legitimation des modernen Staates durch Verfahren und Normen', in *Gute Policey als Politik im 16. Jahrhundert: Die Entstehung des öffentlichen Raumes in Oberdeutschland*, ed. Peter Blickle, Peter Kissling, and Heinrich Richard Schmidt (Frankfurt: Klostermann, 2003), p. 118; Kersten Krüger, *Die landständische Verfassung* (Munich: Oldenbourg, 2003), p. 70.
62. Beat Kümin and Andreas Würgler, 'Petitions, Gravamina and the Early Modern State: Local Influence on Central Legislation in England and Germany (Hesse)', *Parliaments, Estates & Representation* 17, no. 1 (1997), pp. 43–4.
63. Krüger, *Die landständische Verfassung*, pp. 70–1.
64. Volkmar Wittmütz, *Die Gravamina der bayerischen Stände im 16. und 17. Jahrhundert als Quelle für die wirtschaftliche Situation und Entwicklung Bayerns* (Munich: Stadtarchiv München, 1970), p. 61 with FN 5.
65. Saxony: Volckart, *Währung*, no. 2, pp. 8–9., 11; no. 18, p. 60; no. 92, p. 379; the electors on the Rhine: ibid., *Währung*, no. 84, p. 285.
66. Ibid., *Währung*, no. 37, pp. 125–6; no. 86, p. 313.
67. Freist, 'Öffentlichkeit', p. 344.
68. Cf. Whaley, *Germany*, I, p. 12.
69. Blickle, *Der Bauernkrieg*, p. 42.
70. ÖStA, HHStA Wien, Reichshofrat, Miscellanea Münzwesen 2: Münzwesen im Reich, 1551–1564, fol. 52r.
71. Peter Hess, *Resisting Pluralization and Globalization in German Culture, 1490–1540: Visions of a Nation in Decline* (Berlin, Boston: de Gruyter, 2020), p. 256.
72. Enders, *Johann Eberlin von Günzburg: Sämtliche Schriften*, vol. 3, pp. 147–81.
73. Ibid., *Johann Eberlin von Günzburg: Sämtliche Schriften*, vol. 3, p. 159.
74. StAWü, Mainzer Regierungsarchiv 7226 (Münze K 137/1½), fol. 5v.
75. John H. Munro, 'Bullionism and the Bill of Exchange in England, 1272–1663: A Study in Monetary Management and Popular Prejudice', in *The Dawn of Modern Banking*, ed. F. Chiappelli (New Haven and London: Yale University Press, 1979), pp. 174–6; Rössner, 'Monetary Theory', p. 106.
76. Volckart, *Währung*, no. 84, p. 296.
77. Ibid., 'Money and its Technologies, pp. 24–5.
78. Rössner, *Deflation*, pp. 251–3.
79. Winfried Schulze, 'Vom Gemeinnutz zum Eigennutz: Über den Normenwandel in der ständischen Gesellschaft in der frühen Neuzeit', *Historische Zeitschrift* 243 (1986), p. 600. Merchants were mentioned far less often than the common man. Aulinger, *Reichstag zu Worms 1545*, vol. 2, no. 86, pp. 955–6; no. 89, p. 975; Volckart, *Währung*, no. 37, p. 154; no. 86, pp. 304, 313; no. 88, p. 340; no. 99, p. 399.
80. ÖStA, HHStA Wien, Reichshofrat, Miscellanea Münzwesen 2: Münzwesen im Reich, 1551–1564, fol. 57r.
81. Kamann, 'Christoph Fürer', p. 293.

82. Theodor Gustav Werner, 'Ein Münzgutachten Jakob Fuggers des Reichen für Erzherzog Ferdinand von Österreich aus dem Jahre 1524 oder 1525', *Scripta Mercaturae* I (1967), pp. 23–5.
83. Kamann, 'Christoph Fürer', p. 262.
84. E.g., Hermann Kellenbenz, ed., *Das Meder'sche Handelsbuch und die Welser'schen Nachträge* (Wiesbaden: Steiner, 1974), pp. 245–8, 259–99; Eduard Schulte, 'Das Danziger Kontorbuch des Jakob Stöve aus Münster (Hansische Maße, Münzen, Waren, Wege und Zölle um 1560)', *Hansische Geschichtsblätter* 62 (1937), pp. 54–5, 57.
85. Lars Boerner and Oliver Volckart, 'The Utility of a Common Coinage: Currency Unions and the Integration of Money Markets in Late Medieval Central Europe', *Explorations in Economic History* 48 (2011), pp. 59–61; Oliver Volckart, 'Währungsvielfalt, Wechselkurse und Geldmarktintegration im Hanseraum, *c.*1350–1550', in *Hansischer Handel im Strukturwandel*, ed. Stephan Selzer and Rolf Hammel-Kiesow (Trier: Porta Alba Verlag, 2016).
86. Raymond de Roover, *Money, Banking and Credit in Medieval Bruges: Italian Merchant-Bankers Lombards and Money-Changers. A Study in the Origins of Banking* (Cambridge, MA: The Medieval Academy of America, 1948), pp. 48–54; Max Neumann, *Geschichte des Wechsels im Hansagebiete bis zum 17. Jahrhundert* (Erlangen: Ferdinand Enke, 1863).
87. John H. Munro, 'The Medieval Origins of the "Financial Revolution": Usury, Rentes, and Negotiability', *International History Review* XXV, no. 3 (2003), pp. 553–4.
88. Markus A. Denzel, *Das System des bargeldlosen Zahlungsverkehrs europäischer Prägung vom Mittelalter bis 1914* (Stuttgart: Franz Steiner, 2008), pp. 166–171; Sprenger, *Geld*, p. 164.
89. Kellenbenz, *Das Meder'sche Handelsbuch*, pp. 252–8.
90. Volckart, *Währung*, no. 37, pp. 175–6.
91. Paul Münch, 'Grundwerte der frühneuzeitlichen Ständegesellschaft? Aufriß einer vernachlässigten Thematik', in *Ständische Gesellschaft und soziale Mobilität*, ed. Winfried Schulze and Helmut Gabel (Munich: Oldenbourg, 1988), p. 66.
92. Emil Bahrfeldt, *Das Münzwesen der Mark Brandenburg unter den Hohenzollern bis zum grossen Kurfürsten, von 1415 bis 1640* (Berlin: Kühl, 1895), no. 14, p. 411.
93. Heinz Angermeier, *Die Reichsreform 1410–1555: die Staatsproblematik in Deutschland zwischen Mittelalter und Gegenwart* (Munich: Beck, 1984), pp. 173–6, 205.
94. Volckart, *Währung*, no. 103, p. 415.
95. Cf. ibid., *Währung*, pp. LIV–LVI; Rössner, *Deflation*, p. 375.
96. Torsten Fried, 'Schrift und Bild: Münzen als Herrschaftszeichen', in *Turbata per aequora mundi: Dankesgabe an Eckhard Müller-Mertens*, ed. Olaf B. Rader (Hannover: Hahn, 2001), pp. 235–6; cf. Jennifer Bishop, 'Currency, Conversation, and Control: Political Discourse and the Coinage in Mid-Tudor England', *English Historical Review* 131, no. 551 (2016), 766.
97. Aulinger, Eltz, and Machoczek, *Reichstag zu Augsburg 1555*, vol. 2, no. 145, p. 1515.

98. Kamann, 'Christoph Fürer', p. 304.
99. Michael Prestwich, 'Early Fourteenth-Century Exchange Rates', *The Economic History Review* XXXII, no. 4 (1979), p. 471.
100. Leeb, *Reichstag zu Augsburg 1559*, vol. 3 no. 661, pp. 1721–2.
101. David Chilosi and Oliver Volckart, 'Good or Bad money? Debasements, Society and the State in the Late Middle Ages', in *Money and Its Use in Medieval Europe Three Decades On: Essays in Honour of Professor Peter Spufford*, ed. Martin Allen (London: The Royal Numismatic Society, 2017), p. 128. Cf. Munro, *Wool, Cloth, and Gold*, pp. 32–3; ibid., 'Bullion Flows', pp. 109–10.
102. Hans-Ulrich Geiger, 'Entstehung und Ausbreitung des Batzens', *Schweizerische Numismatische Rundschau* 51 (1972), p. 145; *Batzens* had a pure silver content of 1.67 grams, Austrian *Kreuzers* minted according to the ordinance of 1481 one of 0.51 grams. Ibid., *Der Beginn der Gold- und Dickmünzenprägung in Bern: Ein Beitrag zur bernischen Münz- und Geldgeschichte des 15. Jahrhunderts* (Bern: Stämpfli & Cie, 1968), p. 85; Alfred Nagl, 'Die österreichische Münzordnung vom Jahre 1481', *Numismatische Zeitschrift* 41 (1908), p. 159.
103. Schüttenhelm, 'Münzprägung', p. 166.
104. Geiger, 'Entstehung', pp. 146–7.
105. Schüttenhelm, 'Münzprägung', p. 164; cf. Eichhorn, *Strukturwandel*, pp. 62–76.
106. Bairoch, Batou, and Chèvre, *La population*, p. 67; Keyser, *Deutsches Städtebuch*, vol. 4, 2: Württemberg, p. 370; ibid., ed., *Deutsches Städtebuch*, vol. 4, 2: Baden (Stuttgart: Kohlhammer, 1959), p. 276.
107. Regensburg 1527: ÖStA, HHStA Wien, Reichshofrat, Miscellanea Münzwesen 1: Münzwesen im Reich (2. Konvolut), fol. 240r.–240v.; Augsburg 1533: David Thomann von Hagelstein, *Der Röm. Kayserl. Majestät Deß Heil. Röm. Reichs Geist- und Weltlicher Chur-Fürsten, Fürsten und Ständen Acta Publica Monetaria Schrifftliche Handlungen, Constitutiones, Bedencken und Vorschläge, Die Anordnung, Reformation und Verbesserung Deß Müntz-Wesens in Teutschland betreffende* (Augsburg: Kroniger & Göbels Erben, 1692), p. 72; Munich 1539: Lori, Sammlung, 1, p. 217.
108. Eichhorn, *Strukturwandel*, p. 76.
109. Schüttenhelm, 'Münzprägung', p. 166.
110. Rüthing, 'Geschichte', p. 44.
111. Volckart, *Währung*, no. 88, p. 335.
112. Karl Heinrich Kaufhold, 'Neuere Forschungen zur Wirtschaftsgeschichte des Berg- und Hüttenwesens im westlichen Harz in vorindustrieller Zeit: Ein Überblick unter besonderer Berücksichtigung der wirtschaftlichen Wechsellagen', in *Konjunkturen im europäischen Bergbau in vorindustrieller Zeit*, ed. Christoph Bartels and Markus A. Denzel (Stuttgart: Steiner, 2000), pp. 50–1.
113. Cf. e.g., Hirsch, *Münz-Archiv*, 1, no. CLXXXIII, p. 271; no. CLXXXV, pp. 274–5.
114. Wilhelm Böhmer, ed., *Thomas Kantzow's Chronik von Pommern in Niederdeutscher Mundart. Sammt einer Auswahl aus den übrigen ungedruckten Schriften desselben* (Stettin: Friedrich Heinrich Morin, 1835), p. 164; cf.

Joachim Krüger, *Zwischen dem Reich und Schweden: Die landesherrliche Münzprägung im Herzogtum Pommern und in Schwedisch-Pommern in der frühen Neuzeit (c.1580–1715)* (Berlin: LIT, 2006), p. 40.

115. Vorel, *Circulation*, p. 20.
116. Schrötter, 'Münzwesen, Teil II', pp. 99–100; Lennartz, 'Probationstage', p. 1; Kamann, 'Christoph Fürer', p. 259; Blaich, *Wirtschaftspolitik*, p. 15; Probszt, *Geldgeschichte*, p. 397; Schön, 'Münzprobationstage', p. 467.
117. Andrew K. Rose, 'One Money, One Market: Estimating the Effects of Common Currencies on Trade', *Economic Policy* 30 (2000); ibid., 'Currency Unions and Trade: The Effect is Large', *Economic Policy* 33 (2001).
118. Barry Eichengreen and Douglas A. Irwin, 'Trade Blocs, Currency Blocs and the Reorientation of World Trade in the 1930s', *Journal of International Economics* 38 (1995); Nikolaus Wolf and Albrecht Ritschl, 'Endogeneity of Currency Areas and Trade Blocs: Evidence from a Natural Experiment', *Kyklos* 64, no. 2 (2011).
119. Boerner and Volckart, 'Utility', p. 62.
120. Philippe Dollinger, *Die Hanse*, 3 ed. (Stuttgart: Kröner, 1981), pp. 35–6; Ulf Dirlmeier, *Mittelalterliche Hoheitsträger im wirtschaftlichen Wettbewerb* (Wiesbaden: Steiner, 1966), pp. 26–7; Boerner and Volckart, 'Utility', pp. 54, 63.
121. Eltz, *Reichstag von 1544*, vol. 1, no. 70, p. 339.
122. Volckart, *Währung*, no. 86, p. 960.
123. Ibid., 'Power Politics and Princely Debts: Why Germany's Common Currency Failed, 1549–1556', *The Economic History Review* 70, no. 3 (2017), no. 100, p. 405.
124. Aulinger, *Reichstag zu Worms 1545*, vol. 2, no. 86, pp. 959–60.
125. Ibid., *Reichstag zu Worms 1545*, vol. 2, no. 87, p. 962.
126. For the *Rappen*-union see Julius Cahn, *Der Rappenmünzbund: Eine Studie zur Münz- und Geld-Geschichte des oberen Rheinthales* (Heidelberg: Carl Winter's Universitätsbuchhandlung, 1901).
127. ÖStA, HHStA Wien, Reichshofrat, Miscellanea Münzwesen 2: Münzwesen im Reich, 1551–1564, fol. 522v.
128. ÖStA, HHStA Wien, Reichshofrat, Miscellanea Münzwesen 2: Münzwesen im Reich, 1551–1564, fol. 501r.–501v.
129. Volckart, *Währung*, no. 36, p. 102 with FN 4.
130. Eltz, *Reichstag von 1544*, vol. 1, no. 67, p. 332.
131. Electoral Cologne: Ursula Machoczek, ed., *Deutsche Reichstagsakten unter Kaiser Karl V.: Der Reichstag zu Augsburg 1547/48*, vol. 1 (Munich: Oldenbourg, 2006), no. 62, pp. 365, 381, 386. Electoral Cologne and Trier: ibid., *Reichstag zu Augsburg 1547/48*, vol. 1, no. 216, p. 2000. Electoral Mainz: ibid., *Reichstag zu Augsburg 1547/48*, vol. 1, no. 216, p. 2001.
132. Ibid., *Reichstag zu Augsburg 1547/48*, vol. 3, no. 219, p. 2007.
133. Jan de Vries, *European Urbanization 1500–1800* (London: Methuen, 1984), pp. 36, 39; Robert C. Allen, 'Economic Structure and Agricultural Productivity in Europe, 1300–1800', *European Review of Economic History* 4, no. 1 (2000), pp. 8–9.

134. Edward A. Wrigley, 'Urban Growth and Agricultural Change: England and the Continent in the Early Modern Period', *The Journal of Interdisciplinary History* 15, no. 4 (1985), p. 683; cf. Karl Gunnar Persson, 'Labour Productivity in Medieval Agriculture: Tuscany and the Low Countries', in *Land, Labour and Livestock, Historical Studies in European Agricultural Productivity*, ed. Bruce M.S. Campbell and M. Overton (Manchester: Manchester University Press, 1991).
135. Fernand Braudel, *The Mediterranean and the Mediterranean World in the Age of Philip II*, 5 ed., vol. 2 (Glasgow: Fontana, 1949/87), p. 1039.
136. Richard W. Unger, 'Feeding Low Countries Towns: The Grain Trade in the Fifteenth Century', *Revue belge de philologie etd'histoire* 77, no. 2 (1999); Milja van Tielhof, *The 'Mother of all Trades': The Baltic Grain Trade in Amsterdam From the Late 16th to the Early 19th Century* (Leiden, Boston, Cologne: Brill, 2002), p. 7.
137. Ian Blanchard, 'The Continental European Cattle Trades, 1400–1600', *The Economic History Review* XXXIX, no. 3 (1986), pp. 432, 450.
138. Volckart, *Währung*, no. 2, p. 8.
139. Hans-Wolfgang Bergerhausen, '"Exclusis Westphalen et Burgundt": Zum Kampf um die Durchsetzung der Reichsmünzordnung von 1559', *Zeitschrift für historische Forschung* 20 (1993), p. 195; Donald J. Harreld, *High Germans in the Low Countries: German Merchants and Commerce in Golden Age Antwerp* (Leiden, Boston: Brill, 2004), pp. 128–31.
140. Wilfrid Brulez, 'Le commerce international des Pays-Bas au XVIe siècle: Essai d'appréciation quantitative', *Revue belge de philologie et d'histoire* 46, no. 4 (1968), pp. 1205–6.
141. Ibid., 'Le commerce', p. 1219.
142. Artur Attman, 'The Bullion Flow from Europe to the East: 1500–1800', in *Precious Metals, Coinage and the Changes of Monetary Structures in Latin-America, Europe and Asia (Late Middle Ages—Early Modern Times)*, ed. Eddy H.G. van Cauwenberghe (Leuven: Leuven University Press, 1989), p. 67; Michael North, 'Bullion Transfer from Western Europe to the Baltic and the Problem of Trade Balances: 1550–1750', in *From the North Sea to the Baltic* (Aldershot: Variorum Reprints, 1996), pp. X, 59–60.
143. Brulez, 'Le commerce', p. 1220.
144. Volckart, *Münzpolitik*, pp. 232–3; Stanislawa Kubiak, *Monety i stosunki monetarne w Prusach Królewskich w 2 polowie XV wieku* (Wroclaw, Warszawa, Kraków, Gdansk, Lódz: Zaklad Narodowy Imiena Ossolinskich Wydawnictwo Polskiej Akademii Nauk, 1986), p. 136.
145. For Einsiedel's family see Adalbert Elschenbroich, 'Einsiedel, v.', in *Neue deutsche Biographie*, ed. Historische Kommission bei der (Königlich) Bayerischen Akademie der Wissenschaften (Berlin: Duncker & Humblot, 1959); for his attendance at imperial diets Rosemarie Aulinger and Silvia Schweinzer-Burian, 'Habsburgische und reichsständische Präsenz auf den Reichstagen Kaiser Karls V. (1521–1555) im Spiegel der Reichsmatrikel von 1521: Eine

prosopographische Erfassung', in *Handlungsräume: Facetten politischer Kommunikation in der Frühen Neuzeit. Festschrift für Albrecht P. Luttenberger zum 65. Geburtstag*, ed. Franz Hederer et al. (Munich: Martin Meidenbauer, 2011). His encounter with Luther is described in his obituary: Thomas Wyntzer, *Leichpredigt Vber dem Begrebnis des Edlen Gestrengen vnnd Ehrendvhesten Abraham von Einsiedell, Churf. G. zu Sachssen etc. LandRaht, auffm Scharffensteyne etc., Den 20. Martii Anno 1568* (Dresden, 1568).

146. Volckart, *Währung*, no. 5, p. 26.
147. Cf. Karlheinz Blaschke, 'Menge und Gliederung in der Bevölkerungsentwicklung Sachsens: Eine Langzeitbeobachtung vom 10. bis zum 20. Jahrhundert', in *Struktur und Dimension: Festschrift für Karl Heinrich Kaufhold zum 65. Geburtstag*, ed. Hans-Jürgen Gerhard (Stuttgart: Steiner, 1997), pp. 233, 236.
148. Volckart, *Währung*, p. XC; no. 18, p. 58.

CHAPTER 3

1. Friedrich Uhlhorn, 'Die Erfindung des Walzwerkes und seine Förderung durch Graf Reinhard zu Solms-Lich', *Deutsche Münzblätter* 55, no. 388 (1935); Paul Bamberg, 'Weitere Nachrichten zum maschinellen Münzbetrieb des Grafen Reinhard zu Solms', *Deutsche Münzblätter* 55 (1935).
2. Friedrich Uhlhorn, *Reinhard Graf zu Solms, Herr zu Münzenberg 1491–1562* (Marburg: Elwert, 1952), p. 77.
3. ÖStA, HHStA Wien, Reichshofrat, Miscellanea Münzwesen 2: Münzwesen im Reich, 1551–1564, fol. 272r.–276r.
4. Johannes Herrmann, Günther Wartenberg, and Christian Winter, eds., *Politische Korrespondenz des Herzogs und Kurfürsten Moritz von Sachsen*, vol. 5 (Leipzig: Akademie Verlag, 1998), no. 61, p. 147, no. 70, p. 158.
5. Volckart, *Währung*, no. 87, p. 317.
6. Eltz, *Reichstag zu Augsburg 1550/51*, vol. 2, no. 305, p. 1589.
7. Schmidt, *Geschichte*; ibid., 'Das frühneuzeitliche Reich—komplementärer Staat und föderative Nation', *Historische Zeitschrift* 273, no. 2 (2001); ibid., 'State'; Whaley, *Germany*, I, pp. 642–3.
8. Heinz Schilling, 'Reichs-Staat und frühneuzeitliche Nation der Deutschen oder teilmodernisiertes Reichssystem: Überlegungen zu Charakter und Aktualität des Alten Reiches', *Historische Zeitschrift* 272, no. 2 (2001); Bernd Marquardt, *Das Römisch-Deutsche Reich als segmentäres Verfassungssystem (1348–1806/48): Versuch zu einer neuen Verfassungstheorie auf der Grundlage der lokalen Herrschaften* (Zürich: Schulthess Juristische Medien, 1999); cf. Len Scales and Joachim Whaley, 'Rewriting the History of the Holy Roman Empire', *German History* 36, no. 2 (2018) pp. 342–3.
9. Max Weber, 'Politics as a Vocation', in *Max Weber: The Vocation Lectures. 'Science as a Vocation', 'Politics as a Vocation'*, ed. David Owen and Tracy B. Strong (Indianapolis, Cambridge: Hackett, 1918/2004), p. 33.

10. Matthias Weber, *Die Reichspolizeiordnungen von 1530, 1548 und 1577: Historische Einführung und Edition* (Frankfurt: Vittorio Klostermann, 2002), p. 165, §39.2, p. 214, §37.5; cf. Georg Schmidt, '"Aushandeln" oder "Anordnen": Der komplementäre Reichs-Staat und seine Gesetze im 16. Jahrhundert', in *Der Reichstag 1486–1613: Kommunikation—Wahrnehmung—Öffentlichkeiten*, ed. Maximilian Lanzinner and Arno Strohmeyer (Göttingen: Vandenhoeck & Ruprecht, 2006), p. 109; Whaley, *Germany*, I, p. 368.
11. Jürgen Schlumbohm, 'Gesetze, die nicht durchgesetzt werden: ein Strukturmerkmal des frühneuzeitlichen Staates?', *Geschichte und Gesellschaft* 23, no. 4 (1997), pp. 649–50.
12. Cf. Schmidt, 'Aushandeln', pp. 115–16.
13. In any case, no polity can (and does) rely solely on force to implement what its central authority has decided. Typically, those concerned go along with the decisions without having to be forcibly compelled. Niklas Luhmann, *Legitimation durch Verfahren*, 11 ed. (Berlin: Suhrkamp, 1969/2019), p. 28.
14. Ibid., *Legitimation*, p. 11.
15. Ibid., *Legitimation*, pp. 87–9; Michael Sikora, 'Der Sinn des Verfahrens: Soziologische Deutungsangebote', in *Vormoderne politische Verfahren*, ed. Barbara Stollberg-Rilinger (Berlin: Duncker & Humblot, 2001), p. 32.
16. Luhmann, *Legitimation*, pp. 30, 119.
17. Barbara Stollberg-Rilinger, 'On the Function of Rituals in the Holy Roman Empire', in *The Holy Roman Empire 1495–1806*, ed. R.J.W. Evans, Michael Schaich, and Peter H. Wilson (Oxford: Oxford University Press, 2011), p. 371; cf. ibid., *The Emperor's Old Clothes: Constitutional History and the Symbolic Language of the Holy Roman Empire* (New York, Oxford: Berghahn, 2015), pp. 269–70.
18. Luhmann, *Legitimation*, pp. 48–9.
19. Ibid., *Legitimation*, p. 143.
20. Moraw, *Von offener Verfassung*, pp. 155–7, 416–18.
21. Ibid., 'Versuch', pp. 14–16, 24–6; Duncan Hardy, 'Tage (Courts, Councils and Diets): Political and Judicial Nodal Points in the Holy Roman Empire, *c.*1300–1550', *German History* 36, no. 3 (2018).
22. Volckart, *Währung*, no. 92, p. 377; cf. Helmut Neuhaus, *Reichsständische Repräsentationsformen im 16. Jahrhundert: Reichstag—Reichskreistag—Reichsdeputationstag* (Berlin: Duncker & Humblot, 1982), pp. 18–19.
23. Thomas Felix Hartmann, *Die Reichstage unter Karl V.: Verfahren und Verfahrensentwicklung 1521–1555* (Göttingen: Vandenhoeck & Ruprecht, 2017), p. 321.
24. Stollberg-Rilinger, 'Rituals', p. 361.
25. Esp. ibid., 'Rituals'; ibid., *Old Clothes*; cf. Schmidt, 'Aushandeln', p. 97; Scales and Whaley, 'Rewriting', pp. 344–5.
26. Stollberg-Rilinger, 'Rituals', p. 361.
27. Ibid., *Das Heilige Römische Reich Deutscher Nation: Vom Ende des Mittelalters bis 1806* (Munich: Beck, 2006), p. 47.

28. Ibid., 'Rituals', p. 369.
29. Tim Neu, 'Zeremonielle Verfahren: Zur Funktionalität vormoderner politisch–administrativer Prozesse am Beispiel des Landtags im Fürstbistum Münster', in *Im Schatten der Macht: Kommunikationskulturen in Politik und Verwaltung 1600–1950*, ed. Stefan Haas and Mark Hengerer (Frankfurt, New York: Campus, 2008), p. 29.
30. Yehudi A. Cohen, 'Some Aspects of Ritualized Behavior in Interpersonal Relationships', *Human Relations* 11, no. 3 (1958), p. 203; cf. e.g., Ronald F.E. Weissman, *Ritual Brotherhood in Renaissance Florence* (New York, London: Academic Press, 1982), pp. 26, 102–3.
31. Neu, 'Zeremonielle Verfahren', esp. p. 30; Stollberg-Rilinger, 'Rituals', pp. 368–70.
32. Berndt Keller, "Olsons 'Logik des kollektiven Handelns'. Entwicklung, Kritik—und eine Alternative', *Politische Vierteljahresschrift* 29, no. 3 (1988).
33. Mancur Olson, *The Logic of Collective Action: Public Goods and the Theory of Groups* (Cambridge: MA, London: Harvard University Press, 1965/71), pp. 1–2.
34. Ibid., *Logic*, p. 61.
35. Daniel Eek and Anders Biel, 'The Interplay Between Greed, Efficiency, and Fairness in Public-Goods Dilemmas', *Social Justice Research* 16, no. 3 (2003).
36. Cf. Gertrud A. Fremling and Richard Posner, *Market Signaling of Personal Characteristics*, The University of Chicago Law School (Chicago, 1999).
37. Volckart, *Währung*, no. 87, pp. 317–18.
38. Wolfgang Behringer, '"Von der Gutenberg-Galaxis zur Taxis-Galaxis". Die Kommunikationsrevolution: Ein Konzept zum besseren Verständnis der Frühen Neuzeit', *Historische Zeitschrift. Beihefte* 41 (2005), p. 48; Paul Münch, *Lebensformen in der Frühen Neuzeit 1500 bis 1800* (Frankfurt, Berlin: Ullstein, 1996), p. 501.
39. Kamann, 'Christoph Fürer', no. 5, p. 293.
40. Ibid., 'Christoph Fürer', no. 5, pp. 294–5.
41. Braudel, *The Mediterranean*, 1, p. 355. Braudel would have preferred 'public enemy no. 1' to the expression 'first enemy' chosen by the English translator. Geoffrey Parker, *Emperor: A New Life of Charles V* (New Haven, London: Yale University Press, 2019), p. 653 with note no. 25.
42. Wrede, *Reichstagsakten*, vol. 2, no. 7, p. 155.
43. Erwein Eltz, 'Die Reise zum Reichstag', in *Alltag im 16. Jahrhundert: Studien zu Lebensformen in mitteleuropäischen Städten*, ed. Alfred Kohler and Heinrich Lutz (Vienna: Verlag für Geschichte und Politik, 1987), pp. 217–18; Hartmann, *Reichstage*, p. 112; Maximilian Lanzinner, 'Fürsten und Gesandte als politische Akteure beim Reichstag 1566', in *Religiöse Prägung und politische Ordnung in der Neuzeit: Festschrift für Winfried Becker zum 65. Geburtstag*, ed. Bernhard Löffler and Karsten Ruppert (Cologne: Böhlau, 2006), pp. 61–3; Aulinger and Schweinzer-Burian, 'Präsenz'.

44. Christoph Lehmann, *Florilegium Politicum: Politischer Blumengarten Darinn außerlesene Politische Sententz, Lehren, Reguln, und Sprüchwörter auß Theologis, Jurisconsultis, Politicis, Historicis, Philosophis, Poeten und eygener erfahrung unter 286 Tituln . . . zusammen getragen* (s.l.: Impensis autoris, 1630), p. 687.
45. Eltz, 'Die Reise', p. 215.
46. Mark Brayshay, 'Long-Distance Royal Journeys: Anne of Denmark's Journey from Stirling to Windsor in 1603', *The Journal of Transport History* 25, no. 1 (2004), pp. 8–9.
47. Cf. Eltz, 'Die Reise', p. 216.
48. Hamburg's urban accounts contain entries for 68 couriers sent to Speyer between 1532 and 1562. Karl Koppmann, ed., *Kämmereirechnungen der Stadt Hamburg*, vol. 5 (Hamburg: Hermann Grüning, 1883), *passim*; ibid., ed., *Kämmereirechnungen der Stadt Hamburg*, vol. 6 (Hamburg: Gräfe & Sillem, 1892), ibid., ed., *Kämmereirechnungen der Stadt Hamburg*, vol. 7 (Hamburg: Gräfe & Sillem, 1894). Venice paid between 25 and 58 florins for messages to Nuremberg. Braudel, *The Mediterranean*, 1, p. 365.
49. Erich Keyser, 'Preise und Löhne in Hamburg in der ersten Hälfte des 16. Jahrhunderts', *Zeitschrift des Vereins für Hamburgische Geschichte* 49/50 (1964), p. 80.
50. The main altar piece of St John's Church, Lüneburg, painted by Hinrik Funhof *c.*1483, shows a Hamburg messenger delivering a letter.
51. Peter Moraw, 'Franken als königsnahe Landschaft im späten Mittelalter', *Blätter für deutsche Landesgeschichte N.F.* 112 (1976), p. 125; Wilson, *Empire*, p. 180–1.
52. Schmidt, *Geschichte*, p. 87.
53. Aulinger and Schweinzer-Burian, 'Präsenz'.
54. 1521: Wrede, *Reichstagsakten*, vol. 2, no. 56, pp. 424–42; 1545: Aulinger, *Reichstag zu Worms 1545*, vol. 2, no. 113b, pp. 1084–98.
55. Stollberg-Rilinger, *Old Clothes*, p. 25.
56. Ludwig Frohnhäuser, *Geschichte der Reichsstadt Wimpfen, des Ritterstifts St. Peter zu Wimpfen im Thal, des Dominicanerklosters und des Hospitals zum Hl. Geist zu Wimpfen am Berg* (Darmstadt: Historischer Verein, 1870), p. 199; Keyser, *Deutsches Städtebuch*, vol. 4, 2: Württemberg, pp. 308–9.
57. Fritz Reuter, 'Worms um 1521', in *Der Reichstag zu Worms von 1521: Reichspolitik und Luthersache*, ed. Fritz Reuter (Worms: Stadtarchiv Worms, 1981), p. 42; Rosemarie Aulinger, *Das Bild des Reichstages im 16. Jahrhundert: Beiträge zu einer typologischen Analyse schriftlicher und bildlicher Quellen* (Göttingen: Vandenhoeck & Ruprecht, 1980), pp. 174–5; Willi Alter, 'Von der konradinischen Rachtung bis zum letzten Reichstag in Speyer, 1420–1570', in *Geschichte der Stadt Speyer*, ed. Wolfgang Eger (Stuttgart: Kohlhammer, 1982), p. 515.
58. Erich Keyser, ed., *Deutsches Städtebuch*, vol. 4, 3: Rheinland-Pfalz und Saarland (Stuttgart: Kohlhammer, 1964), pp. 391–3, 454. Cologne, Nuremberg, Augsburg, Lübeck, Aachen, Ulm, and Hamburg were all larger than Worms, but Cologne, Lübeck, Aachen, and Hamburg were too much out of the way to be considered for an imperial diet. Ibid., *Deutsches Städtebuch*, vol. 3, 3: Rheinisches

Städtebuch, pp. 33–4, 255; Keyser and Stoob, *Deutsches Städtebuch*, vol. 5,1: Bayern, pp. 391–3; ibid., eds., *Deutsches Städtebuch*, vol. 5,2: Bayerisches Städtebuch (Stuttgart, Berlin, Cologne, Mainz: Kohlhammer, 1974), pp. 65–6; Erich Keyser, ed., *Deutsches Städtebuch*, vol. 1: Nordostdeutschland (Stuttgart, Berlin: Kohlhammer, 1939), pp. 390, 419; ibid., *Deutsches Städtebuch*, vol. 4,2: Württemberg, pp. 264–5.

59. Wolfgang D. Fritz, ed., *Die Goldene Bulle Kaiser Karls IV. vom Jahre 1356* (Weimar: Böhlau, 1972), p. 627–9.
60. Wrede, *Reichstagsakten*, vol. 2, no. 1, pp. 134–5.
61. Helmut Neuhaus, 'Der Augsburger Reichstag des Jahres 1530: Ein Forschungsbericht', *Zeitschrift für historische Forschung* 9, no. 2 (1982), p. 191.
62. Wolfgang Behringer, 'Kaiser, Reichstag und Postwesen (1490–1615)', in *Der Reichstag 1486–1613: Kommunikation, Wahrnehmung, Öffentlichkeit*, ed. Maximilian Lanzinner and Arno Strohmeyer (Göttingen: Vandenhoeck & Ruprecht, 2006); cf. Maximilian Lanzinner, 'Einleitung', in *Der Reichstag 1486–1613: Kommunikation—Wahrnehmung—Öffentlichkeiten*, ed. Maximilian Lanzinner and Arno Strohmeyer (Göttingen: Vandenhoeck & Ruprecht, 2006), p. 18.
63. Behringer, 'Kaiser', p. 121.
64. Ibid., *Thurn und Taxis: Die Geschichte ihrer Post und ihrer Unternehmen* (Munich, Zürich: Piper, 1990), p. 54; Elsas, *Preise*, 1, p. 731.
65. Behringer, 'Kaiser', pp. 121–2.
66. Ibid., 'Kaiser', pp. 122–4.
67. Volckart, *Währung*, no. 37, p. 151; no. 39, pp. 178–9; no. 80, pp. 275–6.
68. Ibid., *Währung*, no. 27, p. 87.
69. Ibid., *Währung*, no. 5, pp. 26–7.
70. Ibid., *Währung*, no. 51, p. 198; no. 64, p. 244.
71. Ibid., *Währung*, no. 84, pp. 281–300.
72. Ibid., *Währung*, no. 78, p. 273.
73. Aulinger and Schweinzer-Burian, 'Präsenz'; Maximilian Lanzinner, 'Juristen unter den Gesandten der Reichstage 1486–1654', in *Das Reichskammergericht im Spiegel seiner Prozessakten: Bilanz und Perspektiven der Forschung*, ed. Friedrich Battenberg and Bernd Schildt (Cologne, Weimar, Vienna: Böhlau, 2010), p. 359.
74. David Stasavage, *States of Credit: Size, Power, and the Development of European Politics* (Princeton, Oxford: Princeton University Press, 2011), pp. 65–8.
75. The results discussed below were derived in a series of regression analyses. For details of the variables and regression outputs see the Appendix.
76. Lanzinner, 'Juristen', pp. 365–73.
77. Volckart, *Währung*, p. XCV, no. 37, pp. 117, 137, 142; no. 46, p. 189; no. 56, p. 212–16; no. 102, p. 412; no. 103, p. 413–16.
78. Armin Kohnle, 'Die Reichstagsgesandten der Fürsten: Projekt einer Prosopographie im Reformationszeitalter', in *Reichspersonal: Funktionsträger für Kaiser und Reich*, ed. Anette Baumann et al. (Cologne, Weimar, Vienna: Böhlau, 2003), p. 335.

79. Horst Rabe, *Reichsbund und Interim: Die Verfassungs- und Religionspolitik Karls V. und der Reichstag von Augsburg 1547/1548* (Cologne: Böhlau, 1971), p. 195.
80. Machoczek, *Reichstag zu Augsburg 1547/48*, vol. 3, no. 226, p. 2021; Volckart, *Währung*, no. 1, pp. 3–4.
81. Ibid., *Währung*, p. XLV.
82. Ibid., *Währung*, no. 5, p. 22.
83. Ibid., *Währung*, no. 5, p. 23.
84. Hartmann, *Reichstage*, p. 114.
85. ÖStA, HHStA Wien, Reichshofrat, Miscellanea Münzwesen 1: Münzwesen im Reich (1. Konvolut), fols. 19.v.–20v.
86. Volckart, *Währung*, no. 32, p. 92.
87. Ibid., *Währung*, p. XLV.
88. Hermine Stiefenhöfer, *Philipp von Flersheim, Bischof von Speyer (1529-1552) und gefürsteter Propst von Weißenburg 1546–1552: Ein Beitrag zur Geschichte der Reformation in der deutschen Westmark* (Speyer: Pilger-Verlag, 1941), pp. 11–35.
89. Volckart, *Währung*, no. 37, pp. 150, 153–5, 164.
90. ÖStA, HHStA Wien, Reichshofrat, Miscellanea Münzwesen 1: Münzwesen im Reich (1. Konvolut), fols. 4.r–4v.
91. ÖStA, HHStA Wien, Reichshofrat, Miscellanea Münzwesen 1: Münzwesen im Reich (1. Konvolut), fols. 19.v.–20v.
92. Volckart, *Währung*, no. 37, p. 103.
93. Lanzinner, 'Juristen', p. 354.
94. Albrecht Luttenberger, 'Reichspolitik und Reichstag unter Karl V: Formen zentralen politischen Handelns', in *Aus der Arbeit an den Reichstagen unter Kaiser Karl V: 7 Beiträge zu Fragen der Forschung und Edition*, ed. Heinrich Lutz and Alfred Kohler (Göttingen: Vandenhoeck & Ruprecht, 1986), p. 42; Karl Härter, 'Das kurmainzer Reichstagsdirektorium: Eine zentrale reichspolitische Schaltstelle des Reichserzkanzlers im Reichssystem', in *Der Mainzer Kurfürst als Reichserzkanzler: Funktionen, Aktivitäten, Ansprüche und Bedeutung des zweiten Mannes im Alten Reich*, ed. Peter Claus Hartmann (Stuttgart: Steiner, 1997), p. 174; Lanzinner, 'Fürsten und Gesandte', p. 75.
95. Karl Heinz Burmeister, 'Jakob Jonas: Humanist und Staatsmann', *Schriften des Vereins für Geschichte des Bodensees und seiner Umgebung* 89 (1971), pp. 90, 92; Aulinger and Schweinzer-Burian, 'Präsenz'.
96. Burmeister, 'Humanist', p. 84.
97. Volckart, *Währung*, no. 5, p. 23.
98. Ibid., *Währung*, Nr. 19, pp. 61–8.
99. Ibid., *Währung*, Nr. 42, pp. 183–4.
100. Ibid., *Währung*, Nr. 37, pp. 105, § 1.5, 107, § 1.13, 110, § 4.1, 115, § 7.2, 118, § 9.3, 119, § 10.2, § 10.8, 120, § 10.9, 122, § 13.4, § 13.6, 125, § 14.9, etc.
101. Whaley, *Germany*, I, pp. 77–9, 274, 321; Dietmar Heil, *Die Reichspolitik Bayerns unter der Regierung Herzog Albrechts V. (1550–1579)* (Göttingen Vandenhoeck & Ruprecht, 1998), p. 25.

102. Cf. Barbara Stollberg-Rilinger, *Cultures of Decision-Making* (London: The German Historical Institute London, 2015), p. 23.
103. Volckart, *Währung*, Nr. 37, p. 128, no. 52, pp. 200–1; ÖStA, HHStA Wien, Reichshofrat, Miscellanea Münzwesen 1: Münzwesen im Reich (1. Konvolut), fol. 271v.
104. Ibid., *Währung*, no. 86, p. 315.
105. ÖStA, Reichshofrat, Miscellanea Münzwesen 1: Münzwesen im Reich (1. Konvolut), fol. 276r.
106. Eltz, *Reichstag zu Augsburg 1550/51*, vol. 1, Nr. 82, pp. 293–4, 387.
107. Barbara Stollberg-Rilinger, 'Die zeremonielle Inszenierung des Reiches, oder: Was leistet der kulturalistische Ansatz für die Reichs Verfassungsgeschichte?', in *Imperium Romanum—irregulare corpus—Teutscher Reichs-Staat*, ed. Matthias Schnettger (Mainz: Philipp von Zabern, 2002), p. 244.
108. Johann Peter Zwengel, *New Groß Formular vnd vollkommlich Cantzlei Buch: von den besten vnd auszerlesenen Formularien aller deren Schrifften, so in . . . Cantzleyen, auch sonst in den Ampten . . . fürfallender geschäfft halben, bräuchlich seindt* (Frankfurt: Christian Egenolffs Erben, 1568), fols. XIII–XXX.
109. Fynes Moryson, *An Itinerary Containing His Ten Yeeres Travell through the Twelve Dominions of Germany, Bohmer-land, Sweitzerland, Netherland, Denmarke, Poland, Italy, Turky, France, England, Scotland & Ireland*, vol. 1 (Glasgow: Glasgow University Press, 1617/1907), p. 46.
110. Volckart, *Währung*, no. 137, pp. 107 (13 Sep.), 114 (18 Sep.), 119 (22 Sep.), 120 (24 Sep.), 123 (27 Sep.), 131 (28 Sep.), 136 (2 Oct.); 139 (4 Oct.), 161 (19 Oct.), 169 (26 Oct.).
111. Ibid., *Währung*, no. 37, p. 175–6.
112. Harry Gerber, 'Die Bedeutung des Augsburger Reichstages von 1547/48 für das Ringen der Reichsstädte um Stimme, Stand und Session', *Elsaß-Lothringisches Jahrbuch* 9 (1930), pp. 181, 208.
113. E.g., Volckart, *Währung*, no. 1, p. 3.
114. Hartmann, *Reichstage*, p. 169.
115. Karl Rauch, ed., *Traktat über den Reichstag: Eine offiziöse Darstellung aus der Kurmainzischen Kanzlei* (Weimar: Böhlau, 1905); for the date and authorship see pp. 28–33; cf. Helmut Neuhaus, 'Der Streit um den richtigen Platz: Ein Beitrag zu reichsständischen Verfahrensformen in der Frühen Neuzeit', in *Vormoderne politische Verfahren*, ed. Barbara Stollberg-Rilinger (Berlin: Duncker & Humblot, 2001), pp. 282–3.
116. Rauch, *Traktat*, pp. 61–2.
117. Gerhard Oestreich, 'Zur parlamentarischen Arbeitsweise der deutschen Reichstage unter Karl V. (1519–1556)', in *Die geschichtlichen Grundlagen der modernen Volksvertretung*, ed. Heinz Rausch (Darmstadt: Wissenschaftliche Buchgesellschaft, 1971/74), p. 252.
118. Rauch, *Traktat*, pp. 67–8.

119. See, e.g., Leeb, *Reichstag zu Regensburg 1556/57*, vol. 1, no. 234, pp. 575–7: On 18 November 1556, Regensburg (where the diet of 1556–7 was held) chaired the meeting and opened the discussion. Then the delegates of Augsburg, Nuremberg, Ulm, Regensburg (again), Straßburg (Strasbourg), Augsburg (again), Nuremberg (again), Ulm (again) and Rothenburg ob der Tauber spoke. Regensburg concluded the discussion.
120. Volckart, 'The Dear Old Holy Roman Realm', p. 378.
121. Abhijit V. Banerjee, 'A Simple Model of Herd Behevior', *The Quaterly Journal of Economics* 107, no. 3 (1992); Rebecca B. Morton and Kai Ou, 'What Motivates Bandwagon Voting Behavior: Altruism or a Desire to Win?', *European Journal of Political Economy* 40, Part B (2015).
122. Sushil Bikhchandani, David Hirshleifer, and Ivo Welch, 'A Theory of Fads, Fashion, Custom, and Cultural Change as Informational Cascades', *Journal of Political Economy* 100, no. 5 (1992); Robert J. Schiller, 'Conversation, Information and Herd Behavior', *Rhetoric and Economic Behavior* 85, no. 3 (1995).
123. Oliver Volckart, 'Voting Like Your Betters: The Bandwagon Effect in the Diet of the Holy Roman Empire', *German History* 49, no. 1 (2023).
124. Klaus Schlaich, 'Maioritas—protestatio—itio in partes—corpus Evangelicorum: Das Verfahren im Reichstag des Heiligen Römischen Reichs Deutscher Nation nach der Reformation', *Zeitschrift der Savigny-Stiftung für Rechtsgeschichte: Kanonistische Abteilung* 63 (1977); ibid., 'Die Mehrheitsabstimmung im Reichstag zwischen 1495 und 1613', in *Gesammelte Aufsätze: Kirche und Staat von der Reformation bis zum Grundgesetz*, ed. Klaus Schlaich (Tübingen: Mohr-Siebeck, 1983/97); Winfried Schulze, 'Majority Decision in the Imperial Diets of the Sixteenth and Seventeenth Centuries', *Journal of Modern History* 58 (1986).
125. Cf. John D. Gould, *The Great Debasement: Currency and the Economy in Mid-Tudor England* (Oxford: Clarendon Press, 1970), p. 11.
126. Volckart, *Währung*, no. 37, pp. 140.
127. Ibid., *Währung*, no. 58, p. 225–9.
128. Ibid., *Währung*, no. 86, p. 302.
129. Hans-Jürgen Becker, 'Protestatio, Protest: Funktion und Funktionswandel eines rechtlichen Instruments', *Zeitschrift für Historische Forschung* 5, no. 4 (1978), pp. 399–400.
130. Schlaich, 'Maioritas', p. 274.
131. Volckart, *Währung*, nos. 27–31, pp. 87–91.
132. Ibid., *Währung*, no. 37, p. 122.
133. Hartmann, *Reichstage*, pp. 262–3.
134. Aulinger, Eltz, and Machoczek, *Reichstag zu Augsburg 1555*, vol. 2, no. 145, pp. 1274–5 (20 Feb. 1555); Leeb, *Reichstag zu Regensburg 1556/57*, vol. 1, no. 122, pp. 450–2; no. 160, pp. 499–504; no. 167, pp. 509–12; no. 170, pp. 515; Maximilian Lanzinner and Dietmar Heil, eds., *Der Reichstag zu Augsburg 1566*, vol. 1 (Munich: Oldenbourg, 2002), no. 86, pp. 578–9.

135. Wrede, *Reichstagsakten*, vol. 2, no. 56, pp. 424–42.
136. Winfried Schulze, *Reich und Türkengefahr im späten 16. Jahrhundert: Studien zu den politischen und gesellschaftlichen Auswirkungen einer äußeren Bedrohung* (Munich: Beck, 1978), p. 77 with FN 19.
137. Albrecht Luttenberger, ed., *Deutsche Reichstagsakten unter Kaiser Karl V.: Der Reichstag zu Regensburg 1541* (Munich: De Gruyter Oldenbourg, 2018), Nr. 941, S. 3620.
138. Neuhaus, 'Streit', p. 285.
139. Statistically, the so-called 'Spearman's rank correlation' value for this sample is 0.302. A perfect match would be indicated by a value of 1.
140. Cf. Aulinger and Schweinzer-Burian, 'Präsenz'.
141. The Spearman's rank correlation value for the poll on 20 Feb. 1555 was 0.733. Later polls: 30 Sep. 1556: 0.616; 22 Dec. 1556: 0.709; 2 Jan. 1557: 0.827; 7. Jan. 1557: 0.616; 19 Apr. 1566: 0.657.
142. Volckart, 'Voting'.
143. Schlumbohm, 'Gesetze'; Joachim Whaley, *Germany and the Holy Roman Empire*, vol. II: The Peace of Westphalia to the Dissolution of the Reich 1648–1806 (Oxford: Oxford University Press, 2012), p. 650.
144. Gerhard Köbler, *Historisches Lexikon der deutschen Länder: Die deutschen Territorien vom Mittelalter bis zur Gegenwart*, 7 ed. (Munich: Beck, 2007), p. 565.
145. Heinz Schilling, 'Veni, vidi, Deus vixit: Karl V. zwischen Religionskrieg und Religionsfrieden', *Archiv für Reformationsgeschichte* 89 (1998), p. 145.
146. Machoczek, *Reichstag zu Augsburg 1547/48*, vol. 3, no. 372b, pp. 2664–5.

CHAPTER 4

1. Christian Meltzer, *Historia Schneebergensis renovata, das ist: erneuerte Stadt- u. Berg-Chronica der im Ober-Ertz-Gebürge Meißens gelegenen Berg-Stadt Schneeberg* (Schneeberg: Heinrich Fulde, 1716), pp. 33–5.
2. Oswald Hoppe, *Der Silberbergbau zu Schneeberg bis zum Jahre 1500* (Freiberg: Gerlachsche Buchdruckerei, 1908); Adolf Laube, *Studien über den erzgebirgischen Silberbergbau von 1470 bis 1546: Seine Geschichte, seine Produktionsverhältnisse, seine Bedeutung für die gesellschaftlichen Veränderungen und Klassenkämpfe in Sachsen am Beginn der Übergangsepoche vom Feudalismus zum Kapitalismus*, 2 ed. (Berlin: Akademie-Verlag, 1976), pp. 22–3.
3. Georgius Agricola, *Bermannus, sive de re metallica* (Basel: Froben, 1530), fol. 25r.
4. Hoppe, *Silberbergbau*, p. 9.
5. Lothar Klappauf, '1000 Jahre Bergbau?', in *Auf den Spuren einer frühen Industrielandschaft: Naturraum – Mensch – Umwelt im Harz*, ed. Christiane Segers-Glocke (Hameln: CW Niemeyer, 2000), pp. 19–20.

6. Wilhelm Stieda, *Das Hausiergewerbe in Deutschland: Vortrag, gehalten in der Gehe-Stiftung zu Dresden am 12. März 1898* (Dresden: Pöschel & Trepte, 1899), pp. 14–15; Eugen Peter Schwiedland, *Die Hausierfrage in Österreich* (Leipzig: Duncker & Humblot, 1899), p. IX; Sheilagh Ogilvie, Markus Küpker, and Janine Maegraith, 'Krämer und ihre Waren im ländlichen Württemberg zwischen 1600 und 1740', *Zeitschrift für Agrargeschichte und Agrarsoziologie* 59, no. 2 (2011), pp. 56–7.
7. Julia Kahleyß, 'Der wirtschaftliche Aufstieg des Martin Römer: Soziale Mobilität im westerzgebirgischen Bergbau des 15. Jahrhunderts', *Vierteljahrschrift für Sozial- und Wirtschaftsgeschichte* 100, no. 2 (2013), p. 160.
8. Tina Asmussen and Pamela O. Long, 'Introduction: The Cultural and Material Worlds of Mining in Early Modern Europe', *Renaissance Studies* 34, no. 1 (2020), pp. 15–16. 26–7.
9. Hermann Kellenbenz, 'Das Römisch-Deutsche Reich im Rahmen der wirtschafts- und finanzpolitischen Erwägungen Karls V. im Spannungsfeld imperialer und dynastischer Interessen', in *Das römisch-deutsche Reich im politischen System Karls V.*, ed. Heinrich Lutz and Elisabeth Müller-Luckner (Munich, Vienna: Oldenbourg, 1982), p. 44.
10. Aulinger, *Reichstag zu Worms 1545*, vol. 2, no. 70, p. 902.
11. Jakob Strieder, *Studien zur Geschichte kapitalistischer Organisationsformen: Monopole, Kartelle und Aktiengesellschaften im Mittelalter und zu Beginn der Neuzeit* (Munich, Leipzig: Duncker & Humblot, 1914), p. 40; Othmar Pickl, 'Kupfererzeugung und Kupferhandel in den Ostalpen', in *Schwerpunkte der Kupferproduktion und des Kupferhandels in Europa 1500–1650*, ed. Hermann Kellenbenz (Cologne, Vienna: Böhlau, 1977), p. 124; Wieland Held, 'Soziale Herkunft und Situation der Mansfelder Bergleute in der ersten Hälfte des 16. Jahrhunderts', *Jahrbuch für Wirtschaftsgeschichte* 4 (1982), p. 115.
12. Laube, *Studien*, p. 115.
13. Adolf Soetbeer, 'Edelmetall-Produktion und Werthverhältniss zwischen Gold und Silber seit der Entdeckung Amerika's bis zur Gegenwart', in *Dr A. Petermanns Mittheilungen aus Justus Perthes' geographischer Anstalt: Ergänzungsband 13*, ed. E. Behm (Gotha: Justus Perthes, 1879–80), pp. 24, 30; Andreas Bingener, Christoph Bartels, and Michael Fessner, 'Die große Zeit des Silbers: Der Bergbau im deutschsprachigen Raum von der Mitte des 15. bis zum Anfang des 17. Jahrhunderts', in *Der alteuropäische Bergbau: Von den Anfängen bis zur Mitte des 18. Jahrhunderts*, ed. Christoph Bartels and Rainer Slotta (Münster: Aschendorf, 2012), pp. 373–86.
14. John H. Munro, 'The Central European Mining Boom, Mint Outputs, and Prices in the Low Countries and England, 1450–1550', in *Money, Coins, and Commerce: Essays in the Monetary History of Asia and Europe (From Antiquity to Modern Times)*, ed. Eddy H.G. van Cauwenberghe (Leuven: Leuven University Press, 1991); Bingener, Bartels, and Fessner, 'Zeit des Silbers'.

15. John Day, 'The Question of Monetary Contraction in Late Medieval Europe', in *The Medieval Market Economy*, ed. John Day (Oxford: Basil Blackwell, 1981/87), p. 71.
16. Christoph Bartels, 'Bergbau und Münzstätten im Harz', *Abhandlungen der Braunschweigischen Wissenschaftlichen Gesellschaft* 60 (2008), p. 36.
17. Lothar Suhling, *Aufschließen, Gewinnen und Fördern: Geschichte des Bergbaus* (Reinbek bei Hamburg: Rowohlt, 1988), pp. 84–9; Karl-Heinz Ludwig, 'Bergbau zwischen ökonomischem Interesse und politischer Macht', in *Metalle und Macht 1000 bis 1600* ed. Karl-Heinz Ludwig and Volker Schmidtchen (Frankfurt: 1992), pp. 37–75; Wolfgang von Stromer, 'Konjunktur im europäischen Bergbau: Wasserkünste', in *Konjunkturen im europäischen Bergbau in vorindustrieller Zeit: Festschrift für Ekkehard Westermann zum 60. Geburtstag*, ed. Christoph Bartels and Markus A. Denzel (Stuttgart: Steiner, 2000), pp. 151–2.
18. Hans Joachim Kraschewski, 'Das Spätmittelalter: Die Zeit des Aufbruchs', in *Der alteuropäische Bergbau: Von den Anfängen bis zur Mitte des 18. Jahrhunderts*, ed. Christoph Bartels and Rainer Slotta (Münster: Aschendorf, 2012), pp. 250, 256.
19. Christoph Bartels, 'Zur Bergbaukrise des Spätmittelalters', in *Konjunkturen im europäischen Bergbau in vorindustrieller Zeit: Festschrift für Ekkehard Westermann zum 60. Geburtstag*, ed. Christoph Bartels and Markus A. Denzel (Stuttgart: Steiner, 2000), p. 167.
20. Neithard Bulst, 'Der Schwarze Tod: demographische, wirtschafts- und kulturgeschichtliche Aspekte der Pestkatastrophe von 1347–1352: Bilanz der neueren Forschung', *Saeculum* 30 (1979), pp. 54–5; Òscar Jordà, Sanjay R. Singh, and Alan M. Taylor, *Longer-Run Economic Consequences of Pandemics*, Federal Reserve Bank of San Francisco (San Francisco, 2020), pp. 8–9.
21. Josef Janáček, 'L'argent tchèque et la Méditerranée (XIVe et XVe siècles)', in *Mélanges en l'honneur de Fernand Braudel: Histoire économique du monde méditerranéen 1440–1650*, ed. Ernest Labrousse (Toulouse: Privat, 1973), p. 255.
22. Bartels, 'Bergbaukrise', pp. 168–9.
23. Philippe Braunstein, 'Innovations in Mining and Metal Production in Europe in the Late Middle Ages', *Journal of European Economic History* 12, no. 3 (1983), pp. 584–6; Christoph Bartels, 'Krisen und Innovationen im Erzbergbau des Harzes zwischen ausgehendem Mittelalter und beginnender Neuzeit', *Technikgeschichte* 63, no. 1 (1996), pp. 6–10.
24. Ekkehard Westermann, 'Zur Silber- und Kupferproduktion Mitteleuropas vom 15. bis zum frühen 17. Jahrhundert: Über Bedeutung und Rangfolge der Reviere von Schwaz, Mansfeld und Neusohl', *Der Anschnitt* 5/6 (1986), p. 187; Kraschewski, 'Das Spätmittelalter', p. 257; Bingener, Bartels, and Fessner, 'Zeit des Silbers', p. 331.
25. Braunstein, 'Innovations', p. 587; Stuart Jenks, 'Von den archaischen Grundlagen bis zur Schwelle der Moderne (*c.*1000–1450)', in *Deutsche Wirtschaftsgeschichte: Ein Jahrtausend im Überblick*, ed. Michael North (Munich: Beck, 2000), p. 66; Kraschewski, 'Das Spätmittelalter', p. 267.

26. Georgius Agricola, *De re metallica* (New York: Dover Publications, 1556/1950), pp. 513–24; Maxime L'Héritier and Florian Téreygeol, 'From Copper to Silver: Understanding the Saigerprozess through Experimental Liquation and Drying', *Historical Metallurgy* 44, no. 2 (2010), p. 136.
27. Johann Mathesius, *Sarepta oder Bergpostill sampt der Jochimßthalischen kurtzen Chroniken* (Nuremberg: vom Berg, 1562), fol. C verso.
28. Danuta Molenda, 'Investments in Ore Mining in Poland from the 13th to the 17th Centuries', *Journal of European Economic History* 5, no. 1 (1976), p. 156; Kraschewski, 'Das Spätmittelalter', pp. 262, 270; Bingener, Bartels, and Fessner, 'Zeit des Silbers', p. 318–20; Guy, *Gresham's Law*, p. 36.
29. Bartels, 'Krisen', p. 8.
30. Hoppe, *Silberbergbau*, pp. 22–3, 27, 36; Hubert Ermisch, *Das sächsische Bergrecht des Mittelalters* (Leipzig: Gieseke & Devrient, 1887), p. 114; Laube, *Studien*, p. 86.
31. There were forerunners in thirteenth-century Siena, Styria, and France. Jonathan Barron Baskin and Paul J. Miranti, *A History of Corporate Finance* (Cambridge: Cambridge University Press, 1999), p. 60.
32. Agricola, *De re metallica*, pp. 89–90; Laube, *Studien*, p. 82; Richard Dietrich, *Untersuchungen zum Frühkapitalismus im mitteldeutschen Erzbergbau und Metallhandel* (Hildesheim: Georg Olms-Verlag, 1991), p. 164.
33. Theodor Gustav Werner, 'Das fremde Kapital im Annaberger Bergbau und Metallhandel des 16. Jahrhunderts (I.)', *Neues Archiv für sächsische Geschichte* 57 (1936), p. 122; Laube, *Studien*, p. 91.
34. Werner, 'Das fremde Kapital', p. 132; ibid., 'Regesten und Urkunden über Beteiligung von Nürnbergern an der Zeche Rappolt und an anderen Schneeberger Bergwerks- und Metallhandelsunternehmungen (II. Teil)', *Mitteilungen des Vereins für Geschichte der Stadt Nürnberg* 60 (1973), p. 170; Laube, *Studien*, p. 83; Franz Irsigler, 'Rheinisches Kapital in Mitteleuropäischen Montanunternehmen des 15. und 16. Jahrhunderts', *Zeitschrift für Historische Forschung* 3, no. 2 (1976), p. 158; Dietrich, *Untersuchungen zum Frühkapitalismus im mitteldeutschen Erzbergbau und Metallhandel*, p. 163.
35. David Chilosi, Max-Stephan Schulze, and Oliver Volckart, 'Benefits of Empire? Capital Market Integration North and South of the Alps, 1350–1800', *The Journal of Economic History* 78, no. 3 (2018), pp. 653, 663.
36. Wolfgang Wüst, *Die 'gute' Policey im Fränkischen Reichskreis* (Berlin: Akademie-Verlag, 2003), pp. 17–19.
37. Laube, *Studien*, p. 84.
38. Werner, 'Das fremde Kapital', p. 134.
39. Volckart, *Währung*, no. 5, p. 24.
40. Ibid., *Währung*, no. 17, p. 55.
41. Ermisch, *Bergrecht*, pp. 153–4; Laube, *Studien*, p. 282.
42. Paul Arnold, 'Das sächsische Münzwesen in der ersten Hälfte des 16. Jahrhunderts—die Wechselbeziehungen zwischen Bergbau und Münzpolitik in Sachsen', in *Georgius Agricola, 500 Jahre: Wissenschaftliche Konferenz vom*

25.–27. März 1994 in Chemnitz, Freistaat Sachsen, ed. F. Naumann (Basel, Boston, Berlin: Birkhauser Verlag 1994), p. 416; Hans Joachim Kraschewski, 'Wirtschaftliche Wechsellagen, ihre Einwirkungen auf den Bergbau des sechzehnten und siebzehnten Jahrhunderts und die bergbauliche Arbeitsverfassung', in *Konjunkturen im europäischen Bergbau in Vorindustrieller Zeit: Festschrift für Ekkehard Westermann zum 60.* Geburtstag, ed. Christoph Bartels and Markus A. Denzel (Steiner: Stuttgart, 2000), 215; ibid., 'Das Spätmittelalter', p. 313.

43. Strieder, *Studien*, p. 27.
44. Richard Ehrenberg, *Das Zeitalter der Fugger: Geldkapital und Creditverkehr im 16. Jahrhundert*, vol. 1: Die Geldmächte des 16. Jahrhunderts (Jena: Fischer, 1896), p. 89.
45. Mark Häberlein, 'Die Fugger'sche Anleihe von 1488: Handelskapital, fürstliche Privilegien und der Aufstieg der süddeutschen Kaufmannsbankiers', in *Schlüsselereignisse der deutschen Bankengeschichte*, ed. Dieter Lindenlaub, Carsten Burhop, and Joachim Scholtyseck (Stuttgart: Steiner, 2013), pp. 17–9.
46. Ehrenberg, *Zeitalter der Fugger*, 1: Die Geldmächte des 16. Jahrhunderts, pp. 90–5.
47. Benedikt Greiff, *Was Kayser Carolus dem Vten die Römisch Künglich Wal cost im 1520 Jar* (no place [Augsburg]: no publisher, 1869); Whaley, *Germany*, I, pp. 158–9.
48. Häberlein, *Die Fugger*, pp. 65–6.
49. Ehrenberg, *Zeitalter der Fugger*, 1: Die Geldmächte des 16. Jahrhunderts, p. 187; Häberlein, 'Die Fugger'sche Anleihe', p. 18.
50. Ehrenberg, *Zeitalter der Fugger*, 1: Die Geldmächte des 16. Jahrhunderts, pp. 190–1.
51. Bingener, Bartels, and Fessner, 'Zeit des Silbers', p. 337.
52. Strieder, *Studien*, p. 27; A. Zycha, 'Zur neuesten Literatur über die Wirtschafts- u. Rechtsgeschichte des deutschen Bergbaues', *Vierteljahrschrift für Sozial- und Wirtschaftsgeschichte* 5, no. 1/2 (1907), pp. 274–5.
53. Braunstein, 'Innovations', p. 589.
54. Soetbeer, 'Edelmetall-Produktion'; John Ulrich Nef, 'Silver Production in Central Europe 1450–1618', *Journal of Political Economy* 49 (1941); Georg W. Schenk, 'Über die Anfänge des Silberbergbaues von St. Joachimsthal', *Der Anschnitt* 20, no. 5 (1968); Janáček, 'L'Argent'; Laube, *Studien*; Oszkár Paulinyi, 'The Crown Monopoly of the Refining Metallurgy of Precious Metals and the Technology of the Cameral Refineries in Hungary and Transsylvania in the Period of Advanced and Late Feudalism (1325–1700) with Data and Output', in *Precious Metals in the Age of Expansion: Papers of the XIVth International Congress of the Historical Sciences*, ed. Hermann Kellenbenz (Stuttgart: Klett-Cotta, 1981); Ekkehard Westermann, *Das Eislebener Garkupfer und seine Bedeutung für den europäischen Kupfermarkt 1460–1560* (Vienna, Cologne: Böhlau, 1971); ibid., 'Zur Brandsilber- und Kupferproduktion des Falkenstein bei Schwaz 1470–1623: Eine Kritik bisheriger Ermittlungen von

Produktionziffern', *Tiroler Heimat* 50 (1986); ibid., 'Silber- und Kupferproduktion'; ibid., 'Über Beobachtungen und Erfahrungen bei der Vorbereitung der Edition einer vorindustriellen Produktionsstatistik: Zur Brandsilberproduktion des Falkenstein bei Schwaz/Tirol von 1470–1623', in *Quantifizierungsprobleme bei der Erforschung der Montanwirtschaft des 15. bis 18. Jahrhundert*, ed. Ekkehard Westermann (St. Katharinen: Scripta Mercaturae Verlag, 1988); ibid., *Die Listen der Brandsilberproduktion des Falkenstein bei Schwaz/Tirol von 1470–1623: Kommentar und Edition* (Vienna, 1988).

55. John H. Munro, 'The Monetary Origins of the "Price Revolution": South German Silver Mining, Merchant-Banking, and Venetian Commerce, 1470–1540', in *Global Connections and Monetary History, 1470–1800*, ed. Dennis O. Flynn, Arturo Giráldez, and Richard von Glahn (Aldershot, Brookfield: Ashgate Publishing, 2003), p. 8; Bingener, Bartels, and Fessner, 'Zeit des Silbers', p. 424.
56. Nef, 'Silver', p. 588.
57. Robert C. West, 'Early Silver Mining in New Spain, 1531–1555', in *Mines of Silver and Gold in the Americas*, ed. Peter J. Bakewell (Abingdon, New York: Routledge, 1995/97), pp. 60–1.
58. Renate Pieper, 'American Silver Production and West European Monetary Supply in the Sixteenth and Seventeenth Century', in *Economic effects of the European expansion: 1492–1824*, ed. José Casas Pardo (Stuttgart: Steiner, 1992), p. 81; West, 'Early Silver Mining in New Spain, 1531–1555', p. 70.
59. Peter J. Bakewell, *Silver Mining and Society in Colonial Mexico: Zacatecas 1546–1700* (Cambridge: Cambridge University Press, 1971), p. 4.
60. Ibid., *Silver Mining*, p. 241. The mark in which the quantities are given was the equivalent of 226.9 grams; ibid., 'Registered Silver Production in the Potosí district, 1550–1735', *Jahrbuch für Geschichte Lateinamerikas – Anuario de Historia de America Latina* 12, no. 1 (1975), p. 69.
61. Ibid., 'Silver Production', pp. 92–3.
62. Earl J. Hamilton, *American Treasure and the Price Revolution in Spain, 1501–1650* (Cambridge: MA: Harvard University Press, 1934), pp. 11–12, 22–4; cf. Michel Morineau, *Incroyables gazettes et fabuleux métaux: Les retours des trésor américains d'après les gazettes hollandaises (XVIe. –XVIIIe. siècles)* (London, New York, New Rochelle, Sydney, Melbourne: Cambridge University Press, 1985).
63. Hamilton, *American Treasure*, p. 42; Bingener, Bartels, and Fessner, 'Zeit des Silbers', pp. 446–7.
64. Oliver Volckart, 'Early Beginnings of the Quantity Theory of Money and their Context in Polish and Prussian Monetary Policies, *c.*1520–1550', *The Economic History Review* 50, no. 3 (1997).
65. Hamilton, American Treasure; Douglas Fisher, 'The Price Revolution: A Monetary Interpretation', *The Journal of Economic History* 49 (1989); Bernd Sprenger, 'Münzverschlechterung, Geldmengenwachstum und Bevölkerungsvermehrung als Einflußgrößen der sogenannten Preisrevolution im 16. und

beginnenden 17. Jahrhundert in Deutschland', in *Theorie und Empirie in Wirtschaftspolitik und Wirtschaftsgeschichte: Festschrift für Wilhelm Abel zum 80. Geburtstag*, ed. K.H. Kaufhold and F Riemann (Göttingen: Schwartz, 1984); Gerhard, 'Ursachen'.

66. Cf. Bingener, Bartels, and Fessner, 'Zeit des Silbers', p. 450.
67. ÖStA, Finanz- und Hofkammerarchiv, Alte Hofkammer, Niederösterreichisches Münz- und Bergwesen, 1524–1750, Akten 01, fol. 124r.
68. Kurt Dülfer, *Die Packschen Händel: Darstellungen und Quellen* (Marburg: Elwert, 1958), pp. 57–60; Whaley, *Germany*, I, pp. 295–6.
69. Leopold von Ranke, *History of the Reformation in Germany* (London: Longman, Brown, Green, and Longmans, 1847), p. 48.
70. Hanns Inama-Sternegg, 'Das Nachlaßinventar des Ambros Mornauer von Lichtenwert 1550', in *Festgabe für Erich Egg zum 65. Geburtstag*, ed. Christina Antenhofer and Richard Schober (Innsbruck: Landesmuseum, 1985).
71. ÖStA, Finanz- und Hofkammerarchiv, Alte Hofkammer, Niederösterreichisches Münz- und Bergwesen, 1524–1750, Akten 01, fol. 124v.
72. Vorel, *Circulation*, pp. 56, 67; Blaich, *Wirtschaftspolitik*, pp. 19, 258; Christmann, *Vereinheitlichung*, pp. 90–1; Bergerhausen, 'Exclusis Westphalen et Burgundt', p. 190; cf. North, 'Reich und Reichstag', p. 223.
73. Adolf Wrede, ed., *Deutsche Reichstagsakten unter Kaiser Karl V.*, vol. 3 (Gotha: Friedrich Andreas Perthes, 1901), no. 106, p. 620.
74. Volckart, 'The Dear Old Holy Roman Realm', pp. 380–1.
75. ÖStA, Finanz- und Hofkammerarchiv, Alte Hofkammer, Niederösterreichisches Münz- und Bergwesen, 1524–1750, Akten 01, fol. 125v.
76. Blaich, *Wirtschaftspolitik*, pp. 19–20; Rosemarie Aulinger, ed., *Deutsche Reichstagsakten unter Kaiser Karl V.: Der Reichstag zu Worms 1545*, vol. 1 (Munich: Oldenbourg, 2003), p. 67.
77. Wolfgang Burgdorf, 'Proto-constitutionalism—The Imperial Constitution in the Electoral Capitulations and Basic Law Guarantees', *German History* 36, no. 3 (2018), pp. 415–16; cf. Whaley, *Germany*, I, p. 160.
78. Wolfgang Burgdorf, ed., *Die Wahlkapitulationen der römisch-deutschen Könige und Kaiser 1519–1792* (Göttingen: Vandenhoeck & Ruprecht, 2015), p. 30.
79. Ibid., *Wahlkapitulationen*, pp. 22–3; Whaley, *Germany*, I, p. 161.
80. Horst Rabe, *Reich und Glaubensspaltung: Deutschland 1500–1600* (Munich: Beck, 1989), pp. 163, 168–9.
81. Wrede, *Reichstagsakten*, vol. 3, no. 105, pp. 599–615, with FN 1, p. 599.
82. Ibid., *Reichstagsakten*, vol. 3, no. 105, p. 600. In England, the golden rose noble was accepted as one-half of the silver pound sterling (that is, as a 120-pence-piece). Spufford, *Money and its Use in Medieval Europe*, p. 409; Christopher Edgar Challis, *The Tudor Coinage* (Manchester: Manchester University Press, 1978), pp. 67–9.
83. Adolf Wrede, ed., *Deutsche Reichstagsakten unter Kaiser Karl V.*, vol. 4 (Gotha: Friedrich Andreas Perthes, 1905), no. 149, p. 601.

84. Hirsch, *Münz-Archiv*, 1, no. CLXVII, pp. 240–3.
85. Vorel, *Circulation*, p. 58.
86. ÖStA, Finanz- und Hofkammerarchiv, Alte Hofkammer, Niederösterreichisches Münz- und Bergwesen, 1524–1750, Akten 01. Fol. 124v.
87. Schrötter, 'Münzwesen, Teil I', p. 154; Blaich, *Wirtschaftspolitik*, p. 19; Rössner, 'Monetary Instability', pp. 310–11.
88. Christine Roll, *Das zweite Reichsregiment 1521–1530* (Cologne, Weimar, Vienna: Böhlau, 1996), p. 370; Schrötter, 'Münzwesen, Teil I', p. 154.
89. Johann Newald, *Das österreichische Münzwesen unter Ferdinand I.: Eine münzgeschichtliche Studie* (Vienna: Kubasta & Voigt, 1883), no. 5, p. 141.
90. Rabe, *Reich*, pp. 164–5.
91. Newald, *Münzwesen*, no. 5, pp. 140–4.
92. Alfred Kohler, *Karl V. 1500–1558: Eine Biographie* (Munich: Beck, 1999/2013), pp. 96–100.
93. Quoted from ibid., *Karl V.*, pp. 79–80.
94. Ibid., *Karl V.*, pp. 80–1.
95. Bartholomäus Sastrow and Gottlieb Mohnike, *Bartholomäi Sastrowen Herkommen, Geburt und Lauff seines gantzen Lebens auch was sich in dem Denckwerdiges zugetragen, so er mehrentheils selbst gesehen und gegenwärtig mit angehöret hat*, vol. 2 (Greifswald: Universitäts-Buchhandlung, 1824), p. 84; cf. Freytag, Pictures of German Life in the Fifteenth, Sixteenth and Seventeenth Centuries, 1, p. 175.
96. Newald, *Münzwesen*, no. 5, p. 141.
97. Cosimo Perrotta, 'Einleitung zum Münzstreit der sächsischen Albertiner und Ernestiner um 1530', in *Die drei Flugschriften* über *den Münzstreit der sächsischen Albertiner und Ernestiner: Vademecum zu drei klassischen Schriften frühneuzeitlicher Münzpolitik*, ed. Karl Heinrich Kaufhold et al. (Düsseldorf: Verlag Wirtschaft und Finanzen, 2000), pp. 121–5.
98. Walther Lotz, *Die drei Flugschriften über den Münzstreit der sächsischen Albertiner und Ernestiner um 1530* (Leipzig: Duncker & Humblot, 1893), p. 61.
99. Aulinger, *Reichstag zu Worms 1545*, vol. 2, no. 71, p. 907.
100. Ibid., *Reichstag zu Worms 1545*, vol. 2, no. 71, p. 908.
101. Volckart, *Währung*, no. 19, pp. 64–5.
102. Aulinger, *Reichstag zu Worms 1545*, vol. 2, no. 86, pp. 951–2.
103. Ibid., *Reichstag zu Worms 1545*, vol. 2, no. 85, p. 943.
104. Sprenger, 'Münzverschlechterung', p. 131.
105. Volckart, *Währung*, no. 19, p. 62.
106. Wilhelm Maurenbrecher, *Karl V. und die deutschen Protestanten, 1545–1555* (Frankfurt: Rütten & Loening, 1865), pp. 91, 104.
107. Eltz, *Reichstag von 1544*, vol. 1, no. 67, p. 328; no 70, pp. 339–40.; no. 71, p. 344.
108. Volckart, *Währung*, no. 18, p. 59.
109. Ibid., *Währung*, no. 18, p. 59.
110. Cf. Kamann, 'Christoph Fürer', p. 294.

111. Volckart, *Währung*, no. 80, p. 276.
112. Eltz, *Reichstag von 1544*, vol. 1, no. 71, p. 343.
113. Volckart, *Währung*, no. 99, p. 403.
114. Eltz, *Reichstag von 1544*, vol. 1, no. 67, p. 337.
115. Ibid., *Reichstag von 1544*, vol. 1, no. 67, p. 335.
116. *Teütscher Nation Notturfft*, pp. 22–3 (original not paginated).
117. Oechsle, *Beiträge*, no. 22, p. 289.
118. Kamann, 'Christoph Fürer', no. 5, pp. 294.
119. Ibid., 'Christoph Fürer', p. 262.
120. Eltz, *Reichstag von 1544*, vol. 1, no. 64, pp. 321–2.
121. Vorel, *Circulation*, p. 87.
122. Braudel, *The Mediterranean*, 1, p. 480; Adon A. Gordus and Jeanne P. Gordus, 'Potosi Silver and Coinage of Early Modern Europe', in *Precious Metals in the Age of Expansion: Papers of the XIVth International Congress of the Historical Sciences*, ed. Hermann Kellenbenz (Stuttgart: Klett-Cotta, 1975), pp. 230–6; Emmanuel Le Roy Ladurie et al., 'Sur les traces de l'argent du Potosí', *Annales. Économies, Sociétés, Civilisations* (1990), pp. 502–5; Renate Pieper, 'Amerikanische Edelmetalle in Europa (1492–1621). Ihr Einfluß auf die Verwendung von Gold und Silber', *Jahrbuch für Geschichte von Staat, Wirtschaft und Gesellschaft Lateinamerikas* 32 (1995), p. 171; Riu Borges et al., 'European Silver Sources from the 15th to the 17th Century: The Influx of "New World" Silver in Portuguese Currency', *Heritage* 1 (2018), p. 465.
123. Hartmann, *Reichstage*, pp. 71–2, 85.
124. Volckart, 'The Dear Old Holy Roman Realm', pp. 377–8.
125. Aulinger, *Reichstag zu Worms 1545*, vol. 2, no. 67, pp. 881–9, no. 68, pp. 890–8.
126. Ibid., *Reichstag zu Worms 1545*, vol. 2, no. 87, p. 962.
127. Ibid., *Reichstag zu Worms 1545*, vol. 2, no. 72, p. 914.
128. Ibid., *Reichstag zu Worms 1545*, vol. 2, no. 72, p. 914; no. 87, p. 964.
129. Ibid., *Reichstag zu Worms 1545*, vol. 2, no. 67, p. 889.
130. ÖStA, Finanz- und Hofkammerarchiv, Alte Hofkammer, Niederösterreichisches Münz- und Bergwesen, 1524–1750, Akten 01, fol. 126r.; StAWü, Mainzer Regierungsarchiv 7226 (Münze K 137/1½), fols. 4r–4v.
131. The insight was perhaps inspired by the French fourteenth-century cleric Nicholas Oresme. Oresme's treatise on minting was available in print since the 1480s. See Charles Johnson, ed., *The De Moneta of Nicholas Oresme and English mint documents* (London, Edinburgh, Paris: Thomas Nelson and Sons, 1956), p. XVI; chapter VI, pp. 11–13.
132. Aulinger, *Reichstag zu Worms 1545*, vol. 2, no. 79, p. 925.
133. Ibid., *Reichstag zu Worms 1545*, vol. 2, no. 86, pp. 947–8.
134. Ibid., *Reichstag zu Worms 1545*, vol. 2, no. 86, p. 955.
135. Cf. Sargent and Velde, 'The Big Problem of Small Change', pp. 18–19; cf. Redish, *Bimetallism*, p. 24.

136. Aulinger, *Reichstag zu Worms 1545*, vol. 2, no. 87, pp. 962–3.
137. Volckart, *Währung*, no. 99., p. 402.
138. Uhlhorn, *Solms*, pp. 95–8.
139. Volckart, *Währung*, no. 26, pp. 86–7.
140. Ibid., *Währung*, no. 39, p. 177.
141. Ibid., *Währung*, no. 37, pp. 123–31; no. 51, pp. 197–8; no. 52, pp. 198–206.
142. Ibid., *Währung*, no. 37, p. 163.
143. Luttenberger, 'Reichspolitik', pp. 24, 46.
144. Eltz, *Reichstag zu Augsburg 1550/51*, vol. 2, no. 118, pp. 861–2.
145. Arthur T. Denzau and Douglass C. North, 'Shared Mental Models: Ideologies and Institutions', *Kyklos* 47 (1994), p. 3.
146. Ibid., 'Mental Models', p. 8.
147. Cf. Douglass C. North, 'A Transaction Cost Theory of Politics', *Journal of Theoretical Politics* 2, no. 4 (1990).

CHAPTER 5

1. Christoph Seidler, 'Schatzsucher heben das Rheingold', *Der Spiegel*, 23/08/2012, online at https://www.spiegel.de/wissenschaft/natur/rohstoffe-in-deutschland-schatzsucher-heben-das-rheingold-a-847742.html (accessed 27/02/2023).
2. Henry Garland and Mary Garland, eds., *The Oxford Companion to German Literature*, 3 ed. (Oxford: Oxford University Press, 1997/2005).
3. Herfried Münkler, *Die Deutschen und ihre Mythen* (Reinbek bei Hamburg: Rowohlt, 2010), pp. 69–107, 389–410.
4. Max Herrmann, 'Die Überlieferung des Liedes vom Hürnen Seyfrid', *Zeitschrift für deutsches Altertum und deutsche Literatur* 46, no. 1/2 (1902), p. 85; Elisabeth Lienert, *Mittelhochdeutsche Heldenepik* (Berlin: Erich Schmidt, 2015), p. 70.
5. https://www.dw.com/de/der-r%C3%A4tselhafte-schatz-der-nibelungen/a-17009071 (accessed 20/02/2023).
6. Zoltán Batizi, 'Mining in Medieval Hungary', in *The Economy of Medieval Hungary*, ed. József Laszlovszky et al. (Leiden: Brill, 2018), pp. 174–6; Day, 'Monetary Contraction', p. 71; Paulinyi, 'Crown Monopoly', pp. 38–9.
7. Kathleen Bickford Berzock, 'Caravans of Gold, Fragments in Time: An Introduction', in *Caravans of Gold, Fragments in Time: Art, Culture, and Exchange across Medieval Saharan Africa*, ed. Kathleen Bickford Berzock (Princeton: NJ: Princeton University Press, 2019), pp. 25–6.
8. E.W. Bovill, *The Golden Trade of the Moors*, 2 ed. (London: Oxford University Press, 1958).
9. John O. Hunwick, *Timbuktu and the Songhay Empire: Al-Sadi's Tarikh al-Sudan Down to 1613 and Other Contemporary Documents* (Leiden: Brill, 2003), pp. 9–10.

10. Black Crofton, 'Leo Africanus's "Descrittione dell'Africa" and its Sixteenth-Century Translations', *Journal of the Warburg and Courtauld Institutes* 65 (2002).
11. Robert Brown, ed., *The History and Description of Africa and the Notable Things Therein Contained, written by Al-Hassan Ibn-Mohammed Al-Wezaz Al-Fasi, a Moor, Baptised as Giovanni Leone, but Better Known as Leo Africanus, Done into English in the Year 1600, by John Pory* vol. 3 (London: Hakluyt Society, 1896), p. 824.
12. The ducat contained about 3.5 grams of pure gold. Frederic C. Lane and Reinhold C. Mueller, *Money and Banking in Medieval and Renaissance Venice*, vol. 1: Coins and Moneys of Account (Baltimore, London: Johns Hopkins University Press, 1985), p. 175.
13. Ghislaine Lydon, *On Trans-Saharan Trails: Islamic Law, Trade Networks, and Cross-Cultural Exchange in Nineteenth-Century Western Africa* (Cambridge: Cambridge University Press, 2009), pp. 54, 58, 61.
14. Andrew M. Watson, 'Back to Gold—and Silver', *The Economic History Review* XX, no. 1 (1967), pp. 23–5, 27.
15. Ivana Elbl, 'Cross-Cultural Trade and Diplomacy: Portuguese Relations with West Africa, 1441–1521', *Journal of World History* 3, no. 2 (1992), p. 168.
16. Ibid., 'Trade and Diplomacy', p. 170.
17. Ralph A. Austen, 'Marginalization, Stagnation, and Growth: The Trans-Saharan Caravan Trade in the Era of European Expansion, 1500–1900', in *The Rise of Merchant Empires: Long Distance Trade in the Early Modern World 1350–1750*, ed. James D. Tracy (Cambridge: Cambridge University Press, 1990), p. 315.
18. John W. Blake, *West Africa: Quest for God and Gold, 1454–1578* (London: Curzon Press, 1977), pp. 79–82; Austen, 'Marginalization', pp. 314, 347.
19. George H.T. Kimble, ed., *Esmeraldo de Situ Orbis by Duarte Pacheco Pereira* (London: Hakluyt Society, 1937), pp. 81, 117, 120.
20. Johann Friedrich Krüger, *Vollständiges Handbuch der Münzen, Masse und Gewichte aller Länder der Erde* (Quedlinburg, Leipzig: Gottfried Basse, 1830), p. 63.
21. Blake, *West Africa*, p. 83.
22. Ibid., *West Africa*, p. 83.
23. Philip D. Curtin, 'Africa and the Wider Monetary World, 1250–1850', in *Precious Metals in the Later Medieval and Early Modern Worlds*, ed. J.F. Richards (Durham, NC: Carolina Academic Press, 1983), pp. 240, 244; Ward Barrett, 'World Bullion Flows, 1450–1800', in *The Rise of Merchant Empires: Long-Distance Trade in the Early Modern World 1350–1750*, ed. James D. Tracy (Cambridge: Cambridge University Press, 1990), p. 247.
24. Ibid., 'Bullion Flows', p. 225.
25. Hamilton, *American Treasure*, p. 42; Harry E. Cross, 'South American Bullion Production and Export 1550–1750', in *Precious Metals in the Later Medieval and Early Modern Worlds* ed. John F. Richards (Durham, NC: Carolina Academic Press, 1983), p. 401.

26. Hamilton, *American Treasure*, p. 42.
27. Friedrich Blendinger and Elfriede Blendinger, eds., *Zwei Augsburger Unterkaufbücher aus den Jahren 1551 bis 1558: Älteste Aufzeichnungen zur Vor- und Frühgeschichte der Augsburger Börse* (Stuttgart: Steiner, 1994), pp. 33–190; London: J. Craig, *The Mint: A History of the London Mint from A.D. 287 to 1948* (Cambridge, 1953), pp. 413–17.
28. Carlo Maria Cipolla, *Money in Sixteenth-Century Florence* (Berkeley, Los Angeles: University of California Press, 1989), pp. 63, 69–70.
29. Harreld, *High Germans In The Low Countries: German Merchants And Commerce In Golden Age Antwerp*, p. 131; Jakob Strieder, 'Negerkunst von Benin und deutsches Metallexportgewerbe im 15. und 16. Jahrhundert', *Zeitschrift für Ethnologie* 64, no. 4/6 (1932), pp. 251, 253.
30. Chilosi and Volckart, 'Money'.
31. Hermen Bote, 'Von der page munte', in *Chroniken der niedersächsischen Städte: Braunschweig*, ed. Historische Kommission bei der Königlichen Akademie der Wissenschaften (Leipzig: S. Hirzel, 1880), p. 427.
32. Chilosi and Volckart, 'Money'.
33. Oliver Volckart and Nikolaus Wolf, 'Estimating Financial Integration in the Middle Ages: What Can We Learn from a TAR-model?', *The Journal of Economic History* 66, no. 1 (2006).
34. Volckart, *Währung*, no. 9, p. 41.
35. Max Bernhart, *Die Münzen und Medaillen der Stadt Kaufbeuren nebst einer münzgeschichtlichen Einleitung* (Halle: Riechmann, 1923), pp. 9–10.
36. Schulten, *Deutsche Münzen*, p. 168.
37. Volckart, *Währung*, no. 88, p. 328.
38. ÖStA, HHStA Wien, Reichshofrat, Miscellanea Münzwesen 1: Münzwesen im Reich—Münzordnung, Münztag zu Speyer - 1549–1551 - 3. Konvolut, fols. 384r.–384v.
39. ÖStA, HHStA Wien, Reichshofrat, Miscellanea Münzwesen 1: Münzwesen im Reich—Münzordnung, Münztag zu Speyer - 1549–1551 - 3. Konvolut, fol. 385r.
40. Volckart, *Währung*, p. XCVII.
41. Aulinger, *Reichstag zu Worms 1545*, vol. 2, no. 66, p. 874.
42. Münch, 'Grundwerte', p. 66.
43. Aulinger, *Reichstag zu Worms 1545*, vol. 2, no. 86, p. 951; cf. ibid., *Reichstag zu Worms 1545*, vol. 2, no. 83, p. 939.
44. Ibid., *Reichstag zu Worms 1545*, vol. 2, no. 83, p. 936.
45. Volckart, *Währung*, no. 52, p. 202.
46. Ibid., *Währung*, no. 84, pp. 296–7.
47. Ibid., *Währung*, no. 37, pp. 103–16; no. 42, pp. 183–4.
48. Ibid., *Währung*, no. 47, p. 192.
49. ÖStA, HHStA Wien, Reichshofrat, Miscellanea Münzwesen 1: Münzwesen im Reich (1. Konvolut), fol. 42r.

50. ÖStA, HHStA Wien, Reichshofrat, Miscellanea Münzwesen 1: Münzwesen im Reich (Münzordnung, Münztag zu Speyer), 1549–1551 (3. Konvolut), fol. 5r.
51. Volckart, *Währung*, no. 50, p. 196.
52. ÖStA, HHStA Wien, Reichshofrat, Miscellanea Münzwesen 2: Münzwesen im Reich, 1551–1564, fol. 41v.
53. Lori, *Sammlung*, 1, no. CXCV, p. 224; Newald, *Münzwesen*, p. 113; Blendinger and Blendinger, *Unterkaufbücher*, p. 33.
54. Aulinger, *Reichstag zu Worms 1545*, vol. 2, no. 66, p. 874.
55. Ibid., *Reichstag zu Worms 1545*, vol. 2, no. 67, p. 882.
56. Volckart, *Währung*, no. 52, p. 199.
57. Ibid., *Währung*, no. 52, p. 200.
58. Ibid., *Währung*, no. 37, p. 124.
59. Ibid., *Währung*, no. 37, p. 126.
60. Ibid., *Währung*, no. 37, p. 126.
61. Adolph Friedrich Johann Riedel, *Codex diplomaticus Brandenburgensis: Sammlung der Urkunden, Chroniken und sonstigen Quellenschriften für die Geschichte der Mark Brandenburg und ihrer Regenten*, vol. 1, X (Berlin: G. Reimer, 1856), no. CCLXI, p. 364.
62. Chilosi, Schulze, and Volckart, 'Benefits', p. 639.
63. Munro, 'Medieval Origins', p. 510.
64. Held, 'Stadt-Land-Beziehungen', p. 114.
65. Willi Alfred Boelcke, 'Zur Entwicklung des bäuerlichen Kreditwesens in Württemberg vom späten Mittelalter bis Anfang des 17. Jahrhunderts', *Jahrbücher für Nationalökonomie und Statistik* 176, no. 4 (1964), p. 330.
66. Kiener, 'Vorgeschichte', pp. 497–8; Hans-Jörg Gilomen, 'Das Motiv der bäuerlichen Verschuldung in den Bauernunruhen an der Wende zur Neuzeit', in *Spannungen und Widersprüche: Gedenkschrift für Frantisek Graus*, ed. Susanna Burghartz, Hans-Jörg Gilomen, and Guy Paul Marchal (Sigmaringen: Thorbecke, 1992), p. 181.
67. Chilosi, Schulze, and Volckart, 'Benefits', p. 647; Gilomen, 'Motiv'; Bentzinger, *Wahrheit*, p. 262.
68. Chilosi, Schulze, and Volckart, 'Benefits', p. 652.
69. Landwehr, 'Mobilisierung', p. 485.
70. Michael Cramer-Fürtig, 'Ottheinrichs "merkliche und beschwerliche Schuldenlast": Finanzkrise und Staatsbankrott im Fürstentum Pfalz-Neuburg 1505–1546', in *Pfalzgraf Ottheinrich: Politik, Kunst und Wissenschaft im 16. Jahrhundert*, ed. Stadt Neuburg an der Donau (Regensburg: Friedrich Pustet, 2002), p. 111; Johannes Papritz, 'Das Handelshaus der Loitz zu Stettin, Danzig und Lüneburg', Baltische Studien 44 (1957), p. 87.
71. Landesarchiv Baden-Württemberg, GLA Karlsruhe 78, no. 1638.
72. Landesarchiv Baden-Württemberg, GLA Karlsruhe 78, no. 1638, fols. 78r.–78v. (original not paginated).

73. Erwein Eltz, ed., *Deutsche Reichstagsakten unter Kaiser Karl V.: Der Speyrer Reichstag von 1544*, vol. 3 (Göttingen: Vandenhoeck & Ruprecht, 2001), no. 177, p. 1233.
74. Cf. Mark Dincecco, 'Fiscal Centralization, Limited Government, and Public Revenues in Europe, 1650–1913', *The Journal of Economic History* 69, no. 1 (2009).
75. Kohler, *Karl V.*, pp. 139–49.
76. Kersten Krüger, *Finanzstaat Hessen 1500–1567: Staatsbildung im Übergang vom Domänenstaat zum Steuerstaat* (Marburg: Elwert, 1981), p. 29.t
77. Uwe Schirmer, *Kursächsische Staatsfinanzen (1456–1656): Strukturen—Verfassung—Funktionseliten* (Stuttgart: Franz Steiner Verlag, 2006); Krüger, *Finanzstaat.*
78. Landesarchiv Baden-Württemberg, GLA Karlsruhe 78, no. 1638; August Beck, *Johann Friedrich der Mittlere, Herzog zu Sachsen: ein Beitrag zur Geschichte des sechzehnten Jahrhunderts*, vol. 1 (Weimar: Böhlau, 1858), pp. 63–5; Rudolf Bütterlin, *Die merkantilistische Geldpolitik im Herzogtum Württemberg von der Reformation bis Napoleon* (Metzingen: Hauser, 1966), p. 25; Francis L. Carsten, *Princes and Parliaments in Germany: From the Fifteenth to the Eighteenth Century* (Oxford: Clarendon, 1959), p. 372; Cramer-Fürtig, 'Ottheinrichs "merkliche und beschwerliche Schuldenlast"', pp. 110–11, 114; Ludwig Häusser, *Geschichte der rheinischen Pfalz nach ihren politischen, kirchlichen und literarischen Verhältnissen*, 2 ed., vol. 2 (Heidelberg: Mohr, 1856), p. 736 with FN 42; Siegfried Isaacsohn, 'Die Finanzen Joachims II. und das ständische Kreditwerk', *Zeitschrift für Preußische Geschichte und Landeskunde* 16 (1879), p. 467; ibid., ed., *Urkunden und Actenstücke zur Geschichte des Kurfürsten Friedrich Wilhelm von Brandenburg*, vol. 10 (Berlin: G. Reimer, 1880), p. 11; Alfred Kohler, *Antihabsburgische Politik in der Epoche Karls V. die reichsständische Opposition gegen die Wahl Ferdinands I. zum römischen König und gegen die Anerkennung seine Königstums (1524–1534)* (Göttingen: Vandenhoeck & Ruprecht, 1982), pp. 33–7; ibid., *Karl V.*, p. 145; Maximilian Lanzinner, *Friedenssicherung und politische Einheit des Reiches unter Kaiser Maximilian II. 1564–1576* (Göttingen: Vandenhoeck & Ruprecht, 1993), pp. 173–8; Georg Mentz, *Johann Friedrich der Grossmütige 1503–1554*, vol. 3: Vom Beginn des Schmalkaldischen Krieges bis zum Tode des Kurfürsten. Der Landesherr. Aktenstücke (Jena: Fischer, 1908), pp. 195, 208–9; Peter Rauscher, 'Reiche Fürsten – armer Kaiser? Die finanziellen Grundlagen der Politik Habsburgs, Bayerns und Sachsens im Vorfeld des Dreißigjährigen Krieges', in *Plus Ultra: Die Welt der Neuzeit. Festschrift für Alfred Kohler zum 65. Geburtstag*, ed. Friedrich Edelmayer et al. (Münster: Aschendorff, 2008), pp. 243, 251; Schirmer, *Staatsfinanzen*, pp. 558, 581; Franz Schneider, *Geschichte der formellen Staatswirtschaft von Brandenburg-Preussen* (Berlin: Duncker & Humblot, 1952), p. 27; Stefan Wagner, *Staatssteuern in Jülich-Berg von der Schaffung der Steuerverfassung im 15. Jahrhundert bis zur Auflösung der Herzogtümer in den Jahren 1801 und 1806* (Cologne: Forschungsinstitut für Sozial- und Wirtschaftsgeschichte an der Univ. zu Köln, 1977), pp. 94–5.

79. Based on the bullion parity with the Pound Sterling after its debasement 1544–51. Pound Sterling: Christopher Edgar Challis, *A New History of the Royal Mint* (Cambridge: Cambridge University Press, 1992), p. 723; Austrian *Gulden*: table 11.
80. English revenues: P.K. O'Brien and P.A. Hunt, European State Finance Database (http://www.esfdb.org/table.aspx?resourceid=11226, accessed 11/03/2023). Crown debts: Ian Blanchard, 'English Royal Borrowing at Antwerp, 1544–1574', in *Finances publiques et finances privees au bas moyen age. Actes du colloque tenu a Gand les 5 et 6 mai 1995*, ed. Marc Boone and Walter Prevenier (Leuven, Apeldoorn: Garant, 1996), p. 67.
81. Guy, *Gresham's Law*, pp. 70–1, 96.
82. Winfried Schulze, 'The Emergence and Consolidation of the "Tax State": I. The Sixteenth Century', in *Economic Systems and State Finance*, ed. Richard Bonney (Oxford: Clarendon, 1995), p. 263; Landwehr, 'Mobilisierung', p. 494.
83. Press, 'Formen', p. 291.
84. Krüger, *Finanzstaat*, pp. 232–5; Alfred Kohler, *Ferdinand I. 1503–1564: Fürst, König und Kaiser* (Munich: Beck, 2003), pp. 177, 192–83; Ulmschneider, *Götz von Berlichingen*, p. 204.
85. Guy, *Gresham's Law*, pp. 51, 66, 77.
86. Peter Schuster, 'Soziale und kulturelle Aspekte des Schuldenmachens im ausgehenden Mittealter', in *Prekäre Ökonomien: Schulden in Spätmittelalter und früher Neuzeit*, ed. Gabriela Signori (Konstanz, Munich: UVK, 2014), pp. 20–2.
87. Sheilagh Ogilvie, Markus Küpker, and Janine Maegraith, 'Household Debt in Early Modern Germany: Evidence from Personal Inventories', *The Journal of Economic History* 72, no. 1 (2012), p. 160; Laurence Fontaine, *The Moral Economy: Poverty, Credit and Trust in Early Modern Europe* (Cambridge: Cambridge University Press, 2014), pp. 217–18.
88. Munro, 'Medieval Origins', pp. 510–11; John Thomas Noonan, *The Scholastic Analysis of Usury* (Cambridge: MA: Harvard University Press, 1957), pp. 53–4.
89. StAA, Bestand: Reichsstadt, Strafamt Nr. 96.1 (Strafbuch 1543–1553), fol. 66v.
90. Richard Doebner, ed., *Urkundenbuch der Stadt Hildesheim*, vol. 8: 1481–1597, mit Nachträgen und Berichtigungen zu Bd. 1–8 (Hildesheim: Gerstenberg'sche Buchhandlung, 1901), no. 861, pp. 691–2.
91. Volckart, *Währung*, no. 52, pp. 201–2.
92. Hamburg: Koppmann, *Kämmereirechnungen*, vol. 5; ibid., *Kämmereirechnungen*, vol. 6; ibid., *Kämmereirechnungen*, vol. 7, passim; Cologne: Rainer Metz, *Geld, Währung und Preisentwicklung: Der Niederrheinraum im europäischen Vergleich 1350–1800* (Frankfurt: Fritz Knapp, 1990), pp. 371–5; Nuremberg: Ernst Scholler, *Der Reichsstadt Nürnberg Geld- und Münzwesen in älterer und neuerer Zeit (Ein Beitrag zur reichsstädtischen Wirtschaftsgeschichte)* (Nuremberg: G. Heydolph, 1916), p. 239; Vienna: Schalk, 'Münzverkehr im 16. Jahrhundert', pp. 261–2, ibid., 'Münzverkehr im XVI. Jahrhundert', pp. 91–2; Augsburg: Benedikt Greiff, ed., *Tagebuch des Lucas Rem aus den Jahren 1494–1541: Ein Beitrag zur*

Handelsgeschichte der Stadt Augsburg (Augsburg: Hartmann'sche Buchdruckerei, 1861), p. 62; Blendinger and Blendinger, *Unterkaufbücher*, passim, Karl Otto Müller, ed., *Quellen zur Handelsgeschichte der Paumgartner von Augsburg (1480–1570)* (Wiesbaden: Franz Steiner, 1955), pp. 26, 240; Peter Geffcken and Mark Häberlein, eds, *Rechnungsfragmente der Augsburger Welser-Gesellschaft (1496–1551): Oberdeutscher Fernhandel am Beginn der neuzeitlichen Weltwirtschaft* (Stuttgart: Steiner, 2014), 105–207.

93. Oliver Volckart, 'Bimetallism and its Discontents: Cooperation and Coordination Failure in the Empire's Monetary Policies, 1549–59', *Vierteljahrschrift für Sozial- und Wirtschaftsgeschichte* 105, no. 2 (2018), p. 210.
94. Ibid., *Währung*, no. 80, p. 276.
95. Landesarchiv Baden-Württemberg, GLA Karlsruhe 78, no. 1638, fols. 78r.–78v. (original not paginated).
96. Volckart, 'Politics', no. 37, p. 133.
97. Peter Rauscher, 'La casa de Austria y sus banqueros alemanes', in *Carlos V: europeísmo y universalidad*, ed. Francisco Sánchez-Montes González and Juan Luis Castellano (Granada: Universidad de Granada, 2001).
98. Volckart, *Währung*, no. 82, p. 278.
99. Rössner, *Deflation*, pp. 556–7.
100. Cramer-Fürtig, 'Ottheinrichs "merkliche und beschwerliche Schuldenlast"', p. 120; Lukas Winder, 'Die Kreditgeber der österreichischen Habsburger 1521–1612: Versuch einer Gesamtanalyse', in *Das 'Blut des Staatskörpers': Forschungen zur Finanzgeschichte der Frühen Neuzeit*, ed. Peter Rauscher, Andrea Serles, and Thomas Winkelbauer (Munich: Oldenbourg, 2012), p. 442.
101. Volckart, *Währung*, no. 81, p. 277. For the cities' opposition to bimetallism see ibid., *Währung*, no. 37, p. 131, no. 66, pp. 247–8.
102. ÖStA, HHStA Wien, Reichshofrat, Miscellanea Münzwesen 1: Münzwesen im Reich (Münzordnung, Münztag zu Speyer), 1549–1551 (3. Konvolut), fols. 191r.–196r.
103. ÖStA, HHStA Wien, Reichshofrat, Miscellanea Münzwesen 1: Münzwesen im Reich (Münzordnung, Münztag zu Speyer), 1549–1551 (3. Konvolut), fols. 194v.–195r.
104. Volckart, *Währung*, no. 37, p. 128.
105. Ibid., *Währung*, no. 37, p. 128.
106. Ibid., *Währung*, p. XCVIII; Jules-Adrien Blanchet and Adolphe Dieudonné, *Manuel de numismatique Française*, vol. 2 (Paris: Picard, 1916), p. 323.
107. Volckart, *Währung*, no. 37, pp. 125–6, 128.
108. Ibid., *Währung*, no. 37, pp. 128–9.
109. Ibid., *Währung*, no. 58, pp. 223–36.
110. Ibid., *Währung*, no. 61, pp. 238–9.
111. Ibid., *Währung*, no. 37, p. 173, no. 69, p. 254.
112. Ibid., *Währung*, no. 71, p. 256.
113. Ibid., *Währung*, no. 84, p. 285, 287.

114. Ibid., *Währung*, no. 84, pp. 285, 298–9.
115. Redish, *Bimetallism*, pp. 30–1.
116. Cf. Marc Flandreau, '"Water Seeks Level": Modelling Bimetallic Exchange Rates and the Bimetallic Band', *Journal of Money, Credit and Banking* 34, no. 2 (2002), pp. 491–2, where the relevant research is referenced.
117. Cf. Redish, *Bimetallism*, pp. 30–3.
118. Volckart, *Währung*, no. 37, p. 107.
119. Paolo Malanima, 'Italy in the Renaissance: A Leading Economy in the European Context, 1350–1550', *The Economic History Review* 71, no. 1 (2018), pp. 6–10.
120. Herman van der Wee, 'Structural Changes in European Long-Distance Trade, and Particularly in the Re-Export Trade from South to North, 1350–1750', in *The Rise of Merchant Empires: Long-Distance Trade in the Early Modern World, 1350–1750*, ed. James D. Tracy (Cambridge: Cambridge University Press, 1990), pp. 16–17.
121. John H. Munro, 'The "New Institutional Economics" and the Changing Fortune of Fairs in Medieval and Early Modern Europe: The Textile Trades, Warfare and Transaction Costs', *Vierteljahrschrift für Sozial- und Wirtschaftsgeschichte* 88, no. 1 (2001), p. 21; Thomas Stuart Willan, *The Inland Trade: Studies in English Internal Trade in the Sixteenth and Seventeenth Centuries* (Manchester: Manchester University Press, 1976), pp. 1–2; Michael North, *Kommunikation, Handel, Geld und Banken in der Frühen Neuzeit* (Munich: De Gruyter & Oldenbourg, 2014), p. 58.
122. Van der Wee, 'Structural Change', p. 18.
123. Munro, 'The "New Institutional Economics'", p. 25.
124. Van der Wee, 'Structural Change', pp. 23–4.
125. Volckart, 'Politics'; ibid., 'Bimetallism'.
126. Ann Radcliffe, *A Journey Made in the Summer of 1794: Through Holland and the Western Frontier of Germany, with a Return Down the Rhine; to which are Added, Observations During a Tour to the Lakes of Lancashire, Westmoreland, and Cumberland* (Dublin: William Porter, 1795), p. 305.
127. Friedrich Pfeiffer, *Rheinische Transitzölle im Mittelalter* (Berlin: Akademie-Verlag, 1997), p. 286.
128. Ibid., *Transitzölle*, pp. 669–70; Hiram Kümper, 'Der Streit um den Rhein und die Freiheit der Flussschiffahrt zwischen Territorialisierung und Nationenbildung, 16.–19. Jahrhundert', in *150 Jahre Mannheimer Akte: Festschrift zum 150jährigen Bestehen der Revidierten Rheinschifffahrtsakte vom 17. Oktober 1868*, ed. Hiram Kümper and Andreas Maurer (Baden-Baden: Nomos, 2018); Theo Sommerlad, *Die Rheinzölle im Mittelalter* (Halle: C.A. Kaemmerer & Co., 1893), p. 62.
129. Johann Nicolaus von Hontheim, *Historia Trevirensis diplomatica et pragmatica: inde a translata Treveri praefectura praetorio galliorum, ad haec usque tempora*, vol. 2 (Augsburg, Würzburg: Martin Veith, 1750), no. DCCCLXXXII, p. 489.

130. Wilhelm John, 'Der Kölner Rheinzoll von 1475–1494', *Annalen des Historischen Vereins für den Niederrhein* 48 (1889), pp. 15–16; Pfeiffer, *Transitzölle*, p. 199.
131. Burgdorf, *Wahlkapitulationen*, p. 27.
132. Hans Mosler, 'Der Düsseldorfer Rheinzoll bis zum Ausgang des 16. Jahrhunderts', *Beiträge zur Geschichte des Niederrheins* 21 (1907), pp. 138–9.
133. Cf. Georg Droege, 'Die finanziellen Grundlagen des Territorialstaats in West- und Ostdeutschland an der Wende vom Mittelalter zur Neuzeit', *Vierteljahrschrift für Sozial- und Wirtschaftsgeschichte* 53 (1966), p. 150 with FN 14.
134. Weisenstein, *Geldwesen*, p. 171.
135. Droege, 'Grundlagen', p. 149.
136. Ernst Schubert, 'Der Mainzer Kurfürst als Erzkanzler im Spätmittelalter', in *Der Mainzer Kurfürst als Reichserzkanzler: Funktionen, Aktivitäten, Ansprüche und Bedeutung des zweiten Mannes im Alten Reich*, ed. Peter Claus Hartmann (Stuttgart: Steiner, 1997), p. 79; Droege, 'Grundlagen', p. 149.
137. Quoted from Sommerlad, *Rheinzölle*, p. 107.
138. Volckart, *Währung*, no. 37, p. 126.
139. Van der Wee, 'Structural Change', p. 28.
140. William Brookes Greenlee, ed., *The Voyage of Pedro Álvares Cabral to Brazil and India from Contemporary Documents and Narratives* (London Hakluyt Society, 1938), pp. 134, 136.
141. Van der Wee, 'Structural Change', pp. 30–1.
142. Braudel, *The Mediterranean*, 1, p. 562.
143. Volckart, *Währung*, no. 82, p. 278; Mosler, 'Rheinzoll', pp. 138–9.
144. Peter Claus Hartmann, 'Der Mainzer Kurfürst als Reichserzkanzler: Einführung in die Problematik und Thematik des Kolloquiums', in *Der Mainzer Kurfürst als Reichserzkanzler: Funktionen, Aktivitäten, Ansprüche und Bedeutung des zweiten Mannes im Alten Reich*, ed. Peter Claus Hartmann (Stuttgart: Steiner, 1997), p. 4; Schubert, 'Der Mainzer Kurfürst', pp. 79–80.
145. Aulinger, *Reichstag zu Worms 1545*, vol. 2, no. 77, p. 921.
146. Volckart, *Währung*, no. 37, p. 133.
147. Ibid., *Währung*, no. 58, pp. 225–9.
148. ÖStA, HHStA Wien, Reichshofrat, Miscellanea Münzwesen 2: Münzwesen im Reich, 1551–1564, fol. 24–8.
149. Volckart, *Währung*, no. 137, p. 141.
150. Aulinger, *Reichstag zu Worms 1545*, vol. 2, no. 87, p. 970.
151. Volckart, *Währung*, no. 46, p. 189.
152. In much the same way many thought they did after the introduction of Euro coins and banknotes in 2002. Hans Wolfgang Brachinger, 'Der Euro als Teuro? Die wahrgenommene Inflation in Deutschland', *Wirtschaft und Statistik* 9 (2005), p. 1007.
153. Volckart, *Währung*, no. 58, pp. 223–36; no. 59, p. 236.
154. Ibid., *Währung*, no. 57, pp. 219–20.

155. Eltz, *Reichstag zu Augsburg 1550/51*, vol. 2, no. 305, p. 1590.
156. Volckart, *Währung*, no. 90, pp. 344–72.
157. Ibid., *Währung*, no. 90, pp. 344–72.
158. Ibid., *Währung*, no. 90, pp. 344–72.

CHAPTER 6

1. ÖStA, HHStA Wien, Reichshofrat, Miscellanea Münzwesen 1: Münzwesen im Reich (2. Konvolut), fol. 320r.
2. ÖStA, HHStA Wien, Reichshofrat, Miscellanea Münzwesen 2: Münzwesen im Reich, 1551–1564, fol. 346r.
3. ÖStA, HHStA Wien, Reichshofrat, Miscellanea Münzwesen 2: Münzwesen im Reich, 1551–1564, fols. 419r.–419v.
4. ÖStA, HHStA Wien, Reichshofrat, Miscellanea Münzwesen 2: Münzwesen im Reich, 1551–1564, fol. 422r.
5. ÖStA, HHStA Wien, Reichshofrat, Miscellanea Münzwesen 2: Münzwesen im Reich, 1551–1564, fols. 437r.–437v.
6. Wir Ferdinand von Gottes genaden, Römischer Khünig, zu allen Zeiten merer des Reichs, in Germanien, (s.l. [Augsburg]: no publisher, 1551). Ferdinand's edict, dated Augsburg 25 Feb. 1551: ÖNB, Sammlung von Handschriften und alten Drucken, F100071-B. Online at https://digital.onb.ac.at/rep/pdfviewer/?10078EF3 (accessed 13/03/2023).
7. Lori, *Sammlung*, 1, no. CXCV, p. 224.
8. Volckart, *Währung*, no. 88, p. 333; no. 90, p. 353.
9. Rabe, *Reich*, pp. 284–5; Whaley, *Germany*, I, p. 330.
10. Karl Erich Born, 'Moritz von Sachsen und die Fürstenverschwörung gegen Karl V.', *Historische Zeitschrift* 191, no. 1 (1960), p. 43; Kohler, *Karl V.*, pp. 328–9.
11. Rabe, *Reich*, p. 284.
12. August von Druffel, ed., *Beiträge zur Reichsgeschichte 1546–1552* (Munich: Rieger'sche Universitätsbuchhandlung, 1873), no. 801, pp. 791–2; Maurenbrecher, *Karl V.*, p. 292; Fritz Hartung, *Karl V. und die deutschen Reichsstände von 1546 bis 1555* (Halle a.S.: M. Niemeyer, 1910), pp. 70–1; Rabe, *Reich*, p. 284; Johannes Herrmann, *Moritz von Sachsen (1521–1553): Landes-, Reichs- und Friedensfürst* (Beucha Sax-Verlag, 2003), pp. 149–50, 161.
13. In 1549/50, the income from silver mining and the mint (which the Saxon treasury registered separately only after 1556) accounted for more than a quarter of Maurice's revenues. Between 1572 and 1582, when mining revenues had shrunk, the revenues that Maurice's successor received from the mint alone equalled more than 100,000 *Guldens* per year, i.e., *c.*12 per cent of his total revenues. Schirmer, *Staatsfinanzen*, pp. 558, 621–3, 917.
14. Volckart, *Währung*, p. LXXII; cf. Whaley, *Germany*, I, p. 330.
15. ÖStA, HHStA Wien, Reichshofrat, Miscellanea Münzwesen 2: Münzwesen im Reich, 1551–1564, fol. 348r.

16. ÖStA, HHStA Wien, Reichshofrat, Miscellanea Münzwesen 2: Münzwesen im Reich, 1551–1564, fols. 390r.–394v.; *Römischer, Auch zů Hungern, vnd Behaim etc. Khünigklicher Mayestat, Ertzherzogen zů Ostereich etc. Newe Müntzürdnung: Sampt Valuierung der Gulden vnd Silberin Müntzen, Vnd darauff eruolgtem Edict* (Vienna: Hans Syngriener, 1552) (online at http://digital.onb.ac.at/OnbViewer/viewer.faces?doc=ABO_%2BZ223524305; accessed 20/02/2023).
17. Rabe, *Reich*, p. 288.
18. Johannes Burkhardt, *Deutsche Geschichte in der frühen Neuzeit* (Munich: Beck, 2009), p. 49; Whaley, *Germany*, I, p. 339; Wilson, *Empire*, pp. 115–17, 121.
19. Rabe, *Reich*, p. 298; Kohler, *Karl V.*, pp. 353–5.
20. Vorel, *Circulation*, pp. 96–9.
21. Romischer, Auch zu Hungern, vnd Behaim, etc. Khünigklicher Mayestat, Ertzhertzogen zu Osterreich, etc. Newe Müntzordnung (Vienna: Hans Syngriener, 1556). Online https://reader.digitale-sammlungen.de//resolve/display/bsb11298048.html (accessed 20/02/2023).
22. ÖStA, HHStA Wien, Reichshofrat, Miscellanea Münzwesen 2: Münzwesen im Reich, 1551–1564, fol. 610r.
23. Eltz, *Reichstag zu Augsburg 1550/51*, vol. 2, no. 82, pp. 296, 299.
24. Volckart, *Währung*, no. 27, p. 88.
25. Ibid., 'Bimetallism', p. 217; cf. Aulinger and Schweinzer-Burian, 'Präsenz'; cf. Volckart, *Währung*, no. 2, p. 5.
26. Eltz, *Reichstag zu Augsburg 1550/51*, vol. 1, no. 72, pp. 224–5.
27. Ibid., *Reichstag zu Augsburg 1550/51*, vol. 1, no. 82, pp. 293–4, 303, 435, 549.
28. Ibid., *Reichstag zu Augsburg 1550/51*, vol. 2, no. 305, p. 1607.
29. Ibid., *Reichstag zu Augsburg 1550/51*, vol. 2, no. 305, pp. 1588–90, 1606.
30. Compare ibid., *Reichstag zu Augsburg 1550/51*, vol. 2, no. 125, p. 876 and Volckart, *Währung*, no. 58, p. 226.
31. See his letter to the Rhenish electors dated 26 Apr. 1550; ibid., *Währung*, no. 85, pp. 300–1.
32. Ibid., *Währung*, no. 86, p. 304.
33. Ibid., *Währung*, no. 90, p. 348.
34. ÖStA, Haus-, HHStA Wien, Reichshofrat, Miscellanea Münzwesen 2: Münzwesen im Reich, 1551–1564, fols. 441r.–441v.
35. Leeb, *Reichstag zu Regensburg 1556/57*, vol. 2, no. 447, p. 992.
36. Ibid., *Reichstag zu Regensburg 1556/57*, vol. 2, no. 577, p. 1404.
37. Volckart, *Währung*, p. XLV.
38. Ibid., *Währung*, no. 96, p. 388.
39. Cf. Aulinger and Schweinzer-Burian, 'Präsenz'.
40. ÖStA, HHStA Wien, Reichskanzlei, Berichte aus dem Reich 5b, fol. 327r.
41. Aulinger, Eltz, and Machoczek, *Reichstag zu Augsburg 1555*, vol. 4, no. 330, p. 2867.
42. Volckart, *Währung*, no. 37, p. 147.
43. Aulinger, Eltz, and Machoczek, *Reichstag zu Augsburg 1555*, vol. 4, no. 330, pp. 2868–70.

44. Ibid., *Reichstag zu Augsburg 1555*, vol. 2, no. 144, p. 1260.
45. Leeb, *Reichstag zu Regensburg 1556/57*, vol. 2, no. 447, p. 992.
46. Ibid., *Reichstag zu Regensburg 1556/57*, vol. 1, no. 102, p. 404; no. 103, pp. 407–8.
47. Peter Fleischmann, *Rat und Patriziat in Nürnberg: Die Herrschaft der Ratsgeschlechter vom 13. bis zum 18. Jahrhundert*, vol. 2: Ratsherren und Ratsgeschlechter (Neustadt an der Aisch: Verein für Geschichte der Stadt Nürnberg, no year (*c.*2008)), p. 987; Theodor Gustav Werner, 'Das Kupferhüttenwerk des Hans Tetzel aus Nürnberg auf Kuba und seine Finanzierung durch europäisches Finanzkapital. I. Teil (1545–1571)', *Vierteljahrschrift für Sozial- und Wirtschaftsgeschichte* 48, no. 3 (1961), pp. 312–14; Ibid., 'Das Kupferhüttenwerk des Hans Tetzel aus Nürnberg auf Kuba (1545–1571) und seine Finanzierung durch europäisches Finanzkapital II. Teil', *Vierteljahrschrift für Sozial- und Wirtschaftsgeschichte* 48, no. 4 (1961).
48. Leeb, *Reichstag zu Regensburg 1556/57*, vol. 2, no. 577, p. 1420.
49. Volckart, *Währung*, p. XCVI.
50. Cf. ibid., *Währung*, no. 90, pp. 347 with FN 88; 350 with FN 90; 352 with FN 91; 356–9 with FN 97–107; 370 with FN 110.
51. Ibid., *Währung*, no. 92, p. 376–7.
52. Ibid., *Währung*, no. 96, pp. 387–90.
53. Ibid., *Währung*, 96, p. 389; no. 98, p. 395; no. 101, p. 409.
54. Ibid., *Währung*, no. 98, p. 396; no. 101, p. 409.
55. Ibid., *Währung*, no. 98, p. 394.
56. Ibid., *Währung*, no. 105, p. 423.
57. Ibid., *Währung*, no. 105, p. 423.
58. Ibid., *Währung*, no. 100, p. 404.
59. Marc von Knorring, 'Reichsverfassung und ständische Interessen: Der Streit um das Verfahren auf dem Deputationstag von 1564. Neue Erkenntnisse aus der Aktenedition', *Parliaments, Estates and Representation* 35, no. 2 (2015), pp. 173–4.
60. Volckart, *Währung*, no. 37, pp. 140–1.
61. Leeb, *Reichstag zu Augsburg 1559*, vol. 3, no. 554, p. 1365.
62. Ibid., *Reichstag zu Augsburg 1559*, vol. 3, no. 555, p. 1371.
63. Rössner, *Martin Luther*, p. 174.
64. Leeb, *Reichstag zu Augsburg 1559*, vol. 3, no. 555, p. 1373.
65. Ibid., ed., *Der Kurfürstentag zu Frankfurt 1558 und der Reichstag zu Augsburg 1559*, vol. 2 (Göttingen: Vandenhoeck & Ruprecht, 1999), no. 182, p. 766; no. 299, p. 951.
66. Ibid., *Reichstag zu Augsburg 1559*, vol. 2, no. 183, p. 766; ibid., *Reichstag zu Augsburg 1559*, vol. 3, no. 556, pp. 1375–6; ibid., *Reichstag zu Augsburg 1559*, vol. 3, no. 557, p. 1380.
67. Schrötter, 'Münzwesen, Teil II', p. 111; Vorel, *Circulation*, p. 88.
68. Leeb, *Reichstag zu Augsburg 1559*, vol. 3, no. 100, p. 403.
69. ÖStA, HHStA Wien, Reichshofrat, Miscellanea Münzwesen 2: Münzwesen im Reich, 1551–1564, fol. 41v.

70. Leeb, *Reichstag zu Augsburg 1559*, vol. 3, no. 557, p. 1381.
71. Ibid., *Reichstag zu Augsburg 1559*, vol. 3, no. 557, p. 1381.
72. Ibid., *Reichstag zu Augsburg 1559*, vol. 3, no. 804, p. 1969.
73. Blendinger and Blendinger, *Unterkaufbücher*, pp. 180, 203.
74. Leeb, *Reichstag zu Augsburg 1559*, vol. 3, no. 804, p. 1959.
75. Ibid., *Reichstag zu Augsburg 1559*, vol. 3, no. 804, pp. 1962–4.
76. Ibid., *Reichstag zu Augsburg 1559*, vol. 3, p. 1994 with FN 10.
77. Ibid., *Reichstag zu Augsburg 1559*, vol. 3, no. 660, pp. 1715–19.
78. Ibid., *Reichstag zu Augsburg 1559*, vol. 2, no. 194, pp. 796–7.
79. Arnold, 'Talerwährung', p. 68.
80. Maximilian Lanzinner and Dietmar Heil, eds., *Der Reichstag zu Augsburg 1566*, vol. 2 (Munich: Oldenbourg, 2002) no. 467, pp. 1554–5.
81. LA Wolfenbüttel, 1 Alt 16, no. 16.
82. Arnold, 'Talerwährung', pp. 70–1.
83. Johann Christoph Hirsch, *Des Teutschen Reichs Münz-Archiv*, vol. 7 (Nuremberg: Adam Jonathan Felßeckers seel. Erben, 1761), no. LXXVII, p. 87; Tielemannus Friese and Cyriacus Spangenberg, *Müntz-Spiegel/das ist: Ein New und Wolaußgeführter Bericht von der Müntz* (Frankfurt: Johann Feyrabendt, 1592), pp. 204–5; cf. Johann Christoph Hirsch, *Des Teutschen Reichs Münz-Archiv*, vol. 2 (Nuremberg: Adam Jonathan Felßeckers seel. Erben, 1756), no. XLVI, p. 102.
84. Volckart, *Währung*, p. LXXIV; Bergerhausen, 'Exclusis Westphalen et Burgundt', p. 192.
85. Prokisch, *Grunddaten*, pp. 1–244.
86. Peter Spufford, 'Mint Organisation in Late Medieval Europe', in *Later Medieval Mints: Organisation, Administration and Techniques. The Eighth Oxford Symposium on Coinage and Monetary History*, ed. Peter Spufford and Nicholas J. Mayhew (Oxford: B.A.R. Publications, 1988), p. 17.
87. Volckart, *Währung*, no. 90, p. 370; no. 99, p. 401.
88. Ibid., *Währung*, no. 101, p. 412.
89. Leeb, *Reichstag zu Augsburg 1559*, vol. 3, no. 804, p. 1985.
90. Spufford, 'Mint Organisation', p. 24; Emmerig, 'Münzbetrieb', p. 9.
91. In the 1520s, the mint of Königsberg in Prussia operated without an assayer. Volckart, *Münzpolitik*, no. 10, p. 409.
92. Leeb, *Reichstag zu Augsburg 1559*, vol. 3, no. 805, pp. 1991–2.
93. Ibid., *Reichstag zu Augsburg 1559*, vol. 3, no. 805, p. 1998.
94. Ibid., *Reichstag zu Augsburg 1559*, vol. 3, no. 804, p. 1980.
95. Ibid., *Reichstag zu Augsburg 1559*, vol. 3, no. 805, p. 1993.
96. Maximilian Lanzinner, ed., *Der Reichstag zu Speyer 1570*, vol. 2: Akten und Abschied (Göttingen: Vandenhoeck & Ruprecht, 1988), no. 567, pp. 1246–7; Hirsch, *Münz-Archiv*, 2, no. XLVI, p. 106.
97. Leeb, *Reichstag zu Augsburg 1559*, vol. 3, no. 805, p. 1993.
98. Ibid., *Reichstag zu Augsburg 1559*, vol. 3, pp. 1954–5 with FN 10.

99. North, 'Reich und Reichstag', p. 224.
100. Ibid., 'Reich und Reichstag', p. 225.
101. Johann Christoph Hirsch, *Des Teutschen Reichs Münz-Archiv*, vol. 3 (Nuremberg: Adam Jonathan Felßeckers seel. Erben, 1757), no. XLVIII, pp. 119–20.
102. Ibid., *Münz-Archiv*, 3, no. XLVIII, pp. 119–20.
103. Thomas Nicklas, *Macht oder Recht: Frühneuzeitliche Politik im obersächsischen Reichskreis* (Stuttgart: Steiner, 2002), p. 128.
104. Krüger, *Reich*, p. 55; North, 'Reich und Reichstag', p. 226.
105. Hirsch, *Münz-Archiv*, 2, no. LI, p. 129; Lennartz, 'Probationstage', p. 12.
106. *Vortrab und gründlicher, warhafftiger, kurtzer Bericht, der guten Reichs-Müntzordnung*, (Munich: Adam Berg, 1572), Introduction (unfoliated).
107. Hirsch, *Münz-Archiv*, 7, no. LXXVII, pp. 87–8.
108. Volckart, *Währung*, no. 44, p. 188; no. 90, pp. 349–50.
109. Bergerhausen, 'Exclusis Westphalen et Burgundt', pp. 193, 196; cf. Lanzinner and Heil, *Reichstag zu Augsburg 1566*, vol. 2, no. 250, p. 1042.
110. P. Verkade, *Muntboek, bevattende de namen en afbeeldingen van munten: geslagen in de zeven voormalig Vereenigde Nederlandsche Provincien, sedert den vrede van Gent tot op onzen tijd* (Schiedam: P.J. van Dijk, 1848), pp. 28, 31–2.
111. Lennartz, 'Probationstage', p. 7.
112. Ibid., 'Probationstage', p. 10; Bergerhausen, 'Exclusis Westphalen et Burgundt', pp. 198–200.
113. Leeb, *Reichstag zu Augsburg 1559*, vol. 3, no. 661, pp. 1721–2.
114. Elizabeth Lamond, ed., *A Discourse of the Commonweal of This Realm of England: First Printed in 1581 and Commonly Attributed to W.S.* (Cambridge: Cambridge University Press, 1929), pp. xii–xiii, xxv, 45; cf. Steven Deng, '"So Pale, So Lame, So Lean, So Ruinous": The Circulation of Foreign Coins in Early Modern England', in *A Companion to the Global Renaissance: English Literature and Culture in the Era of Expansion*, ed. Jyotsna G. Singh (Chichester: Wiley-Blackwell, 2009); Dewar, Mary. 'The Authorship of the "Discourse of the Commonweal"', *The Economic History Review* 19, no. 2 (1966).
115. Denis Richet, 'Le cours officiel des monnaies étrangères circulant en France au XVIe siècle', *Revue Historique* 225, no. 2 (1961), p. 368.
116. Debra Glassman and Angela Redish, 'New Estimates of the Money Stock in France, 1493–1680', *The Journal of Economic History* 45, no. 1 (1985), pp. 44–5. For England, see Deng, '"So Pale, So Lame, So Lean, So Ruinous": The Circulation of Foreign Coins in Early Modern England'.
117. Cf. Gerhard, 'Garten', p. 159.
118. Karl Weisenstein, *Die Kipper- und Wipperzeit im Kurfürstentum Trier* (Koblenz: Numismatischer Verlag Forneck, 1991), pp. 93–4; Carl Friedrich Evers, *Mecklenburgische Münz-Verfassung, besonders die Geschichte derselben*, vol. 1 (Schwerin: Baerensprung, 1798), p. 56; Johann Friedrich Klotzsch, *Versuch einer Chur-Sächschen Münzgeschichte: von den ältesten, bis auf jetzige Zeiten*, vol. 2 (Chemnitz: Johann Christoph Stößel, 1780), pp. 492–4, 521; William Löbe,

Geschichte der Landwirthschaft im Altenburgischen Osterlande (Leipzig: Brockhaus, 1845), p. 37; Hirsch, *Münz-Archiv*, 2, pp. 25, 46, 379; ibid., *Des Teutschen Reichs Münz-Archiv*, vol. 5 (Nuremberg: Adam Jonathan Felßeckers seel. Erben, 1759), pp. 50, 54; ibid., *Münz-Archiv*, 7, pp. 135, 155; Alfred Francis Pribram, *Materialen zur Geschichte der Preise und Löhne in Österreich*, vol. 1 (Vienna: Carl Ueberreuters Verlag, 1938), p. 28; Konrad Schneider, *Frankfurt und die Kipper- und Wipperinflation der Jahre 1619–1623* (Frankfurt: Stadtarchiv, 1990), p. 74; Fritz Popelka, 'Die Lebensmittelpreise und Löhne in Graz vom 16. bis zum 18. Jahrhundert', *Vierteljahrschrift für Sozial- und Wirtschaftsgeschichte* 23 (1930), p. 167; Leonhard Willibald Hoffmann, *Alter und neuer Münz-Schlüssel Oder Beantwort- und Eröffnung CCXXII. Curioser Fragen* (Nuremberg: J. Zieger, 1692), 'Auf- und Absteigungs-Tafel'; Johann Diederich von Steinen, *Westphälische Geschichte*, vol. 3 (Lemgo: Meyer, 1755), pp. 1075, 1090; Jürgen Elert Kruse, *Allgemeiner und besonders Hamburgischer Contorist*, 3 ed., vol. 1 (Hamburg: Eigenverlag, 1766), pp. 163, 193; Konrad Schneider, 'Hamburg während der Kipper- und Wipperzeit', *Zeitschrift des Vereins für hamburgische Geschichte* 67 (1981), p. 54; Hermann Grote, *Osnabrück'sche Geld- und Münz-Geschichte* (Leipzig: Hahn'sche Verlagsbuchhandlung, 1864), p. 38; Hans-Christian Altmann, *Die Kipper- und Wipperinflation in Bayern (1620–1623): Ein Beitrag zur Strukturanalyse des frühabsolutistischen Staates* (Munich: Stadtarchiv München, 1976), p. 272.

119. Schalk, 'Münzverkehr im 16. Jahrhundert', p. 328.
120. Sargent and Velde, *Problem*.
121. Leonid Arbusow, ed., *Akten und Recesse der livländischen Ständetage*, vol. 3 (1494–1535) (Riga: Deubner, 1910), no. 308, p. 799.
122. Sargent and Velde, *Problem*, p. 53; Angela Redish and Warren E. Weber, 'Coin Sizes and Payments in Commodity Money Systems', Macroeconomic Dynamics 15, no. S1 (2011), p. 67.
123. Volckart, *Währung*, no. 101, p. 410; no. 104, p. 419 with FN 102; no. 105, p. 424; no. 106, p. 427.
124. Ibid., *Währung*, no. 105, p. 424.
125. Cf. Redish, *Bimetallism*, p. 30.
126. Leeb, *Reichstag zu Augsburg 1559*, vol. 3, no. 556, p. 1376.
127. Robert Wuttke, 'Die Probationsregister des Obersächsischen Kreises', *Numismatische Zeitschrift* 29 (1897), pp. 248–9.
128. Lennartz, 'Probationstage', pp. 10–11.
129. See Tables A.4 and A.5.
130. Schalk, 'Münzverkehr im 16. Jahrhundert', p. 328.
131. For Nuremberg: Lazarus Carl von Wölkern, *Historia Norimbergensis Diplomatica oder Zusammentrag der Vornehmsten von den Glorwürdigsten Römischen Kaysern und Königen der Reichs-Freyen Stadt Nürnberg Allermildest ertheilten Freyheiten Begnadigungen und Concessionen* (Nuremberg: Endter, 1738), p. 348. Florence and Venice experimented with such a policy in the second half of the fifteenth century. Sargent and Velde, *Problem*, pp. 114–15.

132. Volckart, *Währung*, no. 90, pp. 352–3.
133. Leeb, *Reichstag zu Augsburg 1559*, vol. 3, no. 804, p. 1959.
134. Schmoller, 'Scheidemünzpolitik', pp. 19–20.
135. Ibid., 'Scheidemünzpolitik', p. 20.
136. Redish, *Bimetallism*, p. 28.
137. Rolf Engelsing, *Analphabetentum und Lektüre: Zur Sozialgeschichte des Lesens in Deutschland zwischen feudaler und industrieller Gesellschaft* (Stuttgart: Metzler, 1973), pp. X, 32; Robert W. Scribner, 'How Many Could Read? Comments on Bernd Moeller's "Stadt und Buch"', in *Stadtbürgertum und Adel in der Reformation: Studien zur Sozialgeschichte der Reformation in England und Deutschland (The Urban Classes, the Nobility and the Reformation: Studies on The Social History of the Reformation in England and Germany)*, ed. Wolfgang J. Mommsen (Stuttgart: Klett-Cotta, 1979), p. 44.
138. *Verzeychnus was vermög des H. R. R. Müntzordnungen vnd Abschied vom 1559. 1566. vnnd 1570 Jarn für Silberin vnnd Guldine Müntz Sorten . . . hinfüro zu nemen vnnd zu geben zugelassen . . .* (Straßburg, 1571). ÖNB Sammlung von Handschriften und alten Drucken F120054-B (online at https://search.onb.ac.at/primo-explore/fulldisplay?docid=ONB_alma21226720570003338&context=L&vid=ONB&lang=de_DE, accessed 20/02/2023).
139. Hirsch, *Münz-Archiv*, 2, no. LXVI, pp. 182–3.
140. Volckart, *Währung*, no. 37, p. 143; Wölkern, *Historia*, p. 348.
141. Leeb, *Reichstag zu Augsburg 1559*, vol. 2, no. 204, pp. 836–7.
142. Altenburg: Zacharias Kresse, *Geschichte der Landwirthschaft des Altenburgischen Osterlandes* (Altenburg: H.A. Pierer, 1845), p. 115; Augsburg: Elsas, *Preise*, 1, p. 595; Erfurt: Otto Kius, 'Die Preis- und Lohnverhältnisse des sechszehnten Jahrhunderts in Thüringen I.', *Jahrbücher für Nationalökonomie und Statistik* 1 (1864), pp. 69–70; Frankfurt: Moritz J. Elsas, *Umriss einer Geschichte der Preise und Löhne in Deutschland vom ausgehenden Mittelalter bis zum Beginn des neunzehnten Jahrhunderts*, vol. 2 (Leiden: A.W. Sijthoffs Uitgeversmaatschappij, 1940), p. 464; Lübeck: Johannes Hansen, *Beiträge zur Geschichte des Getreidehandels und der Getreidepolitik Lübecks* (Lübeck: Max Schmidt, 1912), p. 134; Lüneburg: Hans-Jürgen Gerhard and Karl Heinrich Kaufhold, *Preise im vor- und frühindustriellen Deutschland: Grundnahrungsmittel* (Göttingen Schwartz, 1990), p. 229; Munich: Elsas, *Preise*, 1, p. 561; Vienna: Pribram, *Materialien*, 1, pp. 269–71. For the conversion of local units of measurement into bushels: Johann Christian Nelkenbrecher and Mark Rudolph Balthazar Gerhardt, *Nelkenbrechers Taschenbuch der Münz-Maaß und Gewichtskunde für Kaufleute*, 7 ed. (Berlin: Arnold Wever, 1793), pp. 67, 74, 133–4, 154, 208, 263 and Krüger, *Handbuch*, p. 161.
143. Stephen Broadberry et al., *British Economic Growth 1270–1870* (Cambridge: Cambridge University Press, 2015), p. 97.
144. Ibid., *British Economic Growth 1270–1870*, pp. 282, 289.
145. Sargent and Velde, *Problem*, p. 114.

146. Paris: Micheline Baulant, 'Le prix des grains à Paris de 1431 à 1788', *Annales. Économies, Sociétés, Civilisations* 23, no. 3 (1968), p. 538; Lyon: Richard Gascon, *Grand commerce et vie urbaine au XVIe siècle: Lyon et ses marchands (environs de 1520–environs de 1580)* (Paris et La Haye: Ecole pratique des hautes études, 1971), pp. 920–1.
147. Leeb, *Reichstag zu Augsburg 1559*, vol. 2, no. 434, p. 1083.
148. Ibid., *Reichstag zu Augsburg 1559*, vol. 2, no. 434, p. 1082.
149. William Lowndes, *A Report Containing an Essay for the Amendment of the Silver Coins* (London: Charles Bill, 1695), p. 115.
150. Debra Glassman and Angela Redish, 'Currency Depreciation in Early Modern England and France', *Explorations in Economic History* 25, no. 1 (1988), pp. 80–3; Jan de Vries and Ad van der Woude, *The First Modern Economy: Success, Failure, and Perseverance of the Dutch Economy, 1500–1815* (Cambridge: Cambridge University Press, 1997), pp. 82–3; Helleiner, *National Money*, pp. 23–4.
151. See, e.g., Gerhard, 'Garten'.

EPILOGUE

1. Moryson, *Itinerary*, 1, p. xii.
2. Ibid., *Itinerary*, 1, p. 48; ibid., *Itinerary*, 2, pp. 122–3.
3. Ibid., *Itinerary*, 1, pp. 84–7.
4. Ibid., *Itinerary*, 1, p. xxiii.
5. Ibid., *Itinerary*, 2, p. 133.
6. Ibid., *An Itinerary Containing His Ten Yeeres Travell through the Twelve Dominions of Germany, Bohmer-land, Sweitzerland, Netherland, Denmarke, Poland, Italy, Turky, France, England, Scotland & Ireland*, vol. 4 (Glasgow: Glasgow University Press, 1617/1908), p. 172.
7. Modern analyses bear out Moryson's hunch. Cf. Redish and Weber, 'Coin Sizes', pp. 79–80.
8. Moryson, *Itinerary*, 1, p. 34.
9. Bergerhausen, 'Exclusis Westphalen et Burgundt', p. 189; Michael North, 'Von der atlantischen Handelsexpansion bis zu den Agrarreformen 1450–1815', in *Deutsche Wirtschaftsgeschichte: Ein Jahrtausend im Überblick*, ed. Michael North (Munich: Beck, 2001), p. 173; Sprenger, *Geld*, pp. 102–3; Oliver Volckart, 'Die Reichsmünzordnung von 1559: Das Scheitern reichseinheitlichen Geldes', in *Schlüsselereignisse der deutschen Bankengeschichte*, ed. Dieter Lindenlaub, Carsten Burhop, and Joachim Scholtyseck (Stuttgart: Franz Steiner Verlag, 2013), Rössner, 'Monetary Instability', p. 312, but see Volckart, 'The Dear Old Holy Roman Realm' and North, 'Geld- und Ordnungspolitik', pp. 94–5; ibid., 'Reception'; ibid., 'Monetary Reforms in the Holy Roman Empire in the Fifteenth and Sixteenth Centuries', in *Money in the Western Legal Tradition: Middle Ages to Bretton Woods*, ed. David Fox and Wolfgang Ernst (Oxford: Oxford University Press, 2016).

10. Alfred Kohler, 'Das Heilige Römische Reich—Ein Föderativsystem?', in *Föderationsmodelle und Unionsstrukturen: Über Staatenverbindungen in der frühen Neuzeit vom 15. zum 18. Jahrhundert*, ed. Thomas Fröschl (Vienna: Verlag für Geschichte und Politik, 1994); Wilson, *Empire*, p. 9.
11. Christmann, *Vereinheitlichung*, pp. 181–2.
12. Philipp Robinson Rössner, 'Besprechung von Oliver Volckart: Eine Wähung für das Reich. Die Münztage zu Speyer 1549 und 1557', *Vierteljahrschrift für Sozial- und Wirtschaftsgeschichte* 106 (2019), p. 279.
13. Schlumbohm, 'Gesetze', p. 660 with FN 55.
14. E.g., Volckart, *Währung*, no. 24, p. 78; no. 37, pp. 166–7; no. 90, pp. 371–2.
15. Ibid., *Währung*, no. 86, p. 305.
16. Peter Rauscher, *Zwischen Ständen und Gläubigern: Die kaiserlichen Finanzen unter Ferdinand I. und Maximilian II. (1556–1576)* (Vienna, Munich: Oldenbourg, 2004), p. 113.
17. Helleiner, *National Money*, pp. 21–3, 31; cf. Adolf Soetbeer, *Denkschrift betreffend Deutsche Münzeinigung: Den Hohen Deutschen Regierungen* (Berlin: Liebheit & Thiesen, 1869), pp. 9–10.
18. Rössner, 'Monetary Instability', p. 312.
19. Steffen Leins, *Das Prager Münzkonsortium 1622/23: Ein Kapitalgeschäft im Dreißigjährigen Krieg am Rand der Katastrophe* (Münster: Aschendorf, 2012), p. 144.
20. Paul Arnold, 'Die Währungsunionen von Zinna (1667–1690) und Leipzig (1690–1750/63) unter besonderer Berücksichtigung des kursächsischen Münzwesens', in *Währungsunionen: Beiträge zur Geschichte überregionaler Münz- und Geldpolitik*, ed. Reiner Cunz (Hamburg: Museum für Hamburgische Geschichte, 2002).
21. Friedrich Frhr. von Schrötter, *Das Preussische Münzwesen im 18. Jahrhundert: Münzgeschichtlicher Teil*, vol. 2: Die Begründung des preussischen Münzsystems durch Friedrich den Grossen und Grauman: 1740–1755 (Berlin: Parey, 1908), pp. 74–5.
22. Georg Andr. Septim. von Praun, *Grundliche Nachricht von dem Münzwesen insgemein, insbesondere aber von dem Deutschen Münzwesen älterer und neuerer Zeiten: und dann auch von dem Französischen, Spanischen, Niederländschen, Englischen und Dänischen Münzwesen*, 3 ed. (Leipzig: Weygandsche Buchhandlung, 1784), pp. 156–7; Probszt, *Geldgeschichte*, pp. 495–6.
23. Karl Theodor Helfferich, ed., *Ludwig Bamberger: Ausgewählte Reden und Aufsätze über Geld- und Bankwesen* (Berlin: Guttentag, 1900), pp. 188–9.

APPENDIX

1. Austria: Rudolf Geyer, 'Die österreichische Münzordnung von 1524 und ihre Vorläufer', *Numismatische Zeitschrift* 61 (1928), p. 29; Newald, *Münzwesen*, p. 6; Hirsch, *Münz-Archiv*, 1, no. CLXXXIII, pp. 168–271; electoral Saxony:

Arnold, 'Talerwährung', pp. 62, 64, 67; Hirsch, *Münz-Archiv*, 1, no. CCXVIII, pp. 376–83; electors on the Rhine: Weisenstein, *Geldwesen*, p. 227; Burgundy: Pusch, *Münz- und Geldpolitik*, p. 86, Verkade, *Muntboek*, p. 29; Empire-wide ordinances: Hirsch, *Münz-Archiv*, 1, no. CLXVII, pp. 240–8; Volckart, *Währung*, no. 90, pp. 344–72; Leeb, *Reichstag zu Augsburg 1559*, vol. 3, no. 804, pp. 1953–88; Lanzinner and Heil, *Reichstag zu Augsburg 1566*, vol. 2, no. 467, pp. 1554–5.

2. The weight of the mark was reduced by around 0.9 per cent. Hirsch, *Münz-Archiv*, 1, no. CCXVIII, p. 378.
3. Cf. Rössner, 'Monetary Theory', p. 312.
4. Harald Witthöft, 'Die Münzordnungen und das Grundgewicht im Deutschen Reich vom 16. Jahrhundert bis 1871/72', in *Geld und Währung vom 16. Jahrhundert bis zur Gegenwart*, ed. Eckart Schremmer (Stuttgart: Steiner, 1993), p. 62; Gerhard Krug, *Die meißnisch-sächsischen Groschen 1338–1500* (Berlin: VEB Deutscher Verlag der Wissenschaften, 1974), pp. 100–1; John H. Munro, 'The Maze of Medieval Monetary Metrology: Determining Mint Weights in Flanders, France and England from the Economics of Counterfeiting, 1388–1469', *Journal of European Economic History* 29, no. 1 (2000), p. 26; Alfred Nagl, 'Das Tiroler Geldwesen unter Erzherzog Sigismund und die Entstehung des Silberguldens', *Numismatische Zeitschrift* 38 (1906), p. 109.
5. Cf. Rössner, 'Monetary Theory', p. 312.
6. Hirsch, *Münz-Archiv*, 1, no. CLXVII, pp. 240–8.
7. Volckart, *Währung*, no. 90, pp. 344–72.
8. Leeb, *Reichstag zu Augsburg 1559*, vol. 3, no. 804, pp. 1953–88.
9. Hirsch, *Geheimnus*, p. 123.

Archival Sources and Bibliography

ARCHIVAL SOURCES

Archiv der Hansestadt Lübeck (AHL):
 Altes Senatsarchiv, Interna 22782 (ASA Interna—Münzwesen - 23/5).
Geheimes Staatsarchiv Preußischer Kulturbesitz (GStAPK):
 I. HA, Rep. 15, Nr. 1 G.
Landesarchiv Baden–Württemberg:
 Generallandesarchiv Karlsruhe (GLA Karlsruhe) 78, no. 1638.
Landesarchiv Wolfenbüttel (LA Wolfenbüttel):
 1 Alt 16, no. 16.
Österreichische Nationalbibliothek (ÖNB):
 Sammlung von Handschriften und alten Drucken, F100071-B.
Österreichisches Staatsarchiv (ÖStA):
Haus-, Hof- und Staatsarchiv Wien (HHStA):
 Reichshofrat, Miscellanea Münzwesen 1: Münzwesen im Reich (1. Konvolut).
 Reichshofrat, Miscellanea Münzwesen 1: Münzwesen im Reich (2. Konvolut).
 Reichshofrat, Miscellanea Münzwesen 1: Münzwesen im Reich—Münzordnung, Münztag zu Speyer—1549–1551 (3. Konvolut).
 Reichshofrat, Miscellanea Münzwesen 2: Münzwesen im Reich, 1551–1564.
 Reichskanzlei, Berichte aus dem Reich 5b.
Finanz- und Hofkammerarchiv:
 Alte Hofkammer, Niederösterreichisches Münz- und Bergwesen, 1524–1750.
Staatsarchiv Würzburg (StAWü):
 Mainzer Regierungsarchiv 7226 (Münze K 137/1½).
Stadtarchiv Augsburg (StAA):
 Bestand: Reichsstadt.
 00084 Urgichten 1549 VI 18 Silvester Raid.
 Strafamt Nr. 96.1 (Strafbuch 1543–1553).
 Ratsprotokolle 17/II (1543).

PUBLISHED PRIMARY SOURCES AND PREMODERN PRINTS

Agricola, Georgius. *Bermannus, sive de re metallica*. Basel: Froben, 1530.

Agricola, Georgius. *De re metallica*. Translated by Herbert C. Hoover and Lou Henry Hoover. New York: Dover Publications, 1556/1950.

Arbusow, Leonid, ed. *Akten und Recesse der livländischen Ständetage*. Vol. 3 (1494–1535). Riga: Deubner, 1910.

Aulinger, Rosemarie, ed. *Deutsche Reichstagsakten unter Kaiser Karl V.: Der Reichstag zu Worms 1545*. Vols. 1, 2. Munich: Oldenbourg, 2003.

Aulinger, Rosemarie, Erwein Eltz, and Ursula Machoczek, eds. *Deutsche Reichstagsakten unter Kaiser Karl V.: Der Reichstag zu Augsburg 1555*. Vols. 2, 4. Munich: Oldenbourg, 2009.

Bentzinger, Rudolf, ed. *Die Wahrheit muß ans Licht: Dialoge aus der Zeit der Reformation*. Frankfurt: Röderberg, 1983.

Blendinger, Friedrich, and Elfriede Blendinger, eds. *Zwei Augsburger Unterkaufbücher aus den Jahren 1551 bis 1558: Älteste Aufzeichnungen zur Vor- und Frühgeschichte der Augsburger Börse*. Stuttgart: Steiner, 1994.

Böhmer, Johann Friedrich. *Regesta Imperii*. Vol. V: Jüngere Staufer 1198–1272, Innsbruck: Wagner'sche Universitäts-Buchhandlung, 1881.

Böhmer, Wilhelm, ed. *Thomas Kantzow's Chronik von Pommern in Niederdeutscher Mundart. Sammt einer Auswahl aus den übrigen ungedruckten Schriften desselben*. Stettin: Friedrich Heinrich Morin, 1835.

Bollandt, Jürgen, ed. *Hamburgische Burspraken 1346 bis 1594 mit Nachträgen bis 1699*. Vol. 2: Bursprakentexte. Hamburg: Hans Christians Druckerei und Verlag, 1960.

Bote, Hermen. 'Von der pagemunte'. In *Chroniken der niedersächsischen Städte: Braunschweig*, edited by Historische Kommission bei der Königlichen Akademie der Wissenschaften, 409–50. Leipzig: Hirzel, 1880.

Burgdorf, Wolfgang, ed. *Die Wahlkapitulationen der römisch-deutschen Könige und Kaiser 1519–1792*. Göttingen: Vandenhoeck & Ruprecht, 2015.

Des Chürfürsten vnd Hertzog Georgen zu Sachssen etc. Muntz Ordenung. s.l.: no publisher, 1534.

Doebner, Richard, ed. *Urkundenbuch der Stadt Hildesheim*. Vol. 8: 1481–1597, mit Nachträgen und Berichtigungen zu Bd. 1–8. Hildesheim: Gerstenberg'sche Buchhandlung, 1901.

Eberlin von Günzburg, Johann. *15 Bundsgenossen, bearb. und eingerichtet von Michael Holzinger*. Berlin: Holzinger, 1521/2013.

Ein Frag an eynen Müntzer/ wahin doch souil Geltz/ kumme das man alltag müntzet. Augsburg: Wolfgang Rösch, 1530.

Eltz, Erwein, ed. *Deutsche Reichstagsakten unter Kaiser Karl V.: Der Speyrer Reichstag von 1544*. Vols. 1, 3. Göttingen: Vandenhoeck & Ruprecht, 2001.

Eltz, Erwein, ed. *Deutsche Reichstagsakten unter Kaiser Karl V.: Der Reichstag zu Augsburg 1550/51*. Vols. 1, 2. Munich: Oldenbourg, 2005.

Enders, Ludwig, ed. *Johann Eberlin von Günzburg: Sämtliche Schriften*. Vol. 3: Halle: Max Niemeyer, 1902.

Euling, Karl, ed. *Chronik des Johan Oldecop*. Tübingen: Litterarischer Verein in Stuttgart, 1891.

Evers, Carl Friedrich. *Mecklenburgische Münz-Verfassung, besonders die Geschichte derselben*. Vol. 1: Schwerin: Baerensprung, 1798.

Friese, Tielemannus, and Cyriacus Spangenberg. *Müntz-Spiegel/das ist: Ein New und Wolaußgeführter Bericht von der Müntz*. Frankfurt: Johann Feyrabendt, 1592.

Fritz, Wolfgang D., ed. *Die Goldene Bulle Kaiser Karls IV. vom Jahre 1356*. Weimar: Böhlau, 1972.

Fronsberger, Leonhard. *Von Kayserlichem Kriegßrechten, Malefitz vnd Schuldhändlen, Ordnung vnd Regiment*. Frankfurt: Feyerabend, 1564.

Gaebel, Georg, ed. *Des Thomas Kantzow Chronik von Pommern in hochdeutscher Mundart*. Vol. 1: Letzte Bearbeitung. Stettin: Paul Niekammer, 1897.

Gasser, Achilles Pirminius. 'Annales civitatis ac reipublicae Augsburgensis'. In *Scriptores rerum germanicarum, praecipue saxonicarum*, edited by Johannes Burkhard Mencke, 1315–954. Leipzig: Johann Christian Martin, 1728.

Geffcken, Peter, and Mark Häberlein, eds. *Rechnungsfragmente der Augsburger Welser-Gesellschaft (1496–1551): Oberdeutscher Fernhandel am Beginn der neuzeitlichen Weltwirtschaft*. Stuttgart: Steiner, 2014.

Greenlee, William Brookes, ed. *The Voyage of Pedro Álvares Cabral to Brazil and India from Contemporary Documents and Narratives*. London Hakluyt Society, 1938.

Greiff, Benedikt, ed. *Tagebuch des Lucas Rem aus den Jahren 1494–1541: Ein Beitrag zur Handelsgeschichte der Stadt Augsburg*. Augsburg: Hartmann'sche Buchdruckerei, 1861.

Greiff, Benedikt. *Was Kayser Carolus dem Vten die Römisch Künglich Wal cost im 1520 Jar*. no place [Augsburg]: no publisher, 1869.

Haß, Kunz. *Hierin vindet mon die vrsach wodurch alle hendel yetz in der welt verkert und verderbt werden*. Nuremberg: no publisher, *c.*1500.

Hirsch, Johann Christoph. *Des Teutschen Reichs Münz-Archiv*. Vols. 1–7, Nuremberg: Adam Jonathan Felßeckers seel. Erben, 1756-61.

Hirsch, Johann Christoph. *Eröfnetes Geheimnus der practischen Münz-Wissenschafft samt beygefügter Tariffa, über Gold und Silber*. Nuremberg: Adam Jonathan Felßeckers seel. Erben, 1762.

Hoffmann, Leonhard Willibald. *Alter und neuer Münz-Schlüssel Oder Beantwort- und Eröffnung CCXXII. Curioser Fragen*. Nuremberg: J. Zieger, 1692.

Hontheim, Johann Nicolaus von. *Historia Trevirensis diplomatica et pragmatica: inde a translata Treveri praefectura praetorio galliorum, ad haec usque tempora*. Vol. 2: Augsburg, Würzburg: Martin Veith, 1750.

Inama-Sternegg, Hanns. 'Das Nachlaßinventar des Ambros Mornauer von Lichtenwert 1550'. In *Festgabe für Erich Egg zum 65. Geburtstag*, edited by Christina Antenhofer and Richard Schober, 39–59. Innsbruck: Landesmuseum, 1985.

Isaacsohn, Siegfried, ed. *Urkunden und Actenstücke zur Geschichte des Kurfürsten Friedrich Wilhelm von Brandenburg*. Vol. 10: Berlin: G. Reimer, 1880.

Jacobs, J.M., ed. *Works of Martin Luther with Introduction and Notes*. Vol. II: Philadelphia: A.J. Holman, 1916.

Johnson, Charles, ed. *The De Moneta of Nicholas Oresme and English mint documents*. London, Edinburgh, Paris: Thomas Nelson and Sons, 1956.

Kaiser Karl des fünfften Newe Müntzordnung, Sampt Valuierung der Gulden vnd Silberin Müntzen, Vnd darauff eruolgtem Kaiserlichen Edict, zu Augspurg alles im Jar M.D. LI. aufgericht und außgangen. Augsburg: Philipp Ulhart, 1551.

Kellenbenz, Hermann, ed. *Das Meder'sche Handelsbuch und die Welser'schen Nachträge*. Wiesbaden: Steiner, 1974.

Kimble, George H.T., ed. *Esmeraldo de Situ Orbis by Duarte Pacheco Pereira*. London: Hakluyt Society, 1937.

Klotzsch, Johann Friedrich. *Versuch einer Chur-Sächschen Münzgeschichte: von den ältesten, bis auf jetzige Zeiten*. Vol. 2: Chemnitz: Johann Christoph Stößel, 1780.

Kohler, Joseph, and Willy Scheel, eds. *Die Peinliche Gerichtsordnung Kaiser Karls V.: Constitutio Criminalis Carolina*. Halle: Verlag der Buchhandlung des Waisenhauses, 1900.

Koppmann, Karl, ed. *Kämmereirechnungen der Stadt Hamburg*. Vols. 5–7. Hamburg: Hermann Grüning, Gräfe & Sillem, 1883–94.

Krantz, Albert. *Wandalia*. Cologne: no publisher, 1519.

Kruse, Jürgen Elert. *Allgemeiner und besonders Hamburgischer Contorist*. 3 ed. Vol. 1: Hamburg: Eigenverlag, 1766.

Lamond, Elizabeth, ed. *A Discourse of the Commonweal of This Realm of England: First Printed in 1581 and Commonly Attributed to W.S.* Cambridge: Cambridge University Press, 1929.

Lanzinner, Maximilian, ed. *Der Reichstag zu Speyer 1570*. Vol. 2: Akten und Abschied. Göttingen: Vandenhoeck & Ruprecht, 1988.

Lanzinner, Maximilian, and Dietmar Heil, eds. *Der Reichstag zu Augsburg 1566*. Vols. 1, 2. Munich: Oldenbourg, 2002.

Leeb, Josef, ed. *Der Kurfürstentag zu Frankfurt 1558 und der Reichstag zu Augsburg 1559*. Vols. 2, 3. Göttingen: Vandenhoeck & Ruprecht, 1999.

Leeb, Josef, ed. *Der Reichstag zu Regensburg 1556/57*. Vols. 1, 2. Munich: Oldenbourg, 2013.

Lehmann, Christoph. *Florilegium Politicum: Politischer Blumengarten Darinn außerlesene Politische Sententz, Lehren, Reguln, und Sprüchwörter auß Theologis, Jurisconsultis, Politicis, Historicis, Philosophis, Poeten und eygener erfahrung unter 286 Tituln . . . zusammen getragen*. s.l.: Impensis autoris, 1630.

Lori, Johann Georg von. *Sammlung des baierischen Münzrechts*. Vol. 1: s.l.: no publisher, 1768.

Lotz, Walther. *Die drei Flugschriften über den Münzstreit der sächsischen Albertiner und Ernestiner um 1530*. Leipzig: Duncker & Humblot, 1893.

Lowndes, William. *A Report Containing an Essay for the Amendment of the Silver Coins*. London: Charles Bill, 1695.

Luttenberger, Albrecht, ed. *Deutsche Reichstagsakten unter Kaiser Karl V.: Der Reichstag zu Regensburg 1541*. Munich: De Gruyter Oldenbourg, 2018.

Machoczek, Ursula, ed. *Deutsche Reichstagsakten unter Kaiser Karl V.: Der Reichstag zu Augsburg 1547/48*. Vols. 1, 3. Munich: Oldenbourg, 2006.

Mathesius, Johann. *Sarepta oder Bergpostill sampt der Jochimßthalischen kurtzen Chroniken*. Nuremberg: vom Berg, 1562.

Meltzer, Christian. *Historia Schneebergensis renovata, das ist: erneuerte Stadt- u. Berg-Chronica der im Ober-Ertz-Gebürge Meißens gelegenen Berg-Stadt Schneeberg*. Schneeberg: Heinrich Fulde, 1716.

Moryson, Fynes. *An Itinerary Containing His Ten Yeeres Travell through the Twelve Dominions of Germany, Bohmer-land, Sweitzerland, Netherland, Denmarke, Poland, Italy, Turky, France, England, Scotland & Ireland*. Vols. 1, 2, 4. Glasgow: Glasgow University Press, 1617/1907–8.

Müller, Karl Otto, ed. *Quellen zur Handelsgeschichte der Paumgartner von Augsburg (1480–1570)*. Wiesbaden: Franz Steiner, 1955.

Nelkenbrecher, Johann Christian, and Mark Rudolph Balthazar Gerhardt. *Nelkenbrechers Taschenbuch der Münz-Maaß und Gewichtskunde für Kaufleute*. 7 ed. Berlin: Arnold Wever, 1793.

Phillips, Walter Alison. *Selected Poems of Walther von der Vogelweide the Minnesinger*. London: Smith, Elder & Co., 1896.

Praun, Georg Andr. Septim. von. *Grundliche Nachricht von dem Münzwesen insgemein, insbesondere aber von dem Deutschen Münzwesen älterer und neuerer Zeiten: und dann auch von dem Französischen, Spanischen, Niederländschen, Englischen und Dänischen Münzwesen*. 3 ed. Leipzig: Weygandsche Buchhandlung, 1784.

Radcliffe, Ann. *A Journey Made in the Summer of 1794: Through Holland and the Western Frontier of Germany, with a Return Down the Rhine; to which are Added, Observations During a Tour to the Lakes of Lancashire, Westmoreland, and Cumberland*. Dublin: William Porter, 1795.

Rauch, Karl, ed. *Traktat über den Reichstag: Eine offiziöse Darstellung aus der Kurmainzischen Kanzlei*. Weimar: Böhlau, 1905.

Rhegius, Urbanus. *Der XV. Psalm Davids*. Magdeburg: Lotther, 1538.

Riedel, Adolph Friedrich Johann. *Codex diplomaticus Brandenburgensis: Sammlung der Urkunden, Chroniken und sonstigen Quellenschriften für die Geschichte der Mark Brandenburg und ihrer Regenten*. Vol. 1, X, Berlin: G. Reimer, 1856.

Römischer, Auch zů Hungern, vnd Behaim etc. Khünigklicher Mayestat, Ertzherzogen zů Ostereich etc. Newe Müntzürdnung: Sampt Valuierung der Gulden vnd Silberin Müntzen, Vnd darauff eruolgtem Edict. Vienna: Hans Syngriener, 1552.

Romischer, Auch zu Hungern, vnd Behaim etc. Khünigklicher Mayestat, Ertzhertzogen zu Osterreich etc. Newe Müntzordnung. Vienna: Hans Syngriener, 1556.

Ropp, Goswin Frhr. von der, ed. *Hanserecesse von 1431–1476*. Vol. 1 (2. Abt.). Leipzig: Duncker & Humblot, 1876.

Rössner, Philipp Robinson, ed. *Martin Luther: On Commerce and Usury (1524)*. London: Anthem Press, 2015.

Roth, Friedrich, ed. *Die Chroniken der schwäbischen Städte: Augsburg*. Vol. 7: Leipzig: Hirzel, 1917.

Sastrow, Bartholomäus, and Gottlieb Mohnike. *Bartholomäi Sastrowen Herkommen, Geburt und Lauff seines gantzen Lebens auch was sich in dem Denckwerdiges zugetragen, so er mehrentheils selbst gesehen und gegenwärtig mit angehöret hat*. Vols. 1, 2. Greifswald: Universitäts-Buchhandlung, 1823–4.

Scott, Tom, and Bob Scribner, eds. *The German Peasants' War: A History in Documents*. New Jersey, London: Humanities Press, 1991.

Steinen, Johann Diederich von. *Westphälische Geschichte*. Vol. 3: Lemgo: Meyer, 1755.

Stetten, Paul von. *Geschichte Der Heil. Röm. Reichs Freyen Stadt Augspurg: Aus bewährten Jahr-Büchern und Tüchtigen Urkunden gezogen, Und an das Licht gegeben*. Frankfurt: Merz und Mayer, 1743.

Teütscher Nation Notturfft: Die Ordnung vnd Reformation aller Stendt ym Römischen Reych. Durch Kayser Fridrich den dritten Gott zu lob / der gantzen Christenheyt zu nutz vnd säligkeyt fürgenommen. Zwickau: Gastel, 1523.

Thomann von Hagelstein, David. *Der Röm. Kayserl. Majestät Deß Heil. Röm. Reichs Geist- und Weltlicher Chur-Fürsten, Fürsten und Ständen Acta Publica Monetaria Schrifftliche Handlungen, Constitutiones, Bedencken und Vorschläge, Die Anordnung, Reformation und Verbesserung Deß Müntz-Wesens in Teutschland betreffende*. Augsburg: Kroniger & Göbels Erben, 1692.

Verzeychnus was vermög des H. R. R. Müntzordnungen vnd Abschied vom 1559. 1566. vnnd 1570 Jarn für Silberin vnnd Guldine Müntz Sorten . . . hinfüro zu nemen vnnd zu geben zugelassen . . . Straßburg, 1571.

Volckart, Oliver, ed. *Eine Währung für das Reich: Die Akten der Münztage zu Speyer 1549 und 1557*. Stuttgart: Steiner, 2017.

Vortrab und gründlicher, warhafftiger, kurtzer Bericht, der guten Reichs-Müntzordnung. Munich: Adam Berg, 1572.

Weber, Matthias. *Die Reichspolizeiordnungen von 1530, 1548 und 1577: Historische Einführung und Edition*. Frankfurt: Vittorio Klostermann, 2002.

Welser, Marcus, Achilles Pirmin Gasser, and Engelbert Werlich. *Chronica der weitberüempten keyserlichen freyen und deß H. Reichs Statt Augspurg in Schwaben von derselben altem Ursprung, schöne gelegene zierliche Gebäwen unnd namhafften gedenckwürdigen Geschichten*. Vol. 3: Basel: Egenolff, 1596.

Werner, Theodor Gustav. 'Ein Münzgutachten Jakob Fuggers des Reichen für Erzherzog Ferdinand von Österreich aus dem Jahre 1524 oder 1525', *Scripta Mercaturae* I (1967): 23–35.

Werner, Theodor Gustav. 'Regesten und Urkunden über Beteiligung von Nürnbergern an der Zeche Rappolt und an anderen Schneeberger Bergwerks- und Metallhandelsunternehmungen (II. Teil)', *Mitteilungen des Vereins für Geschichte der Stadt Nürnberg* 60 (1973): 153–94.

Westphal, Sina, ed. *Die Korrespondenz zwischen Kurfürst Friedrich dem Weisen von Sachsen und der Reichsstadt Nürnberg*. Frankfurt, Berlin, Bern: Peter Lang, 2009.

Wir Ferdinand von Gottes genaden, Römischer Khünig, zu allen Zeiten merer des Reichs, in Germanien. s.l. [Augsburg]: no publisher, 1551.
Wölkern, Lazarus Carl von. *Historia Norimbergensis Diplomatica oder Zusammentrag der Vornehmsten von den Glorwürdigsten Römischen Kaysern und Königen der Reichs-Freyen Stadt Nürnberg Allermildest ertheilten Freyheiten Begnadigungen und Concessionen*. Nuremberg: Endter, 1738.
Wrede, Adolf, ed. *Deutsche Reichstagsakten unter Kaiser Karl V*. Vols. 2–4. Gotha: Friedrich Andreas Perthes, 1896–1905.
Wyntzer, Thomas. *Leichpredigt Vber dem Begrebnis des Edlen Gestrengen vnnd Ehrendvhesten Abraham von Einsiedell, Churf. G. zu Sachssen etc. LandRaht, auffm Scharffensteyne etc., Den 20. Martii Anno 1568*. Dresden, 1568.
Zarncke, Friedrich, ed. *Sebastian Brants Narrenschiff*. Hannover: Georg Olms, 1854/1961.
Zwengel, Johann Peter. *New Groß Formular vnd vollkommlich Cantzlei Buch: von den besten vnd auszerlesenen Formularien aller deren Schrifften, so in . . . Cantzleyen, auch sonst in den Ampten . . . fürfallender geschäfft halben, bräuchlich seindt*. Frankfurt: Christian Egenolffs Erben, 1568.

SECONDARY SOURCES

Allen, Robert C. 'Economic Structure and Agricultural Productivity in Europe, 1300–1800', *European Review of Economic History* 4, no. 1 (2000): 1–26.
Alter, Willi. 'Von der konradinischen Rachtung bis zum letzten Reichstag in Speyer, 1420–1570'. In *Geschichte der Stadt Speyer*, edited by Wolfgang Eger, 369–570. Stuttgart: Kohlhammer, 1982.
Altmann, Hans-Christian. *Die Kipper- und Wipperinflation in Bayern (1620–1623): Ein Beitrag zur Strukturanalyse des frühabsolutistischen Staates*. Munich: Stadtarchiv München, 1976.
Angermeier, Heinz. 'Die Vorstellung des gemeinen Mannes von Staat und Reich im deutschen Bauernkrieg', *Vierteljahrschrift für Sozial- und Wirtschaftsgeschichte* 53, no. 3 (1966): 329–43.
Angermeier, Heinz. *Die Reichsreform 1410–1555: die Staatsproblematik in Deutschland zwischen Mittelalter und Gegenwart*. Munich: Beck, 1984.
Arnold, Klaus. 'damit der arm man vnnd gemainer nutz iren furgang haben . . . : Zum deutschen "Bauernkrieg" als politischer Bewegung: Wendel Hiplers und Friedrich Weygandts Pläne einer "Reformation" des Reiches', *Zeitschrift für Historische Forschung* 9, no. 3 (1982): 257–313.
Arnold, Paul. 'Die sächsische Talerwährung von 1500 bis 1763', *Schweizerische Numismatische Rundschau* 59 (1980): 50–94.
Arnold, Paul. 'Das sächsische Münzwesen in der ersten Hälfte des 16. Jahrhunderts—die Wechselbeziehungen zwischen Bergbau und Münzpolitik in Sachsen'. In *Georgius Agricola, 500 Jahre: Wissenschaftliche Konferenz vom 25.–27. März 1994 in Chemnitz, Freistaat Sachsen*, edited by F. Naumann, 416–22. Basel, Boston, Berlin: Birkhauser Verlag 1994.
Arnold, Paul. 'Die Währungsunionen von Zinna (1667–1690) und Leipzig (1690–1750/63) unter besonderer Berücksichtigung des kursächsischen Münzwesens'. In *Währungsunionen: Beiträge zur Geschichte überregionaler Münz- und*

Geldpolitik, edited by Reiner Cunz, 221–48. Hamburg: Museum für Hamburgische Geschichte, 2002.

Ash, Timothy Garton. 'Since Reunification, Germany Has Had its Best 30 Years: The Next 30 Will Be Harder', *The Guardian*, 20 Sep. 2020.

Asmussen, Tina, and Pamela O. Long. 'Introduction: The Cultural and Material Worlds of Mining in Early Modern Europe', *Renaissance Studies* 34, no. 1 (2020): 8–30.

Attman, Artur. 'The Bullion Flow from Europe to the East: 1500–1800'. In *Precious Metals, Coinage and the Changes of Monetary Structures in Latin-America, Europe and Asia (Late Middle Ages—Early Modern Times)*, edited by Eddy H.G. van Cauwenberghe, 65–68. Leuven: Leuven University Press, 1989.

Aulinger, Rosemarie. *Das Bild des Reichstages im 16. Jahrhundert: Beiträge zu einer typologischen Analyse schriftlicher und bildlicher Quellen*. Göttingen: Vandenhoeck & Ruprecht, 1980.

Aulinger, Rosemarie, and Silvia Schweinzer-Burian. 'Habsburgische und reichsständische Präsenz auf den Reichstagen Kaiser Karls V. (1521–1555) im Spiegel der Reichsmatrikel von 1521: Eine prosopographische Erfassung'. In *Handlungsräume: Facetten politischer Kommunikation in der Frühen Neuzeit. Festschrift für Albrecht P. Luttenberger zum 65. Geburtstag*, edited by Franz Hederer, Christian König, Kathrin Nina Marth, and Christina Milz, 109–64. Munich: Martin Meidenbauer, 2011.

Austen, Ralph A. 'Marginalization, Stagnation, and Growth: The Trans-Saharan Caravan Trade in the Era of European Expansion, 1500–1900'. In *The Rise of Merchant Empires: Long Distance Trade in the Early Modern World 1350–1750*, edited by James D. Tracy, 311–50. Cambridge: Cambridge University Press, 1990.

Backhaus, Fritz. '"Das größte Siedelwerk des deutschen Volkes": Zur Erforschung der Germania Slavica in Deutschland'. In *Struktur und Wandel im Früh- und Hochmittelalter: Eine Bestandsaufnahme aktueller Forschungen zur Germania Slavica*, edited by Christian Lübke, 17–38. Stuttgart: Steiner, 1998.

Bahrfeldt, Emil. *Das Münzwesen der Mark Brandenburg unter den Hohenzollern bis zum grossen Kurfürsten, von 1415 bis 1640*. Berlin: Kühl, 1895.

Bairoch, Paul. 'Urbanization and the Economy in Preindustrial Societies: The Findings of Two Decades of Research', *Journal of European Economic History* 18 (1989): 239–88.

Bairoch, Paul, Jean Batou, and Pierre Chèvre. *La population des villes européennes: banque de données et analyse sommaire des résultats; 800–1850 (The Population of European Cities)*. Genève: Droz, 1988.

Bakewell, Peter J. *Silver Mining and Society in Colonial Mexico: Zacatecas 1546–1700*. Cambridge: Cambridge University Press, 1971.

Bakewell, Peter J. 'Registered Silver Production in the Potosí district, 1550–1735', *Jahrbuch für Geschichte Lateinamerikas–Anuario de Historia de America Latina* 12, no. 1 (1975): 67–103.

Bamberg, Paul. 'Weitere Nachrichten zum maschinellen Münzbetrieb des Grafen Reinhard zu Solms', *Deutsche Münzblätter* 55 (1935): 317–26, 72–6, 95–8.

Banerjee, Abhijit V. 'A Simple Model of Herd Behavior', *The Quarterly Journal of Economics* 107, no. 3 (1992): 797–817.

Barrett, Ward. 'World Bullion Flows, 1450–1800'. In *The Rise of Merchant Empires: Long-Distance Trade in the Early Modern World 1350–1750*, edited by James D. Tracy, 224–54. Cambridge: Cambridge University Press, 1990.

Bartels, Christoph. 'Krisen und Innovationen im Erzbergbau des Harzes zwischen ausgehendem Mittelalter und beginnender Neuzeit', *Technikgeschichte* 63, no. 1 (1996): 1–19.

Bartels, Christoph. 'Zur Bergbaukrise des Spätmittelalters'. In *Konjunkturen im europäischen Bergbau in vorindustrieller Zeit: Festschrift für Ekkehard Westermann zum 60. Geburtstag*, edited by Christoph Bartels and Markus A. Denzel, 157–72. Stuttgart: Steiner, 2000.

Bartels, Christoph. 'Bergbau und Münzstätten im Harz', *Abhandlungen der Braunschweigischen Wissenschaftlichen Gesellschaft* 60 (2008): 23–50.

Baskin, Jonathan Barron, and Paul J. Miranti. *A History of Corporate Finance*. Cambridge: Cambridge University Press, 1999.

Batizi, Zoltán. 'Mining in Medieval Hungary'. In *The Economy of Medieval Hungary*, edited by József Laszlovszky, Balázs Nagy, Péter Szabó, and András Vadas, 166–81. Leiden: Brill, 2018.

Bauernfeind, Walter, Michael Diefenbacher, and Christine Sauer, eds. *Bilderpracht und Seelenheil: Illuminierte Urkunden aus Nürnberger Archiven und Sammlungen. Begleitband zur gleichnamigen Ausstellung in der Stadtbibliothek im Bildungscampus Nürnberg vom 13. Februar–4. Mai 2019*. Nuremberg: Verlag Ph. C.W. Schmidt, 2019.

Baulant, Micheline. 'Le prix des grains à Paris de 1431 à 1788', *Annales. Économies, Sociétés, Civilisations* 23, no. 3 (1968): 520–40.

Beck, August. *Johann Friedrich der Mittlere, Herzog zu Sachsen: ein Beitrag zur Geschichte des sechzehnten Jahrhunderts*. Vol. 1: Weimar: Böhlau, 1858.

Becker, Hans-Jürgen. 'Protestatio, Protest: Funktion und Funktionswandel eines rechtlichen Instruments', *Zeitschrift für Historische Forschung* 5, no. 4 (1978): 385–412.

Begert, Alexander. *Böhmen, die böhmische Kur und das Reich vom Hochmittelalter bis zum Ende des Alten Reiches: Studien zur Kurwürde und staatsrechtlichen Stellung Böhmens*. Husum: Matthiesen, 2003.

Behringer, Wolfgang. *Thurn und Taxis: Die Geschichte ihrer Post und ihrer Unternehmen*. Munich, Zürich: Piper, 1990.

Behringer, Wolfgang. '"Von der Gutenberg-Galaxis zur Taxis-Galaxis". Die Kommunikationsrevolution: Ein Konzept zum besseren Verständnis der Frühen Neuzeit', *Historische Zeitschrift. Beihefte* 41 (2005): 39–54.

Behringer, Wolfgang. 'Kaiser, Reichstag und Postwesen (1490–1615)'. In *Der Reichstag 1486–1613: Kommunikation, Wahrnehmung, Öffentlichkeit*, edited by Maximilian Lanzinner and Arno Strohmeyer, 117–48. Göttingen: Vandenhoeck & Ruprecht, 2006.

Bellingradt, Daniel. 'Die vergessenen Quellen des Alten Reiches: Ein Forschungsüberblick zu frühneuzeitlicher Flugpublizistik im Heiligen Römischen

Reich deutscher Nation'. In *Presse und Geschichte: Leistungen und Perspektiven der historischen Presseforschung*, edited by Astrid Blome and Holger Böning, 77–95. Bremen: edition lumière, 2008.

Bergerhausen, Hans-Wolfgang. '"Exclusis Westphalen et Burgund": Zum Kampf um die Durchsetzung der Reichsmünzordnung von 1559', *Zeitschrift für historische Forschung* 20 (1993): 189–203.

Berghaus, Peter. 'Umlauf und Nachprägung des Florentiner Guldens nördlich der Alpen'. In *Congresso Internazionale di Numismatica, Roma 11–16 settembre 1961*, 595–607. Rome: Commision Internationale de Numismatique, 1965.

Bernhart, Max. *Die Münzen und Medaillen der Stadt Kaufbeuren nebst einer münzgeschichtlichen Einleitung*. Halle: Riechmann, 1923.

Bickford Berzock, Kathleen. 'Caravans of Gold, Fragments in Time: An Introduction'. In *Caravans of Gold, Fragments in Time: Art, Culture, and Exchange across Medieval Saharan Africa*, edited by Kathleen Bickford Berzock, 23–37. Princeton: NJ: Princeton University Press, 2019.

Bikhchandani, Sushil, David Hirshleifer, and Ivo Welch. 'A Theory of Fads, Fashion, Custom, and Cultural Change as Informational Cascades', *Journal of Political Economy* 100, no. 5 (1992): 992–1026.

Binder, Christian, and Julius Ebner. *Württembergische Münz- und Medaillenkunde*. Vol. 1: Stuttgart: Kohlhammer, 1910.

Bingener, Andreas, Christoph Bartels, and Michael Fessner. 'Die große Zeit des Silbers: Der Bergbau im deutschsprachigen Raum von der Mitte des 15. bis zum Anfang des 17. Jahrhunderts'. In *Der alteuropäische Bergbau: Von den Anfängen bis zur Mitte des 18. Jahrhunderts*, edited by Christoph Bartels and Rainer Slotta, 317–452. Münster: Aschendorf, 2012.

Bishop, Jennifer. 'Currency, Conversation, and Control: Political Discourse and the Coinage in Mid-Tudor England', *English Historical Review* 131, no. 551 (2016): 763–92.

Blaich, Fritz. *Die Wirtschaftspolitik des Reichstags im Heiligen Römischen Reich: Ein Beitrag zur Problemgeschichte wirtschaftlichen Gestaltens*. Stuttgart: Fischer, 1970.

Blake, John W. *West Africa: Quest for God and Gold, 1454–1578*. London: Curzon Press, 1977.

Blanchard, Ian. 'The Continental European Cattle Trades, 1400–1600', *The Economic History Review* XXXIX, no. 3 (1986): 427–60.

Blanchard, Ian. 'English Royal Borrowing at Antwerp, 1544–1574'. In *Finances publiques et finances privees au bas moyen age. Actes du colloque tenu a Gand les 5 et 6 mai 1995*, edited by Marc Boone and Walter Prevenier, 57–74. Leuven, Apeldoorn: Garant, 1996.

Blanchet, Jules-Adrien, and Adolphe Dieudonné. *Manuel de numismatique Française*. Vol. 2: Paris: Picard, 1916.

Blaschke, Karlheinz. 'Menge und Gliederung in der Bevölkerungsentwicklung Sachsens: Eine Langzeitbeobachtung vom 10. bis zum 20. Jahrhundert'. In *Struktur und Dimension: Festschrift für Karl Heinrich Kaufhold zum 65. Geburtstag*, edited by Hans-Jürgen Gerhard, 223–43. Stuttgart: Steiner, 1997.

Blickle, Peter. *Die Revolution von 1525*. Munich: Oldenbourg, 1981.

Blickle, Peter. 'Der Gemeine Nutzen: Ein kommunaler Wert und seine politische Karriere'. In *Gemeinwohl und Gemeinsinn: Historische Semantiken politischer Leitbegriffe*, edited by Herfried Münkler and Harald Bluhm, 85–107. Berlin: Akademie Verlag, 2001.

Blickle, Peter. *Der Bauernkrieg: Die Revolution des Gemeinen Mannes*. Munich: Beck, 2002.

Blickle, Peter. 'Beschwerden und Polizeien: Die Legitimation des modernen Staates durch Verfahren und Normen'. In *Gute Policey als Politik im 16. Jahrhundert: Die Entstehung des öffentlichen Raumes in Oberdeutschland*, edited by Peter Blickle, Peter Kissling, and Heinrich Richard Schmidt, 549–68. Frankfurt: Klostermann, 2003.

Blickle, Peter. *Unruhen in der ständischen Gesellschaft 1300–1800*. 3 ed. Munich: Oldenbourg, 2012.

Bloemendal, Jan, and Arjan van Dixhoorn. 'Early Modern Literary Cultures and Public Opinion: An Epilogue in the Form of a Discussion'. In *Literary Cultures and Public Opinion in the Low Countries, 1450–1650*, edited by Jan Bloemendal, Arjan van Dixhoorn, and Elsa Strietman. Leiden: Brill, 2011.

Boelcke, Willi Alfred. 'Zur Entwicklung des bäuerlichen Kreditwesens in Württemberg vom späten Mittelalter bis Anfang des 17. Jahrhunderts', *Jahrbücher für Nationalökonomie und Statistik* 176, no. 4 (1964): 319–58.

Boerner, Lars, and Oliver Volckart. 'The Utility of a Common Coinage: Currency Unions and the Integration of Money Markets in Late Medieval Central Europe', *Explorations in Economic History* 48 (2011): 53–65.

Boldt, Hans. *Deutsche Verfassungsgeschichte*. 2 ed. Vol. 1: Von den Anfängen bis zum Ende des älteren deutschen Reiches 1806, Munich: dtv, 1990.

Boockmann, Hartmut. *Stauferzeit und spätes Mittelalter: Deutschland 1125–1517*. 4 ed. Berlin: Siedler, 1994.

Borges, Riu, R.J.C. Silva, Luis Alves, et al. 'European Silver Sources from the 15th to the 17th Century: The Influx of "New World" Silver in Portuguese Currency', *Heritage* 1 (2018): 453–67.

Born, Karl Erich. 'Moritz von Sachsen und die Fürstenverschwörung gegen Karl V.', *Historische Zeitschrift* 191, no. 1 (1960): 18–66.

Bovill, E.W. *The Golden Trade of the Moors*. 2 ed. London: Oxford University Press, 1958.

Brachinger, Hans Wolfgang. 'Der Euro als Teuro? Die wahrgenommene Inflation in Deutschland', *Wirtschaft und Statistik* 9 (2005): 999–1013.

Brakensiek, Stefan. 'Akzeptanzorientierte Herrschaft: Überlegungen zur politischen Kultur der Frühen Neuzeit'. In *Die Frühe Neuzeit als Epoche*, edited by Helmut Neuhaus, 395–406. Munich: Oldenbourg, 2009.

Braudel, Fernand. *The Mediterranean and the Mediterranean World in the Age of Philip II*. 5 ed. Vols. 1, 2. Glasgow: Fontana, 1949/86–7.

Braunstein, Philippe. 'Innovations in Mining and Metal Production in Europe in the Late Middle Ages', *Journal of European Economic History* 12, no. 3 (1983): 573–91.

Brayshay, Mark. 'Long-Distance Royal Journeys: Anne of Denmark's Journey from Stirling to Windsor in 1603', *The Journal of Transport History* 25, no. 1 (2004): 1–21.

Broadberry, Stephen, Bruce M.S. Campbell, Alexander Klein, Mark Overton, and Baas Van Leeuwen. *British Economic Growth 1270–1870*. Cambridge: Cambridge University Press, 2015.

Brown, Robert, ed. *The History and Description of Africa and the Notable Things Therein Contained, written by Al-Hassan Ibn-Mohammed Al-Wezaz Al-Fasi, a Moor, Baptised as Giovanni Leone, but Better Known as Leo Africanus, Done into English in the Year 1600, by John Pory* Vol. 3: London: Hakluyt Society, 1896.

Brulez, Wilfrid. 'Le commerce international des Pays-Bas au XVIe siècle: Essai d'appréciation quantitative', *Revue belge de philologie et d'histoire* 46, no. 4 (1968): 1205–21.

Büchmann, Georg. *Geflügelte Worte: Der Zitatenschatz des deutschen Volkes*. Cologne: Atlas-Verlag, 1956.

Buck, Heinrich, and Max von Bahrfeld. *Die Münzen der Stadt Hildesheim*. Hildesheim, Leipzig: Lax, 1937.

Bulst, Neithard. 'Der Schwarze Tod: demographische, wirtschafts- und kulturgeschichtliche Aspekte der Pestkatastrophe von 1347–1352: Bilanz der neueren Forschung', *Saeculum* 30 (1979): 45–67.

Burgdorf, Wolfgang. 'Proto-constitutionalism: The Imperial Constitution in the Electoral Capitulations and Basic Law Guarantees', *German History* 36, no. 3 (2018): 415–31.

Burkhardt, Johannes. 'Europäischer Nachzügler oder institutioneller Vorreiter? Plädoyer für einen neuen Entwicklungsdiskurs zur konstruktiven Doppelstaatlichkeit des frühmodernen Reiches'. In *Imperium Romanum—irregulare corpus—Teutscher Reichs-Staat: Das Alte Reich im Verständnis der Zeitgenossen und der Historiographie*, edited by Matthias Schnettger, 297–316. Mainz: Zabern, 2002.

Burkhardt, Johannes. *Das Reformationsjahrhundert: Deutsche Geschichte zwischen Medienrevolution und Institutionenbildung, 1517–1617*. Stuttgart: Kohlhammer, 2002.

Burkhardt, Johannes. *Deutsche Geschichte in der frühen Neuzeit*. Munich: Beck, 2009.

Burmeister, Karl Heinz. 'Jakob Jonas: Humanist und Staatsmann', *Schriften des Vereins für Geschichte des Bodensees und seiner Umgebung* 89 (1971): 83–94.

Buszello, Horst. 'Gemeinde, Territorium und Reich in den politischen Programmen des Deutschen Bauernkrieges 1524/25', *Geschichte und Gesellschaft: Sonderheft* 1 (1975): 105–28.

Bütterlin, Rudolf. *Die merkantilistische Geldpolitik im Herzogtum Württemberg von der Reformation bis Napoleon*. Metzingen: Hauser, 1966.

Cahn, Julius. *Der Rappenmünzbund: Eine Studie zur Münz- und Geld-Geschichte des oberen Rheinthales*. Heidelberg: Carl Winter's Universitätsbuchhandlung, 1901.

Cahn, Julius. *Münz- und Geldgeschichte von Konstanz und des Bodenseegebietes im Mittelalter bis zum Reichsmünzgesetz von 1559*. Heidelberg: Carl Winter's Universitätsbuchhandlung, 1911.

Carneiro, Robert L. 'A Theory of the Origin of the State', *Science* 169, no. 3947 (1970): 733–38.

Carneiro, Robert L. 'The Circumscription Theory: A Clarification, Amplification, and Reformulation', *Social Evolution & History* 11, no. 2 (2012): 5–30.

Carsten, Francis L. *Princes and Parliaments in Germany: From the Fifteenth to the Eighteenth Century*. Oxford: Clarendon, 1959.

Cassan, Michel. 'Die Krone und die Städte unter Karl IX. und Ludwig XIII'. In *Staatsbildung als kultureller Prozess: Strukturwandel und Legitimation von Herrschaft in der Frühen Neuzeit*, edited by Ronald G. Asch and Dagmar Freist, 135–50. Cologne, Weimar, Vienna: Böhlau, 2005.

Castelin, Karel. 'Zur Entstehung der ältesten "Joachimstaler"', *Numismatische Zeitschrift* 80 (1963): 72–7.

Castelin, Karel. *Grossus Pragensis: Der Prager Groschen und seine Teilstücke; 1300–1547*. 2 ed. Braunschweig: Klinkhardt & Biermann, 1973.

Challis, Christopher Edgar. *The Tudor Coinage*. Manchester: Manchester University Press, 1978.

Challis, Christopher Edgar. *A New History of the Royal Mint*. Cambridge: Cambridge University Press, 1992.

Chilosi, David, Max-Stephan Schulze, and Oliver Volckart. 'Benefits of Empire? Capital Market Integration North and South of the Alps, 1350–1800', *The Journal of Economic History* 78, no. 3 (2018): 637–72.

Chilosi, David, and Oliver Volckart. 'Money, States and Empire: Financial Integration and Institutional Change in Central Europe, 1400–1520', *The Journal of Economic History* 71, no. 3 (2011): 762–91.

Chilosi, David, and Oliver Volckart. 'Good or Bad Money? Debasements, Society and the State in the Late Middle Ages'. In *Money and Its Use in Medieval Europe Three Decades On: Essays in Honour of Professor Peter Spufford*, edited by Martin Allen, 111–28. London: The Royal Numismatic Society, 2017.

Christmann, Thomas. *Das Bemühen von Kaiser und Reich um die Vereinheitlichung des Münzwesens: zugleich ein Beitrag zum Rechtssetzungsverfahren im Heiligen Römischen Reich nach dem Westfälischen Frieden*. Berlin: Duncker & Humblot, 1988.

Cipolla, Carlo Maria. *Money, Prices and Civilization in the Mediterranean World, Fifth to Seventeenth Century*. New York: Gordian Press, 1956.

Cipolla, Carlo Maria. *Money in Sixteenth-Century Florence*. Berkeley, Los Angeles: University of California Press, 1989.

Classen, Peter. 'Das Wormser Konkordat in der deutschen Verfassungsgeschichte'. In *Investiturstreit und Reichsverfassung*, edited by Josef Fleckenstein, 411–60. Sigmaringen: Thorbecke, 1973.

Cohen, Yehudi A. 'Some Aspects of Ritualized Behavior in Interpersonal Relationships', *Human Relations* 11, no. 3 (1958): 195–215.

Craig, J. *The Mint: A History of the London Mint from A.D. 287 to 1948*. Cambridge, 1953.

Cramer-Fürtig, Michael. 'Ottheinrichs "merkliche und beschwerliche Schuldenlast": Finanzkrise und Staatsbankrott im Fürstentum Pfalz-Neuburg 1505–1546'.

In *Pfalzgraf Ottheinrich: Politik, Kunst und Wissenschaft im 16. Jahrhundert*, edited by Stadt Neuburg an der Donau, 108–27. Regensburg: Friedrich Pustet, 2002.

Crofton, Black. 'Leo Africanus's "Descrittione dell'Africa" and its Sixteenth-Century Translations', *Journal of the Warburg and Courtauld Institutes* 65 (2002): 262–72.

Cross, Harry E. 'South American Bullion Production and Export 1550–1750'. In *Precious Metals in the Later Medieval and Early Modern Worlds*, edited by John F. Richards, 397–423. Durham, NC: Carolina Academic Press, 1983.

Cuneo, Pia F. 'Constructing the Boundaries of Community: Nationalism, Protestantism, and Economics in a Sixteenth-Century Broadsheet'. In *Infinite Boundaries: Order, Disorder, and Reorder in Early Modern German Culture*, edited by Max Reinhart, 171–86. Kirksville, MI: Sixteenth Century Journal Publishers, 1998.

Curtin, Philip D. 'Africa and the Wider Monetary World, 1250–1850'. In *Precious Metals in the Later Medieval and Early Modern Worlds*, edited by J.F. Richards, 231–61. Durham, NC: Carolina Academic Press, 1983.

Darley, Rebecca R. 'Money, Art, and Representation: the Powerful and Pragmatic Faces of Medieval Coinage'. In *A Cultural History of Money in The Middle Ages*, edited by Rory Naismith, 99–124. London: Bloomsbury Academic, 2019.

Day, John. 'The Question of Monetary Contraction in Late Medieval Europe'. In *The Medieval Market Economy*, edited by John Day, 55–71. Oxford: Basil Blackwell, 1981/87.

De Roover, Raymond. *Money, Banking and Credit in Medieval Bruges: Italian Merchant-Bankers Lombards and Money-Changers. A Study in the Origins of Banking.* Cambridge, MA: The Medieval Academy of America, 1948.

De Vries, Jan. *European Urbanization 1500–1800*. London: Methuen, 1984.

De Vries, Jan, and Ad van der Woude. *The First Modern Economy: Success, Failure, and Perseverance of the Dutch Economy, 1500–1815*. Cambridge: Cambridge University Press, 1997.

Deng, Steven. '"So Pale, So Lame, So Lean, So Ruinous": The Circulation of Foreign Coins in Early Modern England'. In *A Companion to the Global Renaissance: English Literature and Culture in the Era of Expansion*, edited by Jyotsna G. Singh, 262–78. Chichester: Wiley-Blackwell, 2009.

Denzau, Arthur T., and Douglass C. North. 'Shared Mental Models: Ideologies and Institutions', *Kyklos* 47 (1994): 3–30.

Denzel, Markus A. *Das System des bargeldlosen Zahlungsverkehrs europäischer Prägung vom Mittelalter bis 1914*. Stuttgart: Franz Steiner, 2008.

Dewar, Mary. 'The Authorship of the "Discourse of the Commonweal"', *The Economic History Review* 19, no. 2 (1966): 388–400.

Dietrich, Richard. *Untersuchungen zum Frühkapitalismus im mitteldeutschen Erzbergbau und Metallhandel*. Hildesheim: Georg Olms-Verlag, 1991.

Dincecco, Mark. 'Fiscal Centralization, Limited Government, and Public Revenues in Europe, 1650–1913', *The Journal of Economic History* 69, no. 1 (2009): 48–103.

Dirlmeier, Ulf. *Mittelalterliche Hoheitsträger im wirtschaftlichen Wettbewerb*. Wiesbaden: Steiner, 1966.

Dirlmeier, Ulf. *Untersuchungen zu Einkommensverhältnissen und Lebenshaltungskosten in oberdeutschen Städten des Spätmittelalters (Mitte 14. bis Anfang 16. Jahrhundert).* Heidelberg: Carl Winter Universitätsverlag, 1978.

Dollinger, Philippe. *Die Hanse.* 3 ed. Stuttgart: Kröner, 1981.

Dotzauer, Winfried. *Die deutschen Reichskreise in der Verfassung des Alten Reiches und ihr Eigenleben (1500–1806).* Darmstadt: Wissenschaftliche Buchgesellschaft, 1989.

Droege, Georg. 'Die finanziellen Grundlagen des Territorialstaats in West- und Ostdeutschland an der Wende vom Mittelalter zur Neuzeit', *Vierteljahrschrift für Sozial- und Wirtschaftsgeschichte* 53 (1966): 145–61.

Druffel, August von, ed. *Beiträge zur Reichsgeschichte 1546–1552.* Munich: Rieger'sche Universitätsbuchhandlung, 1873.

Dülfer, Kurt. *Die Packschen Händel: Darstellungen und Quellen.* Marburg: Elwert, 1958.

Eek, Daniel, and Anders Biel. 'The Interplay Between Greed, Efficiency, and Fairness in Public-Goods Dilemmas', *Social Justice Research* 16, no. 3 (2003): 195–215.

Ehrenberg, Richard. *Das Zeitalter der Fugger: Geldkapital und Creditverkehr im 16. Jahrhundert.* Vol. 1: Die Geldmächte des 16. Jahrhunderts, Jena: Fischer, 1896.

Eichengreen, Barry, and Douglas A. Irwin. 'Trade Blocs, Currency Blocs and the Reorientation of World Trade in the 1930s', *Journal of International Economics* 38 (1995): 1–24.

Eichhorn, Hansheiner. *Der Strukturwandel im Geldumlauf Frankens zwischen 1437 und 1610: Ein Beitrag zur Methodologie der Geldgeschichte.* Wiesbaden: Franz Steiner Verlag, 1973.

Eisner, Manuel. 'Modernization, Self-Control and Lethal Violence: The Long-term Dynamics of European Homicide Rates in Theoretical Perspective', *British Journal of Criminology* 41 (2001): 618–38.

Elbl, Ivana. 'Cross-Cultural Trade and Diplomacy: Portuguese Relations with West Africa, 1441–1521', *Journal of World History* 3, no. 2 (1992): 165–204.

Elsas, Moritz J. *Umriss einer Geschichte der Preise und Löhne in Deutschland vom ausgehenden Mittelalter bis zum Beginn des neunzehnten Jahrhunderts.* Vols. 1, 2. Leiden: A.W. Sijthoff's Uitgeversmaatschappij, 1936–40.

Elschenbroich, Adalbert. 'Einsiedel, v'. In *Neue deutsche Biographie*, edited by Historische Kommission bei der (Königlich) Bayerischen Akademie der Wissenschaften, 398–99. Berlin: Duncker & Humblot, 1959.

Eltz, Erwein. 'Die Reise zum Reichstag'. In *Alltag im 16. Jahrhundert: Studien zu Lebensformen in mitteleuropäischen Städten*, edited by Alfred Kohler and Heinrich Lutz, 195–221. Vienna: Verlag für Geschichte und Politik, 1987.

Emmerig, Hubert. 'Der Münzbetrieb in Mittelalter und früher Neuzeit: Personal, Ausrüstung, Tätigkeiten', *Vorträge zur Geldgeschichte* 3 (2006): 5–23.

Emmerig, Hubert. 'Zur Datierung der Gegenstempelung von Prager Groschen in Süddeutschland'. In *Nummi Docent! Münzen—Schätze—Funde. Festschrift für Peter Ilisch zum 65. Geburtstag*, edited by Gerd Dethlefs, Arent Pol, and Stefan

Wittenbrink, 211–25. Osnabrück: Numismatischer Verlag der Münzhandlung Fritz Rudolf Künker, 2012.

Endres, Rudolf. 'Zur sozialökonomischen Lage und sozialpsychologischen Einstellungen des "Gemeinen Mannes": Der Kloster- und Burgensturm in Franken 1525', *Geschichte und Gesellschaft: Sonderheft* 1 (1975): 61–78.

Endres, Rudolf. 'Adel und Patriziat in Oberdeutschland'. In *Ständische Gesellschaft und soziale Mobilität*, edited by Winfried Schulze, 221–38. Munich: Oldenbourg, 1988.

Engel, Evamaria. *Die deutsche Stadt im Mittelalter*. Düsseldorf: Patmos Verlag, 1993/2005.

Engelsing, Rolf. *Analphabetentum und Lektüre: Zur Sozialgeschichte des Lesens in Deutschland zwischen feudaler und industrieller Gesellschaft*. Stuttgart: Metzler, 1973.

Ermisch, Hubert. *Das sächsische Bergrecht des Mittelalters*. Leipzig: Gieseke & Devrient, 1887.

Ferber, Magnus Ulrich. *Augsburg im 16. Jahrhundert*. Munich: Volk Verlag, 2012.

Fisher, Douglas. 'The Price Revolution: A Monetary Interpretation', *The Journal of Economic History* 49 (1989): 883–902.

Fitte, Siegfried. *Das staatsrechtliche Verhältnis des Herzogtums Lothringen zum deutschen Reich seit dem Jahr 1542*. Strassburg: Heitz & Mündel, 1891.

Flandreau, Marc. 'The Economics and Politics of Monetary Unions: A Reassessment of the Latin Monetary Union, 1865–71', *Financial History Review* 7, no. 1 (2000): 25–44.

Flandreau, Marc. '"Water Seeks Level": Modelling Bimetallic Exchange Rates and the Bimetallic Band', *Journal of Money, Credit and Banking* 34, no. 2 (2002): 491–519.

Fleischmann, Peter. *Rat und Patriziat in Nürnberg: Die Herrschaft der Ratsgeschlechter vom 13. bis zum 18. Jahrhundert*. Vol. 2: Ratsherren und Ratsgeschlechter, Neustadt an der Aisch: Verein für Geschichte der Stadt Nürnberg, no year (*c.*2008).

Fontaine, Laurence. *The Moral Economy: Poverty, Credit and Trust in Early Modern Europe*. Cambridge: Cambridge University Press, 2014.

Freist, Dagmar. 'Öffentlichkeit und Herrschaftslegitimation in der Frühen Neuzeit: Deutschland und England im Vergleich'. In *Staatsbildung als kultureller Prozess: Strukturwandel und Legitimation von Herrschaft in der Frühen Neuzeit*, edited by Ronald G. Asch and Dagmar Freist, 321–51. Cologne, Weimar, Vienna: Böhlau, 2005.

Fremling, Gertrud A., and Richard Posner. *Market Signaling of Personal Characteristics*. The University of Chicago Law School (Chicago: 1999).

Freytag, Gustav. *Pictures of German Life in the Fifteenth, Sixteenth and Seventeenth Centuries*. Vol. 1: London: Chapman and Hall, 1862.

Fried, Torsten. 'Schrift und Bild: Münzen als Herrschaftszeichen'. In *Turbata per aequora mundi: Dankesgabe an Eckhard Müller-Mertens*, edited by Olaf B. Rader, 233–52. Hannover: Hahn, 2001.

Frohnhäuser, Ludwig. *Geschichte der Reichsstadt Wimpfen, des Ritterstifts St. Peter zu Wimpfen im Thal, des Dominicanerklosters und des Hospitals zum Hl. Geist zu Wimpfen am Berg*. Darmstadt: Historischer Verein, 1870.

Garland, Henry, and Mary Garland, eds. *The Oxford Companion to German Literature*. Oxford: Oxford University Press, 1997/2005.

Gascon, Richard. *Grand commerce et vie urbaine au XVIe siècle: Lyon et ses marchands (environs de 1520–environs de 1580)*. Paris et La Haye: Ecole pratique des hautes études, 1971.

Geiger, Hans-Ulrich. *Der Beginn der Gold- und Dickmünzenprägung in Bern: Ein Beitrag zur bernischen Münz- und Geldgeschichte des 15. Jahrhunderts*. Bern: Stämpfli & Cie, 1968.

Geiger, Hans-Ulrich. 'Entstehung und Ausbreitung des Batzens', *Schweizerische Numismatische Rundschau* 51 (1972): 145–68.

Geppert, Klaus. 'Die Peinliche Halsgerichtsordnung Karls V. (die "Carolina")', *JURA - Juristische Ausbildung* 37, no. 2 (2015): 143–53.

Gerber, Harry. 'Die Bedeutung des Augsburger Reichstages von 1547/48 für das Ringen der Reichsstädte um Stimme, Stand und Session', *Elsaß-Lothringisches Jahrbuch* 9 (1930): 168–208.

Gerhard, Hans-Jürgen. 'Ursachen und Folgen der Wandlungen im Währungssystem des Deutschen Reiches 1500–1625: Eine Studie zu den Hintergründen der sogenannten Preisrevolution'. In *Geld und Währung vom 16. Jahrhundert bis zur Gegenwart*, edited by Eckart Schremmer, 69–84. Stuttgart: Steiner, 1993.

Gerhard, Hans-Jürgen. 'Ein schöner Garten ohne Zaun: Die währungspolitische Situation des Deutschen Reiches um 1600', *Vierteljahrschrift für Sozial- und Wirtschaftsgeschichte* 81, no. 2 (1994): 156–77.

Gerhard, Hans-Jürgen. 'Neuere deutsche Forschungen zur Geld- und Währungsgeschichte der Frühen Neuzeit: Fragen–Ansätze–Ergebnisse', *Vierteljahrschrift für Sozial- und Wirtschaftsgeschichte* 83, no. 2 (1996): 216–30.

Gerhard, Hans-Jürgen, and Karl Heinrich Kaufhold. *Preise im vor- und frühindustriellen Deutschland: Grundnahrungsmittel*. Göttingen Schwartz, 1990.

Geyer, Rudolf. 'Die österreichische Münzordnung von 1524 und ihre Vorläufer', *Numismatische Zeitschrift* 61 (1928): 28–58.

Gilomen, Hans-Jörg. 'Das Motiv der bäuerlichen Verschuldung in den Bauernunruhen an der Wende zur Neuzeit'. In *Spannungen und Widersprüche: Gedenkschrift für Frantisek Graus*, edited by Susanna Burghartz, Hans-Jörg Gilomen, and Guy Paul Marchal, 173–89. Sigmaringen: Thorbecke, 1992.

Glassman, Debra, and Angela Redish. 'New Estimates of the Money Stock in France, 1493–1680', *The Journal of Economic History* 45, no. 1 (1985): 31–46.

Glassman, Debra, and Angela Redish. 'Currency Depreciation in Early Modern England and France', *Explorations in Economic History* 25, no. 1 (1988): 75–97.

Gordus, Adon A., and Jeanne P. Gordus. 'Potosi Silver and Coinage of Early Modern Europe'. In *Precious Metals in the Age of Expansion: Papers of the XIVth International Congress of the Historical Sciences*, edited by Hermann Kellenbenz, 225–42. Stuttgart: Klett-Cotta, 1975.

Gould, John D. *The Great Debasement: Currency and the Economy in Mid-Tudor England* Oxford: Clarendon Press, 1970.

Groag Bell, Susan. 'Johan Eberlin von Günzburg's Wolfaria: The First Protestant Utopia', *Church History* 36, no. 2 (1967): 122–39.

Groebner, Valentin. *Ökonomie ohne Haus: Zum Wirtschaften armer Leute in Nürnberg am Ende des 15. Jahrhunderts*. Göttingen: Vandenhoeck & Ruprecht, 1993.

Grote, Hermann. *Münzstudien*. Vol. 6, Heft 1, Graz: Akademische Druck- u. Verlagsanstalt, 1857–77/1969.

Grote, Hermann. *Osnabrück'sche Geld- und Münz-Geschichte*. Leipzig: Hahn'sche Verlagsbuchhandlung, 1864.

Günter, Heinrich. *Das Münzwesen in der Grafschaft Württemberg*. Stuttgart: Kohlhammer, 1897.

Guy, John. *Gresham's Law: The Life and World of Queen Elizabeth I's Banker*. London: Profile Books, 2020.

Häberlein, Mark. *Brüder, Freunde und Betrüger: Soziale Beziehungen, Normen und Konflikte in der Augsburger Kaufmannschaft um die Mitte des 16. Jahrhunderts*. Berlin: Akademie Verlag, 1998.

Häberlein, Mark. *Die Fugger: Geschichte einer Augsburger Familie (1367–1650)*. Stuttgart: Kohlhammer, 2006.

Häberlein, Mark. 'Die Fugger'sche Anleihe von 1488: Handelskapital, fürstliche Privilegien und der Aufstieg der süddeutschen Kaufmannsbankiers'. In *Schlüsselereignisse der deutschen Bankengeschichte*, edited by Dieter Lindenlaub, Carsten Burhop, and Joachim Scholtyseck, 17–25. Stuttgart: Steiner, 2013.

Häberlein, Mark, and Christina Dalhede. 'Kraffter (Craffter, Krafter), Kaufmannsfamilie'. In *Augsburger Stadtlexikon*, edited by Günther Grünsteudel, Günter Hägele, and Rudolf Frankenberger. Augsburg: Wißner-Verlag, 2010.

Haldén, Peter. *Stability Without Statehood: Lessons from Europe's History Before the Sovereign State*. London: Palgrave Macmillan, 2011.

Hamilton, Earl J. *American Treasure and the Price Revolution in Spain, 1501–1650*. Cambridge, MA: Harvard University Press, 1934.

Hansen, Johannes. *Beiträge zur Geschichte des Getreidehandels und der Getreidepolitik Lübecks*. Lübeck: Max Schmidt, 1912.

Hardy, Duncan. 'Tage (Courts, Councils and Diets): Political and Judicial Nodal Points in the Holy Roman Empire, *c.*1300–1550', *German History* 36, no. 3 (2018): 381–400.

Harreld, Donald J. *High Germans in the Low Countries: German Merchants and Commerce in Golden Age Antwerp*. Leiden, Boston: Brill, 2004.

Härter, Karl. 'Das kurmainzer Reichstagsdirektorium: Eine zentrale reichspolitische Schaltstelle des Reichserzkanzlers im Reichssystem'. In *Der Mainzer Kurfürst als Reichserzkanzler: Funktionen, Aktivitäten, Ansprüche und Bedeutung des zweiten Mannes im Alten Reich*, edited by Peter Claus Hartmann, 171–203. Stuttgart: Steiner, 1997.

Hartmann, Peter Claus. 'Der Mainzer Kurfürst als Reichserzkanzler: Einführung in die Problematik und Thematik des Kolloquiums'. In *Der Mainzer Kurfürst als Reichserzkanzler: Funktionen, Aktivitäten, Ansprüche und Bedeutung des zweiten Mannes im Alten Reich*, edited by Peter Claus Hartmann, 1–8. Stuttgart: Steiner, 1997.

Hartmann, Peter Claus. *Das Heilige Römische Reich deutscher Nation in der Neuzeit 1486–1806*. Stuttgart: Reclam, 2005.

Hartmann, Thomas Felix. *Die Reichstage unter Karl V.: Verfahren und Verfahrensentwicklung 1521–1555*. Göttingen: Vandenhoeck & Ruprecht, 2017.

Hartung, Fritz. *Karl V. und die deutschen Reichsstände von 1546 bis 1555*. Halle a.S.: M. Niemeyer, 1910.

Häusser, Ludwig. *Geschichte der rheinischen Pfalz nach ihren politischen, kirchlichen und literarischen Verhältnissen*. 2 ed. Vol. 2: Heidelberg: Mohr, 1856.

Heather, Peter. *The Restauration of Rome: Barbarian Popes and Imperial Pretenders*. London: Pan Books, 2013.

Heil, Dietmar. *Die Reichspolitik Bayerns unter der Regierung Herzog Albrechts V. (1550–1579)*. Göttingen Vandenhoeck & Ruprecht, 1998.

Held, Wieland. 'Soziale Herkunft und Situation der Mansfelder Bergleute in der ersten Hälfte des 16. Jahrhunderts', *Jahrbuch für Wirtschaftsgeschichte* 4 (1982): 115–27.

Held, Wieland. 'Geldwirtschaftliche und marktwirtschaftliche Aspekte der Stadt-Land-Beziehungen in Thüringen im 16. Jahrhundert', *Jahrbuch für Wirtschaftsgeschichte* 3 (1983): 107–21.

Helfferich, Karl Theodor, ed. *Ludwig Bamberger: Ausgewählte Reden und Aufsätze über Geld- und Bankwesen*. Berlin: Guttentag, 1900.

Helleiner, Eric. *The Making of National Money: Territorial Currencies in Historical Perspective*. Ithaca, London: Cornell University Press, 2003.

Henning, Friedrich-Wilhelm 'Ländliche Sozialstruktur und soziale Mobilität im Mittelalter'. In *Struktur und Dimension. Festschrift für Karl Heinrich Kaufhold zum 65. Geburtstag*, edited by Hans-Jürgen Gerhard, 195–222. Stuttgart: Steiner, 1997.

Herrmann, Johannes. *Moritz von Sachsen (1521–1553): Landes-, Reichs- und Friedensfürst*. Beucha Sax-Verlag, 2003.

Herrmann, Johannes, Günther Wartenberg, and Christian Winter, eds. *Politische Korrespondenz des Herzogs und Kurfürsten Moritz von Sachsen*. Vol. 5: Leipzig: Akademie Verlag, 1998.

Herrmann, Max. 'Die Überlieferung des Liedes vom Hürnen Seyfrid', *Zeitschrift für deutsches Altertum und deutsche Literatur* 46, no. 1/2 (1902): 61–89.

Hess, Peter. *Resisting Pluralization and Globalization in German Culture, 1490–1540: Visions of a Nation in Decline*. Berlin, Boston: de Gruyter, 2020.

Hindle, Steve. 'Law, Law Enforcement and State Formation in Early Modern England'. In *Staatsbildung als kultureller Prozess: Strukturwandel und Legitimation von Herrschaft in der Frühen Neuzeit*, edited by Ronald G. Asch and Dagmar Freist, 209–33. Cologne, Weimar, Vienna: Böhlau, 2005.

'The Holy Roman Empire: European Disunion done Right', *The Economist*, 22 December, 2012, 78–80.

Hoppe, Oswald. *Der Silberbergbau zu Schneeberg bis zum Jahre 1500*. Freiberg: Gerlachsche Buchdruckerei, 1908.

Hunwick, John O. *Timbuktu and the Songhay Empire: Al-Sadi's Tarikh al-Sudan down to 1613 and Other Contemporary Documents.* Leiden: Brill, 2003.

Irsigler, Franz. 'Rheinisches Kapital in Mitteleuropäischen Montanunternehmen des 15. und 16. Jahrhunderts', *Zeitschrift für Historische Forschung* 3, no. 2 (1976): 145–64.

Isaacsohn, Siegfried. 'Die Finanzen Joachims II. und das ständische Kreditwerk', *Zeitschrift für Preußische Geschichte und Landeskunde* 16 (1879): 455–79.

Isenmann, Eberhard. 'The Holy Roman Empire in the Middle Ages'. In *The Rise of the Fiscal State in Europe c.1200–1815*, edited by Richard Bonney, 243–80. Oxford: Oxford University Press, 1999.

Janáček, Josef. 'L'argent tchèque et la Méditerranée (XIVe et XVe siècles)'. In *Mélanges en l'honneur de Fernand Braudel: Histoire économique du monde méditerranéen 1440–1650*, edited by Ernest Labrousse, 245–61. Toulouse: Privat, 1973.

Jenks, Stuart. 'Von den archaischen Grundlagen bis zur Schwelle der Moderne (*c.*1000–1450)'. In *Deutsche Wirtschaftsgeschichte: Ein Jahrtausend im Überblick*, edited by Michael North, 15–106. Munich: Beck, 2000.

Jesse, Wilhelm. *Der Wendische Münzverein.* Lübeck: Hansischer Geschichtsverein, 1928.

John, Wilhelm. 'Der Kölner Rheinzoll von 1475–1494', *Annalen des Historischen Vereins für den Niederrhein* 48 (1889): 9–123.

Jordà, Òscar, Sanjay R. Singh, and Alan M. Taylor. *Longer-Run Economic Consequences of Pandemics.* Federal Reserve Bank of San Francisco (San Francisco: 2020).

Kahleyß, Julia. 'Der wirtschaftliche Aufstieg des Martin Römer: Soziale Mobilität im westerzgebirgischen Bergbau des 15. Jahrhunderts', *Vierteljahrschrift für Sozial- und Wirtschaftsgeschichte* 100, no. 2 (2013): 154–77.

Kamann, Johann. 'Der Nürnberger Patrizier Christoph Fürer der Ältere und seine Denkwürdigkeiten 1479–1537', *Mitteilungen des Vereins für Geschichte der Stadt Nürnberg* 28 (1928): 209–312.

Kaufhold, Karl Heinrich. 'Neuere Forschungen zur Wirtschaftsgeschichte des Berg- und Hüttenwesens im westlichen Harz in vorindustrieller Zeit: Ein Überblick unter besonderer Berücksichtigung der wirtschaftlichen Wechsellagen'. In *Konjunkturen im europäischen Bergbau in vorindustrieller Zeit*, edited by Christoph Bartels and Markus A. Denzel, 37–72. Stuttgart: Steiner, 2000.

Kellenbenz, Hermann. 'Das Römisch-Deutsche Reich im Rahmen der wirtschafts- und finanzpolitischen Erwägungen Karls V. im Spannungsfeld imperialer und dynastischer Interessen'. In *Das römisch-deutsche Reich im politischen System Karls V.*, edited by Heinrich Lutz and Elisabeth Müller-Luckner, 35–54. Munich, Vienna: Oldenbourg, 1982.

Keller, Berndt. 'Olsons "Logik des kollektiven Handelns". Entwicklung, Kritik—und eine Alternative', *Politische Vierteljahresschrift* 29, no. 3 (1988): 388–406.

Keyser, Erich, ed. *Deutsches Städtebuch.* Vols. 1, 3,3, 4,1, 4,2, 4,3. Stuttgart, Berlin: Kohlhammer, 1939–64.

Keyser, Erich. 'Preise und Löhne in Hamburg in der ersten Hälfte des 16. Jahrhunderts', *Zeitschrift des Vereins für Hamburgische Geschichte* 49/50 (1964): 77–82.

Keyser, Erich, and Heinz Stoob, eds. *Deutsches Städtebuch*. Vol. 5,1, 5,2. Stuttgart, Berlin, Cologne, Mainz: Kohlhammer, 1971–4.

Kiener, Fritz. 'Zur Vorgeschichte des Bauernkriegs am Oberrhein', *Zeitschrift für die Geschichte des Oberrheins* 58 (1904): 479–507.

Kissinger, Henry. *World Order: Reflections on the Character of Nations and the Course of History*. s.l.: Penguin, 2015.

Kius, Otto. 'Die Preis- und Lohnverhältnisse des sechszehnten Jahrhunderts in Thüringen I.', *Jahrbücher für Nationalökonomie und Statistik* 1 (1864): 65–78.

Klappauf, Lothar. '1000 Jahre Bergbau?'. In *Auf den Spuren einer frühen Industrielandschaft: Naturraum—Mensch—Umwelt im Harz*, edited by Christiane Segers-Glocke, 19–27. Hameln: CW Niemeyer, 2000.

Knorring, Marc von. 'Reichsverfassung und ständische Interessen: Der Streit um das Verfahren auf dem Deputationstag von 1564. Neue Erkenntnisse aus der Aktenedition', *Parliaments, Estates and Representation* 35, no. 2 (2015): 171–85.

Köbler, Gerhard. *Historisches Lexikon der deutschen Länder: Die deutschen Territorien vom Mittelalter bis zur Gegenwart*. 7 ed. Munich: Beck, 2007.

Kohler, Alfred. *Antihabsburgische Politik in der Epoche Karls V. die reichsständische Opposition gegen die Wahl Ferdinands I. zum römischen König und gegen die Anerkennung seine Königstums (1524–1534)*. Göttingen: Vandenhoeck & Ruprecht, 1982.

Kohler, Alfred. 'Das Heilige Römische Reich—Ein Föderativsystem?' In *Föderationsmodelle und Unionsstrukturen: Über Staatenverbindungen in der frühen Neuzeit vom 15. zum 18. Jahrhundert*, edited by Thomas Fröschl, 119–26. Vienna: Verlag für Geschichte und Politik, 1994.

Kohler, Alfred. *Karl V. 1500–1558: Eine Biographie*. Munich: Beck, 1999/2013.

Kohler, Alfred. *Ferdinand I. 1503–1564: Fürst, König und Kaiser*. Munich: Beck, 2003.

Kohnle, Armin. 'Die Reichstagsgesandten der Fürsten: Projekt einer Prosopographie im Reformationszeitalter'. In *Reichspersonal: Funktionsträger für Kaiser und Reich*, edited by Anette Baumann, Peter Oestmann, Stephan Wendehorst, and Siegrid Westphal, 335–42. Cologne, Weimar, Vienna: Böhlau, 2003.

Kraschewski, Hans Joachim. 'Wirtschaftliche Wechsellagen, ihre Einwirkungen auf den Bergbau des sechzehnten und siebzehnten Jahrhunderts und die bergbauliche Arbeitsverfassung'. In *Konjunkturen im europäischen Bergbau in Vorindustrieller Zeit: Festschrift für Ekkehard Westermann zum 60. Geburtstag*, edited by Christoph Bartels and Markus A. Denzel, 203–20. Steiner: Stuttgart, 2000.

Kraschewski, Hans Joachim. 'Das Spätmittelalter: Die Zeit des Aufbruchs'. In *Der alteuropäische Bergbau: Von den Anfängen bis zur Mitte des 18. Jahrhunderts*, edited by Christoph Bartels and Rainer Slotta, 249–316. Münster: Aschendorf, 2012.

Kresse, Zacharias. *Geschichte der Landwirthschaft des Altenburgischen Osterlandes*. Altenburg: H.A. Pierer, 1845.

Krug, Gerhard. *Die meißnisch-sächsischen Groschen 1338–1500*. Berlin: VEB Deutscher Verlag der Wissenschaften, 1974.

Krüger, Joachim. *Zwischen dem Reich und Schweden: Die landesherrliche Münzprägung im Herzogtum Pommern und in Schwedisch-Pommern in der frühen Neuzeit (c.1580–1715)*. Berlin: LIT, 2006.

Krüger, Johann Friedrich. *Vollständiges Handbuch der Münzen, Masse und Gewichte aller Länder der Erde*. Quedlinburg, Leipzig: Gottfried Basse, 1830.

Krüger, Kersten. *Finanzstaat Hessen 1500–1567: Staatsbildung im Übergang vom Domänenstaat zum Steuerstaat*. Marburg: Elwert, 1981.

Krüger, Kersten. *Die landständische Verfassung*. Munich: Oldenbourg, 2003.

Krusy, Hans. *Gegenstempel auf Münzen des Spätmittelalters*. Frankfurt: Numismatischer Verlag P. N. Schulten, 1974.

Kubiak, Stanislawa. *Monety i stosunki monetarne w Prusach Królewskich w 2 polowie XV wieku*. Wroclaw, Warszawa, Kraków, Gdansk, Lódz: Zaklad Narodowy Imiena Ossolinskich Wydawnictwo Polskiej Akademii Nauk, 1986.

Kümin, Beat, and Andreas Würgler. 'Petitions, Gravamina and the Early Modern State: Local Influence on Central Legislation in England and Germany (Hesse)', *Parliaments, Estates & Representation* 17, no. 1 (1997): 39–60.

Kümper, Hiram. 'Der Streit um den Rhein und die Freiheit der Flussschiffahrt zwischen Territorialisierung und Nationenbildung, 16.–19. Jahrhundert'. In *150 Jahre Mannheimer Akte: Festschrift zum 150jährigen Bestehen der Revidierten Rheinschifffahrtsakte vom 17. Oktober 1868*, edited by Hiram Kümper and Andreas Maurer, 23–41. Baden-Baden: Nomos, 2018.

L'Héritier, Maxime, and Florian Téreygeol. 'From Copper to Silver: Understanding the Saigerprozess through Experimental Liquation and Drying', *Historical Metallurgy* 44, no. 2 (2010): 136–52.

Landwehr, Achim. *Policey im Alltag: Die Implementation frühneuzeitlicher Policeyordnungen in Leonberg*. Frankfurt: Vittorio Klostermann, 2000.

Landwehr, Achim. '"Normdurchsetzung" in der Frühen Neuzeit? Kritik eines Begriffs', *Zeitschrift für Geschichtswissenschaft* 48 (2000): 146–62.

Landwehr, Götz. 'Mobilisierung und Konsolidierung der Herrschaftsordnung im 14. Jahrhundert'. In *Der deutsche Territorialstaat im 14. Jahrhundert*, edited by Hans Patze, 484–505. Sigmaringen: Thorbecke, 1971/86.

Lane, Frederic C., and Reinhold C. Mueller. *Money and Banking in Medieval and Renaissance Venice*. Vol. 1: Coins and Moneys of Account, Baltimore, London: Johns Hopkins University Press, 1985.

Lanzinner, Maximilian. *Friedenssicherung und politische Einheit des Reiches unter Kaiser Maximilian II. 1564–1576*. Göttingen: Vandenhoeck & Ruprecht, 1993.

Lanzinner, Maximilian. 'Einleitung'. In *Der Reichstag 1486–1613: Kommunikation—Wahrnehmung—Öffentlichkeiten*, edited by Maximilian Lanzinner and Arno Strohmeyer, 9–25. Göttingen: Vandenhoeck & Ruprecht, 2006.

Lanzinner, Maximilian. 'Fürsten und Gesandte als politische Akteure beim Reichstag 1566'. In *Religiöse Prägung und politische Ordnung in der Neuzeit: Festschrift für Winfried Becker zum 65. Geburtstag*, edited by Bernhard Löffler and Karsten Ruppert, 55–82. Cologne: Böhlau, 2006.

Lanzinner, Maximilian. 'Juristen unter den Gesandten der Reichstage 1486–1654'. In *Das Reichskammergericht im Spiegel seiner Prozessakten: Bilanz und Perspektiven der Forschung*, edited by Friedrich Battenberg and Bernd Schildt. Cologne, Weimar, Vienna: Böhlau, 2010.

Laube, Adolf. *Studien über den erzgebirgischen Silberbergbau von 1470 bis 1546: Seine Geschichte, seine Produktionsverhältnisse, seine Bedeutung für die gesellschaftlichen Veränderungen und Klassenkämpfe in Sachsen am Beginn der Übergangsepoche vom Feudalismus zum Kapitalismus*. 2 ed. Berlin: Akademie-Verlag, 1976.

Le Roy Ladurie, Emmanuel, Jean-Noël Barrandon, Bruno Collin, Maria Guerra, and Cécile Morrisson. 'Sur les traces de l'argent du Potosí', *Annales. Économies, Sociétés, Civilisations* (1990): 483–505.

Leins, Steffen. *Das Prager Münzkonsortium 1622/23: Ein Kapitalgeschäft im Dreißigjährigen Krieg am Rand der Katastrophe*. Münster: Aschendorf, 2012.

Lennartz, Peter. 'Die Probationstage und Probationsregister des niederländisch-westfälischen Kreises', *Numismatische Zeitschrift* 46 (1913): 1–84.

Lienert, Elisabeth. *Mittelhochdeutsche Heldenepik*. Berlin: Erich Schmidt, 2015.

Löbe, William. *Geschichte der Landwirthschaft im Altenburgischen Osterlande*. Leipzig: Brockhaus, 1845.

Ludwig, Karl-Heinz. 'Bergbau zwischen ökonomischem Interesse und politischer Macht'. In *Metalle und Macht 1000 bis 1600*, edited by Karl-Heinz Ludwig and Volker Schmidtchen, 37–75. Frankfurt, 1992.

Luhmann, Niklas. *Legitimation durch Verfahren*. 11 ed. Berlin: Suhrkamp, 1969/2019.

Luttenberger, Albrecht. 'Reichspolitik und Reichstag unter Karl V.: Formen zentralen politischen Handelns'. In *Aus der Arbeit an den Reichstagen unter Kaiser Karl V.: 7 Beiträge zu Fragen der Forschung und Edition*, edited by Heinrich Lutz and Alfred Kohler, 18–68. Göttingen: Vandenhoeck & Ruprecht, 1986.

Luttenberger, Albrecht. 'Kirchenadvokatie und Religionsfriede: Kaiseridee und kaiserliche Reichsidee im 16. und 17. Jahrhundert'. In *Legitimation und Funktion des Herrschers: Vom ägyptischen Pharao zum neuzeitlichen Diktator*, edited by Rolf Gundlach and Hermann Weber, 185–232. Stuttgart: Steiner, 1992.

Lutz, Robert Hermann. *Wer war der gemeine Mann? Der dritte Stand in der Krise des Spätmittelalters*. Munich: Oldenbourg, 1979.

Lydon, Ghislaine. *On Trans-Saharan Trails: Islamic Law, Trade Networks, and Cross-Cultural Exchange in Nineteenth-Century Western Africa*. Cambridge: Cambridge University Press, 2009.

Macleod, Henry Dunning. *The Elements of Political Economy*. London: Longman, Brown, Green, Longmans and Roberts, 1858.

Malanima, Paolo. 'Italy in the Renaissance: A Leading Economy in the European Context, 1350–1550', *The Economic History Review* 71, no. 1 (2018): 3–30.

Marquardt, Bernd. *Das Römisch-Deutsche Reich als segmentäres Verfassungssystem (1348–1806/48): Versuch zu einer neuen Verfassungstheorie auf der Grundlage der lokalen Herrschaften*. Zürich: Schulthess Juristische Medien, 1999.

Maurenbrecher, Wilhelm. *Karl V. und die deutschen Protestanten, 1545–1555*. Frankfurt: Rütten & Loening, 1865.

Mentz, Georg. *Johann Friedrich der Grossmütige 1503–1554*. Vol. 3: Vom Beginn des Schmalkaldischen Krieges bis zum Tode des Kurfürsten. Der Landesherr. Aktenstücke, Jena: Fischer, 1908.

Metz, Rainer. *Geld, Währung und Preisentwicklung: Der Niederrheinraum im europäischen Vergleich 1350–1800*. Frankfurt: Fritz Knapp, 1990.

Mierau, Heike Johanna. 'Das Reich, politische Theorien und die Heilsgeschichte: Zur Ausbildung eines Reichsbewußtseins durch die Papst-Kaiser-Chroniken des Spätmittelalters', *Zeitschrift für Historische Forschung* 32, no. 4 (2005): 543–73.

Miskimin, Harry A. 'The Enforcement of Gresham's Law'. In *Cash, Credit and Crisis in Europe, 1300–1600*, edited by Harry Miskimin, IX, 147–61. London: Variorum Reprints, 1985/89.

Moeser, Karl, and Fritz Dworschak. *Die große Münzreform unter Erzherzog Sigmund von Tirol (Die ersten großen Silber- und deutschen Bildnismünzen aus der Münzstätte Hall im Inntal)*. Vienna: Verlag Dr. Eduard Stepan, 1936.

Molenda, Danuta. 'Investments in Ore Mining in Poland from the 13th to the 17th Centuries', *Journal of European Economic History* 5, no. 1 (1976): 151–69.

Moraw, Peter. 'Franken als königsnahe Landschaft im späten Mittelalter', *Blätter für deutsche Landesgeschichte N.F.* 112 (1976): 123–32.

Moraw, Peter. 'Versuch über die Entstehung des Reichstags'. In *Politische Ordnungen und soziale Kräfte im Alten Reich*, edited by Hermann Weber, 1–36. Wiesbaden: Steiner, 1980.

Moraw, Peter. *Von offener Verfassung zu gestalteter Verdichtung: Das Reich im Späten Mittelalter 1250 bis 1490*. Frankfurt, Berlin: Propyläen, 1989.

Morineau, Michel. *Incroyables gazettes et fabuleux métaux: Les retours des trésor américains d'après les gazettes hollandaises (XVIe–XVIIIe siècles)*. London, New York, New Rochelle, Sydney, Melbourne: Cambridge University Press, 1985.

Morton, Rebecca B., and Kai Ou. 'What Motivates Bandwagon Voting Behavior: Altruism or a Desire to Win?', *European Journal of Political Economy* 40, Part B (2015): 224–41.

Mosler, Hans. 'Der Düsseldorfer Rheinzoll bis zum Ausgang des 16. Jahrhunderts', *Beiträge zur Geschichte des Niederrheins* 21 (1907): 97–275.

Mout, Nicolette. 'Die Niederlande und das Reich im 16. Jahrhundert'. In *Alternativen zur Reichsverfassung in der Frühen Neuzeit?*, edited by Volker Press and Dieter Stievermann, 143–68. Munich: Oldenbourg, 1995.

Münch, Paul. 'Grundwerte der frühneuzeitlichen Ständegesellschaft? Aufriß einer vernachlässigten Thematik'. In *Ständische Gesellschaft und soziale Mobilität*, edited by Winfried Schulze and Helmut Gabel, 53–72. Munich: Oldenbourg, 1988.

Münch, Paul. *Lebensformen in der Frühen Neuzeit 1500 bis 1800*. Frankfurt, Berlin: Ullstein, 1996.

Münkler, Herfried. *Die Deutschen und ihre Mythen*. Reinbek bei Hamburg: Rowohlt, 2010.

Munro, John H. *Wool, Cloth, and Gold: The Struggle for Bullion in Anglo-Burgundian Trade, 1340–1478*. Brussels, Toronto: University of Toronto Press, 1972.

Munro, John H. 'Bullionism and the Bill of Exchange in England, 1272–1663: A Study in Monetary Management and Popular Prejudice'. In *The Dawn of Modern Banking*, edited by F. Chiappelli, 169–239. New Haven and London: Yale University Press, 1979.

Munro, John H. 'Bullion Flows and Monetary Contraction in Late-Medieval England and the Low Countries'. In *Precious Metals in the Later Medieval and Early Modern Worlds*, edited by J.F. Richards, 97–158. Durham, NC: Carolina Academic Press, 1983.

Munro, John H. 'The Central European Mining Boom, Mint Outputs, and Prices in the Low Countries and England, 1450–1550'. In *Money, Coins, and Commerce: Essays in the Monetary History of Asia and Europe (From Antiquity to Modern Times)*, edited by Eddy H.G. van Cauwenberghe, 119–83. Leuven: Leuven University Press, 1991.

Munro, John H. 'The Maze of Medieval Monetary Metrology: Determining Mint Weights in Flanders, France and England from the Economics of Counterfeiting, 1388–1469', *Journal of European Economic History* 29, no. 1 (2000): 173–99.

Munro, John H. 'The "New Institutional Economics" and the Changing Fortune of Fairs in Medieval and Early Modern Europe: The Textile Trades, Warfare and Transaction Costs', *Vierteljahrschrift für Sozial- und Wirtschaftsgeschichte* 88, no. 1 (2001): 1–47.

Munro, John H. 'The Monetary Origins of the "Price Revolution": South German Silver Mining, Merchant-Banking, and Venetian Commerce, 1470–1540'. In *Global Connections and Monetary History, 1470–1800*, edited by Dennis O. Flynn, Arturo Giráldez, and Richard von Glahn, 1–34. Aldershot, Brookfield: Ashgate Publishing, 2003.

Munro, John H. 'The Medieval Origins of the "Financial Revolution": Usury, Rentes, and Negotiability', *International History Review* XXV, no. 3 (2003): 505–62.

Nagl, Alfred. 'Das Tiroler Geldwesen unter Erzherzog Sigismund und die Entstehung des Silberguldens', *Numismatische Zeitschrift* 38 (1906): 45–168.

Nagl, Alfred. 'Die österreichische Münzordnung vom Jahre 1481', *Numismatische Zeitschrift* 41 (1908): 157–61.

Nau, Elisabeth. 'Münzumlauf im ländlichen Bereich mit besonderer Berücksichtigung Südwest-Deutschlands'. In *Die Grundherrschaft im späten Mittelalter*, edited by Hans Patze, 97–156. Sigmaringen: Thorbecke, 1983.

Nef, John Ulrich. 'Silver Production in Central Europe 1450–1618', *Journal of Political Economy* 49 (1941): 575–91.

Neu, Tim. 'Zeremonielle Verfahren: Zur Funktionalität vormoderner politisch-administrativer Prozesse am Beispiel des Landtags im Fürstbistum Münster'. In *Im Schatten der Macht: Kommunikationskulturen in Politik und Verwaltung 1600–1950*, edited by Stefan Haas and Mark Hengerer, 23–50. Frankfurt, New York: Campus, 2008.

Neuhaus, Helmut. *Reichsständische Repräsentationsformen im 16. Jahrhundert: Reichstag—Reichskreistag—Reichsdeputationstag*. Berlin: Duncker & Humblot, 1982.

Neuhaus, Helmut. 'Der Augsburger Reichstag des Jahres 1530: Ein Forschungsbericht', *Zeitschrift für historische Forschung* 9, no. 2 (1982): 167–211.

Neuhaus, Helmut. 'Der Streit um den richtigen Platz: Ein Beitrag zu reichsständischen Verfahrensformen in der Frühen Neuzeit'. In *Vormoderne politische Verfahren*, edited by Barbara Stollberg-Rilinger, 281–301. Berlin: Duncker & Humblot, 2001.

Neumann, Max. *Geschichte des Wechsels im Hansagebiete bis zum 17. Jahrhundert*. Erlangen: Ferdinand Enke, 1863.

Newald, Johann. *Das österreichische Münzwesen unter Ferdinand I.: Eine münzgeschichtliche Studie*. Vienna: Kubasta & Voigt, 1883.

Nicklas, Thomas. *Macht oder Recht: Frühneuzeitliche Politik im obersächsischen Reichskreis*. Stuttgart: Steiner, 2002.

Nonn, Ulrich. 'Heiliges Römisches Reich Deutscher Nation: Zum Nationen-Begriff im 15. Jahrhundert', *Zeitschrift für historische Forschung* 9, no. 2 (1982): 129–42.

Noonan, John Thomas. *The Scholastic Analysis of Usury*. Cambridge, MA: Harvard University Press, 1957.

North, Douglass C. 'A Transaction Cost Theory of Politics', *Journal of Theoretical Politics* 2, no. 4 (1990): 355–67.

North, Michael. 'Bullion Transfer from Western Europe to the Baltic and the Problem of Trade Balances: 1550–1750'. In *From the North Sea to the Baltic*. Aldershot: Variorum Reprints, 1996.

North, Michael. 'Münzpolitik in der ersten Hälfte des 16. Jahrhunderts: Das Heilige Römische Reich und Sachsen im europäischen Kontext'. In *Die drei Flugschriften über den Münzstreit der sächsischen Albertiner und Ernestiner*, edited by Bertram Schefold, 83–98. Düsseldorf, 2000.

North, Michael. 'Von der atlantischen Handelsexpansion bis zu den Agrarreformen 1450–1815'. In *Deutsche Wirtschaftsgeschichte: Ein Jahrtausend im Überblick*, edited by Michael North, 107–91. Munich: Beck, 2001.

North, Michael. 'Reich und Reichstag im 16. Jahrhundert: Der Blick aus der angeblichen Reichsferne'. In *Der Reichstag 1486–1613: Kommunikation—Wahrnehmung—Öffentlichkeiten*, edited by Maximilian Lanzinner and Arno Strohmeyer, 221–36. Göttingen: Vandenhoeck & Ruprecht, 2006.

North, Michael. 'Geld- und Ordnungspolitik im Alten Reich'. In *Geld, Handel, Wirtschaft: Höchste Gerichte im Alten Reich als Spruchkörper und Institution*, edited by Anja Amend-Traut, Albrecht Cordes, and Wolfgang Sellert, 93–101. Berlin, Boston: de Gruyter, 2013.

North, Michael. *Kommunikation, Handel, Geld und Banken in der Frühen Neuzeit*. Munich: De Gruyter & Oldenbourg, 2014.

North, Michael. 'The Reception of Imperial Monetary Reforms in 16th-century Northern Germany'. In *Money and Finance in Central Europe During the Later Middle Ages*, edited by Roman Zaoral, 32–41. London: Palgrave Macmillan, 2016.

North, Michael. 'Monetary Reforms in the Holy Roman Empire in the Fifteenth and Sixteenth Centuries'. In *Money in the Western Legal Tradition: Middle Ages to Bretton Woods*, edited by David Fox and Wolfgang Ernst, 191–200. Oxford: Oxford University Press, 2016.

Oechsle, Ferdinand Friedrich. *Beiträge zur Geschichte des Bauernkrieges in den schwäbisch-fränkischen Grenzlanden*. Heilbronn: Carl Drechsler, 1830.

Oestreich, Gerhard. 'Zur parlamentarischen Arbeitsweise der deutschen Reichstage unter Karl V. (1519–1556)'. In *Die geschichtlichen Grundlagen der modernen Volksvertretung*, edited by Heinz Rausch, 242–78. Darmstadt: Wissenschaftliche Buchgesellschaft, 1971/74.

Oestreich, Gerhard. *Verfassungsgeschichte vom Ende des Mittelalters bis zum Ende des alten Reiches*. Munich: dtv, 1982.

Ogilvie, Sheilagh. 'Married Women, Work and the Law: Evidence from Early Modern Germany'. In *Married Women and the Law in Premodern Northwest Europe*, edited by Cordelia Beattie and Matthew Frank Stevens, 213–40. Woodbridge: Boydell & Brewer 2013.

Ogilvie, Sheilagh, Markus Küpker, and Janine Maegraith. 'Household Debt in Early Modern Germany: Evidence from Personal Inventories', *The Journal of Economic History* 72, no. 1 (2012): 134–67.

Ogilvie, Sheilagh, Markus Küpker, and Janine Maegraith. 'Krämer und ihre Waren im ländlichen Württemberg zwischen 1600 und 1740', *Zeitschrift für Agrargeschichte und Agrarsoziologie* 59, no. 2 (2011): 54–75.

Olson, Mancur. *The Logic of Collective Action: Public Goods and the Theory of Groups*. Cambridge, MA, London: Harvard University Press, 1965/71.

Packull, Werner O. 'The Image of the "Common Man" in the Early Pamphlets of the Reformation (1520–1525)', *Historical Reflections/Réflexions Historiques* 12, no. 2 (1985): 253–77.

Pamuk, Şevket, and K. Kıvanç Karaman. 'Different Paths to the Modern State in Europe: The Interaction Between Warfare, Economic Structure, and Political Regime', *American Political Science Review* 107, no. 3 (2013): 603–26.

Pan, David. 'European Union and Holy Roman Empire', *Telos: Critical Theory of the Contemporary* 176 (2016): 202–8.

Papritz, Johannes. 'Das Handelshaus der Loitz zu Stettin, Danzig und Lüneburg', *Baltische Studien* 44 (1957): 73–94.

Parker, Geoffrey. *Emperor: A New Life of Charles V*. New Haven, London: Yale University Press, 2019.

Paulinyi, Oszkár. 'The Crown Monopoly of the Refining Metallurgy of Precious Metals and the Technology of the Cameral Refineries in Hungary and Transsylvania in the Period of Advanced and Late Feudalism (1325–1700) with Data and Output'. In *Precious Metals in the Age of Expansion: Papers of the XIVth International Congress of the Historical Sciences*, edited by Hermann Kellenbenz, 27–39. Stuttgart: Klett-Cotta, 1981.

Perrotta, Cosimo. 'Einleitung zum Münzstreit der sächsischen Albertiner und Ernestiner um 1530'. In *Die drei Flugschriften über den Münzstreit der sächsischen*

Albertiner und Ernestiner: Vademecum zu drei klassischen Schriften frühneuzeitlicher Münzpolitik, edited by Karl Heinrich Kaufhold, Michael North, Cosimo Perrotta, and Bertram Schefold, 101–51. Düsseldorf: Verlag Wirtschaft und Finanzen, 2000.

Persson, Karl Gunnar. 'Labour Productivity in Medieval Agriculture: Tuscany and the Low Countries'. In *Land, Labour and Livestock, Historical Studies in European Agricultural Productivity*, edited by Bruce M.S. Campbell and M. Overton, 124–43. Manchester: Manchester University Press, 1991.

Pfeiffer, Friedrich. *Rheinische Transitzölle im Mittelalter*. Berlin: Akademie-Verlag, 1997.

Pickl, Othmar. 'Kupfererzeugung und Kupferhandel in den Ostalpen'. In *Schwerpunkte der Kupferproduktion und des Kupferhandels in Europa 1500–1650*, edited by Hermann Kellenbenz, 117–47. Cologne, Vienna: Böhlau, 1977.

Pieper, Renate. 'American Silver Production and West European Monetary Supply in the Sixteenth and Seventeenth Century'. In *Economic Effects of the European Expansion: 1492–1824*, edited by José Casas Pardo, 77–98. Stuttgart: Steiner, 1992.

Pieper, Renate. 'Amerikanische Edelmetalle in Europa (1492–1621). Ihr Einfluß auf die Verwendung von Gold und Silber', *Jahrbuch für Geschichte von Staat, Wirtschaft und Gesellschaft Lateinamerikas* 32 (1995): 163–91.

Popelka, Fritz. 'Die Lebensmittelpreise und Löhne in Graz vom 16. bis zum 18. Jahrhundert', *Vierteljahrschrift für Sozial- und Wirtschaftsgeschichte* 23 (1930): 157–218.

Poulsen, Bjørn. 'Die ältesten Bauernanschreibebücher: Schleswigsche Anschreibebücher des 16. und 17. Jahrhunderts'. In *Bäuerliche Anschreibebücher als Quellen zur Wirtschaftsgeschichte*, edited by Klaus Joachim Lorenzen-Schmidt and Bjørn Poulsen, 89–105. Neumünster: Wachholtz, 1992.

Press, Volker. 'Formen des Ständewesens in den deutschen Territorien des 16. und 17. Jahrhunderts'. In *Ständetum und Staatsbildung in Brandenburg-Preußen: Ergebnisse einer internationalen Fachtagung*, edited by Peter Baumgart, 280–318. Berlin, New York: de Gruyter, 1983.

Prestwich, Michael. 'Early Fourteenth-Century Exchange Rates', *The Economic History Review* XXXII, no. 4 (1979): 470–82.

Pribram, Alfred Francis. *Materialen zur Geschichte der Preise und Löhne in Österreich*. Vol. 1: Vienna: Carl Ueberreuters Verlag, 1938.

Probszt, Günther. *Österreichische Münz- und Geldgeschichte von den Anfängen bis 1918*. Vienna, Cologne, Graz: Hermann Böhlaus Nachf., 1973.

Prokisch, Bernhard. *Grunddaten zur europäischen Münzprägung der Neuzeit c.1500–1990*. Vienna: Verlag Fassbaender, 1993.

Pusch, Gottfried. *Staatliche Münz- und Geldpolitik in den Niederlanden unter den burgundischen und habsburgischen Herrschern besonders unter Kaiser Karl V*. Munich: Val. Höfling, 1932.

Pyl, Theodor. 'Sastrow, Bartholomäus'. In *Allgemeine Deutsche Biographie*, edited by Historische Commission bei der Königlichen Akademie der Wissenschaften, 398–408. Leipzig: Duncker & Humblot, 1890.

Quarthal, Franz. 'Verfassung und Verwaltung in südwestdeutschen Städten der Frühen Neuzeit'. In *Recht, Verfassung und Verwaltung in der frühneuzeitlichen Stadt*, edited by Michael Stolleis, 217–39. Cologne: Böhlau, 1991.

Rabe, Horst. *Reichsbund und Interim: Die Verfassungs- und Religionspolitik Karls V. und der Reichstag von Augsburg 1547/1548*. Cologne: Böhlau, 1971.

Rabe, Horst. *Reich und Glaubensspaltung: Deutschland 1500–1600*. Munich: Beck, 1989.

Ranke, Leopold von. *History of the Reformation in Germany*. London: Longman, Brown, Green, and Longmans, 1847.

Rattmann, Cornelis. 'Die Mark kam aus Hamburg'. *Welt am Sonntag*, 09/12/2001.

Rauscher, Peter. 'La casa de Austria y sus banqueros alemanes'. In *Carlos V: europeísmo y universalidad*, edited by Francisco Sánchez-Montes González and Juan Luis Castellano, 411–28. Granada: Universidad de Granada, 2001.

Rauscher, Peter. *Zwischen Ständen und Gläubigern: Die kaiserlichen Finanzen unter Ferdinand I. und Maximilian II. (1556–1576)*. Vienna, Munich: Oldenbourg, 2004.

Rauscher, Peter. 'Reiche Fürsten–armer Kaiser? Die finanziellen Grundlagen der Politik Habsburgs, Bayerns und Sachsens im Vorfeld des Dreißigjährigen Krieges'. In *Plus Ultra: Die Welt der Neuzeit. Festschrift für Alfred Kohler zum 65. Geburtstag*, edited by Friedrich Edelmayer, Martina Fuchs, Georg Heilingsetzer, and Peter Rauscher, 233–58. Münster: Aschendorff, 2008.

Redish, Angela. *Bimetallism: An Economic and Historical Analysis*. Cambridge, New York: Cambridge University Press, 2000.

Redish, Angela, and Warren E. Weber. 'Coin Sizes and Payments in Commodity Money Systems', *Macroeconomic Dynamics* 15, no. S1 (2011): 62–82.

Reuter, Fritz. 'Worms um 1521'. In *Der Reichstag zu Worms von 1521: Reichspolitik und Luthersache*, edited by Fritz Reuter, 13–58. Worms: Stadtarchiv Worms, 1981.

Reuter, Timothy. 'The "Imperial Church System" of the Ottonian and Salian Rulers: A Reconsideration', *The Journal of Ecclesiastical History* 33, no. 3 (1982): 347–74.

Richet, Denis. 'Le cours officiel des monnaies étrangères circulant en France au XVIe siècle', *Revue historique* 225, no. 2 (1961): 359–96.

Richter, Jochen. 'Ländliches Kreditwesen in Mecklenburg 16./17. Jahrhundert', *Jahrbuch für Wirtschaftsgeschichte* 1 (1986): 131–49.

Rohac, Dalibor. 'The Holy Roman Union'. *The American Interest* (Washington, DC), 7 May 2019.

Roll, Christine. *Das zweite Reichsregiment 1521–1530*. Cologne, Weimar, Vienna: Böhlau, 1996.

Rolnick, Arthur J., Francois R. Velde, and Warren E. Weber. 'The Debasement Puzzle: An Essay on Medieval Monetary History', *The Journal of Economic History* 56, no. 4 (1996): 789–808.

Roper, Lyndal. '"The Common Man", "The Common Good", "Common Women": Gender and Meaning in the German Reformation Commune', *Social History* 12, no. 1 (1987): 1–21.

Rose, Andrew K. 'One Money, One Market: Estimating the Effects of Common Currencies on Trade', *Economic Policy* 30 (2000): 7–45.

Rose, Andrew K. 'Currency Unions and Trade: The Effect is Large', *Economic Policy* 33 (2001): 449–61.

Rösener, Werner. 'Die wirtschaftlichen Ressourcen der Fürstenhöfe: Die schwindende Bedeutung der Einnahmen aus den Kammergütern'. In *Hofwirtschaft: Ein ökonomischer Blick auf Hof und Residenz in Spätmittelalter und Früher Neuzeit*, edited by Gerhard Fouquet, Jan Hirschbiegel, and Werner Paravicini, 305–28. Sigmaringen: Thorbecke, 2008.

Rössner, Philipp Robinson. *Deflation—Devaluation—Rebellion: Geld im Zeitalter der Reformation*. Stuttgart: Steiner, 2012.

Rössner, Philipp Robinson. 'Monetary Instability, Lack of Integration, and the Curse of a Commodity Money Standard: The German Lands, *c.*1400–1900 A.D.', *Credit and Capital Markets—Kredit und Kapital* 47, no. 2 (2014): 297–340.

Rössner, Philipp Robinson. 'Monetary Theory and Cameralist Economic Management, *c.*1500–1900 A.D', *Journal of the History of Economic Thought* 40, no. 1 (2018): 99–134.

Rössner, Philipp Robinson. 'Besprechung von Oliver Volckart: Eine Wähung für das Reich. Die Münztage zu Speyer 1549 und 1557', *Vierteljahrschrift für Sozial- und Wirtschaftsgeschichte* 106 (2019): 278–81.

Roth, Friedrich. 'Silvester Raid, der Brand-, Proviant- und spätere Rentmeister des Markgrafen Albrecht Alcibiades von Brandenburg-Kulmbach, und Georg Fröhlich, Verfasser der "Historia belli Schmalcaldici"', *Archiv für Reformationsgeschichte* 9 (1911–12): 1–36.

Rüthing, Heinrich. 'Zur Geschichte des Mariengroschens'. In *Mundus in imagine: Bildersprache und Lebenswelten im Mittelalter. Festgabe für Klaus Schreiner*, edited by Andrea Löther, Ulrich Meier, and Norbert Schnitzler, 35–61. Munich: Fink, 1996.

Sargent, Thomas J., and Francois R. Velde. 'The Big Problem of Small Change', *Journal of Money, Credit and Banking* 31, no. 2 (1999): 137–61.

Sargent, Thomas J., and François R. Velde. *The Big Problem of Small Change*. Princeton, Oxford: Princeton University Press, 2002.

Scales, Len. *The Shaping of German Identity: Authority and Crisis, 1245–1414*. Cambridge: Cambridge University Press, 2012.

Scales, Len, and Joachim Whaley. 'Rewriting the History of the Holy Roman Empire', *German History* 36, no. 2 (2018): 331–48.

Schalk, Carl. 'Die österreichischen Goldgulden im 15. Jahrhundert', *Numismatische Zeitschrift* 11 (1879): 260–83.

Schalk, Carl. 'Der Wiener Münzverkehr im 16. Jahrhundert', *Numismatische Zeitschrift* 13 (1881): 243–329.

Schalk, Carl. 'Der Wiener Münzverkehr im XVI. Jahrhundert', *Numismatische Zeitschrift* 16 (1884): 89–108.

Schenk, Georg W. 'Über die Anfänge des Silberbergbaues von St. Joachimsthal', *Der Anschnitt* 20, no. 5 (1968): 17–27.

Schiller, Robert J. 'Conversation, Information and Herd Behavior', *Rhetoric and Economic Behavior* 85, no. 3 (1995): 181–5.

Schilling, Heinz. 'Veni, vidi, Deus vixit: Karl V. zwischen Religionskrieg und Religionsfrieden', *Archiv für Reformationsgeschichte* 89 (1998): 144–66.

Schilling, Heinz. 'Reichs-Staat und frühneuzeitliche Nation der Deutschen oder teilmodernisiertes Reichssystem: Überlegungen zu Charakter und Aktualität des Alten Reiches', *Historische Zeitschrift* 272, no. 2 (2001): 377–95.

Schirmer, Uwe. *Kursächsische Staatsfinanzen (1456–1656): Strukturen—Verfassung—Funktionseliten*. Stuttgart: Franz Steiner Verlag, 2006.

Schlaich, Klaus. 'Maioritas—protestatio—itio in partes—corpus Evangelicorum: Das Verfahren im Reichstag des Heiligen Römischen Reichs Deutscher Nation nach der Reformation', *Zeitschrift der Savigny-Stiftung für Rechtsgeschichte: Kanonistische Abteilung* 63 (1977): 264–99.

Schlaich, Klaus. 'Die Mehrheitsabstimmung im Reichstag zwischen 1495 und 1613'. In *Gesammelte Aufsätze: Kirche und Staat von der Reformation bis zum Grundgesetz*, edited by Klaus Schlaich, 135–78. Tübingen: Mohr-Siebeck, 1983/97.

Schlumbohm, Jürgen. 'Gesetze, die nicht durchgesetzt werden: ein Strukturmerkmal des frühneuzeitlichen Staates?', *Geschichte und Gesellschaft* 23, no. 4 (1997): 647–63.

Schmidt, Georg. *Geschichte des Alten Reiches: Staat und Nation in der Frühen Neuzeit 1495–1806*. Munich: Beck, 1999.

Schmidt, Georg. 'Das frühneuzeitliche Reich—komplementärer Staat und föderative Nation', *Historische Zeitschrift* 273, no. 2 (2001): 371–99.

Schmidt, Georg. 'Das frühneuzeitliche Reich—Sonderweg und Modell für Europa oder Staat der deutschen Nation?' In *Imperium Romanum—irregulare corpus—Teutscher Reichs-Staat*, edited by Matthias Schnettger, 247–77. Mainz: Philipp von Zabern, 2002.

Schmidt, Georg. "'Aushandeln' oder 'Anordnen': Der komplementäre Reichs-Staat und seine Gesetze im 16. Jahrhundert". In *Der Reichstag 1486–1613: Kommunikation—Wahrnehmung—Öffentlichkeiten*, edited by Maximilian Lanzinner and Arno Strohmeyer, 95–116. Göttingen: Vandenhoeck & Ruprecht, 2006.

Schmidt, Georg. 'The State and Nation of the Germans'. In *The Holy Roman Empire: 1495–1806*, edited by Robert John Weston Evans, Michael Schaich, and Peter H. Wilson, 43–62. Oxford: Oxford University Press, 2011.

Schmoller, Gustav. 'Über die Ausbildung einer richtigen Scheidemünzpolitik vom 14. bis 19. Jahrhundert', *Jahrbuch für Gesetzgebung, Verwaltung und Volkswirtschaft im Deutschen Reich* 24 (1900): 1247–74.

Schneider, Franz. *Geschichte der formellen Staatswirtschaft von Brandenburg-Preussen*. Berlin: Duncker & Humblot, 1952.

Schneider, Konrad. 'Hamburg während der Kipper- und Wipperzeit', *Zeitschrift des Vereins für hamburgische Geschichte* 67 (1981): 47–74.

Schneider, Konrad. *Frankfurt und die Kipper- und Wipperinflation der Jahre 1619–1623*. Frankfurt: Stadtarchiv, 1990.

Schneider, Konrad. 'Norm und Wirklichkeit der rheinischen Goldgulden', *Jahrbuch für westdeutsche Landesgeschichte* 40 (2014): 59–82.

Scholler, Ernst. *Das Münzwesen der Reichsstadt Nürnberg im 16. Jahrhundert: Ein Beitrag zur reichsstädtischen Wirtschaftsgeschichte*. Nürnberg: Benedikt Hilz, 1912.

Scholler, Ernst. *Der Reichsstadt Nürnberg Geld- und Münzwesen in älterer und neuerer Zeit (Ein Beitrag zur reichsstädtischen Wirtschaftsgeschichte)*. Nuremberg: G. Heydolph, 1916.

Scholz, Luca. *Borders and Freedom of Movement in the Holy Roman Empire*. Oxford: Oxford University Press, 2020.

Schön, Gerhard. 'Die Münzprobationstage im Alten Reich', *Abhandlungen der Braunschweigischen Wissenschaftlichen Gesellschaft* 61 (2008): 465–96.

Schrötter, Friedrich Frhr. von. *Das Preussische Münzwesen im 18. Jahrhundert: Münzgeschichtlicher Teil*. Vol. 2: Die Begründung des preussischen Münzsystems durch Friedrich den Grossen und Grauman: 1740–1755, Berlin: Parey, 1908.

Schrötter, Friedrich Frhr. von. 'Das Münzwesen des deutschen Reichs von 1500–1566, Teil I', *Schmollers Jahrbuch für Gesetzgebung, Verwaltung und Volkswirtschaft* 35, no. 4 (1911): 129–72.

Schrötter, Friedrich Frhr. von. 'Das Münzwesen des deutschen Reichs von 1500–1566, Teil II', *Schmollers Jahrbuch für Gesetzgebung, Verwaltung und Volkswirtschaft* 36, no. 1 (1912): 99–128.

Schrötter, Friedrich Frhr. von. 'Der Speierer Reichsmünztag von 1557', *Zeitschrift für Numismatik* 29 (1912): 47–80.

Schubert, Ernst. '"bauerngeschrey": Zum Problem der öffentlichen Meinung im spätmittelalterlichen Franken', *Jahrbuch für fränkische Landesforschung* 34/35 (1975): 883–907.

Schubert, Ernst. 'Franken als königsnahe Landschaft unter Karl IV.', *Blätter für deutsche Landesgeschichte N.F.* 114 (1978): 865–90.

Schubert, Ernst. 'Der Mainzer Kurfürst als Erzkanzler im Spätmittelalter'. In *Der Mainzer Kurfürst als Reichserzkanzler: Funktionen, Aktivitäten, Ansprüche und Bedeutung des zweiten Mannes im Alten Reich*, edited by Peter Claus Hartmann, 77–97. Stuttgart: Steiner, 1997.

Schulte, Eduard. 'Das Danziger Kontorbuch des Jakob Stöve aus Münster (Hansische Maße, Münzen, Waren, Wege und Zölle um 1560)', *Hansische Geschichtsblätter* 62 (1937): 40–72.

Schulten, Wolfgang. *Deutsche Münzen aus der Zeit Kaiser Karls V.: Typenkatalog der Gepräge zwischen dem Beginn der Talerprägung (1484) und der dritten Reichsmünzordnung (1559)*. Frankfurt: Numismatischer Verlag P.N. Schulten, 1974.

Schulze, Winfried. *Reich und Türkengefahr im späten 16. Jahrhundert: Studien zu den politischen und gesellschaftlichen Auswirkungen einer äußeren Bedrohung*. Munich: Beck, 1978.

Schulze, Winfried. 'Majority Decision in the Imperial Diets of the Sixteenth and Seventeenth Centuries', *Journal of Modern History* 58 (1986): S46–S63.

Schulze, Winfried. 'Vom Gemeinnutz zum Eigennutz: Über den Normenwandel in der ständischen Gesellschaft in der frühen Neuzeit', *Historische Zeitschrift* 243 (1986): 591–626.

Schulze, Winfried. 'The Emergence and Consolidation of the "Tax State": I. The Sixteenth Century'. In *Economic Systems and State Finance*, edited by Richard Bonney, 261–79. Oxford: Clarendon, 1995.

Schuster, Peter. 'Soziale und kulturelle Aspekte des Schuldenmachens im ausgehenden Mittealter'. In *Prekäre Ökonomien: Schulden in Spätmittelalter und früher Neuzeit*, edited by Gabriela Signori, 17–34. Konstanz, Munich: UVK, 2014.

Schüttenhelm, Joachim. 'Zur Münzprägung und Silberversorgung süddeutscher Münzstätten im frühen 16. Jahrhundert'. In *Der Anschnitt: Zeischrift für Kunst und Kultur im Bergbau. Beiheft 2: Montanwirtschaft Mitteleuropas vom 12. bis 17. Jahrhundert. Stand, Wege und Aufgaben der Forschung*, edited by Werner Kroker, 159–69. Bochum: Deutsches Bergbau-Museum, 1984.

Schüttenhelm, Joachim. 'Problems of Quantifying the Volume of Money in Early Modern Times: A Preliminary Survey'. In *Precious Metals, Coinage and the Changes of Monetary Structures in Latin-America, Europe and Asia (Late Middle Ages–Early Modern Times)*, edited by Eddy Van Cauwenberghe, 83–98. Leuven: Leuven University Press, 1989.

Schwiedland, Eugen Peter. *Die Hausierfrage in Österreich*. Leipzig: Duncker & Humblot, 1899.

Schwinkowski, Walter. 'Das Geld- und Münzwesen Sachsens', *Neues Archiv für sächsische Geschichte* 38 (1917): 140–81, 355–95.

Scott, Tom. 'The German Peasants' War and the "Crisis of Feudalism": Reflections On a Neglected Theme', *Journal of Early Modern History* 6, no. 3 (2002): 265–95.

Scribner, Robert W. 'How Many Could Read? Comments on Bernd Moeller's "Stadt und Buch"'. In *Stadtbürgertum und Adel in der Reformation: Studien zur Sozialgeschichte der Reformation in England und Deutschland (The Urban Classes, the Nobility and the Reformation: Studies on The Social History of the Reformation in England and Germany)*, edited by Wolfgang J. Mommsen, 44–45. Stuttgart: Klett-Cotta, 1979.

Scribner, Robert W. 'Flugblatt und Analphabetentum: Wie kam der gemeine Mann zu reformatorischen Ideen?' In *Flugschriften als Massenmedium der Reformationszeit: Beiträge zum Tübinger Symposion 1980*, edited by Hans-Joachim Köhler, 65–76. Stuttgart: Klett-Cotta, 1981.

Scribner, Robert W. *Popular Culture and Popular Movements in Reformation Germany*. London: Bloomsbury Academic, 1987.

Seidler, Christoph. 'Schatzsucher heben das Rheingold', *Der Spiegel*, 23/08/2012.

Sikora, Michael. 'Der Sinn des Verfahrens: Soziologische Deutungsangebote'. In *Vormoderne politische Verfahren*, edited by Barbara Stollberg-Rilinger, 25–51. Berlin: Duncker & Humblot, 2001.

Šimek, Eduard. 'Die Zusammenhänge zwischen Währung und Handel im Böhmen des 16. Jahrhunderts'. In *Der Außenhandel Ostmitteleuropas 1450–1650: Die ostmitteleuropäischen Volkswirtschaften in ihren Beziehungen zu Mitteleuropa*, edited by Ingomar Bog, 229–45. Cologne, Vienna: Böhlau, 1971.

Simms, Brendan. 'The Ghosts of Europe Past', *The New York Times*, 09/06/2013.

Soetbeer, Adolf. *Denkschrift betreffend Deutsche Münzeinigung: Den Hohen Deutschen Regierungen*. Berlin: Liebheit & Thiesen, 1869.

Soetbeer, Adolf. 'Edelmetall-Produktion und Werthverhältniss zwischen Gold und Silber seit der Entdeckung Amerika's bis zur Gegenwart'. In *Dr. A. Petermanns Mittheilungen aus Justus Perthes' geographischer Anstalt: Ergänzungsband 13*, edited by E. Behm, 1–143. Gotha: Justus Perthes, 1879–80.

Sommerlad, Theo. *Die Rheinzölle im Mittelalter*. Halle: C.A. Kaemmerer & Co., 1893.

Sprenger, Bernd. 'Münzverschlechterung, Geldmengenwachstum und Bevölkerungsvermehrung als Einflußgrößen der sogenannten Preisrevolution im 16. und beginnenden 17. Jahrhundert in Deutschland'. In *Theorie und Empirie in Wirtschaftspolitik und Wirtschaftsgeschichte: Festschrift für Wilhelm Abel zum 80. Geburtstag*, edited by K.H. Kaufhold and F. Riemann, 127–44. Göttingen: Schwartz, 1984.

Sprenger, Bernd. *Das Geld der Deutschen: Geldgeschichte Deutschlands von den Anfängen bis zur Gegenwart*. 3 ed. Paderborn, Munich, Vienna, Zürich: Schöningh, 2002.

Spruyt, Hendrik. *The Sovereign State and its Competitors: An Analysis of Systems Change*. Princeton: NJ: Princeton University Press, 1994.

Spufford, Peter. 'Mint Organisation in Late Medieval Europe'. In *Later Medieval Mints: Organisation, Administration and Techniques. The Eighth Oxford Symposium on Coinage and Monetary History*, edited by Peter Spufford and Nicholas J. Mayhew, 7–29. Oxford: B.A.R. Publications, 1988.

Spufford, Peter. *Money and its Use in Medieval Europe*. Cambridge, New York, Port Chester, Melbourne, Sydney: Cambridge University Press, 1991.

Sreenivasan, Govind. *The Peasants of Ottobeuren, 1487–1726: A Rural Society in Early Modern Europe*. Cambridge: Cambridge University Press, 2004.

Stasavage, David. *States of Credit: Size, Power, and the Development of European Politics*. Princeton, Oxford: Princeton University Press, 2011.

Stieda, Wilhelm. *Das Hausiergewerbe in Deutschland: Vortrag, gehalten in der Gehe-Stiftung zu Dresden am 12. März 1898*. Dresden: Pöschel & Trepte, 1899.

Stiefenhöfer, Hermine. *Philipp von Flersheim, Bischof von Speyer (1529–1552) und gefürsteter Propst von Weißenburg 1546–1552: Ein Beitrag zur Geschichte der Reformation in der deutschen Westmark*. Speyer: Pilger-Verlag, 1941.

Stollberg-Rilinger, Barbara. 'Die zeremonielle Inszenierung des Reiches, oder: Was leistet der kulturalistische Ansatz für die Reichs Verfassungsgeschichte?' In *Imperium Romanum—irregulare corpus—Teutscher Reichs-Staat*, edited by Matthias Schnettger, 233–46. Mainz: Philipp von Zabern, 2002.

Stollberg-Rilinger, Barbara. *Das Heilige Römische Reich Deutscher Nation: Vom Ende des Mittelalters bis 1806*. Munich: Beck, 2006.

Stollberg-Rilinger, Barbara. 'On the Function of Rituals in the Holy Roman Empire'. In *The Holy Roman Empire 1495–1806*, edited by R.J.W. Evans, Michael Schaich, and Peter H. Wilson, 359–73. Oxford: Oxford University Press, 2011.

Stollberg-Rilinger, Barbara. *Cultures of Decision-Making*. London: The German Historical Institute London, 2015.

Stollberg-Rilinger, Barbara. *The Emperor's Old Clothes: Constitutional History and the Symbolic Language of the Holy Roman Empire*. New York, Oxford: Berghahn, 2015.

Strieder, Jakob. *Studien zur Geschichte kapitalistischer Organisationsformen: Monopole, Kartelle und Aktiengesellschaften im Mittelalter und zu Beginn der Neuzeit*. Munich, Leipzig: Duncker & Humblot, 1914.

Strieder, Jakob. 'Negerkunst von Benin und deutsches Metallexportgewerbe im 15. und 16. Jahrhundert', *Zeitschrift für Ethnologie* 64, no. 4/6 (1932): 249–59.

Stromer, Wolfgang von. 'Konjunktur im europäischen Bergbau: Wasserkünste'. In *Konjunkturen im europäischen Bergbau in vorindustrieller Zeit: Festschrift für Ekkehard Westermann zum 60. Geburtstag*, edited by Christoph Bartels and Markus A. Denzel, 151–55. Stuttgart: Steiner, 2000.

Suhling, Lothar. *Aufschließen, Gewinnen und Fördern: Geschichte des Bergbaus*. Reinbek bei Hamburg: Rowohlt, 1988.

Sussman, Nathan, and Joseph Zeira. 'Commodity Money Inflation: Theory and Evidence from France in 1350–1436', *Journal of Monetary Economics* 50 (2003): 1769–93.

Szabó, Thomas. 'Die Straßen in Deutschland und Italien im Mittelalter'. In *Straßen- und Verkehrswesen im hohen und späten Mittelalter*, edited by Rainer Christoph Schwinges, 71–118. Sigmaringen: Thorbecke, 2007.

Thomas, Heinz. 'Julius Caesar und die Deutschen: Zu Ursprung und Gehalt eines deutschen Geschichtsbewußtseins in der Zeit Gregors VII. und Heinrichs IV.'. In *Die Salier und das Reich*, edited by Stefan Weinfurter, 245–78. Sigmaringen: Thorbecke, 1991.

Trauner, Karl-Reinhart. *Identität in der frühen Neuzeit: Die Autobiographie des Bartholomäus Sastrow*. Münster: Aschendorf, 2004.

Uhlhorn, Friedrich. 'Die Erfindung des Walzwerkes und seine Förderung durch Graf Reinhard zu Solms-Lich', *Deutsche Münzblätter* 55, no. 388 (1935): 297–304.

Uhlhorn, Friedrich. *Reinhard Graf zu Solms, Herr zu Münzenberg 1491–1562*. Marburg: Elwert, 1952.

Ulmschneider, Helgard. *Götz von Berlichingen: Ein adeliges Leben der deutschen Renaissance*. Sigmaringen: Thorbecke, 1974.

Underhill, Geoffrey R.D. 'Multilateralism'. In *A Concise Oxford Dictionary of Politics and International Relations*, edited by Garrett W. Brown, Iain McLean, and Alistair McMillan. Oxford: Oxford University Press, 2018.

Unger, Richard W. 'Feeding Low Countries Towns: The Grain Trade in the Fifteenth Century', *Revue belge de philologie etd'histoire* 77, no. 2 (1999): 329–58.

Van der Wee, Herman. 'Structural Changes in European Long-Distance Trade, and Particularly in the Re-Export Trade from South to North, 1350–1750'. In *The Rise of Merchant Empires: Long-Distance Trade in the Early Modern World, 1350–1750*, edited by James D. Tracy, 14–33. Cambridge: Cambridge University Press, 1990.

Van Tielhof, Milja. *The 'Mother of all Trades': The Baltic Grain Trade in Amsterdam from the Late 16th to the Early 19th Century*. Leiden, Boston, Cologne: Brill, 2002.

Verkade, P. *Muntboek, bevattende de namen en afbeeldingen van munten: geslagen in de zeven voormalig Vereenigde Nederlandsche Provincien, sedert den vrede van Gent tot op onzen tijd*. Schiedam: P.J. van Dijk, 1848.

Vogler, Günter. 'Reichsvorstellungen im Umkreis des Bauernkrieges'. In *Alternativen zur Reichsverfassung in der Frühen Neuzeit?*, edited by Volker Press and Dieter Stievermann, 23–41. Munich: Oldenbourg, 1995.

Voigt, Johannes. 'Musikliebhaberei des Herzogs Albrecht von Preußen', *Allgemeines Archiv für die Geschichtskunde des preußischen Staates* 2 (1830): 69–78.

Volckart, Oliver. *Die Münzpolitik im Deutschordensland und Herzogtum Preußen von 1370 bis 1550*. Wiesbaden: Harrassowitz, 1996.

Volckart, Oliver. 'Early Beginnings of the Quantity Theory of Money and their Context in Polish and Prussian Monetary Policies, *c.*1520–1550', *The Economic History Review* 50, no. 3 (1997): 430–49.

Volckart, Oliver. 'Die Reichsmünzordnung von 1559: Das Scheitern reichseinheitlichen Geldes'. In *Schlüsselereignisse der deutschen Bankengeschichte*, edited by Dieter Lindenlaub, Carsten Burhop, and Joachim Scholtyseck, 26–37. Stuttgart: Franz Steiner Verlag, 2013.

Volckart, Oliver. 'Währungsvielfalt, Wechselkurse und Geldmarktintegration im Hanseraum, *c.*1350–1550'. In *Hansischer Handel im Strukturwandel*, edited by Stephan Selzer and Rolf Hammel-Kiesow, 11–29. Trier: Porta Alba Verlag, 2016.

Volckart, Oliver. 'Power Politics and Princely Debts: Why Germany's Common Currency Failed, 1549–1556', *The Economic History Review* 70, no. 3 (2017): 758–78.

Volckart, Oliver. 'Bimetallism and its Discontents: Cooperation and Coordination Failure in the Empire's Monetary Policies, 1549–59', *Vierteljahrschrift für Sozial- und Wirtschaftsgeschichte* 105, no. 2 (2018): 201–20.

Volckart, Oliver. 'Money and its Technologies: The "Principles of Minting" in the Middle Ages'. In *A Cultural History of Money in the Medieval Age*, edited by Rory Naismith, 15–35. London, New York, Oxford, New Delhi, Sydney: Bloomsbury Academic, 2019.

Volckart, Oliver. 'The Dear Old Holy Roman Realm: How Does it Hold Together? Monetary Policies, Cross-cutting Cleavages and Political Cohesion in the Age of Reformation', *German History* 38, no. 4 (2020): 365–86.

Volckart, Oliver. 'Voting Like Your Betters: The Bandwagon Effect in the Diet of the Holy Roman Empire', *German History* 49, no. 1 (2023): 1–20.

Volckart, Oliver, and Nikolaus Wolf. 'Estimating Financial Integration in the Middle Ages: What Can We Learn from a TAR-model?', *The Journal of Economic History* 66, no. 1 (2006): 122–39.

Vorel, Petr. *Monetary Circulation in Central Europe at the Beginning of the Early Modern Age: Attempts to Establish a Shared Currency as an Aspect of the Political Culture of the 16th Century (1524–1573)*. Pardubice: Univerziteta Pardubice, 2006.

Wagner, Stefan. *Staatssteuern in Jülich-Berg von der Schaffung der Steuerverfassung im 15. Jahrhundert bis zur Auflösung der Herzogtümer in den Jahren 1801 und 1806*. Cologne: Forschungsinstitut für Sozial- und Wirtschaftsgeschichte an der Univ. zu Köln, 1977.

Watson, Andrew M. 'Back to Gold—and Silver', *The Economic History Review* XX, no. 1 (1967): 1–34.

Weber, Max. 'Politics as a Vocation'. In *Max Weber: The Vocation Lectures. 'Science as a Vocation', 'Politics as a Vocation'*, edited by David Owen and Tracy B. Strong, 32–94. Indianapolis, Cambridge: Hackett, 1918/2004.

Weisenstein, Karl. *Die Kipper- und Wipperzeit im Kurfürstentum Trier*. Koblenz: Numismatischer Verlag Forneck, 1991.

Weisenstein, Karl. *Das Kurtriersche Münz- und Geldwesen vom Beginn des 14. bis zum Ende des 16. Jahrhunderts: Auch ein Beitrag zur Geschichte des Rheinischen Münzvereins*. Koblenz: Numismatischer Verlag Forneck, 1995.

Weissman, Ronald F.E. *Ritual Brotherhood in Renaissance Florence*. New York, London: Academic Press, 1982.

Wensky, Margret. 'Städtische Führungsschichten im Spätmittelalter'. In *Sozialer Aufstieg: Funktionseliten im Spätmittelalter und in der frühen Neuzeit*, edited by Günther Schulz, 17–27. Munich: Harald Boldt, 2002.

Werner, Theodor Gustav. 'Das fremde Kapital im Annaberger Bergbau und Metallhandel des 16. Jahrhunderts (I.)', *Neues Archiv für sächsische Geschichte* 57 (1936): 113–79.

Werner, Theodor Gustav. 'Das Kupferhüttenwerk des Hans Tetzel aus Nürnberg auf Kuba und seine Finanzierung durch europäisches Finanzkapital. I. Teil (1545–1571)', *Vierteljahrschrift für Sozial- und Wirtschaftsgeschichte* 48, no. 3 (1961): 289–328.

Werner, Theodor Gustav. 'Das Kupferhüttenwerk des Hans Tetzel aus Nürnberg auf Kuba (1545–1571) und seine Finanzierung durch europäisches Finanzkapital II. Teil', *Vierteljahrschrift für Sozial- und Wirtschaftsgeschichte* 48, no. 4 (1961): 444–502.

West, Robert C. 'Early Silver Mining in New Spain, 1531–1555'. In *Mines of Silver and Gold in the Americas*, edited by Peter J. Bakewell, 57–73. Abingdon, New York: Routledge, 1995/97.

Westermann, Ekkehard. *Das Eislebener Garkupfer und seine Bedeutung für den europäischen Kupfermarkt 1460–1560*. Vienna, Cologne: Böhlau, 1971.

Westermann, Ekkehard. 'Zur Silber- und Kupferproduktion Mitteleuropas vom 15. bis zum frühen 17. Jahrhundert: Über Bedeutung und Rangfolge der Reviere von Schwaz, Mansfeld und Neusohl', *Der Anschnitt* 5/6 (1986): 187–211.

Westermann, Ekkehard. 'Zur Brandsilber- und Kupferproduktion des Falkenstein bei Schwaz 1470–1623: Eine Kritik bisheriger Ermittlungen von Produktionziffern', *Tiroler Heimat* 50 (1986): 109–25.

Westermann, Ekkehard. 'Über Beobachtungen und Erfahrungen bei der Vorbereitung der Edition einer vorindustriellen Produktionsstatistik: Zur Brandsilberproduktion des Falkenstein bei Schwaz/Tirol von 1470–1623'. In *Quantifizierungsprobleme bei der Erforschung der Montanwirtschaft des 15. bis 18. Jahrhundert*, edited by Ekkehard Westermann, 27–42. St. Katharinen: Scripta Mercaturae Verlag, 1988.

Westermann, Ekkehard. *Die Listen der Brandsilberproduktion des Falkenstein bei Schwaz/Tirol von 1470–1623: Kommentar und Edition*. Vienna, 1988.

Whaley, Joachim. 'The Old Reich in Modern Memory: Recent Controversies Concerning the "Relevance" of Early Modern German History'. In *German Literature, History and the Nation: Papers from the Conference 'The Fragile Tradition', Cambridge 2002*, edited by Christian Emden and David Midgley, 25–49. Oxford: Peter lang, 2004.

Whaley, Joachim. *Germany and the Holy Roman Empire*. Vols. I, II. Oxford: Oxford University Press, 2012.

Willan, Thomas Stuart. *The Inland Trade: Studies in English Internal Trade in the Sixteenth and Seventeenth Centuries*. Manchester: Manchester University Press, 1976.

Wilson, Peter H. *The Holy Roman Empire: A Thousand Years of Europe's History*. London: Allen Lane, 2016.

Wilson, Peter H. 'The Holy Roman Empire Can Help Inspire a Different European Union'. *Financial Times*, 20/01/2016.

Wind, Marlene. 'The European Union as a Polycentric Polity: Returning to a Neo-Medieval Europe?' In *European Constitutionalism Beyond the State*, edited by J.H.H. Weiler, 103–31. Cambridge: Cambridge University Press 2004.

Winder, Lukas. 'Die Kreditgeber der österreichischen Habsburger 1521–1612: Versuch einer Gesamtanalyse'. In *Das 'Blut des Staatskörpers': Forschungen zur Finanzgeschichte der Frühen Neuzeit*, edited by Peter Rauscher, Andrea Serles, and Thomas Winkelbauer, 435–58. Munich: Oldenbourg, 2012.

Witthöft, Harald. 'Die Münzordnungen und das Grundgewicht im Deutschen Reich vom 16. Jahrhundert bis 1871/72'. In *Geld und Währung vom 16. Jahrhundert bis zur Gegenwart*, edited by Eckart Schremmer, 45–67. Stuttgart: Steiner, 1993.

Wittmütz, Volkmar. *Die Gravamina der bayerischen Stände im 16. und 17. Jahrhundert als Quelle für die wirtschaftliche Situation und Entwicklung Bayerns*. Munich: Stadtarchiv München, 1970.

Wohlfeil, Rainer, and Trudl Wohlfeil. 'Verbildlichungen ständischer Gesellschaft: Bartholomäus Bruyn d.Ä.—Petrarcameister (mit Exkursen von Marlies Minuth und Heike Talkenberger)'. In *Ständische Gesellschaft und soziale Mobilität*, edited by Winfried Schulze and Helmut Gabel, 269–331. Munich: Oldenbourg, 1988.

Wolf, Nikolaus, and Albrecht Ritschl. 'Endogeneity of Currency Areas and Trade Blocs: Evidence from a Natural Experiment', *Kyklos* 64, no. 2 (2011): 291–312.

Wrigley, Edward A. 'Urban Growth and Agricultural Change: England and the Continent in the Early Modern Period', *The Journal of Interdisciplinary History* 15, no. 4 (1985): 683–728.

Wüst, Wolfgang. *Die 'gute' Policey im Fränkischen Reichskreis*. Berlin: Akademie-Verlag, 2003.

Wuttke, Robert. 'Die Probationsregister des Obersächsischen Kreises', *Numismatische Zeitschrift* 29 (1897): 237–302.

Zycha, A. 'Zur neuesten Literatur über die Wirtschafts- u. Rechtsgeschichte des deutschen Bergbaues', *Vierteljahrschrift für Sozial- und Wirtschaftsgeschichte* 5, no. 1/2 (1907): 238–92.

Index

For the benefit of digital users, indexed terms that span two pages (e.g., 52–53) may, on occasion, appear on only one of those pages.

Persons

Places

Concepts